Argument
Today

RICHARD JOHNSON-SHEEHAN
Purdue University

CHARLES PAINE
University of New Mexico

Boston   Columbus   Indianapolis   New York   San Francisco   Upper Saddle River
Amsterdam   Cape Town   Dubai   London   Madrid   Milan   Munich   Paris   Montréal   Toronto
Delhi   Mexico City   São Paulo   Sydney   Hong Kong   Seoul   Singapore   Taipei   Tokyo

Senior Acquisitions Editor: Brad Potthoff
Senior Development Editor: David B. Kear
Executive Marketing Manager: Roxanne McCarley
Senior Supplements Editor: Donna Campion
Executive Digital Producer: Stefanie Snajder
Digital Editor: Sara Gordus
Production/Project Manager: Eric Jorgensen
Project Coordination, Text Design, and Electronic Page Makeup: PreMediaGlobal USA, Inc
Cover Design Manager: Heather Scott
Cover Image: Tetiana Yurchenko/Shutterstock
Senior Manufacturing Buyer: Roy L. Pickering, Jr.
Printer/Binder: RR Donnelley Harrisonburg
Cover Printer: RR Donnelley Harrisonburg

Credits and acknowledgments borrowed from other sources and reproduced, with permission, in this textbook appear on the appropriate page within text or on pages 483–485.

Library of Congress Cataloging-in-Publication Data
Johnson-Sheehan, Richard.
  Argument today with readings / Richard Johnson Sheehan, Charles Paine.—First Edition.
      pages   cm
  Includes bibliographical references and index.
  ISBN-13: 978-0-205-20968-2 (alk. paper)
  ISBN-10: 0-205-20968-8 (alk. paper)
  1. Persuasion (Rhetoric)—Problems, exercises, etc. 2. Debates and debating—Problems, exercises, etc. 3. English
  language—Rhetoric—Problems, exercises, etc. 4. College readers. I. Paine, Charles. II. Title.
  PE1431.J643 2014
  808.53—dc23

                                                                              2013041764

Student Edition ISBN 10: 0-205-20968-8
Student Edition ISBN 13: 978-0-205-20968-2
A la Carte Edition ISBN-10: 0-321-96032-7
A la Carte Edition ISBN-13: 978-0-321-96032-0

Contents

4 Critical Reading and Rhetorical Analysis   67

PART 2

Genres of Argument   87

5 Descriptions—Arguing about People, Places, Things, and Events   88

PART 3

The Research Project

16 Developing Your Research Process

17 Crediting, Quoting, Paraphrasing, and Summarizing

PART 4
Style, Design and Medium   429

Welcome to Argument Today

Argument is war. That's the underlying metaphor that has muddied the field of argumentation for centuries. Traditionally, argument has been advertised to students as a tool to defend their claims, confront the ideas of others, attack weak points, and reinforce their positions. Students are promised that learning to argue will help them stand up for themselves and, in doing so, shield or inoculate themselves against the possibly harmful ideas of others. Even books that include chapters on "alternative" approaches to argument, such as Rogerian rhetoric or Toulmin's system, usually end up spending most of their time defaulting to the combative approach.

Unfortunately, the war metaphor permeates today's media and culture. Instead of news or debates, public figures and private citizens engage in pointless "Yes it is!" "No it isn't!" kinds of quarrels. Personal attacks and name calling are the mainstays of news websites, blogs, Twitter feeds, editorial pages, and talk radio. Our politicians and public figures have come to view argument as trench warfare. Never give in. Never surrender. Hold your position at all costs, even when the other side has some good ideas.

Like you, we have witnessed the consequences of this antagonistic approach to argument in our classrooms. Classroom discussions have turned into battles of media sound bites and clichés. Students dismiss and even deride alternative viewpoints. But what troubles us most, and perhaps you too, is the silence. Many students refuse to participate in discussions about important issues because they don't want to get into some kind of pitched battle with others. Silence is a way to keep the peace with their classmates, their friends, their families, and others. After all, if argument is a war of attrition, why would anyone bother taking part, especially if they could avoid it?

Of course, arguments are not wars, and one side is almost never declared the winner and the other the loser. In some instances, people do need to take a stand and defend their beliefs, but these instances are more the exception than the norm. The majority of arguments are really just conversations among people who agree more than they disagree, sharing most of their beliefs and values in common.

So, instead of training your students how to attack and defend, we want to help you teach them how to listen carefully, critically analyze all sides of an issue, weigh the available evidence, figure out what they believe, and express their ideas clearly. Properly taught, argumentation becomes a "habit of mind" that your students can transfer to their other college courses, their careers, and their civic lives.

We also want to help your students succeed in a world that is dramatically changing due to new media. A new approach to argument seems especially important as virtual classrooms and workplaces, social networking, and multimodality change the way all of us argue. Because we are in continual conversations with others, teaching your students how to argue collaboratively in networks of others is ever more important.

In this book, your students will learn argument from a different and more productive perspective. In Chapter 1, we start by telling them that people engage in two basic types of argument, *generative arguments* and *persuasive arguments*:

> **Generative arguments,** which we refer to as "power with" arguments, are designed to build understanding and consensus among people who share many values in common. These kinds of arguments often don't look like arguments because the participants focus on talking with each other, figuring out where they agree, discussing their differences, and working together to solve common problems. Generative arguments allow people to sort out their beliefs, work as a team, and take action together. People use generative arguments to have *power with* each other.

> **Persuasive arguments,** which we refer to as "power over" arguments, use reasoning, authority, and emotion to try to convince others to believe something or take a specific action. Persuasive arguments help people clarify their views and work together toward changing the minds of others. In many cases, persuasive arguments are used to convince others to do something they probably wanted to do in the first place. In these kinds of arguments, people try to use words and images to exert *power over* others.

These types of argument are the two ends of the same spectrum: Any generative argument will include some elements of persuasion, and any persuasive argument will contain generative elements. We have found this basic "power with" and "power over" dichotomy helps students remember that argument has a wide range of purposes. In each particular situation, they first need to determine where on the spectrum the argument lies. Then, they can interpret complex rhetorical situations and use a variety of generative and persuasive forms of argument to express their ideas.

Another major premise of this book is that people argue through genres, which we define as "the ways people in communities and cultures get things done." There are unlimited and always-evolving genres in any given culture. With help from instructors and reviewers, we have settled on a *genre set* that we believe students will find most helpful in their advanced college courses, their careers, and their lives. The argument genres featured in this book will transfer to other courses, workplaces, and public situations. Your students will learn that genres are adaptable and "stretchy," meaning they can be adapted for a variety of everyday purposes. We encourage your students (and you) to play with genres to figure out how they work and how they can be used to meet society's ever-evolving needs.

Finally, we want to help your students learn how to argue successfully in networks using multimodal strategies. Networked computers, mobile phones, and social media have dramatically shifted how people argue today. Your students need to learn how to communicate effectively in physical *and* virtual environments. They need to learn how to argue in a variety of media, including paper, websites, social media, presentations, and mixed media. To succeed in college and the workplace, your students need to know how to shape the flow of information as it moves through these networks. Genres are helpful tools for creating order within these often chaotic networks.

Writing this book has been a pleasure and a humbling experience for both of us. It's been a labor of love as we strive to shift how argumentation is taught to college students.

How This Book Is Organized

The flexible and adaptable organization of *Argument Today* is designed to help you get your students writing arguments right away. It's also designed to let you decide how the chapters of this book will fit into your syllabus.

PART 1

Fundamentals of Argument

Part 1 gives your students a brief overview of argument theory and explains how genres are used to develop successful arguments. Chapters 1 through 3 define the concept of genres and explain generative and persuasive approaches to argument.

PART 2

Genres of Argument

Part 2 introduces them to eleven genres (i.e., a *genre set*) that they will find useful in college and their careers. These genres move progressively from generative arguments, such as description arguments, to increasingly persuasive arguments, such as proposals. We put these genre chapters up front in the book, because we want to help you get your students writing arguments as quickly as possible.

PART 3

The Research Project

Part 3 brings together the chapters on research into one place, so you can use them together as a "research unit" or access an individual chapter any time you want to discuss research in your class.

PART 4

Style, Design, and Medium

Part 4 shows your students how to use techniques of plain and persuasive style, visual design and graphics, and multimedia. These chapters will help them write stronger prose and use visual design to make their arguments clearer and more engaging. Then they will learn how you use a variety of media to present their arguments to others.

Features of This Book

Interactive writing style works best with today's students. Instruction is to the point: key concepts are immediately defined and reinforced; paragraphs are short and supported by instructional visuals. This interactive style helps students ask questions and access knowledge—*when they are ready for it*—putting them in control of their learning.

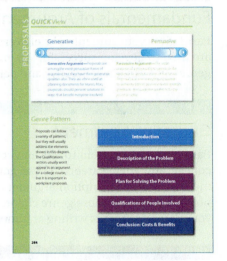

QuickView illustrates how writers might organize each kind of writing and positions each genre in the context of both persuasive and generative arguments. Students are immediately and visually oriented to the kind of writing they'll be analyzing and producing.

Moves for Arguing offer intuitive and memorable real-world argument strategies. The "Moves for Arguing" in each genre chapter will motivate your students to experiment on various arguments, allowing them to see the moves everywhere and go beyond skill-and-drill writing practices.

Features of This Book

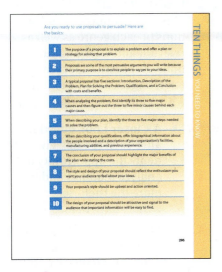

Ten Things You Need to Know offers specific, to-the-point summary to get students developing their own arguments. Every chapter ends with a useful review of key concepts, moves, and strategies that reinforces the chapter's instruction.

End-of-chapter activities give students opportunities to practice what they have read. At the close of every chapter, students have plentiful occasions to "learn by doing" in two ways:

- **Let's Talk about This** exercises prompt classroom discussion, especially in small groups.
- **Let's Argue about This** prompts provide opportunities for formal writing and longer projects.

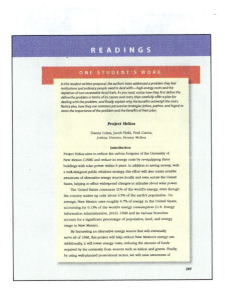

One Student's Work presents model compositions. A student-authored sample in each genre chapter demonstrates how student writers have approached the genre and helps students understand their peers' rhetorical choices.

Readings and prompts

illustrate common organizations of each genre as well as relevant and engaging variations. Apparatus after readings encourages students to interact with readings in a critical way.

- **A Closer Look** questions after each reading give students the opportunity to analyze readings and to explore the rhetorical choices writers have made.

- **Ideas for Arguing** prompts after each reading give students the chance to write responses, analyses, and the specific genre taught in the chapter.

Multimodal strategies and assignments teach

twenty-first-century composing skills. Strategies for composing arguments with electronic and visual tools are offered in each of the genre chapters, along with assignments that offer multimodal opportunities. Chapter 23, "Arguing in Virtual Spaces," encourages students to use Web 2.0 platforms and technologies to publish their arguments and engage in generative arguments.

Supplements

The Instructor's Manual

The Instructor's Manual opens by discussing how genre theory can be applied to argumentative writing and speaking. Subsequent chapters discuss classroom management, syllabus building, and teacher–student communication in traditional, hybrid, or online learning spaces. The second section is a collection of syllabi that facilitates rhetorical strategies/patterns approaches or purposes-/aims-based approaches. The third section offers teaching strategies and support for *every* chapter in the book, as well as discussion of how each chapter aligns with WPA Outcomes. The last section provides additional support for teaching the readings and using the activities and prompts in the Anthology.

MyWritingLab: Now Available for Composition

MyWritingLab is an online homework, tutorial, and assessment program that provides engaging experiences for today's instructors and students. MyWritingLab's hallmark features are now combined with new features designed specifically for composition instructors and their course needs: a new Composing Space for students; customizable Rubrics for assessing and grading student writing; multimedia instruction on all aspects of composition, not just grammar; analyze class performance through advanced reporting. For students who enter the course under-prepared, MyWritingLab offers assessments and personalized remediation so they see improve results and instructors spend less time in class reviewing the basics. Rich multimedia resources are built in to engage students and support faculty throughout the course. Visit www.mywritinglab.com for more information.

Acknowledgments

A book like this one is a team effort with many people involved. We would like to thank our colleagues for allowing us to bounce ideas off them, including David Blakesley, Scott Sanders, Linda Bergmann, Irwin Weiser, Cristyn Elder, and Bethany Davila. Our research assistants, Gracemarie Mike, Mary McCall, Daniel Cryer, Lindsey Ives, and Ana Knutson, deserve special praise for helping us locate materials and developing the Instructor's Manual. There are too many undergraduates and graduate students to name, but we would like to thank them for listening patiently and offering their own ideas as we worked through the concepts in this book. Finally, we would like to thank our editors, David Kear, Brad Potthoff, and Lauren Finn, for guiding us through a complex writing process.

And, we would like to thank our families, including Susan, Kellen, and Dana, as well as Tracey, Emily, and Collin.

We are appreciative of our thoughtful reviewers, whose feedback helped us articulate, shape, and sharpen our vision:

Teresa Aggen, *Pike Peaks Community College*
Robert Alexander, *Point Park University*
Maria K. Barron, *West Virginia University*
Holly Lynn Baumgartner, *Lourdes University*
Britt Benshetler, *Northwest Vista College*
Rochelle Becker Berstein, *Seminole State College of Florida*
Jade Bittle, *Rowan-Cabarrus Community College*
Ron Brooks, *Oklahoma State University*
Michael Callaway, *Mesa Community College*
Susan Dalton, *Alamance Community College*
Elizabeth Delf, *Oregon State University*
Allison M. Dieppa, *Florida Gulf Coast University*
Annette R. Dolph, *Southwestern Michigan College*
Taylor Donnelly, *Clackamas Community College*
Peter Dorman, *Central Virginia Community College*
Megan Edwards, *Old Dominion University*
Carrie Emerson, *Old Dominion University*
Denice Fregozo, *Arizona Western College*
Victoria Gay, *Columbia State Community College*
Rochelle Gregory, *North Central Texas College*

Ryan K. Guth, *University of Memphis*
Tasha Haas, *Kansas City Kansas Community College*
Tara Hembrough, *Southern Illinois University Carbondale*
Christy Kinnion, *Wake Tech Community College*
Linda Cooper Knight, *College of the Albemarle*
Jacqueline McGrath, *College of DuPage*
Vicki Moulson, *College of the Albemarle*
Courtney Mustoe, *University of Nebraska at Omaha*
Matt Oliver, *Old Dominion University*
Amber Pagel, *Eastfield College*
Gary Randolph, *Central Virginia Community College*
Kay Siebler, *Missouri Western State University*
Tom Treffinger, *Greenville Technical College*
Elizabeth West, *Central Piedmont Community College*
William Zhang, *Des Moines Area Community College*

About the Authors

Richard Johnson-Sheehan is a professor of rhetoric and composition at Purdue University. At Purdue, he has directed the Introductory Composition program, and he has mentored new teachers of composition for many years. He teaches a variety of courses in composition, professional writing, and writing program administration, as well as classical rhetoric and the rhetoric of science. He has published widely in these areas. His prior books on writing include *Writing Today*, now in its second edition, *Technical Communication Today,* now in its fourth edition, and *Writing Proposals,* now in its second edition. Professor Johnson-Sheehan was awarded 2008 Fellow of the Association of Teachers of Technical Writing and has been an officer in the Council for Writing Program Administrators.

Charles Paine is a professor of English at the University of New Mexico, where he teaches undergraduate courses in first-year, intermediate, and professional writing as well as graduate courses in writing pedagogy, the history of rhetoric and composition, and other areas. At UNM, he is director of the Rhetoric and Writing Program and the First-Year Writing Program. He is an active member of the Council of Writing Program Administrators and has served on its Executive Board and other committees. His prior books on writing include *The Resistant Writer*, *Writing Today* (now in its second edition), and his coedited collection of essays, *Teaching with Student Texts*. He cofounded and coordinates the Consortium for the Study of Writing in College, a joint effort of the National Survey of Student Engagement and the Council of Writing Program Administrators.

Fundamentals of Argument

The word argue *originates from the Latin word,* arguere, *which means to "make clear." The ability to make your ideas clear and support them with good evidence is the essence of successful argumentation.*

1 Starting an Argument

IN THIS CHAPTER, YOU WILL LEARN—

1.1 How argument has changed recently

1.2 About two approaches to argument: the generative approach (power with) and persuasive approach (power over)

1.3 How to start inventing an argument by identifying the five elements of the rhetorical situation: topic, angle, purpose, audience, and context

1.4 Strategies for developing a main claim or working thesis

1.5 How genres are used to invent, organize, draft, design, and edit arguments

Often, people associate the word *argument* with winning, as in "winning the argument" or "losing the argument." For this reason, when taking a course on argument, they hope to learn how to argue better because they want to win and they don't like to lose.

The word *argue*, though, originates from the Latin word, *arguere*, which means to "make clear." The ability to make your ideas clear and support them with good evidence is the essence of successful argumentation, not winning or losing. In fact, the vast majority of arguments don't determine who wins or who loses. Instead, most arguments involve people striving to reach a common understanding or consensus.

1.1 How argument has changed recently

Arguing Today

The way people argue has been changing during your lifetime. Not long ago, argument primarily relied on a person's ability to *persuade* others to agree with a particular point. These kinds of arguments were typically one directional: A writer or speaker would argue for a specific position, and the readers or audience would

FIGURE 1.1 Arguing in Networks Is Crucial to Your Success
Arguing effectively today means being able to persuade and participate in ongoing conversations.

decide whether they agreed with it. These one-directional arguments happened in essays, editorials, political speeches, closing arguments, advertisements, and business proposals. The ability to make these kinds of arguments is still important, but now arguments are much more complex and dynamic.

Today, we live in a world in which arguments are multidirectional. Arguments flow in real time through networks such as e-mail, Facebook, Twitter, Reddit, YouTube, blogs, chat rooms, conference calls, and video conferencing, as well as virtual and in-person meetings. Mobile phones and electronic networks allow us to stay in constant communication, so you will be expected to work effectively with others in teams while participating in ongoing conversations (Figure 1.1). These real-time arguments flow, evolve, and shift directions, so you need to stay light on your feet. You need to know how to manage the flow of conversations and generate new ideas as events are happening.

In college, your professors will expect you to learn and interact with others through these kinds of networks. College courses are becoming increasingly collaborative and team-centered. Likewise, in your career, you will also need to work in these kinds of networks. Today, employers consistently report that they are looking for people who know how to work in teams and who communicate effectively. Your ability to argue in person and through a variety of media will help you succeed in today's networked workplaces. Meanwhile, as a citizen, you need to engage in the important conversations happening all around you. That's what arguing today is about.

Generative Arguments and Persuasive Arguments

To help you succeed in college, in your career, and as a citizen, this book will teach you two fundamental approaches to argument: the *generative approach* and the *persuasive approach*.

Generative Approach (Power With)

Generative arguments are conversations that happen within groups, teams, or networks, both large and small. In generative arguments, people discuss issues, generate new ideas, share experiences, and strive toward consensus in an open-ended way. These kinds of arguments include discussions, team projects, negotiations, brainstorming sessions, planning meetings, and social networking. They happen in meeting rooms, in cafes, through e-mail or blogs, on Facebook or Twitter, and other places where people gather to talk about issues. Generative arguments are sometimes called "power with" arguments because the people involved are working together to build a mutual understanding and sort out their differences.

Persuasive Approach (Power Over)

Persuasive arguments happen when an individual, a team, or an organization is trying to influence other people to believe something or take specific actions. Persuasive arguments include advertisements, opinion essays, legal cases, political speeches, sales pitches, business proposals, recommendation reports, and sermons. These arguments happen in political events, news websites, law courts, legislatures, corporate boardrooms, and on television. They are sometimes called "power over" arguments because the writer or speaker is attempting to exert power over others with words and images.

These two approaches are basically two ends of the same argument spectrum (Figure 1.2). In any argument, you will need to use both generative and persuasive strategies to achieve your purpose.

However, you might also find it helpful to view generative arguments and persuasive arguments as different, because they pursue different goals:

- In a generative argument, you and others are sharing opinions and information in an open-ended way, striving toward consensus. You're having a conversation because your minds aren't made up yet. Your common goal is to reach an understanding on the issue being discussed.

- When making a persuasive argument, you have mostly decided what you believe and what you want to do. You are trying to persuade others to agree with your opinions. You want to win them over to your side.

When you get into an argument, you first need to figure out whether you are in a generative (*power with*) or persuasive (*power over*) situation (Figure 1.3). This decision will help you figure out the best way to argue in that particular moment.[1]

---

[1] This division is an ancient one, but William Covino created this vocabulary for distinguishing between the "generative" approach and "arresting" approach in his book *Magic, Rhetoric, and Literacy* (1994).

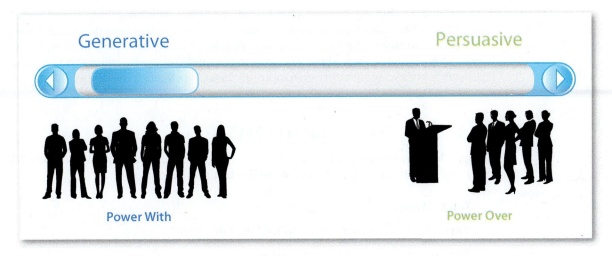

FIGURE 1.2
Two Types of Argument: Generative and Persuasive
Almost all arguments fall somewhere between having a generative conversation and trying to win people over with persuasion.

FIGURE 1.3 Arguing in Generative and Persuasive Ways
Generative arguments tend to happen in groups or teams, where people are striving toward consensus. Persuasive arguments usually involve one person or a team trying to influence others to think or act a particular way.

Throughout this book, you will learn how to argue in both generative and persuasive ways. Specifically, Chapter 2 will show you how to use generative argument strategies to be successful in conversations and work more effectively in groups and teams. Then Chapter 3 will show you how to persuade others by using good reasoning, establishing your authority on a topic, and making effective use of emotions.

1.3 How to start inventing an argument by identifying the five elements of the rhetorical situation: topic, angle, purpose, audience, and context

Starting an Argument

All right, let's say you're in an argument or you're getting ready for one. Where should you start? You should begin by answering five basic questions:

Topic: *What exactly am I arguing about?*

Angle*: What new perspective can I bring to this issue?*

Purpose: *What am I trying to achieve?*

Audience*: Who is reading or listening to my argument?*

Context: *How will place, time, and medium shape my argument?*

Experts in argument call these five elements the "rhetorical situation." These elements give you a starting place for *inventing* your argument. They help you figure out what you are arguing about and what you are trying to achieve (Figure 1.4). Let's look at these elements individually.

FIGURE 1.4 The Five Elements of the Rhetorical Situation
When you are preparing for an argument, you should consider these five elements.

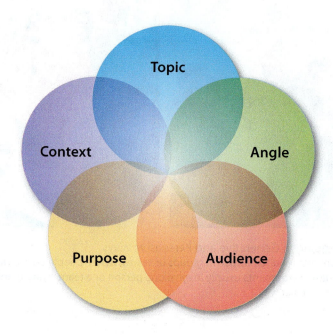

Topic: What Exactly Am I Arguing About?

Your first task is to figure out what exactly you are arguing about. In college and the work-place, your professors and supervisors will usually assign you topics to write or speak about. If you are able to pick your own topic, make sure it's something that interests you.

Once you figure out your topic, you should explore it and narrow the topic down to something you can handle in a brief argument.

Exploring Your Topic

To explore your topic, you should begin with some prewriting, such as freewriting, making a brainstorming list, or creating a concept map. Prewriting will help you figure out what you already know about the issue.

Freewriting—Spend about five minutes writing everything you know about your topic. Don't stop to correct or change anything. Just keep typing or writing. Sometimes it helps to not look at the screen as you are typing. You might even turn off or darken your screen so you can write without revising. Then, when you turn on your screen, you will find that you have written quite a bit about your topic already.

Brainstorming List—Put your topic at the top of your screen or piece of paper. Then, for about three minutes, make a list of everything you know about that topic. Keep typing or writing everything that comes to mind and don't cross out or delete anything.

Concept Map—Write your topic in the center of a piece of paper or your screen. Circle it. Then, for about three minutes, write down everything you can think of on your sheet or screen. Circle each item and connect them to other items.

Figure 1.5 shows how you might use a concept map or a brainstorming list to explore the same topic (minimum age for drinking alcohol). Whether you prefer free-writing, brainstorming, or mapping depends on you. All three of these invention tools are useful for getting your ideas out on your screen or a piece of paper.

Narrowing Your Topic

After freewriting, brainstorming, or drawing a concept map, you should look for ways to narrow your topic. Underline or put stars next to the few items that seem most interesting to you in your freewrite, brainstorming list, or concept map. Then spend a few minutes creating a second freewrite, brainstorming list, or con-cept map around those starred issues.

A second pre-writing activity is the secret to finding a great topic. It will help you focus your topic to an issue you can handle in a college-length paper or pre-sentation. Similarly, in the workplace, narrowing your topic will help you pin-point exactly what your supervisors or clients need to know about the issue.

Brainstorm: Minimum Age for Alcohol

- Full citizen at 18
- Drinking and driving
- Alcoholism
- Drinking in high school
- Binge drinking increasing
- Prohibition doesn't work
- Discrimination is wrong
- Force drinking outside
- Canada's drinking age is 18
- People drink and drive more!
- Bars and homes are safer
- Age 21 makes alcohol more desirable
- We're adults. Treat us that way.

- Forbidden fruit
- Fight in wars but not have beer?
- Alcohol and illegal drugs not same
- Drinking in controlled environments
- People learn to break laws
- Flaunting of laws sets bad precedent
- Would be less social pressure to drink
- Statistics don't back up 21 age limit
- Drinking becomes a rite of passage
- Makes drinking an underground activity
- College presidents support lower drinking age
- Much advertising pitched at college students
- Drink too much when you have it
- Other countries have lower age limits

FIGURE 1.5
Concept Mapping and Brainstorming Concept maps and brainstorming lists are good ways to narrow your topic.

Angle: What New Perspective Can I Bring to This Issue?

Mistakenly, people often assume they need to find a *new* topic. They waste hours looking for something "new" that they can write an argument about. Truth is, new topics are rare because almost all topics have been argued about before. However—and this is important—you can always find new *angles* on existing topics.

A new angle is a fresh perspective that allows you to see an established topic in a new light. To find your angle, answer the following two questions:

What has happened recently that makes this topic especially interesting or important *right now*?

What new perspective can I personally bring to this topic?

What Has Happened Recently?

For example, the topic of underage drinking has been around for decades, so it's not a new topic. If you want to write about this topic, you should first ask yourself, "What's new about this topic that makes it interesting or important right now?" Here are a few possible answers:

Possible Angle 1: The recent fad of combining energy drinks and alcohol is increasing the number of people who are binge drinking, because the caffeine makes people feel more sober than they are.

Possible Angle 2: Binge drinking has become entrenched in some parts of the 18- to 20-year-old culture because my generation has now grown up with the 21-year minimum age limit. College students are still drinking alcohol, but they have changed their drinking practices to skirt and even rebel against the law. Binge drinking is one of those changes.

Possible Angle 3: Last Saturday, two underage college students drowned in Tennessee because they were drinking near a river when a flash flood happened. They were drinking in this remote area because it's an "illegal" activity even though the product is legal.

Possible Angle 4: In August, the government reported that binge drinking among 18- to 20-year-olds has actually increased over the three decades since the 21-year minimum age law passed.

Each of these new angles puts this "old" topic in a new light. They all refer to something that happened recently, which makes this topic interesting or important.

What Has Happened to Me Personally with This Topic?

You can also find a new angle by reflecting on your own experiences with an issue. Has something happened to you that caused you to change your mind or see your topic from a new perspective? You could use your own experiences as a basis for discussing your topic in a new and interesting way. For example,

Possible Angle 1: Within 48 hours of stepping onto this campus, I was offered my first beer even though I was only 18 years old. That night, I went to my first college party, where people were binge drinking. Needless to say, the 21-year-old minimum age was not a deterrent. To be honest, nobody even thought about it. What I thought I learned that night was that some laws could be ignored by college students. That was a bad lesson to learn.

Possible Angle 2: Mike Hampton was a kid who grew up with me in Franklin, Georgia. We didn't hang out together much, but we played football and had mutual friends.

He liked to party a bit more than me, but I did my share. Last month, Mike was out drinking with his college roommates. He ran a stop sign at a rural intersection and smashed into another car, killing one person and injuring two others. Mike's now out of jail on bail, awaiting trial for vehicular homicide. Since then, I keep thinking about how that could have been me. An age limit hadn't kept Mike from driving drunk, and it hadn't kept those people from getting hurt. Surely, I keep thinking, there must be a better way to stop young people from drinking and driving.

Here's a hint: Even if your professor asks you to write about a traditional college essay topic, you should look for new angles on that topic. Don't just offer the same predictable response to the assignment prompt. That's what the others in your class will do. Your argument will stand out if you respond to the assigned topic in a way that reflects current issues or your own experiences.

The same is true in the workplace. The innovators and entrepreneurs are the people who are always looking for new angles or perspectives on existing problems. Completely new products and services are rare, but there are always new ways to innovate on existing products and services. Your colleagues and supervisors will appreciate your efforts to be creative and solve problems in new ways.

Purpose: What Am I Trying to Achieve?

Your purpose is what you want your argument to accomplish. Any time you make an argument, you should have a clear sense of *why* you are arguing and *what* you want to achieve. You should be able to state your purpose in one sentence.

Writing a Purpose Statement

Your purpose needs to be focused, and it needs to be clear about what you are trying to do. For example, an initial purpose statement might be something like, "I'm trying to get the drinking age reduced from 21 to 18 years old." That may be your long-term goal, but is that *really* the purpose of the argument? Could a single argument really accomplish that? No, of course not.

You need to focus your purpose statement on something that could be actually achieved. It's fine to start with a broad purpose statement, but then you need to sharpen it. For example,

> **Broad Purpose Statement:** In this paper, I am arguing that the minimum drinking age should be reduced from 21 to 18 years old.

> **More Focused Purpose Statement:** In this paper, I am arguing that the minimum drinking age does not decrease incidents of binge drinking or drunk driving; therefore, it is an unnecessary law.

> **Even More Focused:** In this paper, I am arguing that the rights of adult citizens between the ages of 18 and 21 are being infringed upon by a minimum drinking age law that does not decrease incidents of binge drinking or drunk driving; therefore, as full citizens who are being discriminated against, we should work toward overturning this unnecessary law.

The "Even More Focused" purpose statement is a bit long, but it sets an achievable and specific purpose for the argument.

Try to boil your purpose statement down to one sentence. This will help you keep your argument narrow enough to be handled in a college-length paper.

Audience: Who Is Reading or Listening to My Argument?

Your audience includes the people who are discussing an issue with you or reading or listening to your argument. Obviously, different people will react to your argument in different ways. Think about your audience's needs, values, and attitudes (Figure 1.6). Doing so will help you select information that is most important to them and present it in ways that they will find most helpful or persuasive.

FIGURE 1.6 Analyzing Your Audience
Each audience is different and will respond to your ideas in a different way. Before writing or speaking, you should analyze their needs, values, and attitudes.

What Do They Need?

Make a list of the information your audience *needs* in order to understand your topic, make a decision, or take action. Meanwhile, think about which of these "needs" will motivate them. At a basic level, people need material things like food, security, health, money, and shelter. At a more complex level, they need immaterial things like friendship, respect, self-esteem, confidence, dignity, and love.

What Do They Value?

Make a list of your audience's values and the things they value. In other words, try to figure out what your audience values and where those values come from. On a social level, their values might be based on their experiences, personalities, faiths, social expectations, or cultures. On a personal level, one person might value creativity while someone else values predictability. Another person prefers an emotional attachment to an issue, while someone else prefers a logical approach. Making a list of your audience's social and personal values will help you determine how to appeal to them.

What Is Their Attitude?

Try to figure out your audience's attitude toward you and your topic. Are they positive, wary, hopeful, careful, concerned, skeptical, or excited about what you have to say? If they have a positive attitude toward you and your topic, you will probably find it easier to reach consensus or persuade them. But if they have a negative attitude toward your topic or you, you are going to need to work around their negative attitude to present your ideas in ways that appeal to them.

This thorough audience analysis might seem like additional work, but it really only takes a few minutes. You can even use Internet search engines like Google, Bing, or Yahoo to help you learn more about your audience and their needs, values, and attitudes.

Context: How Will the Place, Time, and Medium Shape This Argument?

The context is the place, time, and medium in which your argument will be accessed by your audience. An argument that works in one place and time might not work in a different place and time. Likewise, an argument that works in one medium, such as a website, a blog, paper document, or podcast, might not work as well in another medium.

You need to shape your argument to the context in which your audience will experience it. Here are some factors to consider:

What Is the Physical Context?

Think about the physical places in which people will most likely read or hear your argument. Are they at home or in a meeting? Are they in a café or in a classroom? Could they be reading on a bus or airplane? Each of these physical contexts would require adjustments to the content, organization, style, and design of the argument.

How Does the Medium Affect the Message?

Today, most arguments happen in electronic media, not on paper. Obviously, an argument uploaded to YouTube will have a different effect on the audience than a traditional 1-inch-margin, double-spaced college essay (Figure 1.7). Each medium has its strengths and weaknesses, so you should find out how the medium you choose will influence how your audience interprets and understands your argument.

What Is the Economic Context?

Think about how monetary concerns and other financial issues impact your audience's decision making. Even the best ideas won't be accepted if there isn't money or resources to put them into action. So consider the costs involved with your ideas.

What Is the Political Context?

Consider the ways in which your argument changes the political landscape on a personal level. When people make decisions, their choices affect their relationships with others in both positive and negative ways. Even the best ideas won't be accepted if they dramatically alter a person's relationships in an overly negative way.

FIGURE 1.7 The Choice of Medium Will Affect Your Argument
Using a medium like YouTube will change the nature of your argument and the ways your audience reacts to it.

As with audience analysis, this deep thinking about your argument's context probably seems like extra work. But it only takes a couple minutes to identify the contextual forces that shape how your audience thinks about your topic or makes decisions. You want to make sure you are aware of all the factors that might influence the direction of the argument and how people react to what you are arguing.

Developing Your Main Claim (Working Thesis)

1.4 Strategies for developing a main claim or working thesis

The heart of an argument is its *main claim*, which usually begins as a *working thesis*. Once you have figured out your topic, angle, purpose, audience, and context, you can begin to develop the working thesis that will guide your research. There are four major types of thesis statements for an argument:

Generative Thesis—A generative thesis statement tells your audience, "Here's what I believe right now, but I'm open to hearing what others believe and modifying my views." A generative thesis usually highlights the common values, beliefs, and experiences that will help people reach a common understanding or consensus. For example,

> **Working Thesis:** As college students, we see first hand the negative consequences of the under-21 age restriction on alcohol consumption. By working with legislators, administrators, the public, and other students, we can work toward developing a solution to this problem.

Highlights common values and experiences

Stresses a willingness to consider different ideas

Working Thesis: Human-caused climate change is something that will impact our generation, but we need to keep an open mind about the many pathways available to achieving sustainability.

These generative thesis statements are seeking common understanding and consensus with the audience.

Persuasive Thesis—A persuasive thesis statement tells your audience, "Here's what I believe, and I'm going to try to persuade you to believe it, too." A persuasive thesis presents an argumentative claim that the readers or audience can choose to agree or disagree with. This kind of thesis typically has two parts, an *assertion* and *support*.

Assertion

Support

Working Thesis: Politicians won't lower the drinking age as long as students stay silent; therefore, we need to become much more active in the political system by registering to vote, getting our message out there, and rallying for laws that benefit us.

Assertion

Support

Working Thesis: In this proposal, we argue that Knapp University should convert completely to sustainable energy sources and end its dependence on fossil fuels. That way, we can do our share to minimize human-caused climate change while making Knapp into a forward-thinking, elite university that attracts top faculty and students.

An effective persuasion thesis needs to be *reasonable*, meaning at least two defensible sides are available and your audience should feel able to agree or disagree with your claim.

Question Thesis—In some arguments, you might want to hold off stating your thesis until the conclusion, especially if you are making a controversial argument or your audience might be resistant to your views. In these situations, you might pose your thesis as a question:

Working Thesis: Is the current under-21 drinking age reducing the amount of alcohol that young people consume, or is it really causing more harm than good?

Working Thesis: Would the benefits of converting to sustainable energy sources be worth the costs for Knapp University?

If you use a question thesis in your introduction, you need to include a generative or persuasive thesis statement in the conclusion of your argument. For example, the following thesis statements could appear in the conclusion.

Concluding Thesis: The current under-21 drinking age causes more harm than good, so it is vital that we work toward changing laws and attitudes in ways that promote a lower age and a healthier relationship between young people and alcohol.

Concluding Thesis: The costs of fossil-fuel energy will soon rise dramatically, so a conversion to sustainable energy, though seemingly expensive now, will eventually save Knapp University a great amount of money and make it more competitive for top faculty and students.

These kinds of concluding thesis statements answer in a definitive way the thesis questions that were posed in the introduction.

Implied Thesis—In some kinds of arguments, you may choose to not state your thesis explicitly. An implied thesis lets the readers or audience figure out the meaning of your argument for themselves. This kind of thesis is especially common in a narrative argument, because you want the audience to figure out the meaning of your story without explicitly telling them.

An implied thesis can be tricky, though, so you should use this kind of thesis only in special situations. After all, if you don't explicitly state a thesis in your argument, your audience could interpret what you write or say in ways you didn't expect. So, if you choose to use an implied thesis, you need to make sure the main point of your argument comes through clearly for the audience, even though you aren't stating that main point directly.

Using Genres to Argue Effectively

In this book, you will also learn how to use *genres* to argue clearly and compellingly. You may have learned how to use genres in a previous writing or public speaking course. If so, in this book you will learn a new "genre set" that is especially useful for developing arguments.

If the concept of genres is new to you, you are about to learn a very useful tool for writing and speaking. Genres are helpful for generating, organizing, editing, and designing arguments. Knowing how to use genres will save you time while helping you write and speak more effectively in almost any situation.

What Is a Genre?

That's not an easy question to answer. Traditionally, the concept of genres has been used to sort literary texts into categories (e.g., novels, poems, dramas, comedies, tragedies, biographies, epics). Genres can be used to sort other things like movies (e.g., horror, romantic comedy, buddy flick, science fiction), video games (e.g., shooter, adventure, role-playing, racing, strategy, trivia), or music (e.g., hip-hop, country, bluegrass, heavy metal, jazz, classical).

More recently, though, genres have been used to understand how people use familiar patterns to communicate in recurring situations. For example, a movie review is a common argument genre. Let's imagine you are looking for reviews of a recently released movie on Rotten Tomatoes (rottentomatoes.com). Before you begin reading a review, you already have expectations about its content, organization, style, and design. Both you and the review writer is already familiar with the movie review genre, so you are both able to use this genre to make meaning together.

In other words, a movie review is a genre because it is a familiar social pattern that occurs over and over. You, as the reader, know what to expect. If one of the reviewers decides to ignore the genre, you're going to be confused or annoyed. For instance, let's say one of the reviewers on Rotten Tomatoes spends most of her time

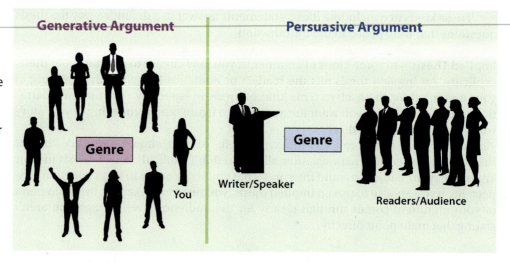

FIGURE 1.8 Genre as a Place Where People Make Meaning Together People make meaning together with genres. Therefore, genres need to be flexible to fit the needs of various situations and people.

complaining about her "dull" weekend while offering only a few comments about the movie she was supposed to be reviewing. You're going to be irritated. She just wasted your time because she didn't use the genre properly.

Genres are more than organizational structures. They do provide helpful patterns for organizing arguments, but they also offer much more. Instead, genres should be understood as *meeting places where people make meaning together* (Figure 1.8). You, as a writer or speaker, supply the words and images that support your argument. Meanwhile, your audience is responsible for interpreting those words and images to figure out your meaning. The genre is a familiar space in which you and your audience create this common understanding together.

OK, Got It. So, What Is a Genre?

Here's a bottom-line definition of genre: *Genres reflect recurring social activities and the ways people in communities and cultures get things done.* Genres help you make choices about the following:

- the information you should include in your argument
- how the information in your argument should be organized
- what style would be appropriate for your argument
- how the argument should look
- what medium would work best for the argument

You already use genres every day. They are the familiar patterns you use when you communicate with others, whether you are talking on the phone, ordering coffee at a café, or debating politics with your friends. Even more than that, though, genres

What do you need to do?	Try this genre.
Describe a person, object, place, or event from a specific perspective.	Description (Chapter 5)
Compare two or more similar people, places, or objects.	Comparison (Chapter 6)
Explain what caused something else to happen.	Causal Analysis (Chapter 7)
Use images and graphics to explain something.	Visual Essay (Chapter 8)
Tell a story that argues a point.	Narrative (Chapter 9)
Review or critique something.	Review (Chapter 10)
Express an opinion on a current event.	Commentary (Chapter 12)
Evaluate or review someone or something.	Evaluation (Chapter 11)
Challenge an argument made by someone else.	Refutation (Chapter 13)
Propose a new idea, product, or plan.	Proposal (Chapter 14)
Research an issue and explain my findings.	Research Paper or Report (Chapter 15)

FIGURE 1.9
Figuring Out the Appropriate Genre
The best genre for your paper or presentation depends on what you need to do.

also reflect the common values, practices, beliefs, and expectations of the groups and cultures to which you belong.

So, when you need to write or present an argument, you should first figure out which genre would be best for achieving your purpose and getting your message across to your audience. Once you figure out which genre is appropriate, writing your paper or creating your presentation becomes much easier. Similarly, when you are analyzing or responding to someone else's argument, you should figure out which genre the writer or speaker is using. Once you recognize the genre, you can better understand, challenge, or respond to that person's argument.

Choosing the Best Argument Genre

Choosing the right genre for an argument depends on what you are trying to achieve. Figure 1.9 lists the most common argument genres you will use in college, the workplace, and public life.

When you know your purpose, you can then figure out which genre or genres would be appropriate for that kind of argument. Keep in mind, though, that more than one genre might be available to help you accomplish your goals. So you should consider a couple possible genres before settling on one that will work.

Fortunately, your professors and supervisors will usually signal to you which genre they want you to use.

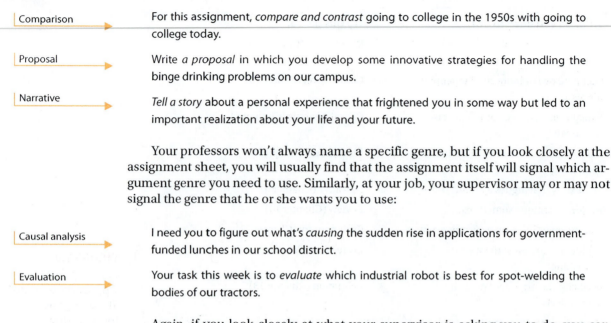

Comparison → For this assignment, *compare and contrast* going to college in the 1950s with going to college today.

Proposal → Write *a proposal* in which you develop some innovative strategies for handling the binge drinking problems on our campus.

Narrative → *Tell a story* about a personal experience that frightened you in some way but led to an important realization about your life and your future.

Your professors won't always name a specific genre, but if you look closely at the assignment sheet, you will usually find that the assignment itself will signal which argument genre you need to use. Similarly, at your job, your supervisor may or may not signal the genre that he or she wants you to use:

Causal analysis → I need you to figure out what's *causing* the sudden rise in applications for government-funded lunches in our school district.

Evaluation → Your task this week is to *evaluate* which industrial robot is best for spot-welding the bodies of our tractors.

Again, if you look closely at what your supervisor is asking you to do, you can usually figure out which genre will help you get the project done.

1.5 How genres are used to invent, organize, draft, design, and edit arguments

Using Genres and the Five Elements of the Rhetorical Situation

We threw quite a bit at you in this chapter, so let's wrap up with a simple takeaway. You need to learn how to argue in both generative and persuasive situations. The five elements of the rhetorical situation will help you figure out your topic, angle, purpose, audience, and context. Then choosing the right genre will help you invent your ideas, organize them, create the appropriate style, design your argument, and pick the best medium.

This is one of those "work smarter, not harder" kinds of situations. You are going to save time and argue more effectively if you spend a few minutes thinking about the elements of the rhetorical situation, developing a working thesis, and choosing the appropriate genre.

Yes, this kind of preparation takes time, and your time is valuable. Try out what you learned in this chapter. You will find that the ten minutes you spend preparing to argue will save you a great amount of time and effort, because you won't waste your time going down dead ends. Meanwhile, this kind of preparation will make you a much more effective writer and presenter, which will help you succeed in your classes and your career. The extra time you spend on preparation will be worth it.

Are you ready to get going right now? Here are some basic ideas to help you prepare for an argument:

1 There are two approaches to argument: *generative arguments* (power with) and *persuasive arguments* (power over).

2 The differences between these approaches to argument are not clear cut. Persuasive arguments sometimes happen in groups, and generative arguments can be persuasive.

3 Generative arguments happen when people discuss issues and strive toward *consensus* in groups. People work together to build common ground and decide what to do.

4 Persuasive arguments happen when one side is trying to convince others to take action or believe something.

5 The five elements of the rhetorical situation include topic, angle, purpose, audience, and context.

6 Genres reflect recurring social activities and ways people in communities and cultures get things done.

7 A genre is a place where people—both the writer/speaker and the audience—meet to make meaning together.

8 Genres help you make choices about the information you should include, how that information should be organized, what style would be appropriate, and how the document or presentation should look.

9 In most cases, your professors or supervisors will signal directly or indirectly which genre would be suitable for an assignment.

10 Genres and the five elements of the rhetorical situation work together in both generative and persuasive arguments to help you develop an effective argument.

TEN THINGS YOU NEED TO KNOW

1. With your group, look over the list of genres that are included in Figure 1.9. Ask each member of your group to choose one of these genres and find three examples of that genre. The Internet is a good place to start searching, but you will also find examples in newspapers, magazines, and other print sources. Then have each member compare and contrast the three examples, explaining their content, organization, style, and design.

2. Ask each member of your group to find an example of a document or presentation that was *not* appropriate for its audience or context. How did the writer or speaker misunderstand his or her audience? What were some of the problems created by this misunderstanding? How, if possible, could the writer or speaker have adjusted the argument to fit this audience?

3. Think of two advertising campaigns aimed at college students, one effective and one ineffective, that you have seen on television or on the Internet. How did the effective advertising campaign target you or people like you in a persuasive way? Did the advertising agency properly anticipate your needs, values, and attitude? Why did the ineffective campaign fail? What did the advertisers not understand about people like you that led them to design an ineffective campaign?

**LET'S ARGUE
ABOUT THIS**

1. Choose a contentious issue that is in the news right now. Write one page in which you describe how people could use a generative approach to talk about this contentious issue. Then write one page that describes how someone might use a persuasive approach to influence the opinions of others. Write a reflection in which you talk about the differences and similarities between these two approaches to argument.

2. Make a list of five topics that interest you personally. Then come up with a new angle for each of these five topics. Your new angle should refer to something that has happened recently or a personal experience that gives you a unique insight into this topic. Choose the best topic and narrow it down to something very specific. Then develop a thesis statement that would give you the basis of an interesting argument. Hand in your thesis statement with notes to your professor.

3. Choose a topic that interests you. Come up with a new angle on this topic. Then develop a thesis statement that you could support or prove. Look through the table of genres in Figure 1.9. Which genres on this list could be used to make an argument that supports your thesis statement? Why do you believe some genres would work better than others? Now choose a genre that would not be appropriate for your topic. Why would this genre not work well? In a brief e-mail to your instructor, explain why you believe some genres would work better than others to help you make the argument you have in mind.

CHAPTER 2

Generative Arguments

IN THIS CHAPTER, YOU WILL LEARN—

2.1 How generative arguments can be used to communicate successfully with others

2.2 How to encourage others to identify with you

2.3 How to frame issues positively and avoid negative frames

2.4 How to tell good, engaging stories

2.5 How to negotiate with others

2.6 Techniques for encouraging consensus while valuing constructive dissensus

Most arguments happen within conversations, so your ability to argue effectively in groups, teams, organizations, and networks will be critical in college and your career. We live in a media-centered world in which ongoing conversations are happening all around us. You probably already join these conversations through Facebook, Twitter, Reddit, Tumblr, websites, listservs, blogs, and e-mail. Likewise, in college and your career, you will participate in face-to-face conversations, such as class discussions, staff meetings, brainstorming sessions, strategic planning summits, and video conferences.

These conversations are called *generative arguments* because you and others are collaboratively using spoken and written discourse to come up with new ideas, share your opinions, compare experiences, build understanding, sort out differences, and figure out what each other believes (Figure 2.1). In generative arguments, you need to think creatively, sort out your beliefs, and make decisions about the best way forward.

Ordinarily, most generative arguments don't *feel* like arguments. In most conversations, people usually aren't openly disagreeing with each other or trying to win others over to their side. Instead, they are working together to develop a common

FIGURE 2.1
Generative Arguments
Generative arguments happen when people get together to discuss issues in person or through electronic media.

understanding or consensus. Generative arguments are also called "power-with" arguments because participants are working together to clarify what they believe, resolve differences, and manage how others view them and their ideas. The arguments might be subtle, but they're still there.

In this chapter, you will learn how to speak and write effectively in these generative situations. Your ability to use generative strategies to argue in groups, teams, organizations, and networks will be vital to your success in college, the workplace, and the public sphere.

2.1 How generative arguments can be used to communicate successfully with others

Four Strategies for Generative Arguments

Generative arguments rely on your ability to develop a common understanding with others while striving toward consensus. Here are four basic strategies that you can use to communicate effectively in face-to-face and electronic conversations:

Strategy 1: Build a sense of identification.

Strategy 2: Frame the issue to your advantage.

Strategy 3: Tell interesting stories.

Strategy 4: Negotiate disagreements with Rogerian methods.

These strategies will also help you generate new ideas and plan effectively with others. Once you learn how to use these strategies, you will find that you can speak and write with more influence in group or team situations.

2.2 How to encourage others to identify with you

Strategy 1: Build a Sense of Identification

Kenneth Burke, an influential American rhetorician, pointed out that people rarely change their minds based on good reasoning and facts alone. Instead, most people are influenced by their *identification* with others. They tend to trust and believe people who are similar to them in backgrounds, beliefs, attitudes, and experiences.

So, if you can demonstrate that you share a common identity with others (e.g., common values or interests, same economic class, similar culture, common upbringing, membership in the same groups, and so on), they are more likely to trust you and agree with your ideas.

Of course, at some level we all identify with each other as human beings. You can, however, look for opportunities to build a stronger sense of identification with others by paying attention to the specific qualities you hold in common with them.

This isn't as complicated as it sounds. As a member of a culture, society, or peer group, you share something in common with just about anyone. So, to build a sense of common identity with someone else, you should be clear about your shared values, interests, or background.

Identify Yourself with the Audience

Burke used the word *consubstantial* to explain why people identify with each other. He defined consubstantial as uniting people through "common sensations, concepts, images, ideas and attitudes."[1] People identify with each other by "acting-together."

In a generative argument, using identification means first showing others that you share or at least respect their values, upbringing, experiences, or status. If people accept you as one of their own (i.e., identify with you), they are more likely to believe what you have to say. Even if you are very different from them in some ways, demonstrating that you respect and understand their values will help them better respect and understand your values.

Let's consider an example. Evangelical Christians tend to be highly skeptical about the existence of human-caused climate change, even though the Bible and religious dogma have almost nothing to say about environmental issues, especially climate change. So why do many evangelicals believe climate change is a hoax?

Here's one possible answer. A majority of evangelicals are *social conservatives*, so they tend to identify with *economic conservatives*, who are usually probusiness and anti-regulation. Economic conservatives generally argue against government regulations, including most environmental policies aimed at regulating greenhouse gasses. So due

---

[1] Kenneth Burke, *Rhetoric of Motives* (Berkeley: U of California, 1969) 21.

to identification, evangelical Christians are more likely to side with other conservatives who are skeptical about climate change. They identify with economic conservatives more than environmentalists, because they trust conservatives who they believe share their values (Figure 2.2).

FIGURE 2.2
Identifying with Others
In some cases, people will identify with groups that hold similar but not the same values.

Of course, this example doesn't tell the whole story. Increasingly, many evangelical Christians are coming to believe that climate change exists, especially evangelicals in the Creation Care movement. Meanwhile, there are a few environmentalists who don't believe in climate change. In other words, people usually agree with people they identify with—but not always. Individuals have good reasons for identifying themselves with specific groups on some issues and identifying themselves with other groups on other issues.

Identify with the Audience Against a Shared Problem

Burke also suggested that *division* is an effective way to build identification with others. He pointed out that when people feel physically or economically threatened, highlighting issues you and they are commonly *against* is an effective way to unify groups of people who might otherwise not identify with each other.

A good example would be collective efforts against drunk drivers. People who drive while intoxicated are a commonly acknowledged menace on the roadways. Efforts to stop people from driving while intoxicated often bring together groups with widely different backgrounds and values, such as Mothers Against Drunk Driving, state police, college students, brewing companies, lawyers, teachers, and politicians. Drunk drivers are a common problem that all these groups can identify themselves against.

Natural and human-made disasters also offer opportunities for people to identify with each other and unify to achieve common ends (Figure 2.3). When hurricane Sandy ravaged downtown New York and much of New Jersey in 2012, politicians like Chris Christie, a Republican New Jersey governor, and Barack Obama, a president from the Democratic Party, set aside their differences to work together on storm recovery. Just weeks earlier, Governor Christie had been campaigning vigorously against the reelection of Obama, but the two leaders could set aside their differences to address the common problem of a devastating hurricane.

FIGURE 2.3 Building Identification by Unifying Against a Problem Natural and human-made disasters often bring people together against a common threat.

Don't Scapegoat or Pander

Identification can be a powerful tool, but when misused it can also be exploited to scapegoat victims or pander to audiences. Burke pointed out that war and violence can be used to unify people while highlighting differences with others. For example, think about the unity and division that were felt after terrorists brought down the World Trade Center and attacked the Pentagon on September 11, 2001. After the attacks, a large majority of Americans felt unified because they identified with each other against a common threat—terrorism. In a good way, they temporarily overlooked their differences out of compassion for the victims and their common fear of terrorism.

However, this identification also had a dark side. After September 11, there were shocking racist incidents in which mosques in the United States were vandalized and people who appeared to be of Middle Eastern descent were scapegoated, targeted, profiled, and harassed. To suppress dissent, people were told, "You are either with us or you are against us." Division can be a powerful tool for unifying people who feel threatened, but it can also be exploited by public figures who are fearmongering and scapegoating.

Another risk of identification is pandering. If you are trying too hard to identify with others, you risk losing a sense of your own identity. You tell them what they want to hear rather than express your own views. Or worse, you come off as a phony who is trying too hard to appeal to them. When using identification as an argument strategy, it's important to draw attention to shared values, interests, or backgrounds, but you should not fabricate or exaggerate these shared characteristics. Most people can spot phonies or fakes.

Strategy 2: Frame the Issue to Your Advantage

When discussing an issue with others, you should be aware of how the issue is being "framed." A frame is a mental structure that shapes how people interpret and talk about an issue. How an issue is framed often determines what people believe and how they express their ideas. Frames also help us understand why people sometimes draw very different conclusions from the same body of facts (Figure 2.4).

FIGURE 2.4 Different Attempts to Frame an Issue
The Occupy Wall Street movement tried to show that the growing wealth gap between the rich and poor was not in line with American beliefs in equality and fairness. The Tea Party movement, similarly, argued effectively that taxation was curbing American freedoms.

For example, "economic inequality" has become an important social issue in American culture. While America has more billionaires than ever, we also have a swelling number of employed people who have fallen below the poverty line. Advocates for the poor would frame this issue as one of "economic inequality." They would argue that it is morally wrong and socially harmful for economic power to be concentrated exclusively in the hands of a few wealthy people. Defenders of free enterprise, meanwhile, would frame this issue in terms of "economic freedom." The freedom to pursue wealth, they would argue, is a creative force that leads to more prosperity for everyone.

When you are aware of how an issue is being framed, you can better use that frame to express your ideas. Or, in some cases, you can reframe the issue in a way that better suits your own beliefs and values. Here are some strategies for framing issues to your advantage.

Listen for Frames

When discussing an issue with other people, listen carefully to how the issue is being framed. For example, in American culture, "freedom" is a common frame. We hear arguments about the freedom of speech, freedom to bear arms, freedom to choose, freedom to marry, and even the freedom to fail. Being free to make our own choices is something almost all Americans value.

As a result, you will hear many arguments being framed in terms of *freedom*. "Increased taxes restrict our economic freedom." "People who love each other should have the freedom to marry." "We should have the freedom to smoke pot." "Speed limits take away our freedom to drive as fast as we want."

Another common frame, *fun*, is widely used with college-age audiences. As a student, you are regularly promised, "This class will be fun." Advertisements imply that you will have more fun if you buy a specific phone (or car, or clothing, or food). Your friends encourage you to "loosen up and have some fun." Having fun is something that college-aged people tend to value, so many arguments are framed in terms of fun.

Other common frames include the following:

security	competitive	creative
success	responsible	reform
self-reliance	low-cost	rights
fairness	realistic	investment
a balanced approach	practical	choice
faith-based	innovative	healthy
middle-class	"green"	high-quality
environmental	honesty	self-sacrifice
being active	independent	achievement

If you listen carefully while you are talking to others, you can identify the frames at work beneath the conversations.

Frame the Conversation

To frame a conversation, you first need to figure out what you value and what others in the conversation value. With these values in mind, choose a frame that will help you *positively* shape that conversation in your favor. Then, as you discuss the issue, you should associate yourself with the positive aspects of the frame.

For example, let's say you and your friends are discussing whether the wealthy (the so-called 1 percent) have too much political and economic power in American society (Figure 2.4). If you think the wealthy have too much power already, you could frame the discussion around issues of fairness and social responsibility, pointing out that American political and economic systems should be fair to everyone and the wealthy should be asked to pay their fair share.

If you take the other side by defending free enterprise, you might frame the conversation in terms of freedom by suggesting that restraining the wealthy would ultimately harm economic independence and creativity. You could talk about how taxes take away people's freedom to compete, their freedom to be successful, or their freedom to create new businesses.

As you discuss this issue, you should frame the conversation in ways that make your views seem more positive and reasonable to your audience. Meanwhile, avoid using frames that put your views in a negative light. If you can get the others in the group to accept your frame for the issue, then there is a good chance they will accept your views.

George Lakoff, a linguist and political consultant, suggests that the keys to effective framing are to a) know your values and b) frame the debate in positive, constructive terms.[2] In other words, good framing begins by first understanding what you and others value. Then you need to choose a frame that allows you to express those values in positive terms.

A simple way to evoke a frame is to use positive words that fit the frame. To find those words, put a key idea that signals the frame in the middle of your screen or a piece of paper. Use concept mapping to discover other words and phrases that are evoked by that frame (Figure 2.5). Then train yourself to use these words as much as you can when you are talking about this particular issue.

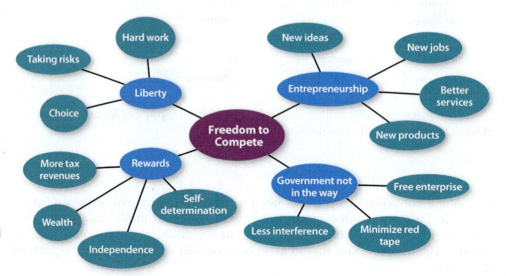

FIGURE 2.5 Using Concept Mapping to Frame an Issue Concept mapping is a helpful tool for developing words and themes that will help you frame an issue.

When used together, these framed clusters of ideas become *themes*. If you keep using specific words over and over, your audience will connect them into larger themes that frame the issue you are discussing.

---

[2] George Lakoff, *Don't Think of an Elephant: Know Your Values and Frame the Debate* (White River Junction, VT: Chelsea Green, 2004) 4.

Reframe the Conversation

As much as possible, you also want to avoid adopting negative frames that cast your views in an unfavorable light. For example, if you want to argue that wealthy people have too much power in American society, you would not be effective if you argued, "Maybe we need to take away people's freedom to pursue wealth." This negative frame would structure the conversation in a way that makes you sound unreasonable. After all, most Americans would react negatively to taking away the freedom of others.

Likewise, defenders of free enterprise would be ineffective if they stated, "It's all right to treat some people unfairly because they are poor." This negative frame would be resisted by most Americans because treating others unfairly goes against their cultural values.

A common mistake in generative arguments is to let others frame the debate in a way that puts you on the defensive or in a negative light. Others say something like, "We need to protect people's freedom to accumulate as much wealth as they can." If you respond, "No, we need to take that freedom away, because the wealthy already have all the advantages in our society," you are arguing ineffectively from a negative frame.

Instead, you should reframe the conversation by responding from a positive frame of your own choosing: "What we really need is economic fairness and political equality that supports a healthy economy and a sustainable democracy. It's unfair for a small number of wealthy people to control our economy and government simply because they have more money."

Use a Metaphor to Frame or Reframe the Conversation

A metaphor is a special kind of framing device that urges people to visualize an issue from a specific or new perspective. For example, the metaphor "Taxes are chains that hold down America's job creators" establishes a visual frame. With this metaphor, the audience can actually imagine people (those job creators) being weighed down by heavy chains. Of course, the wealthy aren't being put in chains (nor are they always job creators), but the metaphor encourages the audience to visualize them that way. It creates a frame by creating a particular perspective.

Some metaphorical frames become so common that we don't view them as metaphors anymore. For instance, the "war on drugs" is a metaphor that has long shaped the United States' policies toward drug abusers and suppliers (Figure 2.6). Instead of seeing drug abuse as a health issue, the war on drugs frames the argument in militaristic terms, implying

FIGURE 2.6 Using a Metaphor to Frame an Argument
The *"War on Drugs"* metaphor has shaped how Americans view the drug abuse problem. Americans tend to view drug abuse in militaristic terms rather than as a health issue.

that high-power weaponry, security sweeps, and armed intervention are needed to stop drug use and trafficking. Metaphors can be used to frame arguments in powerful ways.

Some other commonly used metaphors include, "Our team/company is a family," "Children are wild animals," "Morality is strength," "An election is a campaign," "Love is a game," and "Addiction is a disease." Each of these metaphorical frames encourages you and others to think and talk about issues in specific ways.

2.4 How to tell good, engaging stories

Strategy 3: Tell Interesting Stories

The third generative argument strategy involves using stories to illustrate and reinforce your beliefs and values. People enjoy listening to stories, so narrative is a particularly effective way to explain your beliefs and describe important events to others. When you're dealing with someone who is especially hostile to your perspectives, a good story can open them up a little so they'll at least give your ideas a fair hearing.

Tell a Funny, Tragic, or Instructive Story

Many of your beliefs and values came about because you or someone you know experienced something funny, tragic, or enlightening. Describing your experience with a story is a good way to explain why you hold some beliefs or opinions to be true.

Most stories have five parts:

Set the scene—Identify the people (the characters) involved and the time and place in which the story happened.

Introduce a conflict or problem to be solved—Stories typically focus on a conflict or problem that alters the characters' lives in some way.

Describe how you and others reacted to the conflict—The people involved evaluate the conflict, event, or problem, trying to figure out what happened.

Describe how you and others resolved the conflict—Your characters come up with a way of resolving or responding to the conflict.

Explain what you or others learned—Not all stories end with a "Here's what we learned" ending. However, explaining how the experience shaped your beliefs or values can be a good way to clarify the meaning of your story.

For example, here is a brief story that makes a simple point:

Sets scene →

One summer, my friends and I were backpacking in the mountains of northern New Mexico. We were exhausted because we had hiked nearly fifteen miles through rough terrain. So, when we arrived at our campsite, we dumped our packs, stripped off our sweaty shirts and shoes, and collapsed under some trees for a rest.

Before long, a large mother black bear and her two cubs ambled out of the forest to check out their new neighbors. It didn't take them long to catch the scent of our food. Before we could head them off, they were tearing into our packs and dining on the food for the rest of our trip. Our yelling and screaming couldn't drive them off. The mother bear would snarl and make feint charges at us. So we had to sit patiently and watch them eat, hoping our unwelcome guests would leave us something for the rest of the trip.

Introduces conflict

Evaluates conflict

Eventually, the bears had their fill and sauntered back into the woods. We went over to see how much of our food was left. They had eaten about half of the food and damaged much of the rest. As a result, we needed to end our trip a couple days early because we ran out of supplies.

Resolves conflict

That day, we learned that no matter how tired we were after a day of backpacking, we should always secure our food before doing anything else.

What was learned

Try the narrative pattern out. Next time you want to make a specific point, look for a story from your or someone else's life that illustrates your point in a meaningful way.

Use Anecdotes to Describe or Clarify

Anecdotes are small stories that can be used in an argument to illustrate specific points. You can draw anecdotes from your own experiences, someone else's experiences, or a historical event. Here is an anecdote about anorexia nervosa from "Kathy Carey" by Teresa Joerger:

Kathy Carey used to rise each morning before her husband and children, even before the sun, to go on a ten-mile run. Many of her friends admired her for her athleticism and physical appearance. She often heard people comment, "I'd love to have legs like yours." Her husband frequently told her how proud he was of how she looked. Even her doctor said that she was impressed with her ability to drop the weight so quickly after giving birth to her third child. What these people did not realize was that they were reinforcing Kathy's beliefs that she had to be athletic and thin to be accepted. They did not realize that Kathy, at 5'4", had gradually dropped from 115 to 85 pounds.

An anecdote like this one could be used within a larger argument about the importance of eating disorder awareness.

Illustrate with Hypothetical Examples

In some situations, you can also use a hypothetical story to connect with your audience. A hypothetical story is designed to put the readers into a story, so it needs to be realistic, and it needs to be something people might actually experience:

Imagine you and your friends have been drinking at a party. You're all under 21, and you all had a few more drinks than you intended. The host of the party, who you don't know, is kicking everyone out, and it's a twelve-mile drive home. There isn't public transportation in the area, and taxis aren't available. Now what?

Hypothetical stories often use the "you" style to put the readers into the story. That way, your readers can identify with the main characters and their problem. Hypothetical examples are a good way to illustrate the dilemmas that people face.

Use Fables or Parables

Though not common in arguments today, fables and parables are still good ways to make a point in an argument. Most people know fables like "The Tortoise and the Hare," "Goldilocks and the Three Bears," or the "The Ant and the Grasshopper." These familiar fables can be referenced or modernized to fit a current problem or issue (Figure 2.7).

In religious and some secular arguments, parables are also useful. Parables can be drawn from scriptural texts, such as the Bible, Quran, Bhagavad Gita, Tripitaka, Tao Te Ching, or Book of Mormon. A parable, like a fable, illustrates a point though a fictionalized story. Unlike a fable, though, a parable almost always uses humans as the characters.

Modern-day fables and parables can also be found in popular television shows or movies. People will often use scenes from *The Office, Glee,* or *Modern Family* to explain a point in a funny way. Popular movies, such as *Star Wars, Monty Python and the Holy Grail,* and *The Big Lebowski* are also common places from which to draw fictional stories that make a point. In many ways, these shows are the myths and parables of our time.

FIGURE 2.7 Using a Fable to Make a Familiar Point
Fables are a good way to make a simple point with widely known tales.

2.5 How to negotiate with others

Strategy 4: Negotiate Differences with Rogerian Methods

You can negotiate differences by focusing on *issues* rather than personalities or feelings. An effective negotiation strategy is to use a form of argument called Rogerian rhetoric, which is based on the theories of psychologist Carl Rogers.

According to Rogers, the problem with most overt attempts to persuade is that persuasive appeals force people to decide whether they agree or disagree with someone else's views.[3] This kind of persuasion is threatening because people feel they are

---

[3] Carl Rogers, "Communication: Its Blocking and its Facilitation." *On Becoming a Person.* (Boston: Houghton Mifflin, 1961) 329–337. Also, see the discussion of Rogerian Rhetoric in Richard Young, Alton Becker and Kenneth Pike, *Rhetoric: Discovery and Change* (New York: Harcourt, 1970).

being asked to change their self-image or worldview. That's why people tend to reject new or different ideas without fully considering them. Given a choice to agree or disagree, most will stay with what they already believe, even if agreeing with something new would be advantageous to them.

Rogers believed that an effective argument needs to first remove this threat to a person's self-image before he or she will consider new ideas or alternate perspectives. Therefore, all sides should strive to listen carefully and understand what others believe. By striving for *understanding* rather than agreement, negotiation allows people to feel less threatened and more open to new ideas and points of view. All sides have the freedom to consider a variety of worldviews and then choose the ideas that fit their own needs and experiences.

According to Rogerian rhetoric, you should follow four steps when negotiating with others:

1. Introduce the problem and demonstrate that you understand and value the others' positions.

2. Identify situations in which the others' positions are valid.

3. Identify situations in which your position is valid.

4. Explain how both you and the others would benefit if you adopted elements from all positions. Stress the places in which the different viewpoints complement and strengthen each other.

When negotiating, your goal is not to *persuade* the others to agree with you in an overt way. Instead, you want to show them that you understand their views and recognize that there are situations in which their views make sense (Figure 2.8). Likewise, you should help them understand your views and imagine situations in which your views make sense. Then, when all sides understand the others' views, everyone involved can work toward consensus rather than trying to win the others over.

In this way, all sides cooperate to come up with an understanding or plan that is acceptable and beneficial to all. More than likely, everyone won't agree on all points, but each person understands the others' points of view. All sides can then agree to move forward together.

FIGURE 2.8 Negotiation as a Form of Generative Argument
The best negotiators are people who can focus on issues and negotiate differences. The best outcomes happen when both sides feel like they received something while not giving up too much.

2.6 Techniques for encouraging consensus while valuing constructive dissensus

Consensus and Dissensus

In generative arguments, people are usually striving to reach some kind of consensus. Consensus doesn't mean you and the others will agree completely about an issue. It simply means you are identifying places you agree while openly discussing places you disagree. A disagreement doesn't mean one side or the other is right or wrong. Disagreement only means that full consensus hasn't been reached on the issue.

Striving for Consensus

Consensus happens when people figure out where they agree on a particular issue. For example, you and your friends might be talking about a hot-button issue, such as whether abortion should be legal (Figure 2.9). This issue tends to bring out strong differences in opinion, even among people who agree on most other issues.

Nevertheless, you and the others should be able to reach consensus on some important points. For example, almost all people can agree on the following points:

- Unintended pregnancies should be prevented as much as possible.

- The number of abortions should be as few as possible, ideally zero.

- Adoption should be offered as an alternative to abortion, but no one should be forced or pressured to give a baby away for adoption.

- Abortion is acceptable in very rare cases in which the pregnancy is likely to cause the death of the pregnant woman.

FIGURE 2.9 Lack of Consensus About a Divisive Issue
Even on the most divisive issues, a measure of consensus is possible.

This is what we mean by striving *toward* consensus. There is a good chance you and the others won't reach full agreement about an issue like abortion, especially if you hold opposite opinions. However, discussing this issue in a reasonable way is still important. In fact, you will usually find that people who strongly disagree with you about highly contentious issues can reach consensus on some major points.

When you and the others reach consensus on some major points, you can then figure out how you as a group might achieve common goals. For instance, even though people disagree strongly about abortion, they can agree about preventing unintended pregnancies, reducing the number of abortions, making adoption more available, and defining when a woman's life is threatened by a pregnancy.

Most issues are not as contentious as abortion. You will find that consensus is much easier to reach about issues that are less contentious or polarizing.

Valuing Dissensus

The ability to disagree, or dissent, is important, too. In generative arguments, people should be able to express a disagreement in a reasonable way. Unfortunately, in our polarized and partisan society, many people feel uncomfortable disagreeing with others. So they change the topic, stop listening, walk away, or change the channel instead of actually engaging with the beliefs of others. That's too bad, because even on the most controversial issues, people tend to agree more than they disagree.

Dissensus is important because it urges people to be creative and develop better awareness of issues. All citizens should have the freedom to offer their own viewpoints, even if they know others will disagree with them. Meanwhile, you should encourage people to speak up if they disagree with you or others. That way, you can better understand all points of view.

It takes courage to dissent. When you speak up, people might disagree with you, and they may even get angry. In the end, though, silence and being silenced are the real enemies of civil

FIGURE 2.10 Silence Is Worse Than Disagreement
Putting duct tape over the mouth has become a common symbol for protesters who feel they are being silenced.

discourse, not the people who have the courage to speak up. A generative argument fails when people cannot say what they believe or, even worse, are being silenced by others (Figure 2.10). We are all better off when people are allowed to express alternative views, because these disagreements often lead to innovative solutions, stronger plans, and better understanding.

Writing generative arguments can help you argue better in groups and teams. Here is what you need to know from this chapter.

1 Conversations are generative arguments in which people share ideas, compare experiences, build understanding, and figure out the best way forward.

2 Generative arguments are often called "power-with" arguments because people are working together to figure out what to believe or what to do.

3 There are four basic strategies for making a successful generative argument: (1) build a sense of identification, (2) frame the issue, (3) tell an interesting story, and (4) negotiate disagreements.

4 Identification involves demonstrating to others that you share their ideas, values, and experiences.

5 To frame an issue, choose an organizing idea or theme that fits your worldview and use it to promote a specific way of looking at an issue.

6 Telling an interesting story allows you to exhibit and reinforce your or your culture's values.

7 Some common types of stories include (a) funny, tragic, or instructive stories, (b) anecdotes, and (c) fables and parables.

8 Negotiation involves understanding the views of others while sharing your views.

9 Generative arguments strive toward consensus rather than winning people over to one side.

10 Dissensus should be valued rather than avoided because expressing differences often opens the door for creativity and better awareness of issues.

1. With a small group in class, have a conversation about a current topic or issue that is important right now. You could talk about sports, music, movies, commercials, or anything that the entire group knows something about. Ask one member of the group to silently record the kinds of arguments that happen. Talk for about five minutes. Then ask the person who recorded the arguments to list all the moments when he or she felt people were working out differences and shifting their views.

2. If you have an account on a social networking site, such as Facebook, Google+, or Tumblr, look at the postings over the previous month. What kinds of arguments are happening among your friends and family? Are people openly disagreeing with each other? How are they reaching understanding or resolving differences? What happens when people aren't willing to talk about issues that they disagree about?

3. Think about a situation in which you actually changed your mind about an important issue. Then figure out what brought you to a moment when you could change your mind. Did you feel like you were persuaded by facts or logic? Or did you change your mind because you identified with someone else or reached an understanding by sharing ideas with other people? Share your experience with a group of people from your class. How were your experiences similar to the experiences of others in your group? How were your experiences different?

Let's TALK About This

1. List five issues that people find difficult to talk about with a group of others. Pick one of these topics and have a conversation about it with a group of others in your class. Where do people agree? Where do they disagree? At what points did you notice people becoming uptight about this issue? What triggers their negative responses? Using this conversation for support, write an e-mail to your professor in which you describe how people struggle to hold conversations about difficult issues.

2. Pick an issue that interests you. Write a brief argument (200 words) in which you use one of the four generative argument strategies described in this chapter. Then rewrite the argument using a different generative argument strategy (another 200 words). Finally, write an analysis in which you compare these two strategies, discussing their strengths and weaknesses as ways to argue about an issue.

3. List three issues about which you believe people are unable to speak freely. In other words, what are three issues that others will resist talking about? Choose one of these issues. Looking at the four generative argument strategies discussed in this chapter, what strategy would be most effective for talking about this issue with someone who disagrees with you? Write a single-page, single-spaced memo to your instructor in which you describe how you might use this strategy to open a dialogue about this issue with someone who would be uncomfortable talking about it.

Let's ARGUE About This

3 Persuasive Arguments

IN THIS CHAPTER, YOU WILL LEARN—

3.1 How persuasive arguments are used to influence others to change their minds or take action

3.2 Five strategies for developing successful persuasive arguments

3.3 How to use the Toulmin method for analyzing and inventing arguments

The purpose of a persuasive argument is to influence the beliefs of others and motivate them to do what you think should be done. Aristotle, the ancient Greek philosopher, offered one of the first known definitions of rhetoric (and argument) when he wrote,

> Rhetoric is an ability in each particular case to see the available means of persuasion.[1]

In this definition, you can see the essence of a persuasive argument. To persuade others, you first need to *envision* or *imagine* the available paths for winning them over to your side. Then you need to choose one or more paths and use your abilities to write, speak, and design to convince them that you know the best way forward.

Persuasive arguments are sometimes called "power-over" arguments. When trying to persuade others, you are trying to exert power over them. You are trying to change their minds or influence them to take a specific action. Persuasive arguments are not bullying or trying to "win at all costs." Quite the opposite. To be persuasive, you need to listen carefully to all sides of an issue and respond fairly to any reasonable alternatives. You need to be flexible, adjusting your argument as you gain more information and hear other sides of the issue.

---

[1] This definition is a variation found in George Kennedy's translation of Aristotle's *On Rhetoric,* 2nd ed. Oxford: Oxford, UP, 2007, p. 37.

Persuasive arguments *feel* like arguments. There are usually two or more sides, and people disagree about what to believe and what to do. Your audience understands that you are trying to persuade them to believe or do something. Your job as the writer or speaker is to state your claims clearly and give your audience good reasons and evidence to see things your way (Figure 3.1).

The ability to persuade others will be vital to your success in college, your career, and your life as a citizen. In advanced college courses, you will often be asked by professors to argue for or against specific views. In the workplace, you will need to persuade your supervisors, coworkers, and clients that you have good ideas and know the best way forward. And, as a citizen of a democracy, you will need to take a stand for what you believe.

FIGURE 3.1 Persuasive Arguments
Persuasive arguments involve a speaker or writer trying to convince others to believe or do something specific.

Strategies for Successful Persuasive Arguments

3.1 How persuasive arguments are used to influence others to change their minds or take action

When you make a *persuasive argument*, you are in a position of power. You "have the floor" or you are holding the attention of the audience. There are five main strategies you can use to argue persuasively:

Strategy 1: State a reasonable and specific claim (your thesis).

Strategy 2: Support your claim with reasoning, authority, and emotion.

Strategy 3: Support your claim with existing evidence.

Strategy 4: Use commonplaces to structure your argument.

Strategy 5: Avoid fallacious arguments.

In any persuasive argument, you will use a combination of these strategies to build a convincing argument.

3.2 Five strategies for developing successful persuasive arguments

Strategy 1: State a Reasonable and Specific Claim (Your Thesis)

Using a persuasive thesis is one of the surest ways to cue your audience that you are making a persuasive argument. Your thesis is the moment in your argument at which you are going to tell your audience exactly what you are trying to prove. A good persuasive thesis signals to your audience that you will be asking them to decide whether they agree or disagree with your claim.

A version of your thesis will typically appear in two places in your persuasive argument:

Introduction—State the claim you are trying to prove, or you will ask a key question that you intend to answer.

Conclusion—Restate your thesis with more emphasis. This concluding thesis statement drives home your main claim for the audience.

Here are a few examples of persuasive thesis statements:

Thesis statement: The death penalty is necessary because execution is still the only way to ensure that the worst criminals will never walk free and won't be able to harm others.

Thesis statement: The 2012 remake of *Red Dawn* is one of the worst action movies of all time because of its farfetched plot, unconvincing characters, and blatant xenophobia.

Sometimes the best way to express your thesis is with a thesis question in your argument's introduction and a thesis statement in your conclusion.

Thesis question (in the introduction): Has cheating on exams become so common that college students no longer view cheating as dishonest or unethical?

Thesis statement (in the conclusion): As I have shown in this report, students still believe cheating is dishonest, but the pressure to do well on exams sometimes causes them to put their ethics aside.

Thesis Question (in the introduction): Shakespeare's *Hamlet* has been remade in just about every imaginable way, so is it possible for the Millennium Theater to give this old classic new life?

Thesis Statement (in the conclusion): The Millennium Theater's production of Hamlet uses contemporary political themes and stunning imagery to put an exciting new spin on Shakespeare's *Hamlet*.

An effective thesis question opens the door by identifying an issue to be investigated. Then the thesis statement in the conclusion closes the door by stating your final response to that issue.

A Reasonable Thesis: Choosing Sides

Your thesis is reasonable if your audience is able to agree or disagree with it in a logical way. In other words, at least two defensible sides to the issue need to be available.

A reasonable thesis tends to exist somewhere between personal judgments and proven facts (Figure 3.2). After all, statements based on proven facts, such as "The Earth is a round planet" or "The Battle of Hastings happened in 1066 ADE," are not really worth arguing about. If we stopped to quarrel about every proven fact, our arguments would soon become trifling and meaningless. Likewise, matters of personal taste, such as "I hate cold weather!" or "Cold pizza is my favorite breakfast food," are also not worth arguing about because people are entitled to their personal likes and dislikes.

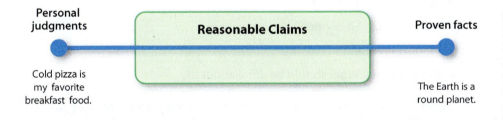

FIGURE 3.2 The Region of Reasonable Claims An effective persuasive argument begins with a reasonable claim. These claims lie in the region between personal judgments and proven facts.

Can you still argue about proven facts or matters of personal taste? Sure. In a sense, you can argue about anything. Some people still argue that the Earth is flat, and your friends might be skeptical that you really like cold pizza for breakfast. You could argue about these topics just for fun, but it's unlikely you would argue about these topics in a serious way.

Therefore, your first task is to state a reasonable claim that you will try to persuade your readers to accept as probably true. For example, here are three claims that take three opposing sides of an issue (other sides are possible as well).

Thesis 1: If we can educate American consumers about the immorality and unsustainability of the palm-oil industry, they will be less likely to buy these products, which will reduce the exploitation of Indonesians and reduce the amount of deforestation.

Thesis 2: While it's true that the palm-oil industry exploits Indonesians and causes massive deforestation, anything that reduces American consumption of palm oil will only make matters worse for the Indonesians by depriving them of employment.

Thesis 3: We must enact federal laws that severely limit the use of palm oil in American food and cosmetic products because American consumers care more about price and convenience than about ethics or saving the planet.

While these claims reflect the personal opinions of the writers, they turn those opinions into reasonable claims. All three sides want to persuade you, the reader, that they are *probably* right.

To test whether your thesis is reasonable, try to come up with at least one opposing thesis statement that disagrees with it. If someone might reasonably support this opposing thesis, then your thesis is addressing an issue worthy of an argument.

A Specific Thesis: Focusing Your Argument

Your persuasive thesis also needs to be specific, meaning it is focused enough for you to prove it in the space and time you have available.

The Roman orator Cicero believed that every argumentative claim could be viewed as hinging on a main question, or *issue*. He suggested that there are four kinds of issues that people argue about:

- Definition: What is it?

- Causation: Why did it happen?

- Evaluation: How good or bad is it?

- Recommendation: What should be done about it?

Typically, one of these four issues will be the main focus of your argument (Figure 3.3). For example, let's say you want to defend an American citizen's right to bear arms while developing some sensible guidelines about the kinds of weaponry people can own. The first version of your thesis might be something like the following:

Rough thesis statement: United States citizens should have the right to bear arms.

This rough thesis statement is way too broad, but it's a start. Let's use Cicero's four issues to focus it. Ask yourself whether your argument is based on an issue of *definition, causation, evaluation,* or *recommendation.* Then narrow your thesis statement by focusing on one of these issues:

Definition thesis: A clearer definition of the Second Amendment is needed because most people agree that some kinds of arms, such as rifles and shotguns, should be allowed, while almost all of us agree that other kinds of arms, such as grenades, machine guns, howitzers, and chemical weapons, don't belong in the hands of citizens.

Causation thesis: Politically motivated gun laws take weapons out of the hands of law-abiding people who want to protect themselves and their homes while ensuring that only criminals and gang members have access to weapons.

Evaluation thesis: The failure of the 1994 Federal Assault Weapons Ban demonstrated that these kinds of sweeping gun laws don't really keep semiautomatic firearms off the streets because such laws are easily subverted or undermined.

Recommendation thesis: My recommendation is that we put the emphasis on gun owners, not guns, by creating a licensing system that reinforces safety, responsible gun ownership, and earned access to more powerful forms of weaponry.

Each of these thesis statements focuses the argument a different way. Which one is most persuasive? That depends on your argument's topic, angle, purpose, audience, and context of use. You might find it helpful to write a thesis statement that fits each of these four issues. Then choose the one that seems the most persuasive.

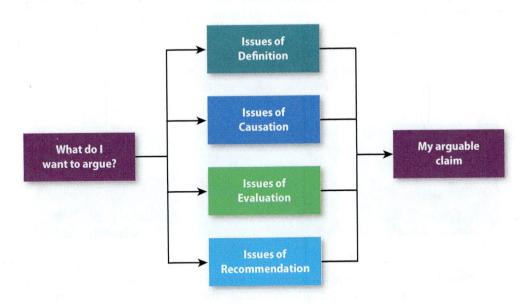

FIGURE 3.3
Developing a Specific Thesis
First, figure out what you want to argue. Then sharpen your claim by figuring out which type of argument you are making. The result will be a much more focused thesis statement.

Strategy 2: Use Appeals to Reason, Authority, and Emotion (*Logos*, *Ethos*, and *Pathos*)

After you finish crafting a reasonable and specific thesis, you should start thinking about how you will support your claim. Aristotle suggested that three kinds of "invented" proofs could be used to support argumentative claims:

Reasoning *(logos)*—using logical statements and examples to reason with your audience

Authority *(ethos)*—using your reputation or the authority of others to demonstrate to your audience that you are knowledgeable, fair, and practical

Emotion *(pathos)*—using emotional appeals to influence your audience to sympathize with your cause or reject another point of view

You may have been told that an argument should rely exclusively on solid reasoning while avoiding appeals to authority or emotion. That's not true. Almost all persuasive arguments rely on a combination of reasoning, authority, and emotion to persuade people to believe or do something (Figure 3.4).

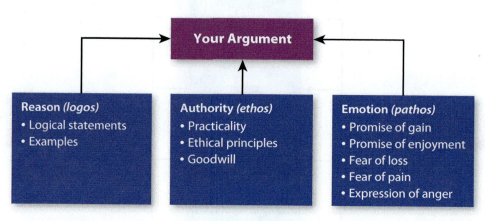

FIGURE 3.4
Supporting Claims with Reason, Authority, and Emotion
Three kinds of appeals can be used to support a claim: appeals to reason, to authority, or to emotion.

These three proofs, which are commonly known by the Greek terms *logos, ethos,* and *pathos,* are called "invented" proofs because they depend on you, the writer or speaker, to create or invent them. In other words, these proofs didn't exist before you or someone else came up with them. As such, they are different from already existing evidence, such as proven facts, artifacts, physical evidence, data, contracts, photographs, testimonials, and so on. (You will learn about using these noninvented proofs later in this chapter.)

Using Reason (*Logos*): Employing Logical Statements and Examples

When you appeal to reason, you are trying to convince your audience that your claim is based on logic and common sense. There are two kinds of reasoning: logical statements and examples.

Logical Statements

When using logical statements, you should use the beliefs, evidence, and facts that your audience already accepts to build your claims.

Logical Pattern	Example
If...then. "If you believe X, then you should also believe Y."	If you agree that biodiversity is essential for the survival of humanity, then you should support the ratification of the Biodiversity Convention.
Either...or. "Either you believe X or Y; you can't logically believe both."	Either you believe that *both* abortion and the death penalty are immoral, or you are not truly prolife.
Cause and effect. "X causes Y" or "Y is caused by X."	The teen-girl media actively peddle the "boyfriend story," which teaches young women that their happiness ultimately depends upon their attractiveness to boys.
Costs and benefits. "The benefits A, B, and C show that X is worth the costs."	Because online learning enhances interactions among students and affords greater flexibility for working students, colleges should invest in online learning despite the significant start-up costs.
Better and worse. "Y is better than X" or "Y is worse than X."	The *Halo* video game franchise is showing its age, but its rich storyline still makes it superior to the more simplistic *Call of Duty* series.
Possible and impossible. "If X is/is not possible, then Y (which is easier/harder by comparison) is/is not possible."	If we could put a human being on the moon at a time when the handheld calculator hadn't yet been invented, then surely we should be able to put humans on the surface of Mars with today's computers and biomedical advances.
Opposites. "If A is X, then its opposite B is Y."	If civil political discourse generally leads to responsible governance, then uncivil and combative political discourse generally leads to irresponsible governance.

Examples

Using examples is also an effective way to support your arguments with real or realistic cases or illustrations.

Type of Example	Illustration
Historical examples	For example, on September 11, 2001, terrorists took advantage of our free society to launch a devastating attack.
Personal experiences	Last summer, I witnessed other employees at the restaurant picking up dropped food from the floor and serving it to customers because they were afraid the manager would yell at them for falling behind.
Facts and data	Data from the 2012 election revealed that that Hispanics are now a rapidly growing 10 percent of the voters; therefore, they can no longer be ignored or abused by candidates who want to win ("Election" 23).
Patterns of experiences	In every national election since 1996, people have reported less resistance to the decriminalization of marijuana, and we see no reason for that trend to change (Ramirez 87).
Quotes and opinions of experts	Dr. Shirley Hampton, a presidential historian at Rutgers University, says, "Eisenhower is often viewed as a popular President who didn't do much, but he actually exerted great influence on the rapidly-changing American society of the 1950s" (54).

In-text citations should be used to signal the source for each fact.

Note: Keep in mind that each of these examples relies on preexisting facts. If those facts were taken from another source, then the original source and the page numbers should be cited.

Authority (*Ethos*): Establishing Credibility

People tend to be persuaded by individuals they trust. If your audience trusts you and your sources, you will speak with more authority and your argument will be more persuasive (Figure 3.5). If they don't trust you or your sources, reasoning alone will not win them over to your side.

FIGURE 3.5
Authority through Reputation Celebrities are often used to promote causes because their credibility with the public is already established. If you're not a celebrity or expert, you will need to work harder to establish your authority with the audience.

You can build or strengthen your authority by showing your audience that you are practical, follow ethical principles, and are a person of goodwill.

Practicality

Being practical means putting an emphasis on solving problems, being resourceful, and getting things done.

Keep it simple—People prefer straightforward solutions that they can understand. Avoid giving them long lectures or spinning out complicated theories that explain the issue. Instead, put the emphasis on taking action and keeping things as simple as possible.

Be resourceful—Try to be as resourceful as possible, and show that you are willing to endure some hardship yourself. Being practical means being mindful of costs and the sacrifices people will need to make if they agree to your argument.

Know your stuff—Demonstrate through your sources that you have researched the topic thoroughly and know the facts and major issues accurately and in depth.

Accept disagreement—You should acknowledge that reasonable people can disagree about the issue. Being practical involves being realistic about what is possible, not idealistic about what should happen in a perfect world.

Ethical Principles

Demonstrate that you are arguing for an outcome that meets a consistent set of ethical principles.

Know your rights (and the rights of others)—When appropriate, use established constitutional rights or human rights to back up your claims. You can turn to documents like the U.S. Constitution or the United Nations Universal Declaration of Human Rights to support your positions.

Find the laws that fit your argument—Refer to local, state, or national laws that support your argument. You can also appeal to any rules or bylaws that govern your university or the organizations you belong to.

Be utilitarian—Utilitarianism means doing what is best for the majority of people. In some cases, you might find it helpful to argue that your position is better because it is beneficial to the most people. Keep in mind, though, that the rights and interests of the minority should also be protected.

Show that you care—The ethics of care stresses that rigid ethical standards can be especially harmful to vulnerable people. In situations that involve people at risk, compassion or understanding might be needed when rigid laws or practices can cause undue harm.

With some audiences and contexts, you might also demonstrate that your position is consistent ethically with your own and your readers' religious beliefs or cultural values.

Goodwill

Goodwill involves being helpful, friendly, and cooperative. It means you are showing that you care for your audience and others.

Understand your audience's needs—Demonstrate that you have your audience's needs in mind, not just your own. Of course, you are likely arguing for something that benefits you. That's a given. Show your readers or listeners that you understand and care about their needs, too.

Stress the benefits to others—Explain to your audience how your approach will be beneficial to them or someone they care about. They should be able to see that the benefits of your approach outweigh the costs.

Show how your position is a win-win—Point out how everyone benefits from your approach. In other words, demonstrate that all sides will be better off if everyone agrees with your position. Don't, however, give the impression that they will win and you will lose. People tend not to believe writers or speakers who seem overly willing to accept a loss.

Arguments that rely on *ethos* often use a combination of appeals to practicality, ethical principles, and good will.

Emotion (*Pathos*): Preparing Your Audience to Make a Decision

Using emotions to persuade your audience is appropriate if the feelings you draw upon are suitable for your subject and your audience. Aristotle wrote that emotions were appropriate if they helped *prepare* the audience to make a decision. However, he pointed out that emotional appeals are inappropriate if used merely to manipulate and warp the audience's judgment.

As you develop your argument, think about the positive and negative emotions that are associated with your topic.

Positive Emotions

Using positive emotions is the best way to motivate your audience to do something they are inclined to do already.

Promise of gain—Demonstrate to your audience that agreeing with your position will help people gain things they need or want, such as trust, time, money, love, advancement, reputation, comfort, popularity, health, beauty, or convenience.

Promise of enjoyment—Show your audience that accepting your position will lead to more personal satisfaction, including joy, anticipation, surprise, pleasure, leisure, or freedom.

Negative Emotions

Like it or not, people can be motivated by fear or anger, especially when they are reluctant to do something. You should be very careful about overusing negative emotions in your arguments, though, because people who are afraid or anxious often end up being more defensive and more hesitant to make a decision or take action.

Fear of loss—Suggest that the alternative to your position might cause the loss of things your audience values, such as time, money, love, security, freedom, reputation, popularity, health, or beauty.

Fear of pain—Hint that the alternative to your position might cause feelings of pain, sadness, frustration, humiliation, embarrassment, loneliness, regret, shame, vulnerability, or worry.

Expressions of anger or disgust—Demonstrate that you share your audience's feelings of anger or disgust about a particular event or situation.

You should avoid threatening or attempting to frighten your readers, because people tend to reject bullying or scare tactics. Instead, use positive emotions as much as you can, because these emotions will build a sense of goodwill in your readers (Figure 3.6). Generally, people like to feel good and believe that agreeing with you will bring them gains, enjoyment, and happiness.

FIGURE 3.6 Using Emotions in an Argument Animals are often used to add an emotional element to advertisements. The American Society for the Prevention of Cruelty to Animals (ASPCA) used this photo on the homepage of its Web site to remind people about the importance of the organization's mission.

Combining All Three Appeals

Aristotle's three-appeals system of using reasoning (*logos*), credibility (*ethos*), and emotion (*pathos*) offers a useful way of inventing proofs for your arguments. This three-part system will help you invent your own argument or analyze an argument written by someone else. Most arguments use a combination of all three kinds of appeals.

When inventing your argument, you might find it helpful to draw three columns on a sheet of paper. Put "Reasoning," "Authority," and "Emotions" at the top of these columns. Then spend some time listing out possible proofs from all three areas that will help you create a balanced argument. The strongest arguments typically draw proofs from all three kinds of appeals.

Usually, an argument focuses more on one of the three kinds of proofs (*logos, ethos, pathos*) than the other two. For example a scientific argument may depend more on reasoning (*logos*), while appeals to authority (*ethos*) and emotion (*pathos*) play secondary and supportive roles.

Strategy 3: Support Your Claim with Existing Evidence

The basis of a good argument is solid evidence, usually gathered from doing research. The evidence for your argument should include factual information that already exists, such as proven facts, physical evidence, artifacts, data, contracts, photographs, and other material items. Evidence can also include testimonials and quotes from witnesses or authoritative sources.

In Chapter 16, you will learn some helpful research methods for collecting electronic, print, and empirical evidence about your topic. For now, let's talk about how to determine what kinds of evidence will be helpful to your argument.

The STAR Approach to Evaluating Evidence

Some researchers use the STAR acronym (sufficient, typical, accurate, and reliable) to help them determine whether they have gathered adequate and appropriate support for their argument.[2]

Sufficient—Do you have enough evidence to support your argument? If you are relying on only one or two sources, then the answer is probably "no." You need to collect a variety and an adequate number of sources. The types and number of sources you will need depend on your argument's subject and your audience. A controversial subject or a skeptical audience will require more evidence than a noncontroversial subject or favorable audience.

Typical—Are you able to find similar kinds of evidence in a variety of sources? If a source seems to be offering evidence that contradicts what other sources are saying, you should take a closer look at how the information was gathered or why its conclusion contradicts other sources. It's always possible that the majority is wrong, but usually sources are more reliable when they are saying what other sources are saying.

---

[2]This approach is adapted from Richard Fulkerson's STAR approach in *Teaching the Argument in Writing* (NCTE, 1996).

Accurate—Did the author of the source use trustworthy methods to gather the information? If the author's methods are unsound or questionable, then the information is probably not accurate. And, if authors don't explain their information-gathering methods at all, then you should be highly skeptical of their so-called evidence.

Reliable—Is the organization or author who wrote the information someone you can trust? Neutral sources are usually the most reliable because they aren't trying to profit from the information. If organizations or authors have something to gain, then you should be more skeptical about the information they are providing. Above all, follow the money. If someone will gain financially from others agreeing with him or her, then you should question whether the source is reliable.

In Chapter 16, you will learn how to "triangulate" sources to help you determine whether your evidence is sufficient, typical, accurate, and reliable. The STAR approach is best used as a way to double-check whether you have gathered the evidence you need to support your argument and persuade your audience.

Images as Evidence

You have often been told to "show, don't just tell." In today's visual society, the ability to argue with images is more important than ever. As you collect information for your argument, you should also be searching for images that will help you explain your subject and support your argument (Figure 3.7).

FIGURE 3.7

Images as Evidence Images should add something beyond mere decoration. They can drive home a point by intensifying emotions or making your point memorable.

Choose images that reinforce your words. Images should be more than "eye candy" or "decorations" for your argument. They should improve understanding, provoke interest, or arouse curiosity. They could stress an important point by evoking emotional responses that stay in your reader's memory. Images can also clarify an issue or even express a unique point that is difficult to make in writing (Figure 3.8). Finally, they can provide alternative access points for readers to skip around through your document or search for specific kinds of information.

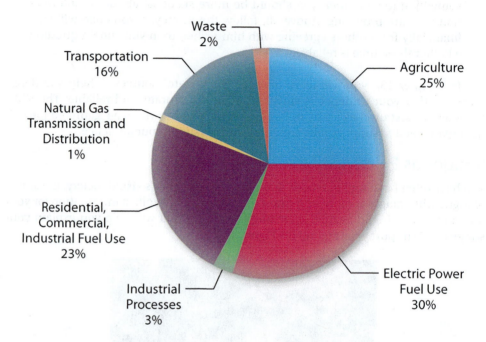

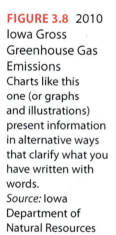

FIGURE 3.8 2010 Iowa Gross Greenhouse Gas Emissions Charts like this one (or graphs and illustrations) present information in alternative ways that clarify what you have written with words. *Source:* Iowa Department of Natural Resources

In Chapter 21, you will learn more about how to create and use images that support your arguments.

Strategy 4: Use Commonplaces to Structure Your Case

More than two thousand years ago, ancient Greek and Roman orators identified a variety of *commonplaces*—strategies or "moves"—that writers and speakers could use to structure their arguments. These patterns can help you present information in logical and efficient ways, especially at the sentence and paragraph levels.

There are two types of commonplaces: *asserting* commonplaces and *responding* commonplaces. The table in Figure 3.9 summarizes these types of commonplaces.

Asserting Commonplaces	Responding Commonplaces
Definition	Better and worse
Negation	Qualification
Two sides	Rephrasing the opposition position
Comparison and contrast	Counterstatement
Classification	Refutation
Cause and effect	Concession and absorption
Division	
Narration	
Proposal	

FIGURE 3.9
Asserting and Responding Commonplaces
Commonplaces can be used to assert new ideas or respond to potential criticisms or questions.

Asserting Commonplaces

You should use asserting commonplaces when you are stating something you believe is true. Here are the most commonly used asserting commonplaces:

Definition *(X is...)*
When defining a word or term, you should state the class to which it belongs and the features that distinguish it from that class:

A _____ is a _____ that has _____ and _____ .

Negation *(X is not...)*
A negation is similar to a definition, except a negation defines something by stating what it is not.

A _____ is not a _____ , because it has _____ and

_____ .

Two Sides *(X can be viewed two ways: A or B)*
In some arguments, you might find it helpful to divide the issue into two sides.

There are two ways to look at this issue: _____ or _____ .

People tend to respond to this situation in one of two ways. They either

_____ or they _____ .

Comparison and Contrast *(X is similar to/different from Y)*

Comparing and contrasting two things is a good way to help people understand something new or unique.

_____ is similar to _____, because they both have _____ and _____ .

However, _____ is different from _____, because it doesn't have _____ and _____ .

Cause and Effect *(X causes Y, or Y is caused by X)*

Identifying causes is a good way to explain why something happened. A cause-and-effect statement is an effective way to argue that an issue addressed now will have positive or negative effects in the future:

_____ was caused by _____ and _____ .

If we do _____, then it will cause _____ and _____ to happen.

Classification *(X can be sorted into Y number of groups)*

Classification means sorting people or items into groups. Classification can be especially helpful when you are trying to discuss a complex issue or something that involves many different kinds of people or things.

_____ can be divided into _____ types: _____ , _____ , and _____ .

By paying attention to how they respond to _____differently, we can sort _____ into the following groups: _____ , _____ , and _____ .

Division *(X can be divided into Y parts)*

You can also examine or describe something in more depth by first dividing it into its major parts.

_____ has _____ major parts, which include _____ , _____ , and _____ .

Then you can divide each major part into minor parts.

Its major part _____ can then be further divided into smaller parts, including _____ , _____ , and _____ .

Narration *(X happened, so they decided to do Y)*
The narration commonplace uses a miniature story or anecdote to support part of your argument.

One time, _____ happened, and we needed to do _____ .

Our experience with _____ was similar to the time when _____

happened and they needed to _____ .

Proposal *(X is a problem, so we should do Y)*
A proposal statement usually identifies the problem and then offers a solution to that problem.

_____ is happening, so our best way forward is to do _____ .

In order to achieve _____ , we will first need to address the problems

with _____ .

Responding Commonplaces

You can use responding commonplaces to counteract or neutralize real or anticipated objections to your argument.

Better and Worse *(X is better than Y)*
When two or more options are available, you should argue that yours is better or that others are worse.

We believe _____ is the better way to go, because it has advantages

like _____ , _____ , and _____ .

Other options may look attractive in some ways, but they would be worse be-

cause they would lead to _____ , _____ , and _____ .

Qualification *(X might not be true when Y happens)*
No solution or plan is perfect, so you should point out any limitations to your audience. That way, you can anticipate and perhaps neutralize criticisms from opponents.

One limitation of our approach is _____ , but we feel the advantages outweigh this minor problem.

It is possible that _____ could happen, but that's unlikely when you

consider _____ , _____ , and _____ .

Rephrasing the Opposing Position *(The other side believes X, Y, and Z)*
When responding to an opponent, you should first rephrase their position in your own words. That way, you can avoid sounding defensive when you argue for your views and against theirs.

Here's what the other side really wants you to believe: _____,

_____, and _____.

Just so we are clear about what _____ believe, they seem to be

saying _____ .

Counterstatement *(X might be true in rare cases, but Y is also almost always true)*
More than likely, the opposing side has some points that are valid. You should identify where you agree with them and then extend their argument in the direction you want to go.

The other side is correct when they argue that _____ , and we believe

the proper way to handle the situation is to _____.

We agree on many points, including _____ and _____;

therefore, we think the best way forward is to _____.

Refutation *(X is not true because of Y)*
If you need to refute an opposing statement that is untrue, you should point out any errors or omissions in facts or logic in an opposing argument.

It's not possible for _____ to be true, because the facts, which

include _____ and _____ , prove that it cannot be true.

The opposing side's argument has left out some key facts, such as _____,

_____ , and _____.

If _____ is true, as they claim, then it would not be logically

possible for _____ to be true also.

Concession and Absorption *(X is true, but Y is still the better way)*
In some situations, the opposing side has produced factual evidence that you must concede to be true. In these cases, a good strategy is to absorb their argument.

Due to the current circumstances, we need to admit _____ is true, but

we still believe that in the long run _____ is the better way forward.

The other side makes some good points, and we grant that they are right

about _____ and _____; however, being right about a few

minor issues does not address the larger issue that involves _____.

Commonplaces are not recipes or templates to follow in a fixed or mechanical way. Instead, they are flexible patterns and phrasings you should adapt to suit your argument. They are especially helpful at the sentence and paragraph levels because they allow you to skillfully assert your ideas and respond effectively to the ideas of others. You can use a combination of these moves to help you prove your thesis.

Strategy 5: Avoid Fallacies

Logical fallacies indicate errors in reasoning or weak spots in an argument. You should avoid using logical fallacies in your arguments because they are vulnerable places that can be exploited by your opponents. Plus, they can lead you or others to draw inaccurate or unsupported conclusions.

Meanwhile, if you find a logical fallacy in the opposing side's argument, that doesn't necessarily mean they are automatically wrong or being unethical. It simply means there is a weak spot or faulty assumption in their argument that you might challenge.

The table in Figure 3.10 lists some of the most common logical fallacies and offers examples. Fallacies tend to occur for the following three reasons:

False or Weak Premises

Fallacious conclusions happen when the original assumptions are false or unproven. In these situations, the speaker or writer is usually stretching the truth or overreaching in some way. He or she might be supporting the argument on a shaky premise (bandwagon, *post hoc* reasoning, slippery slope, or hasty generalization). Or the speaker or writer may be making flimsy comparisons or relying on "facts" from sources that aren't credible (weak analogy, false authority).

Irrelevance

When people realize that their argument is weak or difficult to prove, they may try to distract the audience or change the topic. They will use name calling (*ad hominem*) or bring up unrelated issues (red herring, *tu quoque, non sequitur*) to put the other side on the defensive or distract them.

Ambiguity

Some people will also try to confuse the audience by clouding the issue with circular reasoning (begging the question) or arguing against a position that no one is defending (straw man). They might also try to present two choices (either/or) to the audience with one unreasonable choice that almost no one would accept. That way, given what seems to be a choice between a bad and a worse option, the audience feels impelled to choose the bad option rather than the worse one.

You should closely study the logical fallacies shown in Figure 3.10 so you recognize them when they happen. Again, finding a logical fallacy in an argument doesn't mean you will expose someone else's ideas as wrong or false. However, a fallacy does signal a potential weak spot or faulty logic. In some cases, the speaker or writer may be consciously trying to deceive or distract the audience. In most cases, though, logical fallacies happen accidentally when a speaker or writer has not fully thought through his or her argument.

You should try to memorize these fallacies and also play around with them so you can strengthen your own arguments. Being able to recognize logical fallacies in your own arguments will help you eliminate weaknesses and identify places at which your opposition could undermine your case. Even more importantly, though, by testing your own arguments against these logical fallacies, you will develop a deeper and richer understanding of your own beliefs.

Logical Fallacy	Definition	Example
Bandwagon (*Ad populum*)	Suggesting that a person should agree to something because it is popular.	"Over one thousand people have decided to sign up, so you should, too."
Post hoc reasoning	Arguing that one event caused another when they are unrelated.	"Each time my roommate is out of town, it causes my car to break down and I can't get to work."
Slippery slope	Suggesting that one event will automatically lead to a chain of other events.	"If we allow them to ban assault weapons, soon handguns, rifles, and all other guns will be banned, too."
Hasty generalization	Using a part to make an inaccurate claim about a whole.	"The snowboarder who cut me off proved that all snowboarders are rude."
Begging the question	Using circular reasoning to prove a conclusion.	"Conservatives believe in hard work and strong values. That's why most Americans are conservatives."
Weak analogy	Making an improper comparison between two things that share a common feature.	"Paying taxes to the government is the same as handing your wallet over to a mugger in the park."
False authority	Defending a claim with a biased or untrustworthy source.	"My mother read my paper, and she thinks it deserves an A."
Ad hominem	Attacking the character of the arguer rather than the argument.	"Mary has no credibility on the smoking ban issue because she was once a smoker herself."
Red herring	Saying something that distracts from the issue being argued about.	"So, because books can now be found on the Internet, you're suggesting we burn our libraries?"
Tu quoque	Improperly turning an accusation back on the accuser.	"If you cared about global warming, as you claim, you wouldn't have driven a car to this meeting."
Non sequitur	Stating a conclusion that does not follow from the premises.	"Watching *30 Rock* each week will make you smarter and more popular."
Straw man	Arguing against a position that no one is defending.	"Letting children play soccer on a busy highway is wrong, and I won't stand for it."
Either/or	Presenting someone with a limited choice when other choices are possible.	"We either buy this car now, or we spend the rest of the year walking to school."

FIGURE 3.10 Common Logical Fallacies

Logical fallacies signal weak points in an argument. Look for them in opposing arguments and avoid using them in your own.

The Toulmin System of Argument

3.3 How to use the Toulmin method for analyzing and inventing arguments

In the late 1950s, British philosopher Steven Toulmin grew concerned that argument was becoming too impractical and too dependent on rigid forms of logic. He pointed out that formal logic could be successfully used to prove or disprove the claims of philosophers, but many of these "arguments" were not persuasive because they didn't reflect how ordinary people debated issues in their everyday lives. Rigid logical arguments were not flexible enough to handle common concerns and issues.

Elements of Toulmin's System

To develop a more practical form of argument, Toulmin devised a system that relied on six interconnected elements:

Claim—An assertion or conclusion that the argument will try to prove: "China will continue to grow as an important economic power in the twenty-first century."

Grounds—The empirical evidence or data that can be used to support or provide a foundation for the claim: "China's economy has been expanding about ten percent each year for three decades, and analysts believe it will continue expanding at this rate. Meanwhile, China's gross domestic product (GDP) makes it the second-largest economy in the world."

Warrant—The assumption that forms a bridge between the claim and the ground. The warrant is often not stated in an argument, but the audience needs to be able to connect the claim to the ground for the argument to be persuasive: "A quickly expanding economy that has a large and growing GDP will be influential in worldwide economics."

Backing—The facts that are needed to support, or "back," the warrant, especially if the warrant's core assumption is not immediately obvious to the audience: "Money means power in world economics, so an expanding economy and increasing GDP mean an increase in economic influence."

Rebuttal—A statement that points out any limitations or qualifications that temper the claim: "However, China's economic growth may be slowed by the growth of organized labor, increasing competition with other nations that also have cheap labor, and its dependence on foreign energy sources."

Qualifiers—The use of words or phrases that speakers or writers use to signal the strength of their cases and show readers you're not overreaching. Some of these words include *perhaps, unless, in all probability, maybe*, and the like. Qualifiers allow speakers or authors to signal the gray areas in the argument and identify places at which movement or compromise is possible. Qualifiers also remind audiences that all arguments are based on what is probably true, not what is absolutely true.

The Warrant

The *warrant* is an especially important component of Toulmin's system of argument. It is the bridge that connects the evidence with the claim that the arguer wants to make.

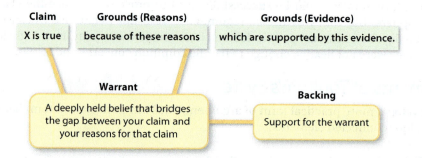

In most arguments, the warrant is typically not stated directly, while other features of the argument like the claim, reasons, and evidence are stated directly. Instead, the warrant is something that the writer or speaker assumes is true without explanation or additional proof. For example,

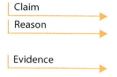

Domestic terrorists should not be tortured or tried in secretive military courts because terrorism is a crime against civilians; therefore, putting the accused on trial through our civilian courts demonstrates to the world our democracy's respect for judicial transparency and basic human rights.

Unstated Warrant: *An accused person, no matter how heinous the crime, deserves a fair trial and is innocent until proven guilty.*

Toulmin believed that warrants should be revealed, acknowledged, and occasionally challenged, because their unspoken nature can allow speakers or writers to support claims or draw conclusions that may or may not be true. Toulmin used a diagram like the one in Figure 3.11 to explain what he had in mind.

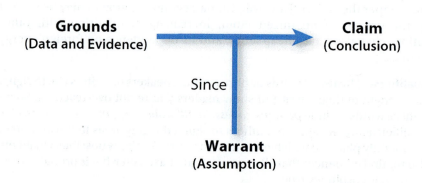

FIGURE 3.11
Toulmin's System of Argument
In Toulmin's system, a key assumption (a warrant) holds together the grounds and the claim.

Using Toulmin's System to Form Solid Arguments

When using Toulmin's system, you might find it helpful to break down your argument into the six elements, answering the following kinds of questions:

1. **Claim:** What claim am I trying to prove? What is my thesis?

2. **Grounds:** What reasoning and evidence (empirical facts or data) support my claim?

3. **Warrant:** What is the unstated assumption that connects the grounds to my claim?

4. **Backing:** What facts are available to support my warrant?

5. **Rebuttal:** What are the possible exceptions or limitations of my claim?

6. **Qualifiers:** How strong is my argument and what words would appropriately signal my confidence in the claim?

Answering these questions will help you put together your argument while revealing any of its weaknesses. The following student example demonstrates an argument using Toulmin's system of argument. This example argument demonstrates how the Toulmin system stresses the importance of paying attention to unstated assumptions while relying on solid evidence.

Sally Reynolds

English 105

April 24, 2013

Boston Marathon Bombing: Can Democracy Pass the Test?

Last week's bombings of the Boston Marathon brought out the best and worst of America. On our screens, we saw ordinary people doing extraordinary things, including risking their own lives to help victims who had lost legs or were severely burned. Certainly, these brave heroes must have known that other bombs might be waiting to go off. And yet, they ran to help, rather than run away. We saw Boston police and firefighters quickly restoring order and helping people to safety. Within a few days, investigators released photos of the suspects, who were then killed or captured the following day in a dramatic manhunt.

Our worst was also on display. The alleged bombers turned out to be two brothers. The older and now dead brother was a violent hothead who was called a "loser" by his own uncle. The younger and still alive brother was a pothead who apparently could not say 'no' to his crazy brother but could say 'yes' to killing and maiming innocent people (Martinez, 2013). Our other worsts included a demand by Greg Ball, a New York state senator, to "use torture on this punk" and calls by Senator Lindsey Graham to consider trying the surviving bomber, who is a U.S. citizen, in a military tribunal as an "enemy combatant." Talk radio buzzed with similar calls for revenge on Muslims and fear-driven doubts whether civilian courts can successfully try terrorism cases.

Qualifier →

There is no doubt that this crime is a heinous incident of terrorism, and if proven guilty the surviving brother deserves life in prison or even the death penalty. However, these kinds of incidents are also a test of our democracy. They help us measure whether we are still a nation of laws and human rights, or whether we are devolving into a society where laws and human rights are casually set aside when people get

Reason →

scared. Domestic terrorists should not be tortured or tried in secretive military courts because terrorism is a crime against civilians. Putting the

Claim →

accused on trial in our civilian courts demonstrates to the world our democracy's respect for judicial transparency and basic human rights.

Review of the Evidence

Let's review the facts. The older brother, Tamerlan Tsarnaev, was an amateur boxer who took classes at a community college, beat up his girlfriend, and became radicalized through a friend and an anti-American

Evidence →

al-Qaida affiliated website. The younger brother, Dzhokar, was a student at UMass-Dartmouth, who friends say was passive, friendly, and liked to smoke pot. Both brothers, especially Tamerlan, were struggling to assimilate to American life, even though they had lived in the United States since they were young boys. Detectives believe the two brothers were not connected to any terrorist networks, instead acting on their own

Grounds →

in a "lone-wolf" attack. The day of the Boston Marathon, they ignited two homemade bombs that killed three people, including a 10-year-old boy, and maimed over a hundred more. Then, while trying to escape, they assassinated an MIT campus police officer. These crimes are, by any measure, horrific forms of terrorism.

Torture Would be Wrong

Given these facts, torturing the younger brother would be wrong. Torture would serve no purpose other than sating some blood-thirsty need for revenge. For one thing, the effectiveness of torture as an interrogation tactic is questionable and perhaps even counterproductive. Research has shown that people being tortured will say anything they believe their torturers want to hear ("Tortured," par. 2). As a result, the "intelligence" gathered may indeed confirm what the torturers wanted to hear, but there is a good chance the information is not accurate or true. Even more problematic, neuropsychologists have shown that a traumatized person, including someone under torture, has impaired cognitive function and confused working memory (Morgan, Doran, Steffian, Hazlett, & Southwick, 2006). In other words, even if a terrorist had something to reveal, the trauma of torture itself may cause him or her to forget or mix up the facts.

Grounds

Torturing the younger brother would show that American society is fear-ridden, reactionary, and hypocritical, abandoning our core values because a "loser" and his submissive brother detonated a couple crude bombs. What kind of message would torturing the younger brother send to other parts of the world? To the developed world, it would signal that the United States is no longer the primary defender of human rights. All our high-mindedness about human dignity and inalienable rights would be proven hollow. Meanwhile, petty tyrants and ruthless oligarchs would see that torture is something condoned, even in advanced nations like the United States.

Backing

Military Tribunals Would be Inappropriate

Likewise, trying the surviving bomber in a secretive military tribunal would show that we do not believe in our own courts or legal system. A military tribunal is a process for trying enemy soldiers and agents during a declared war (Napolitano, 2009, par. 6). In these tribunals, military officers serve as inquisitors, judges, and jury. Using this kind of military court may be appropriate for war criminals or spies, but trying a domestic terrorist

Backing

Rebuttal

Backing →

in a military tribunal would demonstrate a fundamental distrust of an American jury to determine the truth and dispense justice. Meanwhile, to the rest of the world, a panel of uniformed military officers sitting in judgment of an American citizen would look like some kind of showtrial with a predetermined outcome.

Conclusion: Passing the Test

Claim →

Instead of reacting to this heinous crime in a knee-jerk way, let's show the world we are a nation of laws that respects human rights. We can use this tragedy as a way to honor those citizens in Boston who bravely ran to help the injured, even though they knew the risks. We can honor the victims by demonstrating that terrorism does not work and did not fracture our democracy. Let's demonstrate that a democracy is stronger than a couple homemade bombs made by losers. In other words, let's show the world that our nation and our Constitution are strong enough to give even accused terrorists their day in court, being judged by their peers. Let's pass this test.

References

Martinez, M. (2013). Uncle calls Boston Marathon bombers 'losers.' *CNN.com*. Retrieved from http://www.cnn.com/2013/04/19/us/marathon-suspects-uncle

Morgan, C., Doran, A., Steffian, G., Hazlett, G., & Southwick, S. (2006). Stress-induced deficits in working memory and visuo-constructive abilities in special operations soldiers. *Biological Psychiatry 60*, 722–729. doi: 10.1016/j.biopsych.2006.04.021

Napolitano, A. (2009). The case against military tribunals. *Los Angeles Times*. Retrieved from http://articles.latimes.com/2009/nov/29/opinion/la-oe-napolitano29-2009nov29

The tortured brain. (2009). *Newsweek*. Retrieved from http://www.thedailybeast.com/newsweek/2009/09/21/the-tortured-brain.html

Writing persuasive arguments can be challenging and fun.
Here is what you need to know from this chapter:

1 Persuasive arguments are often called "power-over" arguments because they aim to influence the beliefs and actions of others.

2 To persuade effectively, you need to understand the beliefs your audience already holds as true and treat the issues fairly.

3 Persuasive arguments have three basic elements: a claim, reasons that support the claim, and evidence that backs up those reasons.

4 There are five strategies for successful persuasive arguments: (1) State a reasonable and specific claim (your thesis); (2) use appeals to reasoning, authority, and emotion; (3) find evidence, facts, and data for support; (4) use commonplaces to structure your case; and (5) discuss objections and exceptions. Also, avoid fallacies.

5 A persuasive argument's thesis needs to be reasonable, meaning it is a claim that a reasonable person might agree or disagree with.

6 A persuasive argument's thesis can be sharpened by asking questions about definition, causation, evaluation, or recommendation.

7 Three kinds of basic appeals can be used to support claims: reasoning (*logos*), authority (*ethos*), and emotion (*pathos*).

8 Evidence can be evaluated using the STAR model: sufficient, typical, accurate, and relevant.

9 The Toulmin model of argument is helpful for inventing your arguments and finding out if there are unstated assumptions that you need to clarify.

10 Every persuasive argument should take the views of others into account and deal with them fairly.

1. With a small group in class, analyze an argument that clearly aims to persuade its audience. Find one that appears in your local or school newspaper, in an online magazine or newspaper, in this book, or in an online video (e.g., on YouTube). Analyze it using the five persuasive strategies described in this chapter. Finally, determine if you find it a sound argument overall.

2. Visit The Living Room Candidate, which is an online museum of more than 300 presidential campaign television commercials since 1952 (www.livingroom candidate.org). Take some time to explore the website and watch several commercials from past elections, or choose "Type of Commercial" and choose "Children" or "Fear." Every one of these commercials clearly aims to persuade, but how many of them state a specific claim and how many instead make an implied claim ("You should vote for X")?

3. In a small group, choose a topic you all care about. First, compose one or two thesis *questions* (which your group note taker will record). Now compose thesis *statements* that are reasonable and specific, offering at least one major reason for each statement that supports the claim. Share your questions and theses with the class for further discussion.

1. Choose a highly polarized argument that is happening right now. (It could be a national argument or something very local.) In polarized arguments, each side does not want to budge, and perhaps they don't even want to really listen to the other sides' arguments. Now try to identify the very basic questions (issues) that each side considers most important. Write a brief report on this polarized argument in which you discuss whether the issue is a matter of *definition, causation, evaluation,* or *recommendation.*

2. Images can be persuasive, but they rarely make *explicit* claims that are supported by explicit reasons. Instead, those claims and reasons tend to be *implied* by the image itself. Find an image on the Internet that makes an argument. You might use Google to search for images with the words "pregnant smoking," "teen drug addiction," or "natural gas fracking in the United States." Now take that image's argument and write a brief analysis (200 to 300 words) that uses two or three of the strategies discussed in this chapter to describe the image's argument in explicit terms.

3. Analyze a television show that brings advocates on two sides of issues to debate head to head. You can find these highly combative debates on FOX News, MSNBC, CNN, and other national stations. Although each side argues passionately and clearly aims to persuade, are they really persuasive arguments as they are defined in this chapter? Write a brief report in which you discuss whether you think these kinds of shows really engage in persuasive argument or whether they are doing something else.

Critical Reading and Rhetorical Analysis

CHAPTER 4

IN THIS CHAPTER, YOU WILL LEARN—

4.1 Why critical reading is an important skill that you will use in college and your career

4.2 How to "look through" and "look at" an argument

4.3 A simple six-step method for reading and responding to an argument critically

4.4 How to write a rhetorical analysis

You have probably met people who *claim* they like to argue but don't seem to fully understand the issues they want to argue about. Soon, you realize they don't have much support for their opinions, and they don't seem to have good reasons for believing what they believe. In other words, they haven't thought critically about their own beliefs and they don't know how to critically analyze the opinions of others.

4.1 Why critical reading is an important skill that you will use in college and your career

In this chapter, you will learn how to read arguments critically and how to analyze them fairly. These critical reading skills will help you better understanding both generative and persuasive arguments, because critical reading and rhetorical analysis help you figure out why people believe what they believe and why they say what they say.

Critical reading goes beyond simply deciding whether you agree with an argument. Instead, it helps you pull arguments apart to better understand how they work and the motivations behind them.

Later in this chapter, you will learn how use a *rhetorical analysis* to investigate the effectiveness of an argument. This kind of analysis uses rhetorical concepts to closely examine how an argument works and whether it is effective. In college, your professors will ask you to write analyses that investigate why specific historical, technological, theoretical, or political arguments were successful. And, in your career, you and your colleagues will use rhetorical concepts to analyze the behavior of customers, clients, competitors, and markets (Figure 4.1). This kind of analysis will help you better understand why some kinds of messages work and why some don't.

The purpose of this chapter is to help you interpret and understand arguments at a deeper level. That way, you can better understand what motivates people and how to effectively present your own ideas and beliefs.

FIGURE 4.1
Presenting an Analysis in the Workplace
In the workplace, rhetorical analyses are called a variety of names, like "marketing research," "impact studies," or "message testing."

4.2 How to "look through" and "look at" an argument

Looking at and Looking through Arguments

In the past, you have been told to read critically or think critically, but you probably weren't given much advice about how to do it. So let's start out with a few basics.

Richard Lanham, a leading American rhetorician, suggests that critical reading means analyzing an argument on two levels, which he calls "looking through" and "looking at."[1]

> ***Looking through* an argument**—Most of the time, people *look through* an argument to acquire the information it contains. They look through the words at *what* the author is saying, paying attention to the author's facts, reasoning, statistics, examples, evidence, quotations, descriptions, and other information.

---

[1] Richard Lanham, *The Electronic Word* (Chicago: U of Chicago P, 1993) 5–14.

Looking at **an argument**—When people *look at* an argument, they are trying to figure out *how* the argument works, what the argument *does* to readers. They pay attention to its organization, style, and design, as well as its generative and persuasive strategies. They look for the author's motives and values while highlighting any uses of framing, identification, narrative, and negotiation. They look at how the author uses reasoning, authority, and emotion to support his or her claims.

To read critically, you should toggle back and forth between these two kinds of reading. You need to *look through* the argument to figure out what the author is arguing and then *look at* the argument to understand the author's underlying values and argumentative strategies (Figure 4.2).

Looking at the Argument
How

Looking through the Argument
What

• Organization
• Style design
• Motives
• Values
• Framing
• Identification
• Narrative
• Negotiation

• Main point
• Facts
• Reasoning
• Evidence
• Quotations
• Descriptions
• Definitions

FIGURE 4.2
Toggling between *Looking through* and *Looking at* an Argument
Reading critically involves both looking through and looking at an argument.

A Simple Method for Reading Critically

4.3 A simple six-step method for reading and responding to an argument critically

Let's keep this simple. Here are six steps that will help you *look through* and *look at* an argument in a critical way.

Step 1: Read the Argument, Asking Basic Questions

Read through the argument once, primarily paying attention to the information provided by the author and the point the author is trying to make. Then ask some of the following questions:

What Is the Argument's Rhetorical Situation?

An argument's rhetorical situation has five elements: *topic, angle, purpose, audience,* and *context.* You learned about these five elements in Chapter 1, so they will be reviewed briefly here.

- **Topic**—What specifically is the argument about and what are the topic's boundaries or scope?

- **Angle**—What new perspective, if any, is the author bringing to this topic? What has happened recently that makes this topic interesting to the author and to the intended audience?

- **Purpose**—What exactly is the author trying to achieve in this argument? What is the main point or thesis of the argument and where is it stated?

- **Audience**—Who is the primary audience for this argument? What are their needs, values, and attitudes about what the author is saying? How did the author adjust the argument to meet their needs, values, and attitudes?

- **Context**—How have physical, economic, and political influences shaped the author's decisions about the content, organization, style, design, and medium of the argument? How has the author adjusted or designed the argument to fit these contextual influences?

What is the Argument's Genre?

Once you have identified the elements of the rhetorical situation, you can then explore which genre the argument is using. Figure 4.3 lists the argument genres that are covered in this book. If you think you have identified the argument's genre, you can flip to that chapter to find a helpful overview of the genre.

When you identify which genre the argument is using, ask the following questions:

- **Content**—Is the content appropriate for this particular genre? What additional information would be helpful to the audience? What unnecessary information did the author include that isn't helpful or need to know?

- **Organization**—What is the structure of the argument? What are the argument's major sections? Is this argument's organization common for the genre it is using? Where is the author stretching or bending the typical organizational pattern for this genre?

- **Style**—How would you characterize the author's writing style or voice? Is the style quarrelsome or friendly? Is it fast paced or plodding? In one word, how would you describe the tone or voice of the argument? Is this tone or voice appropriate for this argument and its genre?

- **Design**—In what ways does the author use design and images effectively or ineffectively? What tone does the argument's design evoke? How does the author use graphics, such as photos, illustrations, charts, or graphs, to support the written text? Are these design features appropriate for this argument's genre?

- **Medium**—How does the medium of the argument (e.g., newspaper, magazine, blog, podcast, poster presentation, website, social networking, etc.) shape how the argument is presented and how the audience receives it? How might the argument be different if it appeared in a different medium?

Description (Chapter 5)	Evaluation (Chapter 11)
Comparison (Chapter 6)	Commentary (Chapter 12)
Causal Analysis (Chapter 7)	Refutation (Chapter 13)
Visual Essay (Chapter 8)	Proposal (Chapter 14)
Narrative (Chapter 9)	Research Paper or Research Report (Chapter 15)
Review (Chapter 10)	

FIGURE 4.3
Common Argument Genres
Once you identify the genre of the argument you are analyzing, you can go to the chapter in this book that discusses that genre.

Analyzing the content, organization, style, and design of the argument will help you decide whether the author has used the genre effectively.

Why is figuring out the genre important? Knowing the genre of an argument helps you better understand what the author is trying to achieve. Each genre reflects how a community gets something done. So, if you can figure out which genre is being used, you can better understand how the argument works and why the author has chosen to argue a particular way.

Step 2: Play the Believing and Doubting Games with the Argument

Peter Elbow, another American scholar of rhetoric, offers a critical reading strategy called the Believing and Doubting Game that will help you to gain some distance from the argument.[2] These "games" will help you see the text from other perspectives, so you will understand it more fully.

The Believing Game—As you read the argument, imagine you are someone who accepts without question what the author is trying to prove. Highlight the argument's strong points and note the places where it seems well reasoned and well supported. Identify and mark places where someone who is inclined to accept this argument would be most enthusiastic about it.

The Doubting Game—Read the argument again, but this time imagine you are someone who is deeply skeptical and even negative about it. Search out and highlight the argument's factual shortcomings and logical flaws. Find any places where the author is overgeneralizing, drawing biased conclusions, or using fallacious reasoning. Repeatedly ask "So what?" as you read the argument to challenge whether the author is saying something important.

Elbow's term, *game*, is a good choice for this kind of critical reading. You are role playing with the argument, first analyzing it in a sympathetic way and then analyzing it in a skeptical way (Figure 4.4).

---

[2]Peter Elbow, *Writing Without Teachers* (Oxford: Oxford UP, 1973) 147–190.

FIGURE 4.4 Playing the Believing Game and Doubting Game
The Believing Game and Doubting Game can help you analyze an argument from different sides. Then you can synthesize both positions to help you decide what you believe.

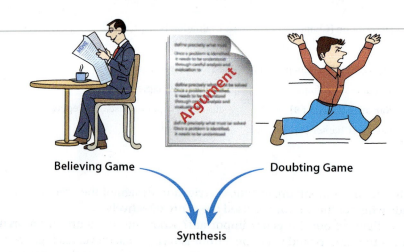

Believing Game   Doubting Game

Synthesis

After you study the argument from both the believing and doubting perspectives, you can create a *synthesis* that helps you build your own response to the argument. This synthesis of the two perspectives will help you see the argument from different sides so you can figure out how your own opinions compare to the author's views.

Step 3: Look for Features of Generative Arguments

In Chapter 2, you learned about the features of *generative arguments*. These "power with" arguments tend to be conversation based, and the people involved are typically striving to reach a common understanding or consensus. Usually, generative arguments are open-ended conversations, so look for places in which the author is inviting people to participate in the argument.

Using identification—In what ways is the author trying to build trust by identifying with the audience? Is the author highlighting any common beliefs or values that are shared with the audience? Is the author trying to build identification by drawing attention to a common problem or shared adversary? Do you think the author is inappropriately scapegoating or pandering to get the audience's attention or trust?

Using framing—How is the author framing the argument for the audience? What are the positive frames he or she is using to shape the argument? Is the author using any negative frames that put her or him on the defensive? Can you think of any other ways that this issue might be better framed or reframed?

Using stories—How is the author using narratives (stories, anecdotes, or made-up scenarios) to support or illustrate important points? Are these stories appropriate to the topic, or are they being used to gloss over significant issues or problems?

Using negotiation—In what ways is the author trying to negotiate with the audience? According to the author, what are the major issues that need to be resolved? Has the author identified any situations in which alternative approaches would be valid? Does the argument highlight points on which all sides can agree?

All arguments, even the most obvious attempts to persuade, will have some features of generative arguments. You should identify these features because they will help you better understand how the author is attempting to build understanding and consensus with the audience.

Step 4: Look for Features of Persuasive Arguments

In Chapter 3, you learned about features of *persuasive arguments*. These "power over" arguments tend to be more one sided because the author is trying to persuade the audience to believe something or take a specific kind of action. Persuasive arguments tend to be constructed with three forms of proof: reasoning (*logos*), authority (*ethos*), and emotion (*pathos*).

Reasoning (*logos*)—In what ways is the author using logic and examples to support the argument's major claims? Highlight the places in which the author is using the following kinds of logical moves:

If…then: "If you believe X, then you should believe Y also."

Either…or: "Either you believe X or you believe Y."

Cause and effect: "X is why Y happens."

Costs and benefits: "The benefits of doing X are worth/not worth the cost of Y."

Better and worse: "X is better/worse than Y because…"

Examples: "For example, X and Y demonstrate that Z happens."

Facts and data: "These facts/data support my argument that X is true (or Y is not true)."

Anecdotes: "X happened to these people, thus demonstrating Y."

Authority (*ethos*)—How is the author trying to establish or draw upon his or her own authority to persuade the audience? How is the author using the authority of experts to support the argument? Highlight the places in which the author is making the following kinds of authority-based moves:

Personal experience: "I have experienced X, so I know it's true and Y is not."

Personal credentials: "I have a degree in Z" or "I am the director of Y." "So I know a lot about the subject of X."

Good moral character: "I have always done the right thing for the right reasons, so you should believe me when I say that X is the best path to follow."

Appeal to experts: "According to Z, who is an expert on this topic, X is true and Y is not true."

Identification with the readers: "You and I come from similar backgrounds and we have similar values; therefore, you would likely agree with me that X is true and Y is not."

Admission of limitations: "I may not know much about Z, but I do know that X is true and Y is not."

Expression of goodwill: "I want what is best for you, so I am recommending X as the best path to follow."

Use of "insider" language: Using jargon or referring to information that primarily insiders would understand.

Emotion (*pathos*)—How is the author trying to inject emotions into the argument? What emotions does the author want the audience to feel as they consider the argument? In what ways is the author using words or images to try to evoke those emotions? Highlight the places in which the author is making some of the following emotional moves:

Promise of gain: "By agreeing with us, you will gain trust, time, money, love, advancement, reputation, comfort, popularity, health, beauty, or convenience."

Promise of enjoyment: "If you do things our way, you will experience joy, anticipation, fun, surprises, enjoyment, pleasure, leisure, or freedom."

Fear of loss: "If you don't do things this way, you risk losing time, money, love, security, freedom, reputation, popularity, health, or beauty."

Fear of pain: "If you don't do things this way, you may feel pain, sadness, grief, frustration, humiliation, embarrassment, loneliness, regret, shame, vulnerability, or worry."

Expressions of anger or disgust: "You should be angry or disgusted because X is unfair to you, me, or others."

Any argument will use a combination of *logos*, *ethos*, and *pathos*. Advertising, of course, relies heavily on *pathos*, but ads also use *logos* and *ethos* to persuade. Scientific texts, meanwhile, are dominated by *logos*, but scientists can draw upon their reputation (*ethos*) and they will occasionally even show emotion (*pathos*) about their topic (Figure 4.5).

FIGURE 4.5 Using Emotion in a Scientific Argument Emotional proofs can be a significant part of any argument even when the topic is scientific. In this picture, scientist Jane Goodall is using emotion to make an important point.

Step 5: Reflect on Your Own Reactions to the Argument

Here's the really tough part. Reflect critically on your own responses and reactions to the argument. No matter how unbiased or impartial you tried to be, as you were reading you still relied on your own existing values and knowledge to help you decide whether the argument was effective. Here are a few questions you can ask yourself:

- What was my first reaction when I started reading the argument?

- How did my first reaction influence how I interpreted the remainder of the argument?

- Where does the argument seem to be agreeing with my views?

- Where is it disagreeing with my views?

- When was I agreeing most with the argument?

- When did I want to argue against it?

- Now that I have spent time analyzing the argument, have my views on this issue changed at all?

Ultimately, critical reading isn't really about the argument you're analyzing. It's about you. Without you, an argument is just ink on a page or pixels on a screen. The argument relies completely on you to interpret and make sense of what the author or presenter is trying to say.

The key to effective critical reading is to continually rethink and reevaluate your own knowledge, values, and beliefs. If an argument challenges you, that's a good thing. If you agree or disagree with it, perhaps the argument will strengthen your convictions. Or maybe you will shift your views or change your mind. Either way, you come away from the experience stronger and better able to understand and articulate the things you believe in.

Step 6: Respond to the Argument

When responding to an argument, you should do more than conclude whether you agree or disagree. In any argument, both sides will have some merit—otherwise, the topic is not really worth arguing about. So you need to explain your response and where your views align with or diverge from the author's views. Here are some questions that will help you form your own response:

Why Does the Argument Matter?

Explain why you think people should care about the argument and why.

_____ is an important issue because _____.

While _____ might not seem important on first glance, it has several important consequences, such as _____, _____, and _____.

Example response: Although childhood obesity might seem like it's just a matter of childhood health that will resolve itself over time, public health studies show that obese children are far more likely to become obese adults, which leads to lifelong health issues for the individuals and skyrocketing healthcare costs for society.

Where and Why Do You Disagree with the Argument?

Describe exactly where the various sides disagree. In Chapter 3 you learned about four categories of issues on which people tend to agree: definition, causation, evaluation, or recommendation.

At the heart of this debate is a disagreement about that nature of _____, whether it was _____ or _____ . **(Definition)**

While most people agree that _____ is caused by _____ , they disagree whether we should _____ or _____ . **(Causation)**

_____ is something we should pay attention to, but it's not important enough for us to do _____ . **(Evaluation)**

I agree that _____ is an issue that needs to be addressed, and I believe the best way forward is to do _____ . **(Recommendation)**

Example response: Although childhood obesity is an important issue that is caused primarily by Americans' junk-food and fast-food habits, I disagree that the problem can be solved by imposing taxes on these foods. Instead, the better solution is to educate Americans and provide positive incentives for adopting healthy dietary habits.

Where and Why Do You Personally Agree with the Argument?

Finally, describe exactly where and why you and others agree with the argument you are analyzing. It's unlikely you agree completely with the author, but you can find places at which your values and beliefs align with the author's values and beliefs. Joseph Harris offers a useful four-point system for demonstrating why you agree with an argument. In *Rewriting: How to Do Things with Texts*, he identifies four key activities:

Illustrating—Use points, descriptions, or stories provided by the argument to support your own views. An author may make a point, provide facts, and provide other evidence that strengthen your argument.

Authorizing—Use the authority, expertise, or experience of the author to strengthen your own position and give it more validity. You can cite the author as support for your own argument.

Borrowing—Use a term, definition, or idea developed in the argument. If your own opinion hinges on a technical concept, key term, definition, or idea, you can borrow and cite what the author says.

Extending—Use the author's argument as starting place for launching your own argument. Your argument might extend the author's argument in a new direction or apply it to topics that the author did not consider.

Reacting and responding to an argument is more than a matter of agreeing or disagreeing. Whether the argument is generative or persuasive, you should feel free to add something to the conversation or explain why you agree or disagree with the author.

Writing a Rhetorical Analysis

4.4 How to write a rhetorical analysis

A rhetorical analysis takes critical reading a step further. The purpose of a rhetorical analysis is to use rhetorical concepts to closely examine how an argument works and determine whether it is *effective* or *ineffective*. You're not figuring out whether the argument is true or false. Instead, you are investigating its effectiveness.

There are a variety of analytical methods available for writing a rhetorical analysis of an argument, but here are a few of the most common:

Analysis of *logos, ethos*, and/or *pathos*—examines how reasoning, credibility, and emotional proofs are used to support an argument, especially a persuasive argument. All three kinds of proofs can be discussed together in the rhetorical analysis, or you can focus on just one of them.

Audience analysis—researches how the argument was written to reflect the needs, values, and attitudes of the targeted audience. An audience analysis also pays attention to how the argument's context (physical, economic, political, and medium) influences how the message was received by the audience.

Genre analysis—studies how an argument uses or deviates from a common genre. You can use the genre to discuss how a specific argument works and whether it is effective.

Narrative analysis—uses elements of narrative (see Chapter 9 on narrative argument) to investigate how a story or stories were used to deliver the argument's message.

Metaphor analysis—pays special attention to the author's or presenter's attempts to frame or reframe an argument through the use of metaphors (see Chapter 20 for more on metaphor).

Stylistic analysis—looks closely at an argument's use of stylistic devices, such as metaphors, similes, analogies, personification, onomatopoeia, rhythm, voice, and tone (see Chapter 20 for more on style).

Visual analysis—uses principles of visual design and visual rhetoric (see Chapter 21 on visual design) to study how the appearance of an argument shapes its message and its impact on the audience.

You can organize a rhetorical analysis in a variety of ways. One of the most common patterns is shown in Figure 4.6. In this pattern, after a brief introduction, the

FIGURE 4.6

Organizing a Rhetorical Analysis
Rhetorical analyses tend to follow a pattern similar to this one. After one or more rhetorical concepts are defined and explained, they are used to analyze the argument.

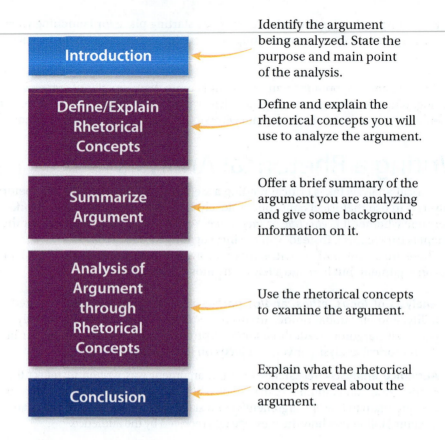

Introduction — Identify the argument being analyzed. State the purpose and main point of the analysis.

Define/Explain Rhetorical Concepts — Define and explain the rhetorical concepts you will use to analyze the argument.

Summarize Argument — Offer a brief summary of the argument you are analyzing and give some background information on it.

Analysis of Argument through Rhetorical Concepts — Use the rhetorical concepts to examine the argument.

Conclusion — Explain what the rhetorical concepts reveal about the argument.

rhetorical concepts are explained and the argument is summarized. Then the selected rhetorical concepts are used to analyze the argument. Typically a rhetorical analysis ends by explaining what the rhetorical concepts reveal about the argument.

The aim of a rhetorical analysis is to extend your critical reading beyond response into a thorough analysis that can be shared with others. A rhetorical analysis lets you use one or more rhetorical concepts to explore and examine how an argument works. It also helps you explain why an argument was effective or ineffective.

Even more importantly, though, a rhetorical analysis helps you and others understand how certain rhetorical techniques, such as identification, framing, narrative, or the use of *logos*, *ethos*, and *pathos*, can make an argument more effective.

Just want the basics? Here's what you need to know about critical reading and rhetorical analysis.

1   Critical reading gives you the ability to examine arguments to figure out how they work and whether they are reasonable.

2   A rhetorical analysis uses rhetorical concepts to closely examine how an argument works and whether it is effective.

3   When you *look through* an argument, you are paying attention to *what* someone else is saying, and when you *look at* an argument, you are paying attention to *how* that person is arguing.

4   Step 1: Read the argument and ask basic questions about its rhetorical situation and genre.

5   Step 2: Play the Believing and Doubting Games to interpret the argument from two opposite perspectives.

6   Step 3: Look for features of generative arguments.

7   Step 4: Look for features of persuasive arguments.

8   Step 5: Reflect on your own reactions to the argument to help you manage your own bias for or against the argument.

9   Step 6: Develop your own response to the argument, explaining where you agree, where you disagree, and the reasons that you disagree.

10   A rhetorical analysis allows you to discuss why an argument is effective or ineffective.

1. In your group, discuss what you have been taught previously about critical thinking or critical reading. Have you been given strategies for critical reading before? If so, share them with the group and discuss how they differ from the strategies discussed in this chapter. Then discuss the difference between uncritical reading/thinking and critical reading/thinking. Do you know anyone who does not think or read critically? Describe how that person behaves during an argument. Describe how people who don't read or think critically tend to argue.

2. Ask each member of your group to bring an argument from the Internet to class. Using the six critical reading strategies discussed in this chapter, analyze two of the arguments. What do the strategies in this chapter reveal about both arguments? In what ways do they allow you to *look through* and *look at* the argument?

3. List five ways that the ability to read critically will be important to your future career. Think about the kinds of analysis you will need to do at your job. How will the ability to analyze arguments critically help you better understand the arguments at your workplace? Then list three workplace activities that are similar to doing a rhetorical analysis. Share and discuss your two lists with your group.

1. Find a written argument on the Internet or in a print source. Fold a piece of paper in half lengthwise and play the Believing Game and the Doubting Game with the argument. First, imagine that you are completely sold on the argument. On one half of the paper, write down all the positive things you can think of. Second, imagine you are completely skeptical of the argument. Write down all your doubts, questions, and concerns about the argument. Then open the sheet of paper and look at both lists. In an e-mail to your instructor, summarize both your positive and skeptical views of the argument. Then discuss where your own views fit between these two positions.

2. With two other people in your class, use the six critical reading strategies discussed in this chapter to analyze one of the arguments that appears at the end of the genre chapters in this book (Chapters 5-15). You and your teammates should divide up the six strategies, with each of you handling two of them. Then, when you are finished analyzing the argument, get together and share your analyses. Take special note of places your analyses seemed to complement each other and places the analyses seemed to contradict. Combine your notes and present your findings to the class.

3. Find an argument that you disagree with on the Internet or in a print source. Write a rhetorical analysis in which you try to be as objective as possible. You don't need to be completely neutral, but you need to fairly consider the author's ideas and analyze his or her text. Use rhetorical concepts to show why you felt the argument was ineffective or not persuasive. If you haven't written a rhetorical analysis before, you might consider following the pattern shown in Figure 4.6 to guide your writing.

Effective Diplomacy: Examining the Rhetorical Elements of Obama's 2009 Cairo Speech

Jeremy Dellarosa, English 102

Over the course of his first term (and now well into a second), President Barack Obama has proven himself to be an effective and inspiring orator, the likes of which has not been seen perhaps since the presidencies of John F. Kennedy and Ronald Reagan. Time and again, through the power of the spoken word, he has walked a delicate line to reach across the diverse viewpoints that make up this country (and the world). In his most memorable speeches, Obama manages to strike a balance between two rhetorical goals: rousing the emotions of his supporters while simultaneously calming his opponents.

Of all of the speeches that Obama has delivered, he faced perhaps the most difficult challenge in his 2009 address from Cairo University in Egypt, where he needed to acknowledge the validity of Muslims' displeased feelings toward the United States while simultaneously portraying his nation and his presidency as strong and just. In just shy of an hour, the president managed to address the strained feelings at the heart of U.S.–Muslim relations, acknowledging tensions, conceding mistakes, and painting a hopeful landscape of a potential future for the Muslim world.

The Speech: Acknowledging the Strain Between Cultures

Throughout his speech, President Obama systematically addresses the myriad issues that will affect the future of the Islamic world. Furthermore, he manages to confront the uneasy (in some cases, contemptuous) relationship that has existed between the Islamic world and America, particularly since 9/11, "nursing the grievances of decades sharpened by the blows of the past

Identifies the background and rhetorical situation

identifies the purpose and states main point of the rhetorical analysis

Elaborates on the rhetorical situation and summarizes the rhetorical strategies used in the speech

81

eight years that preceded Obama's presidency—the invasion and occupation of Iraq, the collapse of the Arab-Israeli peace process" (Schleifer, 2009, para. 13). He even acknowledges problems going back to the Eisenhower era (Herman, 2009, para. 4–5). Needless to say, acknowledgement of these issues would be an audacious move for any contemporary U.S. politician. Yet Obama does not approach these topics in the same haughty, arrogant, disconnected manner that Americans had grown accustomed to during the previous administration. Instead, the tone of the speech is humble, perhaps even entreating at times, yet it is still full of resolve. Furthermore, the potency of the speech is bolstered by its structure, utilizing simultaneous and overlapping appeals to *ethos, logos,* and *pathos* in order to make a meaningful and effective case for improved American relations with this turbulent region.

Using *Ethos* to Establish Credibility and Goodwill

Almost immediately, President Obama begins his speech with an appeal to *ethos,* establishing his own credibility and his goodwill toward the Islamic world. He shows he understands Islamic culture, recounting his own experience with Islam, from his father's Muslim heritage and his childhood years in Indonesia to his time spent working in and among Muslim communities in Chicago. He develops this display of *ethos* to the Muslim world while simultaneously using *logos,* through reasoning and examples, to remind the West about the significant historical contributions of Islam to the rest of the world. He speaks of "civilization's debt to Islam," saying, "It was Islam … that carried the light of learning through so many centuries, paving the way for Europe's renaissance and enlightenment" (Obama, 2009, para. 13.) He describes the invaluable progress made by Muslims in the areas of mathematics and science, medicine, literature, art, and architecture. He also supports his point by stating, "throughout history, Islam has demonstrated through words and deeds the possibilities of religious tolerance and racial equality" (para. 12–14). Lastly, Obama shows his knowledge of the Quran, not merely displaying how much he knows, but more importantly employing its authority to back up the points he wants to make:

Describes how *ethos* is used to establish authority and credibility

Quotes Obama to illustrate his use of *ethos,* showing goodwill to both sides

The Holy Quran teaches that whoever kills an innocent... it is as if   5
he has killed all mankind. And the Holy Quran also says whoever
saves a person, it is as if he has saved all mankind. (para. 42)

Using *Logos* to Set Common Goals

At this point, Obama turns more directly to using *logos* to urge Americans
and Muslims to work together toward a common goal. First he offers
several historical examples of Muslims succeeding in and contributing to
America:

> They have fought in our wars. They have served in our government.
> They have stood for civil rights. They have started businesses. They have
> taught at our universities. They've excelled in our sports arenas. They've
> won Nobel Prizes, built our tallest building and lit the Olympic torch.
> And when the first Muslim American was recently elected to Congress,
> he took the oath to defend our Constitution using the same holy Quran
> that one of our founding fathers, Thomas Jefferson, kept in his personal
> library. (para. 17)

In terms of *logos*, Obama is using reason to argue: If these
collaborations are possible, then so are others. By beginning seven
consecutive brief sentences with the word *they*, these examples seem
to come in rapid-fire succession, suggesting that there are many other
examples he could cite.

Then, President Obama continues to deploy *logos*-based appeals alongside
pathos and *ethos* in order to entreat his audience to follow his suggested
course of action. He encourages a mutual understanding between Muslims and
the U.S., saying that a "partnership between America and Islam must be based
on what Islam is, and not what it isn't" (para. 18). He follows up on this point
by stating that he considers it to be part of his "responsibility as president of
the United States to fight against negative stereotypes of Islam wherever they
appear" (para. 18). Nevertheless, he points out that this level of respect must go
both ways, saying,

Analyzes how logical statements and examples (*logos*) are used to good effect

Describes how style can drive home the *logos* of an argument

10   Just as Muslims do not fit a crude stereotype, America is not the crude
stereotype of a self-interested empire. The United States has been one of
the greatest sources of progress that the world has ever known. We were
born out of revolution against an empire. (para. 18–20)

Explains how
reasoning, emotion,
and authority *(logos,
pathos, and ethos)*
are combined

This particular statement serves a similar purpose as the
aforementioned reminder to the West, giving an emotional *pathos*-laden nod
to Americans while using *logos* to remind the Islamic world of America's
mutually humble beginnings and meaningful contributions.

The president then furthers his appeal by calling on both Islam
and the West to act in favor of the common good and against common
ills. He points out that people throughout the world are inextricably
bound by consequences, mutually hurt by things like economic crises,
new diseases, and the threat posed to the global community by nuclear
proliferations. He mentions the "stain on our collective conscience" caused
by historical acts of violence, and clearly states, "Our problems must
be dealt with through partnership, our progress must be shared" (para.
28–32). Having virtually prompted a shaking of hands between Islam and
America, Obama set the stage for addressing the larger issues of common
importance.

Later in the speech, President Obama also appeals to *logos* by making
use of simple reasoning and strong conviction to confront matters pertaining
to current affairs in the Middle East, as well as those that stand to affect
American relations with the Muslim world. He dives directly into the deep end
of the foreign affairs pool with the discussion of Islamic extremism, voicing
his continued commitment to the pursuit of terrorists waving the Islamic flag.
Nevertheless, he reassures his audience that this is not out of any feeling of
spite toward Islam, but rather "because we reject the same thing that people
of all faiths reject, the killing of innocent men, women, and children" (para.
35). He follows this by reiterating that his primary responsibility as president
is to the continued safety of the American people, but that the harm caused by
violent extremism reaches far beyond American borders, saying the following
of Al Qaida:

They have killed people of different faiths but, more than any other, they have killed Muslims. Their actions are irreconcilable with the rights of human beings, the progress of nations, and with Islam. (para. 33–40)

With this direct use of common logic, Obama is able to display how the issue of violent religious extremism is widespread, even affecting those of a faith that it claims to stem from. Thus, continued commitment to the problem in places like Afghanistan and Pakistan is necessary, not simply for the safety of America, but for the safety of the world. Obama employs logic in order to instill a sense of community between nations affected by a single problem. Despite his soothing and sympathetic rhetoric earlier in the speech, President Obama makes clear that he has an unwavering resolve to do what is necessary to address the problems at hand while still taking into account the common interest of nations everywhere.

15

Conclusion: The Speech Was Effective

Obama's purpose is to urge both Muslim nations and America to work together diplomatically. Likewise, his main rhetorical strategies—reason, goodwill, and level-headed *pathos*—are themselves highly diplomatic. One might liken Obama's America to the grammar-school bully who, now in college, has had ample opportunity to reflect on the error of his past ways and who wishes to reconcile his actions with those whom they affected. But how to go about such reconciliation? Clearly, the same old displays of force and aggression would not be effective in this situation. Thus, humility and kindness are far more viable options. In the same way, America can no longer rely on the forceful approach that it has adopted in the past. Good rapport with the international community is not something to be established and enforced. It is something to be nurtured. Such rapport can only come through respect, and although our reputation may not permit such a humble response, we have reached a significant and hopeful turning

Summarizes and explains what the rhetorical concepts reveal about the argument, concluding with an overall assessment of the speech's effectiveness

point in our life-course as a country. Perhaps we may be able to move forward with a sense of progress, a progress that can only occur through cooperation. In closing, President Obama summarizes in cooperative and conciliatory fashion, quoting the Quran to directly state his main point for his audience in Cairo and his American audience:

> We have the power to make the world we seek, but only if we have the courage to make a new beginning. The Holy Quran tells us, "Mankind, we have created you male and female. And we have made you into nations and tribes so that you may know one another."… The people of the world can live together in peace. We know that is God's vision. Now that must be our work here on Earth. (para. 134–137)

Regardless of differences in faith or ideology, neither side should shoulder the burden of change alone themselves. After all, as the Quran points out, with so many people sharing so small a world, no one is ever acting alone.

References

Herman, C. (2009, November 21). US overthrew Iran's democracy 1953–1979, helped Iraq invade 1980–1988, now US lies for more war. *Examiner.com*. Retrieved from http://www .examiner.com/article/us-overthrew-iran-s-democracy-1953-1979-helped-iraq-invade-1980-1988-now-us-lies-for-more-war

Obama, B. (Speaker). (2009, June 4). Full text of Obama's speech in Cairo. *NBC News*. Retrieved from http://www.nbcnews .com/id/31102929/ns/politics-white_house/#.URnuyTl0vrM

Schleifer, A. S. (2009, June 5). Tears and hard truths in Cairo. *Al Jazeera*. Retrieved from http://www.aljazeera.com/news /middleeast/2009/06/20096503523590820.html

Genres of Argument

GENRES *reflect the ways people get things done in the world. They give you the power to build consensus and persuade others.*

5

Descriptions— Arguing about People, Places, Things, and Events

IN THIS CHAPTER, YOU WILL LEARN—

5.1 How to argue by describing people, places, things, and events

5.2 Strategies for inventing the content of your description with definitions, division, comparisons, and stories

5.3 Ways to organize and draft descriptions with clear introductions, bodies, and conclusions

5.4 How to use style and design to help readers and audiences visualize people, places, things, and events

5.1 How to argue by describing people, places, things, and events

Almost every day, you need to describe people, places, things, and events. If someone asks you about one of your friends, you probably describe what she looks like, how she dresses, and her personality. If someone asks you where you grew up, you would likely describe where your hometown is located, its prominent features, and what it is known for. If someone asks you about an event, you probably describe what happened and the place where it happened.

There are four types of subjects that you will be asked to describe:

People—friends, family members, coworkers, clients, interesting people, research subjects, yourself

Places—research sites, homes, locations, scenes, neighborhoods, zones, regions, countries, territories, habitats

Things—artifacts, tools, machinery, artwork, music, software, hardware, appliances, products, services, clothing, symptoms

Events—concerts, news events, natural phenomena, criminal activities, accidents, artistic openings, procedures, activities, performances

Your ability to use clear and persuasive descriptions in arguments will be an important skill in college and your career. In college, you will need to accurately describe historical events, important people, scientific experiments, diseases, artifacts, human behavior, and natural phenomena. In the workplace, you will need to describe products, services, clients, artistic performances, events, and a variety of other things (Figure 5.1).

FIGURE 5.1 Writing a Description Argument
Describing someone or something is a common form of generative argument in college and the workplace.

Descriptions may not seem like arguments. After all, when describing someone or something, you usually aren't trying to win people over to your side. Instead, descriptions tend to be more generative than persuasive, because you are trying to help others understand a person, place, thing, or event in the same way you understand it. The argument in a description is subtle, but how you illustrate your subject can determine how people react to and interact with it.

Generative

Persuasive

Generative Argument—Descriptions are primarily generative forms of argument, because you will need to work with others to figure out what something is and the best way to describe it. When arguing through description, your goal is to reach a common understanding with others about the nature of something.

Persuasive Argument—Descriptions have a mildly persuasive side, too. When describing your subject, you want your audience to view it in a particular way. You need to be selective about how you define it, what you reveal, and your choice of words.

Genre Patterns

Descriptions tend to follow a version of these two patterns. The pattern on the left is for describing people, places, or things. The pattern on the right is for describing events. You should modify and adapt one of these patterns to the specific needs of your description.

Introduction	**Introduction**
Major Part 1	**Scene 1**
Major Part 2	**Scene 2**
Major Part 3	**Scene 3**
Conclusion	**Conclusion**

Inventing the Content of Your Description

The core of a description is a solid *sentence definition*. After you define your subject, your argument will then expand to describe the person, place, thing, or event in greater depth by dividing it into features or stages, comparing and contrasting it with something else, or telling stories about it. Here are some strategies for inventing the content of your description argument.

Use a Sentence Definition to Frame the Subject

Most descriptions begin with a sentence definition that frames the topic. A typical sentence definition has three parts: (a) the subject, (b) the class in which the subject belongs, and (c) characteristics that distinguish the subject from its class.

> Subject   Class
> Susan, my roommate, is a normal <u>college student</u> in almost all ways, except one: she's a superhero.
>   Distinguishing characteristic

> Subject   Class
> Seattle is a major American city that is in the northwestern state of Washington and near the Pacific Ocean. It's also my hometown.
>   Distinguishing characteristic

> Subject   Class
> Facebook is a social networking website that has the following features: a wall, notes, timeline, chat, friends, and photos.
>   Distinguishing characteristic

A sentence definition is a frame that helps your readers or audience view your subject from a particular perspective. Sentence definitions can be found in a variety of sources, or you can just create your own. You might look in an online dictionary or search the Internet for various definitions of your subject. You will notice that subtle differences exist among the definitions you find.

> *Note*: If you want to use a definition word for word from a source, you need to cite it properly. Even though the definition appears in a dictionary or on a website, it still needs to be properly quoted and cited.

For some topics, you might decide to come up with your own sentence definition, which incorporates the best elements you found among the existing definitions available.

Something to keep in mind is that preexisting frames or identifications are often used to define and describe people, places, things, or events. You should look for those frames and identifications to see if they hold up to scrutiny. In other words, just because something or someone has "always been defined that way" doesn't mean you cannot reframe your subject by defining it from a new perspective.

Likewise, if you are describing people or places, you might find it interesting to challenge how you or others identify with your subject. In some cases, you might even challenge how your subject might identify himself or herself. As with framing, sometimes the most interesting and insightful descriptions challenge existing perspectives or stereotypes.

Divide Your Subject into Features or Stages

Once you have defined your subject, your next task is to identify your subject's major features or stages.

A person—Describe someone by focusing on her or his major features: face, body, clothing, how this individual moves, and the places where this person lives, works, or plays.

A place—Divide the place into its major areas, such as its neighborhoods, regions, rooms, prominent structures, major landforms, or climate.

A thing—Partition the object by identifying its major features, such as essential parts, supplementary parts, decorative features, oddities, and imperfections.

An event—Identify the major stages or scenes in the event: before the event, what caused it, what happened then, what happened next, and how it ended.

FIGURE 5.2 Describing a Person
You might find it helpful to first divide your subject into three to five major features. Then, describe each of these major features separately.

Here's a helpful tip: Divide your subject into two to five major features or stages—no more than seven. Doing so will help you make decisions about its most important features. Then divide each of these major features or stages into two to five minor ones.

For example, to describe the person in Figure 5.2, you might first focus on her major features, such as her face, body, clothing, and the backdrop. Then, for each of these major features, describe three to five other minor features. While describing her face, for instance, you could describe her hair, eyes, nose, mouth, and skin.

Compare and Contrast Your Subject with Something Familiar

Throughout your description, you can compare and contrast your subject with someone or something that your audience will already find familiar.

contrast →

comparison →

My roommate isn't your typical superhero. She isn't tall or glamorous like Wonder Woman. She can't climb walls like Spiderwoman. She's not amazingly strong like Supergirl. However, she does have a clear sense of purpose and values, and she cares deeply about people who are being abused by others. I've seen her do things that can only be called heroic, even superheroic.

comparison →

Seattle is similar to San Francisco, another Pacific Coast city with tall buildings, unique neighborhoods, funky subcultures, and a cool music scene. However, the people in

Seattle are nicer, even the panhandlers, and Seattle's downtown is edgier and less developed. In Seattle, they like their coffee and beer to have more get-up-and-go.   contrast

comparison using a simile
Facebook is like a big reunion for all your friends, family, classmates, and coworkers, all in one confusing place.

As you look for something to compare and contrast with your subject, think about people or things your readers or audience already understand. Then highlight any similarities or differences between your subject and these known people, places, things, or events.

Use Narrative to Tell a Story

You can also use one or more brief anecdotes to illustrate particular aspects of your subject.

One time when we were walking by a bar, Susan saw a large guy pushing around his girlfriend and getting in her face. Even though she's just 5'4", Susan marched across the street, put herself between the two, and told the guy to back off. He stepped back and looked surprised—like "who is this crazy woman?"—then he stalked away.

When I was last back in Seattle, I made my regular pilgrimage to Pike Place Market, where they sell fish, vegetables, and just about anything else you can eat, drink, or smoke. Fish sellers were hosing off the street, and the flower stands were in bloom. I was on my own with a newspaper under my arm, but before long I was in the original Starbucks—yeah, the first one—sipping coffee and debating whether Seattle was still the software mecca of the world. A couple of software developers from Microsoft jumped into the discussion and then a few college students. A quick hour went by with my newspaper still folded on the table.

Last year, one of my friends came down with a life-threatening form of cancer. Her insurance covered the treatments, but she and her husband could not afford daycare for their kids. On Facebook, I reached out to our mutual friends for help, and within a day we had a whole team of volunteers who stepped in to help. This experience showed me the potential of social networking sites to help others.

In a description, you should use stories to make specific points that support your overall description of your subject. Make sure you include plenty of details that add movement and color to each story.

Anticipate Other Descriptions

You should always keep in mind that others can and will describe your subject differently. Try to anticipate these differences and any possible objections to your description. Then deal with them fairly and objectively in your argument.

Some people might view Susan as a meddler or a nuisance. Her strict moral values and her brashness can sometimes make her seem judgmental or pushy. Even Susan agrees that she can be a difficult friend to have.

In the post–grunge era, with the global expansion of Starbucks and Microsoft, many people complain that Seattle has lost its edge. The downtown has been cleaned up a bit, and those Microsoft millionaires are more into fine white wines these days than dark roasts. I agree that the music isn't quite so angry (or loud) anymore. All that head-bobbing and mosh pits probably weren't good for us anyway. Cities, like people, can't stay young forever—but they can still be cool.

Facebook skeptics, like Winkler, often point out that using the site is not really free (par. 2). Some of Facebook's hidden costs include a loss of privacy, loss of intellectual property, more exposure to targeted advertising, vulnerability to a mob mentality, and the potential for data sharing by corporations that want money. Plus, Facebook can be a huge waste of time.

You should research print sources and the Internet for alternative descriptions of your subject. Then you can compare and contrast your description with the descriptions of others. In some cases, you can openly disagree with their descriptions, using their views to clarify and distinguish your own understanding. Make sure you properly quote and cite the works of others if you are using their words or ideas.

MOVES for Arguing

Description is something we do every day. Here are some quick moves for describing a person, place, thing, or event.

_____ has _____ major features, including _____, _____, and _____.

The event happened in _____ stages: (1) _____, (2) _____, (3) _____, …

When I experienced _____, I saw _____, I heard _____, I tasted _____, I smelled _____, and I touched _____.

In many ways, a _____ is like a _____.

A _____ is a _____ that has these unique characteristics.

A _____ might seem similar to a _____, but they are different in several important ways.

Organizing and Drafting Your Description

The organization of a description is normally straightforward, with a distinct introduction, body, and conclusion.

Introduction: Set a Context for the Description

The introduction of a description, as in most any argument, will usually make some or all of the following moves:

Use a Grabber or Lead.

Start out your description with an interesting story or statement about your topic. Many descriptions start out with a *sentence definition* of the topic.

Identify Your Topic.

If your grabber didn't identify the topic, make sure you mention it soon afterward. You want your readers to know what you are describing.

Indicate Your Purpose.

You don't need to explicitly say something like, "My purpose is to describe Seattle," though in some cases stating your purpose directly would be helpful. Instead, make sure the purpose of your argument (i.e., to describe someone, something, somewhere, or an event) is clear to the audience.

State Your Main Point or Thesis.

The thesis of a description typically makes an argumentative claim that reveals your angle on your topic:

> **Weak thesis:** Seattle is a great city.

> **Stronger thesis:** Even though Seattle is no longer that software whiz kid by day and coffee-fueled grunge kid at night, this city is still edgy and unrefined in all the right ways.

Offer Background Information on the Topic.

Offer just enough history or details about the setting to help your audience imagine your topic in a particular place and time period.

Stress the Importance of Your Topic.

Briefly, tell your readers why they should care about your topic. Find a way to answer their "So what?" question up front.

Here's an example introduction that starts with a sentence definition:

Sentence definitions

A superhero is a person who has superhuman powers and uses those powers to do good in a corrupt world. Most of us are familiar with the stock superheroes like Superman, Batman, or Wonder Woman. The archetype superhero, Superman, is amazingly strong, impervious to bullets, and can fly. Batman is exceptionally intelligent, has great weapons,

Background
information

Topic and Purpose

Stresses importance

Main point (thesis)

and drives a really cool car. Wonder Woman can sense the feelings of others, flies in an invisible plane, and has an incredibly useful Lasso of Truth. Deep down inside, though, they all have an innate sense of good and a desire to help the weak and victimized.

It's this deep-down quality that makes my friend Susan a superhero. She doesn't have superpowers, and she doesn't have a cool car or Lasso of Truth. But she knows good from evil and she is quick to take action to protect and support others in a superhuman way. She is the kind of superhero all of us should have watching over our lives.

In this introduction, this author makes all the typical moves while offering a sentence definition that helps define her subject (her friend Susan).

Body: Expand on the Description

The body of your description should support the main point or thesis that you stated in the introduction. Here are a few ways you can generate that support.

Describe your subject's parts or stages—Divide your subject into its two to five major parts or stages of development and describe each separately.

Use your senses—Use your five senses to describe how something looks, sounds, feels, smells, or tastes. Try to use as much detail as you can to help your audience experience your subject.

Use similes or analogies—Compare your subject to something your audience will find familiar. A simile makes a simple comparison (X is like Y), while an analogy makes a somewhat more complex comparison (A is to B as X is to Y).

Describe with negation—Tell your audience what your subject isn't. Negation allows you to explain how your subject is different from people, things, places, or events that might otherwise be similar.

Offer some examples—Use examples of your subject to show its different variations, appearances, or uses.

Include one or more anecdotes—Offer one or more anecdotes that illustrate your subject in action.

Add a few images—Include images, such as photographs or drawings, to give your audience a visual sense of your subject.

Usually, the body of a description will employ several of these methods to help the audience "see" the subject.

Conclusion: Restate Your Main Point (Thesis)

The conclusion of your description should be brief. You should make some or all of the following moves:

Use a concluding transition—With a heading or the first sentence of your conclusion, use a transitional word or phrase to signal clearly that you are ending description (e.g. "Overall," "In conclusion.")

Identify your main point (thesis)—Include a version of the main point of your description.

Restress the importance of your subject—Explain or hint why your subject should be important to your audience.

Look to the future—Explain briefly why your subject will continue to be interesting in the future.

Here is an example conclusion to a description argument:

To conclude, we all know comic book superheroes, dressed in red tights and endowed with muscles, don't really exist. But I have discovered that there are everyday superheroes, like my friend Susan, who have an innate sense of good and a desire to help others. They make all of our lives better by standing up for us, offering a helping hand, and stopping injustice. Now that I have found one superhero, I will be looking for others—and I hope to become one myself.

Signals conclusion

Restates main point

Stresses importance

Looks to the future

This paragraph makes all the moves expected in a conclusion. Notice that the main point, or thesis, is slightly broader than the one in the introduction, giving it additional emphasis.

Style and Design in Description Arguments

5.4 How to use style and design to help readers and audiences visualize people, places, things, and events

Descriptions are primarily visual, so the style and design of your argument should feature visual details and images that reflect and illustrate your subject.

Use Style to Make Your Description Visual

Most descriptions are written in a plain, just-the-facts style, but they don't need to be boring. Depending on your audience or places your description might be read, you can use style to energize and enliven the text.

Show, don't tell—You've heard this one before. Help your readers visualize your subject by using visual detail, such as colors, shapes, textures, and movement. You want them to be able to "see" your subject through your words.

Use plain sentences—Keep your sentences plain by putting the subjects earlier in the sentences. Where possible, put the persons or objects that are doing something in the subjects of your sentences. Then state the action of the sentence in the verb.

Use metaphors and similes to create mental images—Metaphors and similes can be used to create images in the minds of your readers or audience. For example, you could use a metaphor like "Facebook is a vast and expanding universe in which there are brighter and dimmer stars." This kind of metaphor is used to create an image in the mind of the reader. Likewise, similes can be useful for making brief visual comparisons: "The NCAA basketball tournament is like the *Hunger Games*. Many teams come to play for our entertainment, but only one team can win—after lots of carnage."

Use Images and Document Design

Descriptions live or die on your readers' ability to visualize what you are talking about. So a really good way to help your readers see your subject is to show them a picture, drawing, or other image.

Add one or more photographs—You can include a picture of the person, place, object, or event you are describing. You could also include pictures of aspects of your subject, such as the person's face, an object's most interesting feature, or an action shot from a scene. Pictures add personality, color, and movement to your description. You should label any pictures with a figure number and title. Then refer to each picture with a figure number in the written text.

Design the written text—Your description doesn't need to be a one-column, double-spaced text unless your instructor specifically required that format. You might try a two- or three-column page design (Figure 5.3). You can use a title and headings that help your readers locate specific information and recognize the structure of the document or presentation.

Choose an appropriate font—Look for a font that fits the nature of your subject. A sans serif typeface like Arial, Helvetica, or Futura would fit a modern subject. A serif typeface like Times, Bookman, or Garamond would be suitable for a more traditional subject. In some situations, you could choose a playful typeface for the title and headings, such as Chalkboard, Hobo, or Rockwell. Experiment with fonts and see what happens, but don't overdo it.

Check with your instructor before you go too far with images and document design. Some instructors welcome these kinds of innovations and visual expression. Others might have more restrictive formatting guidelines in mind.

FIGURE 5.3 Using Images and Document Design
In workplace descriptions, images and document design are expected visual features.

Now it's your turn to describe something.
This is what you need to know:

1 A description depicts a person, place, thing, or event from a specific perspective.

2 Writing descriptions is an important part of college courses and careers, because all majors and careers will ask you to describe what you see and experience.

3 A sentence definition, especially in the introduction, provides a frame from which you can describe your subject.

4 A typical sentence definition has three parts: (a) the subject, (b) the class of the subject, and (c) characteristics that distinguish the subject from its class.

5 You can use comparison and contrast as well as narrative to fill out your description.

6 A description, like most arguments, has an introduction, body, and conclusion.

7 The introduction and conclusion of a description argument usually contain a sentence definition that can also serve as the main point or thesis. The thesis in the conclusion is usually enhanced in some way to emphasize it.

8 The body of a description typically includes the following kinds of information: descriptions of parts or stages, descriptions with the senses, descriptions with similes and analogies, and description by negation. It can also include examples, anecdotes, and images.

9 The style of your description will tend to be plain; however, you should use sensory details and metaphors to bring a more visual element to the text.

10 The design of the text can enhance the reader's or audience's understanding and use of the document or presentation. Photographs are especially helpful to help people see and understand the subject.

1. Send each member of your group out to find a description of some kind. Many descriptions are available on the Internet, but you should look for descriptions in print sources, too. With your group, talk about the argumentative nature of the descriptions you found. More than likely, most of them won't seem overtly argumentative. Nevertheless, how is even the most straightforward description still an argument? What are its argumentative features?

2. Ask a member of your group to bring in a unique object. Then have each member of your group write a separate description of that object. Remember to describe your subject's major parts. Use your senses and try to find a good simile or analogy that captures the object in words. When the group is finished compare your description with the others. What are some features that you all seemed to notice? What are some features that some people, perhaps you, did not notice? Why do you think each person found different things to focus on?

3. Look on a website that sells reasonably expensive products, such as cars, houses, or high-end electronics. Read through the descriptions they offer. Many of these descriptions will be persuasive, because they are urging you to buy the product. What are some of the elements of persuasion that are built into these descriptions? How are they different from a straightforward description?

1. Find a person, place, object, or event on campus that you can describe for readers or an audience. Write a straightforward description of that subject, trying to be as objective as possible. Then pick an angle on that subject. What is something that has happened or changed recently that gives you a new perspective on this subject? Or what is something unique about you that offers you a unique perspective? Write a second description of your subject in which you use this angle to *argue* for your own view or interpretation.

2. Choose a person, place, object, or event that you can describe through a story (i.e., a narrative or anecdote). Write your description as a story. In a reflection to your instructor, answer the question: How does describing someone or something as a story change what you pay attention to and what you choose to include? Hand in your story and reflection together.

3. Using the Internet, find a description that you disagree with in some way. You might look for descriptions of your hometown, a sports team, a famous person, or a historical or current event. Using this deficient description as a jumping-off point, write an argument in which you show why the description you found is inaccurate. Then offer a better description of your subject that reflects your understanding of it.

In this description argument, student Emily Johnson explains why zombies are so popular in movies and video games. Pay attention to how she uses details, especially color and motion, to bring her subject to life.

Portrait of a Zombie

Emily Johnson

It seems like zombies are everywhere these days. They're in movies and shows like *World War Z, 28 Days Later*, and *The Walking Dead*. They are the baddies in video games like *The Last of Us, Resident Evil*, and even *Minecraft*. But what are zombies and why are we so fascinated with them? I decided to find out.

The word zombie comes from the Haitian word "zombi," which means a near-dead person who has been animated by witchcraft (Merriam-Webster). In real life, Haitian zombies are victims who have been poisoned with a nerve toxin made from the porcupine fish. Somewhat different, cinematic zombies are corpses that have been animated through supernatural means such as sorcery, errant technology, or environmental cataclysm.

The physical appearance of a zombie is usually the dead giveaway. As undead humans, zombies' bodies are steadily decomposing. So, their hair, skin, and the occasional limb will fall off. Zombies' hair and skin have a grey tint, and their eyes are usually filled with a milky-white substance obscuring their pupils. Unfortunately, this milky substance does not obstruct a zombie's sight. Zombies have terrible posture because of their limited muscle control. They tend to stoop over with straight legs, and their heads slump to one side. Their postures steadily deteriorate over time because they are constantly exposed to the elements. Sunscreen and lip balm might help, but zombies usually exist during a shadowy apocalypse so skin care isn't a priority.

Zombie behavior is distinctly different from their living counterparts. Their overriding obsession is to eat human flesh, especially brains. They tend to stagger around aimlessly until they see potential prey. At that point, zombies will begin to moan and walk relentlessly toward their prey, often dragging a leg. "Fast" zombies, like the ones in *World War Z* and *28 Days Later* are able to run, but purists argue that these creatures are not zombies but just infected humans who have gone berserk. Either way, zombies are persistent and they have a tendency to reach their arms mindlessly through broken windows and holes in walls. Because they are low functioning, they cannot use weapons or tools, instead using their bare hands and teeth to attack their prey. Sometimes it appears zombies move in packs, but that's not true. Each zombie is only looking out for himself or herself. The availability of human flesh is merely a common focal point that gives the appearance of collective action.

5   Zombies have some key advantages over other monsters. They aren't refined and debonair like vampires, but they also don't suffer from mood swings, guilty consciences, and love interests. Unlike werewolves, they aren't ADD and don't suffer from identity issues. That's why zombies make such good baddies in movies and video games. There are plenty of them in all shapes and sizes, and nobody cares if mindless corpses get blown away. Their numbers and mindless devotion to the task makes them terrifying and kind of cool—like a corpse.

If you encounter a zombie you need to keep a few things in mind. Zombies are slow. Use that. Zombies have only one way to catch you, their hands. Stay out of arm's reach. Zombies also do not feel pain, so even a zombie that is missing an arm or a leg is dangerous. Aim for the head. However, my best advice is to steer clear of any undead whenever possible.

A CLOSER LOOK AT
Portrait of a Zombie

1. A good description allows you to "see" what the author is describing. What are three techniques Johnson uses to make her description visual?

2. What are two to three things that Johnson could have used to fill out her description of zombies further?

3. Locate the thesis in the introduction and conclusion? How do they work together?

1. A common game on college campuses is Zombies vs. Humans in which people shoot each other with Nerf guns. Some people might say that a game like Humans vs. Zombies is a waste of college students' time. Write a rebuttal or counterstatement (see Chapter 13) in which you defend these kinds of games on campus.

2. Write a description of an event or activity happening on your campus. Tell your readers about the who, what, where, when, and how of the event. Describe the event with as many sensory details as possible.

From J. K. Rowling's Harry Potter Novels to Real Life: The Sport of Quidditch Takes Flight

JACE LACOB

Jace Lacob offers a blow-by-blow description of a popular new sport, Ground Quidditch, that is becoming popular on college campuses. One of the difficulties of describing Ground Quidditch is that the sport needs to compete with the fantasy version in J. K. Rowling's Harry Potter novels and movies. Plus, as you will see, Lacob finds himself arguing against the idea that Ground Quidditch is for nerds and Harry Potter fans. Pay attention to his use of details to bring the scenes to life.

The bone-crushing thud of a body hitting the ground. The splintering sound of a broom breaking. I'm at my first Quidditch match and am discovering it's not for the faint-hearted.

The sport, brought to life from J.K. Rowling's seven-volume *Harry Potter* novel series, has quickly become a permanent fixture on many college campuses, including UCLA, which last weekend hosted the third annual Western Cup. Nineteen teams—including the Power Grangers, Dirigible Plums, Narwhals, and The Prisoners of Kickasskaban—faced off in a grueling two-day tournament that pitted their strength, speed, endurance, and hand-eye coordination—not to mention the ability to keep a broomstick between their legs at all times.

Quidditch, as *Harry Potter* fans know, is played *flying* atop broomsticks. While I saw no one soar through the air, experiencing the nascent and theatrical sport firsthand gives you the opportunity to see just how brutal, competitive, and unique it is—a combination of rugby, basketball, and dodgeball, mixed in a witch's cauldron.

Despite misconceptions about "Muggle" (i.e., nonmagical types) or "Ground" Quidditch, it is not a sport for nerds. "It's really competitive and it's not a sissy sport," said UCLA freshman Sarah Coleman, a beater—they play defense—on the Wizards of Westwood team. "There's blood ... It is full-contact, with no pads, and it's more intense than rugby." Many Quidditch players are serious athletes who, to borrow parlance from the books, look more like Cedric Diggory than, say, Neville Longbottom.

5   Keeper (goalie) and chaser (point-scorer) Zach Lewis, who towers over many of his teammates, is a former high school basketball and baseball player, who joined the team because it seemed like a "great way to work out." He stressed that it is a physical sport, that there is tackling. As for the broom? "It seemed strange at the beginning but you get over it quickly," he said. "You just think, yeah, I'm holding a broom."

Still, even the players admit that there is a geeky element to the sport. "We *are* a bunch of nerds: we're running around on broomsticks," said UCLA sophomore Katelynn Kazane, a chaser. "You have to suspend some of your seriousness, [but] it's one of the roughest sports I've ever played ... It's not just jocks or just a bunch of nerds who dress up and go to conventions.

Some of us do, but some of us haven't read the books and aren't into videogames. It's a combination of two worlds."

Asher King Abramson, UCLA Quidditch president and beater, agreed. "A lot of teams start out as community Harry Potter clubs, run around with capes and wands," he said. "But when you get to higher levels of competition, Quidditch becomes more of a sport and less of an extension of the Harry Potter universe."

It's also coed, and many of the women are only too happy to knock the wind out of their male adversaries. "For the first two weeks [of playing], the guys don't want to tackle a girl: 'I might break them or something,'" said Kazane. "When you knock a guy down, they say, 'OK, we have to guard you.'"

The players on the field are part of a generation of young adults who grew up reading Rowling's novels and who dreamed of one day taking to the sky in a Quidditch match. "It's a childhood dream fulfilled," said Coleman, who checked which schools had Quidditch teams when she was applying to college. "Something clicked," Kazane said of the first time she played. "I don't want to say it was magical, because that's lame, but it was like falling in love."

Yet, there is magic there. "Quidditch is a 10 magical game that, by all rights, shouldn't exist," said Abramson. "We've managed to maintain the spirit of the game from the book and turn it into a physical experience that makes people chuckle, gasp, cringe, and, most importantly, want to get involved ... It's a balance of liberalartsy craziness and all-out competition that you can't find in any other activity on earth."

In 2005, Middlebury College student Alexander Manshel—who would become the first Quidditch commissioner—devised a way to take Rowling's creation and transform it into a physical sport. There are now more than 1000 Quidditch teams around the world recognized by the sport's governing body, the International Quidditch Association.

Stripping away the spells and remembering the immutable laws of gravity, Manshel kept the basics of Rowling's rules of Quidditch while creating a playable sport. In the books, Quidditch is a high-flying game in which the players zoom around a three-dimensional pitch on brooms, casting spells, pummeling each other with dodgeball-like bludgers, and trying to score goals by throwing a volleyball-like quaffle through three round goals. (And, oh, occasionally, the golden snitch—a flying spherical ball—will flutter into the proceedings, creating chaos.)

In Muggle Quidditch, players maneuver around a field with one hand on their broomsticks at all times. The match begins with all players on bended knee, their eyes closed (so as not to see the golden snitch—here embodied by a person dressed in yellow—leave the field of play), until the ref gives the order of "Brooms up!" Then, all hell breaks loose.

Watching it, it's an exciting blur: the quaffle is forcefully hurled through goals (mounted hula-hoops); players are hit—hard—by fast-moving bludgers while others are tackled; a broom handle injures one male player in a very difficult-to-watch way. But despite the seeming chaos, it takes skill to make it through the crucible and score a goal. The proceedings are cloaked in a degree of whimsy: one ref wears a paper crown, and another is dressed in the robes of a Hogwarts professor; suited representatives from the IQA have feathers in their hats, while the snitch, on a break, dons a kilt.

15   UCLA freshman Brady Stanley, a musical-theater major dressed in head-to-toe gold, performed the role of one of the snitches at the Western Cup. A tennis ball in a sock was affixed to his lower back à la flag football, and he was given about a square mile of the campus to hide out in before returning to the field with the seeker in hot pursuit. Once there, he did everything he could to disrupt the game while the seeker tried to grab the snitch. (Capturing the golden snitch gives the winning team an extra 30 points and ends gameplay.)

"A good snitch is somebody who can run well, fight well, or both," said Stanley. "But not only do they have to be able to defend themselves in some sort of physicalized form, but they have to be somewhat entertaining to the audience. We're sort of the mascot and it turns into a game of 'chase the mascot' and eventually 'tackle the mascot.'"

As for Rowling, she's been rather quiet about Quidditch. Rowling's publicist confirmed that the author is aware of the real-life existence of the sport, but said that the *Harry Potter* creator wouldn't comment further.

"I've heard different things," said James Luby, captain of UCLA's B team, the Wizards of Westwood. "That she's against it, that she's happy about it. I would say that if I were to write a book and this were to happen, I would be pretty thrilled."

Rowling should at least be happy that Quidditch, like her books, has a way of bringing people together in some very unexpected ways. More than 1,000 spectators attended the Western Cup and there was a sense of true diversity—gender, ethnicity, and body type—among both the crowd and the players themselves.

The UCLA team, who placed eighth 20 overall in last year's World Cup, made it all the way to the final match of the Western Cup, where, bruised and battered, they faced off with their crosstown rivals USC, but the Trojans ultimately flew away with the Western Cup title after a vicious match. "There was no question that we were fatigued in the finals," said Abramson. "That being said, USC totally deserved their win. They matched up well with us and caught the snitch when it counted most. We'll be bringing over the Golden Remembrall—the Quidditch version of the UCLA-USC Victory Bell—soon."

It's part of the good sportsmanship that marks the game. "Winning isn't everything," said Kazane. "We could lose every game and still have a great time. OK, maybe not every game, but we're going to have a great time no matter what."

While it is an intense sport, the heart of the game is the magic and camaraderie that comes from being part of this unique experience. The goal at the end isn't just to win, but to put your broom down and acknowledge, in Rowling's words, "mischief managed," something embodied in the unpredictability of the golden snitch.

"You can be as mischievous as you want," said Stanley, "but the No. 1 rule of Quidditch is, 'Don't be a dick.'"

A CLOSER LOOK AT
From J. K. Rowling's Harry Potter Novels to Real Life: The Sport of Quidditch Takes Flight

1. An important part of writing a good description is paying close attention to people or things that are moving. Find three places where Lacob describes movement in this article. What effects does movement have on the readers of a description like this one?

2. Obviously, there are significant differences between Ground Quidditch and the descriptions of Quidditch in the Harry Potter novels. What are three differences highlighted by Lacob in this description?

3. In some ways, Lacob seems to believe Ground Quidditch is better than other intercollegiate sports. What are five advantages of Ground Quidditch over some of the more traditional sports played among universities?

IDEAS FOR
Arguing

1. By the end of the article, Lacob seems to be focusing on sportsmanship as the best aspect of Quidditch. Write a commentary (see Chapter 12) in which you argue that college sports should encourage more sportsmanship among players and coaches. Or you could argue that sportsmanship isn't important in intercollegiate sports.

2. Write a description of a sport or other campus activity that you have never watched before. As someone who basically doesn't understand the sport or activity, write a description of it for people like yourself who are learning about it for the first time. How can you make sense of this sport or activity for your readers without also confusing them? What are some ways you can compare the sport or activity to things your audience would understand?

Comparisons— Arguing by Comparing and Contrasting

IN THIS CHAPTER, YOU WILL LEARN—

6.1 How to compare and contrast both similar and different subjects

6.2 Strategies for inventing the content of a comparison

6.3 The difference between a point-by-point comparison and a comparison of similarities and differences

6.4 Ways to use style and design to put the emphasis on the subjects of your comparison

C omparison arguments explore the similarities and differences between two or more people, places, things, or events. Usually, the subjects being compared are alike in an obvious way (e.g., celebrities, supercars, college campuses, historical events). A comparison gives you and your audience the opportunity to investigate the ways in which these subjects are alike or distinct.

6.1 How to compare and contrast both similar and different subjects

Sometimes it is also interesting to compare subjects that are very different. For instance, you might compare your high school prom to a zombie movie (Figure 6.1). You could compare *The Hunger Games* to your childhood summer camp experiences. The best comparisons are often ones that draw your audience's attention to interesting and unexpected similarities between two or more things.

Comparisons are primarily generative, because they usually explain how different subjects are understood in our society. Often, the similarities between two objects, places, or events are due to the common frames we use to describe them. Likewise, when two or more people are compared, we often explore how their identities are similar or different. When a writer or speaker compares two very different things or people, they are often challenging the traditional cultural frames and identities that are used to understand these subjects.

Comparing people, places, things, and events will be something you do regularly in your college courses and career. In college, you will be asked to compare a variety of subjects, such as important people, historical events, diverse ecosystems,

Generative

Persuasive

Generative Argument—Comparisons are mostly generative arguments, since you are primarily trying to make factual statements about your subjects. You want others to understand your subjects by recognizing the same similarities and differences as you do.

Persuasive Argument—Some persuasion is needed in comparisons, especially if you are arguing that one of your subjects is superior in some ways to others. You will need to support your claims about your subjects' strengths and weaknesses.

Genre Patterns

Comparisons can follow a variety of patterns. Here are two common patterns that will help you compare and contrast two subjects. You should modify one of these patterns to fit the specific needs of your comparison.

Point by Point

- Introduction
- Description of Subject 1
- Description of Subject 2
- Point 1 Comparison
- Point 2 Comparison
- Conclusion

Similarities and Differences

- Introduction
- Description of Subject 1
- Description of Subject 2
- Similarities
- Differences
- Conclusion

FIGURE 6.1 Comparing and Contrasting Two Very Different Things
Sometimes it's fun to compare and contrast things that are very different to explore their similarities.

natural phenomena, literary works, human behaviors, technologies, and so on. In the workplace, you will need to write comparisons of products, software, services, artistic performances, experiments, architecture, machinery, procedures, and events. The ability to write or present comparisons is a fundamental skill that will be useful to you right now and in the future.

Inventing the Content of Your Comparison

6.2 Strategies for inventing the content of a comparison

Most comparison argument assignments ask you to explore the similarities and differences between subjects. Occasionally, you may be asked to compare and contrast three or more subjects, which can make this kind of assignment more challenging. However, when you know a few basic strategies for comparing things, the task gets much easier.

Using a Diagram to Identify Similarities and Differences

Your first goal is to identify the major ways in which your subjects are similar and different. For example, let's say you are comparing two fast-food restaurants, like Five Guys and McDonald's. There are many obvious similarities between these two burger places and some important differences.

Here's where you might use a visual tool, like a Venn diagram, to help you identify those major similarities and differences (Figure 6.2). On a sheet of paper or your computer screen, draw two overlapping circles. In the overlapping part of the diagram, write down any similarities that are shared by your two subjects. Then write any differences in the parts of the circles that don't overlap.

At this point, don't worry about whether the things you write down in the diagram are absolutely true. Right now, you're generating ideas, so keep an open mind as you fill in the diagram. You will have plenty of time to check facts, change your mind, add some new ideas, and cross out some of the things that aren't true. You should spend about five minutes writing down anything that comes to mind.

FIGURE 6.2 Using a Diagram to Find Major Points of Comparison
A diagram is a good way two identify what two subjects have in common and what makes them different.

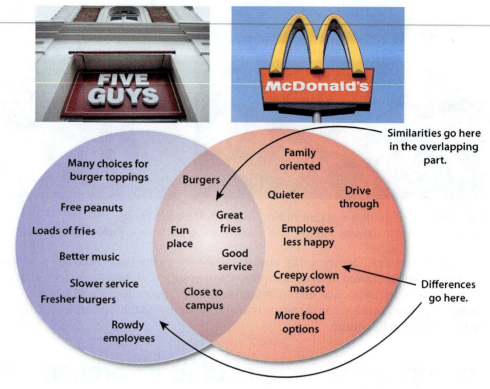

Identifying Frames and Identifications in the Major Points of Comparison

When you are finished adding subjects to the Venn diagram, you will notice that some similarities and differences are more meaningful or interesting than others. Look at your diagram and pick out the two to five major similarities and differences that seem to stand out. These are called the major points of comparison.

Usually, these major points of comparison are based on common frames or identities that people use to discuss these subjects. For example, the concept of a fast-food restaurant is a frame. It determines our expectations for these kinds of places and the kinds of experiences people will have in them.

Likewise, if you are comparing people, pay attention to how they identify themselves, how you identify with them, and how societies or cultures define them. You will often see that there are gendered, cultural, racial, occupational, geographical, and class-based identifications at work, which are worth exploring.

The diagram in Figure 6.2, for instance, brings out some interesting features that you could use to compare and contrast Five Guys with McDonald's. Both fast-food restaurants, of course, offer burgers and fries. Both are fun places near campus with good service. However, these two restaurants are different in some key ways. McDonald's caters to families and people on the go. Five Guys targets those 20-somethings and 30-somethings who want to personalize their burger with a variety of toppings. Five Guys almost exclusively offers burgers, with hot dogs and melted cheese sandwiches as alternatives—which few people order. McDonald's has a full menu of salads, fish sandwiches, chicken nuggets, shakes, and other items.

Try to sort these major similarities and differences into two to five major points of comparison. For example, some points that you could use to compare Five Guys and McDonalds might include:

- Burgers and fries
- Dining atmosphere
- Service
- Typical customers
- Other food options on menu

Discussion of these points of comparison will be the content of your argument's body.

Figure Out Your Angle

Finding a good angle is the secret to writing a successful comparison. If you don't have an angle, your comparison of two or more subjects will probably be a bit dry and boring. An angle will help you compare and contrast your subjects in a unique and interesting way.

For example, you might compare Five Guys and McDonald's by looking at them from the angle of a hungry college student on a tight budget.

> **My Angle:** McDonald's was fine when you were a 10-year-old kid and any burger was good as long as it had ketchup on it and there was a PlayPlace nearby. But college students aren't interested in Happy Meals or PlayPlaces. (OK, some still are.) So, for a college student who wants to eat well on a tight budget, Five Guys is a great place to get a burger and fries.

Or, following a different angle, you might compare these two restaurant chains' impacts on the environment or society. It might even be interesting to evaluate both of these red-meat restaurants from a vegetarian point of view, researching which one is best if you or one of your friends doesn't eat meat.

> If you have vegetarian friends, you need to be sensitive to their needs and find restaurants that cater to a variety of tastes and lifestyles. But, hey, sometimes you just need a burger. Veggie burgers just won't do! So, which burger joint, Five Guys or McDonald's, would be the better choice if you're taking along a vegetarian friend?

A good angle will put your subjects in an interesting light, allowing you to explore their similarities and differences from a new and interesting perspective.

Research Your Subjects

Even if you thoroughly know your subjects, you need to do some research. Begin collecting information with Internet search engines. You should also gather print sources, usually available at your library, and collect empirical evidence on your own.

Electronic sources—A variety of websites are available that will discuss your subjects and even compare them. Don't, however, rely on just one or two

FIGURE 6.3
Doing Empirical
Research Can Be
Fun
Go out and
experience your
subjects. Take
others with you
to see what they
think.

sources. Instead, make sure you collect information about your subjects from a variety of reliable electronic sources.

Print sources—If you are writing about present-day people, places, things, or events, magazines and newspapers might be your most useful print sources. If you are writing about historical people or events, books or academic journals should be available that you can consult. Use your campus library website to help you find these print sources.

Empirical sources—You should go out and experience your subjects first hand (Figure 6.3). Take a notebook to write down your observations. You could also interview experts or survey other people to gather their opinions on your subjects.

MOVES for Arguing

To compare two or more subjects, you need to do more than look at them side by side. Here are some moves that will help you make deeper comparisons.

A _____ is a _____, while a _____ is a _____.

A _____ and a _____ have a few major characteristics in common: (a) _____, (b) _____, (c) _____, ...

_____ and _____ also differ in a few significant ways, such as _____ and _____.

These similarities and differences are important because _____.

Both _____ and _____ have their strengths and weaknesses, which I will demonstrate in this analysis.

Overall, _____ is better than _____ because it has some helpful features and strengths.

While doing research, you will often discover that the apparent similarities and differences between two things have deeper meanings than expected. If you are comparing two fast-food burger joints, for example, your electronic and print research might show that the two chains follow completely different business philosophies and missions. Your research might also confirm your hunch that their marketing strategies intentionally target two different kinds of customers. Meanwhile, your visits to both restaurants might help you discover some similarities and differences that you didn't expect.

When gathering information to write a comparison argument, your research doesn't always need to be formal. You can use informal sources from the Internet or your own experiences to fill in your comparison. You will, however, need electronic, print, and empirical evidence to back up the substantive claims you make about your subjects.

Organizing and Drafting Your Comparison

6.3 The difference between a point-by-point comparison and a comparison of similarities and differences

The organization of a comparison argument should put your subjects side by side so you can highlight their similarities and differences.

Introduction: Setting a Context for Comparison

Your introduction should clearly identify the subjects you are comparing while offering a brief description of them. Typically, a comparison's introduction will make up to five moves:

Use a Grabber or Lead That Identifies the Subjects.

Look for an anecdote or interesting way to put the people, places, things, or events you are comparing into the same space or side by side.

Signal Your Purpose.

Usually, your purpose (i.e., to compare two or more subjects) is obvious to the audience. Nevertheless, make sure your purpose is not hidden. If needed, you can state your purpose directly.

State Your Main Point or Thesis.

A comparison's thesis typically makes an argumentative claim that rates one of the subjects above the other.

> **Weak Thesis:** There are many similarities and differences between McDonald's and Five Guys.

> **Stronger Thesis:** When you were a kid, McDonald's was the coolest place to go; but if you're a hungry college student who wants a great burger and a mountain of fries, Five Guys is your place.

Offer Background Information on Your Subjects

Briefly describe your subjects or offer historical information to help your audience understand the people or things you are comparing.

Stress the Importance of Your Subjects

Somewhere in your introduction, you should directly or indirectly explain or indicate to your audience why they should care about your subjects.

Here is an example introduction that makes all these moves:

Background information

Topic

Stresses importance

Purpose of comparison

Main point (thesis)

Recently, a new Five Guys opened in the Village just off campus. If you're a burger hound who has never tried Five Guys, you are in for a treat. But this upstart burger chain isn't for everyone. If places like McDonald's automatically come to mind whenever you crave a burger and fries, then Five Guys is going to be a little out of your comfort zone. Even though these two chains' basic menu items are burgers and fries, Five Guys and McDonald's are distinctly different in many ways, including their atmospheres, service, typical customers, and the other food options on the menu. When you were a kid, McDonald's was the coolest place to go; but if you're a hungry college student who wants a great burger and a mountain of fries, Five Guys might be your new burger place.

You don't need to make all five moves in your introduction, and you don't need to make them in a specific order. Minimally, a comparison's introduction should identify your topic, purpose, and main point (thesis). The other moves are helpful for building the audience's background understanding of the subjects you are comparing.

The Body: Discussing Similarities and Differences

The body of your comparison should support your main claim (thesis) with the evidence you found. The genre patterns in the QuickView (p. 108) of this chapter shows two common ways to organize a comparison: a *point-by-point comparison* and a *similarities and differences* comparison. Of course, these patterns aren't the only ones available, and you might devise a pattern that better fits the subjects you are comparing.

Describe the subjects being compared—Your first task in the body is to describe your subjects as objectively as possible. You can describe each subject separately by depicting it part by part or stage by stage. When describing something part by part, divide it into its major three to five parts and then describe each of those parts separately. When describing something stage by stage, divide it into its three to five stages of development and then describe each stage separately.

Compare subjects point by point—In a point-by-point comparison, you are going to compare and contrast your subjects by paying attention to three to five major points of comparison. A point-by-point comparison allows you to highlight the similarities and differences.

Compare subjects by their similarities and differences—In some cases, you might want to talk about how your subjects are similar and then discuss how they are different.

The Similarities: Deep Down, They're Still Both Burger Places—In many ways, McDonald's and Five Guys are basically offering the same core products. Despite McDonald's other offerings, people really go there for the burgers and fries. As a result, the two restaurants actually have a great amount in common. For example,…

The Differences: But Then, They're Not the Same At All—The core products may be the same, but there are also some important differences between McDonald's and Five Guys. Most importantly, McDonald's caters to a family-centered consumer, which means they offer a broader selection of products and try to set a family-friendly atmosphere. For example,…

In a short comparison, you might be able to devote one paragraph to similarities and one paragraph to differences. In a longer comparison, the discussions of similarities and differences could each run a few paragraphs (or more).

Conclusion: State or Restate Your Main Point

The primary goal of your conclusion is to state or restate your main point (your thesis) and look to the future. A conclusion will make a few common moves:

Make an obvious transition—Signal to your audience that you are wrapping up. You can use a heading to signal the conclusion, or you can use a transitional phrase (e.g., "In conclusion," "In the end," or "Overall"). In some cases, a transitional sentence might be needed (e.g., "Let me conclude by giving my overall opinion.")

State or restate your main point (thesis)—Tell your audience which item was better according to your analysis.

Restress the importance of the subjects to the audience—Explain briefly why your audience should care about the similarities and differences in your subjects.

Look to the future—Briefly discuss the future of these subjects and how they might continue to be similar and different in key ways.

Your goal is to restate your main point and wrap up.

Developing a Style and Design: Keep It Plain and Simple

6.4 Ways to use style and design to put the emphasis on the subjects of your comparison

In most cases, the style and design of a comparison should be straightforward. As much as possible, you want your comparison's style and design to help your audience focus on the facts.

Using Plain Style

For most comparison arguments, the plain style is most appropriate because your voice will sound straightforward and fair to the audience.

Put the subjects you are comparing in the subjects of your sentences—You want your subjects, not you, to be the focal point of your argument.

Original: I ordered french fries at Five Guys and found them delicious because they were hand cut and deep fried in peanut oil.

Revised: The french fries at Five Guys tasted delicious because they are hand cut and fried in peanut oil.

Use plenty of sensory detail—You also want your audience to see, hear, smell, taste, and feel the subjects you are comparing. So when you are describing each or your subjects, add sensory details that help your audience experience the people, places, things, or events you are comparing.

Eliminate nominalizations where possible—When comparing and contrasting, you might feel the urge to sound more authoritative by using nominalizations (e.g., *evaluate* becomes *evaluation* or *decide* becomes *decision*). Really, though, nominalizations just make the text harder to read. So, where possible, turn these awkward nominalizations into active verbs:

Original: We did <u>an evaluation</u> of the service at both restaurants, and <u>our decision</u> was that McDonald's service was slightly better.

Revised: We <u>evaluated</u> the service at both restaurants, and we <u>decided</u> that McDonald's service was slightly better.

Nominalizations are often called "shun" words because they usually end in *-tion* or *-sion*, which make that "shun" sound.

Designing for Easy Comparisons

The design of your comparison argument should allow your audience to make easy visual comparisons between your subjects.

Use photos, preferably placing them side by side—If possible, put photos of the two subjects side by side so the audience can make direct visual comparisons. Figure 6.4, for example, allows the audience to compare directly the interiors of Five Guys and McDonald's.

Use graphs to help your audience make comparisons—If you are comparing your subjects by using data (e.g., sales figures, sizes, growth), a graph or chart will you make direct comparisons between the different sets of numbers.

Use headings to highlight the structure of the text—A comparison is usually not intended to be pleasure reading. So you want the structure of your argument to be obvious to your audience in a visual way. You should use headings to signal what is being described, compared, or discussed. Your audience should be able to use the headings to skim the text for the information they need.

In most comparisons, the style and design of your document should not be too prominent. You want your audience's attention to be on the subjects you are comparing and contrasting, not on your tone or design.

FIGURE 6.4
Putting Two
Photos Side by
Side
In these two photos,
taken from the
Internet, the visual
differences between
the two subjects are
easy to see.

Ready to compare people, places, things, or events? Here's the basic information you need to know:

1 Typically, comparisons highlight the similarities and differences between two or more subjects, sometimes explaining why one is better (or worse) than the others.

2 The subjects of comparisons are usually similar in an obvious way, but sometimes you will find it fun and challenging to compare subjects that are very different.

3 When inventing your argument, a Venn diagram can be a useful visual tool to identify some of the major similarities and differences between subjects you are comparing and contrasting.

4 Identify two to five major *points of comparison* between the subjects you are comparing. These points will be the major categories you will use in your argument to compare and contrast your subjects.

5 Find an *angle* on your subjects that helps you compare and contrast your subjects in a unique way. What has happened recently that makes your subjects especially interesting? Is there something about you that allows you to provide a unique perspective on these subjects?

6 Don't skimp on the research. Use electronic, print, and empirical sources to help you make comparisons. If you try to use only your experiences or memory, your comparison will lack detail and insight.

7 The two most common structures of a comparison are (a) point by point and (b) similarities and differences. Both highlight the subjects in different ways.

8 Comparisons are organized to put the subjects side by side, so their similarities and differences are obvious to the audience.

9 In most cases, the style of your comparison should be plain with lots of detail. Where possible, make the subjects you are comparing the subjects of your sentences.

10 You can use photos and graphs to help your audience visualize the similarities and differences between the two subjects. Put images side by side where possible.

1. With your group, make a list of five pairs of products, places, or people that you can compare. Each member of your group should choose one of these pairs. Then ask each person to create a Venn diagram that highlights the similarities and differences between these subjects.

2. With your group, make a list of twenty randomly chosen subjects on a sheet of paper. The more different they are, the better. Cut up the sheet with one item per slip. Then have each member of the group choose two slips without looking. In teams of two, use Venn diagrams to compare and contrast these very different subjects.

3. On the Internet, find an example of a comparison. Hint: A good example probably won't be called a comparison. Instead, look for articles that compare products, services, or people. When you find one, use the concepts in this chapter to analyze it. Is it effective or not?

1. Write a comparison from the perspective of a college student. What kind of unique perspective could you bring to the following kinds of subjects?

High school to college	Harry Potter and Percy Jackson	Two popular movies
Being wealthy to being poor	Two video games	New vs. used car while at college
John Deere vs. IH combines	Traditional to online classes	Types of college professors
Spring break: skiing or beach?	Disney World to a camping trip	Clothing stores
Two fast-food restaurants	iPhone vs. Android phones	Dracula vs. Edward Cullen
Two college sports teams	Yoga vs. weightlifting	Democracies and dictatorships
Two religions	Football vs. rugby	Evolution vs. intelligent design

2. Find a comparison on the Internet that compares two or more things you know well. Then write a rebuttal or counterstatement in which you critique and challenge the author's evaluation of these subjects.

3. Write a comparison in which you compare and contrast the college student experiences of people from different cultures, genders, or age groups. For instance, you could compare the experiences of a traditional student (18–22 years old) to a nontraditional student (more than 30 years old). Or you might explore how college is different for men and women. Or you could explain why going to college as a Hispanic student differs from going to college as an African American or European American student. As you are developing your argument, you need to be careful not to use stereotypes or rely on preconceived assumptions about race, class, gender, or age. You should do research on the Internet and use print sources from the library. You might interview or survey people who are in these different demographic groups. *Important: This kind of comparison requires an added level of sensitivity.*

Riley Schenck, a student, takes on a touchy topic in this comparison argument when she tries to sort out the differences between conservatives and liberals. Of course, comparisons like this one are risky because they often generalize broadly about why people think and behave the way they do. And yet, these kinds of comparisons help people better understand where others are coming from. This comparison is biased, but if you read more closely, you will see how the frames used to describe conservatives and liberals create this feeling of bias.

Conservatives Are from Mars, Liberals Are from Venus

Riley Schenck

Earlier this month, science and politics journalist Chris Mooney came out with a new book entitled *The Republican Brain, The Science of Why They Deny Science—and Reality*, a book that is much more insightful and objective than its partisan title would suggest. In the book, Mooney links a number of genetic and physiological studies that paint a picture of the differences between how liberals and conservatives think, and how these differences affect our behavior.

The studies prove empirically what many of you have probably already assumed: Differences in political ideology tend to arise from real differences in people's brains. Studies have begun to show that liberals and conservatives have fundamentally different patterns of how they perceive the world and how they respond to those perceptions. These psychological differences that help shape core values and beliefs "spill over" into many different areas, politics included. In sum, psychological differences in the way we think result in personality traits that predispose us to supporting one ideology or another.

The findings prove that there is actually a lot of truth to many political stereotypes. For example, a 2003 study by John Jost found that people who scored highly on a scale measuring the fear of death were almost four times more likely to hold conservative views (the ignorant, God-fearing Republican stereotype). On the other hand, those who expressed interest in new experiences tended to be liberal (those God-damned free-loving hippie stoners). Jost even found that conservatives prefer simple and unambiguous paintings, poems and songs (country music, anyone?).

Other studies have begun to show how deep-rooted psychological reasons explain these differences. A 2012 study by the University of Nebraska–Lincoln measured the emotional response to different images by measuring the subjects' sweat gland response compared to their eye movement when shown different images and found that conservatives had much stronger reactions to negative images (such as a spider crawling on a person's face or maggots in an open wound), while liberals had stronger reactions towards positive images (a smiling child or a bunny rabbit). Conservatives' eye movements were more quickly drawn to the negative images and spent a longer time fixated on them, while liberals spent more time looking at the positive images.

5   These behavioral differences are likely caused by actual physical differences in conservative and liberal brains. A 2011 study at University College London took MRI scans of the brains of 90 young adult volunteers. They found that liberal students tended to have larger anterior cingulate cortices, an area of the brain that processes conflicting information, while conservatives tended to have larger amygdalas, an area that processes fear and identifies threats.

When you apply these findings to conservative and liberal ideologies, everything begins to fall into place. Thinking about any issue and how it is portrayed by liberals and conservatives, chances are that liberals will focus on positives while conservatives focus on negatives. On abortion, conservatives frame the issue with the negative imagery of baby-killing (if you are not "pro-life," then you must be "pro-death"). Liberals frame their arguments positively with the "pro-choice" idea of women's "freedom to choose." On gay rights, liberals focus on the positive images of tolerance and acceptance while conservatives focus on the (subjectively) "disgusting" image of anal sex and the "destruction of family values." On Obamacare, liberal arguments are framed on the positive image of helping others achieve access to health care, while conservatives focus on the negative ideas of declining quality of care, with some even going so far as to claim that the law would result in "death panels." Liberals find conservative assertions like the "death panels" laughable, but this growing body of research shows that these fear-evoking assertions actually hit home with many conservative voters and are an effective campaign strategy for conservative politicians.

Mooney contends that liberal reactions to positive imagery, along with larger regions of the brain that process conflicting information, lead to much higher degrees of openness, a personality Mooney defines as "a broad personality trait that covers everything from intellectual flexibility and curiosity to an enjoyment of the arts and creativity. It denotes being experimental, a risk taker in one's way of living and one's choices, and wanting to sample variety across the range of life's experiences." Respondents who scored highest in "openness" had more liberal ideologies than 71 percent of the other respondents.

Political conservatives, on the other hand, tended to rate higher in "Conscientiousness" ratings. Mooney states, "Those who rate high on this trait tend to prize orderliness and having a lot of structure in their lives—being on time, working hard, sticking to a predictable schedule, and keeping one's home or office neat or clean. … The conscientious are highly goal-oriented, competent, and organised—and, on average, politically conservative."

Obviously, just because you are goal-oriented doesn't necessarily make you conservative, or a risk-taker a liberal (look at rodeo jockeys). However, I can't help but notice some striking similarities in my own life: Two of the most organized, cleanest people I've ever met were two conservative frat bros I lived with sophomore year (frats don't typically conjure up images of cleanliness), while try as I might, my own room seems to always trend toward entropy.

10   Mooney's book reveals plenty of interesting trends and makes us reconceptualize political ideology. It does not, however, tackle the explanation as to why liberal and conservative thinking is so different.

A CLOSER LOOK AT
Conservatives Are from Mars, Liberals Are from Venus

1. According to this article, what are three to five major ways in which conservatives and liberals think and react differently to issues? List these issues and discuss them with your group in class. Do these differences ring true to your own experiences?

2. This article feels biased, but a closer look reveals that the sense of bias is due primarily to word choice. Specifically, positive words are being associated with liberals, and negative words are being associated with conservatives. How do frames (see Chapter 2) such as the ones used here shape how people describe other people?

3. Find three places in which the author of this comparison argument uses scientific sources to back up the argument. In what ways do these scientific sources support the argument? In what places did Riley use sources effectively? Where could Riley have used more sources to balance the coverage of this issue?

IDEAS FOR
Arguing

1. A critic of this article might point out that the author too easily accepts the frames traditionally associated with conservatives and liberals. Generally, the author, admittedly a liberal, seems to favor the "liberal" frames. Write a counterstatement (see Chapter 13) in which you argue that the conservative frame is beneficial in a variety of circumstances. Or write a rebuttal in which you reject these generalizations about conservatives and liberals.

2. Choose a political party (e.g., Republican, Democratic, Libertarian, Socialist). Write a comparison argument in which you show how that party's political ideologies have changed from the past to today. For example, you might show how Republicans or Democrats have changed their views since the U.S. Civil War or perhaps the Great Depression. At the end of your comparison argument, explain why you think the ideology of the party you studied has evolved in some ways and stayed the same in others.

Why 'The Hunger Games' Isn't 'Twilight' (and Why That's a Good Thing)

KATE ERBLAND

In this comparison argument, Kate Erbland discusses the similarities and differences between two series of movies in which young women are central characters. Erbland favors The Hunger Games, *but the basis of her argument is that the promoters of these movies are following similar strategies, even though the movies themselves are quite different. As you read, look for the points on which the two movies are compared and contrasted.*

The conceptual similarities between Suzanne Collins's *The Hunger Games* series and Stephenie Meyer's *The Twilight Saga* series are slim—and anyone who tells you otherwise is delusional, illiterate, and incapable of complex thoughts related to literary exploration. However, while their content does differ, their initial appeal to a YA audience, the insistence of declaring "teams" for romantic paramours, and their large-scale cinematic adaptations do beg for some discussion about their surface similarities, and how those will translate into stuff like audience appeal and ultimate impact on readers and viewers.

While I find *Twilight* to be the infinitely weaker and less compelling of the two properties, I'm not some sort of blind *Twilight* hater—I've read all the books and seen all the movies, and I get why it's appealing to all sorts of readers and watchers, particularly those looking to consume something that provides escape—but I also think that there is far better material out there for public consumption. Smarter, wiser, more applicable to the real world, and more compelling material—like *The Hunger Games.*

Let's put it this way—if I had a fifteen-year-old daughter, I'd want her to read *The Hunger Games*, and here's why.

The Hunger Games Stands Without the "Team" Mentality

The Twilight Saga is rooted in its central romance(s). These are not books or movies about strong, independent, bold characters—it's a series about how obsessive love can make one weak, and how that's not only a bad thing, it's something to turn away from. Bella, Edward, and Jacob are all slaves to love, a trope in the series that even applies to supporting characters (werewolves "imprinting" on unsuspecting humans, leaving them unable to ever love another, for example). The appeal of *Twilight* has much to do with the force of first love—or, at least, what people perceive as the force of first love. All-consuming, all-desiring, fated in an otherworldly manner, Bella and Edward's love is the central theme and conflict of the series.

It doesn't matter to either one of them the havoc their affection can wreak on others, from innocent bystanders to their own family, they must be together. When they're

5

not together, Bella is unable to function as a human being (remember the first half of *New Moon*?), and her pain eventually reaches the point that she can no longer be human. So, well, Team Edward, right? That's what Bella wants? Right?

Sorry, Team Jacob. Despite the fact that Bella never actually engages with Jacob in a wholly romantic manner or that she pointedly chooses Edward every chance she gets or even that she goes ahead and (spoiler alert?) births a baby who appears to have been conceived principally to love Jacob, the "team" mentality of both *Twilight* and its fans stays strong. And while Katniss Everdeen also has two suitors to choose from, choosing sides isn't central to the story—because it's not central to her character.

Bella doesn't exist without Edward and Jacob battling for her mortal soul—there's literally no reason for the books to exist without that conflict. And while the battles fought in the final Twilight story have further-reaching consequences and involvement than just a boring old love triangle, every thing that has pushed us to that point is thanks to romantic entanglements. Imagine *Twilight* without Edward or Jacob. You can't. Because it would not exist. Imagine *The Hunger Games* without its hard-won romances. You can. Surely, some of the emotion is deflated from certain parts of the story, but what the books are ultimately about are Katniss Everdeen and the world of Panem. Katniss is a fully formed human being who remains independent even without the definition of Peeta Mellark or Gale Hawthorne pining for her.

Fans of *The Hunger Games* do, however, have their own teams (I'm Team Peeta myself), but in reality, what everyone should be is Team Katniss or, as fellow critic James Rocchi tossed off in a tweet a few weeks back, Team She Is Herself. Katniss is a strong, independent, admirable woman who exists far beyond her dueling romances, whereas Bella is absolutely defined by her more tender desires and the two beasts who fight for them.

Katniss Is Driven By Forces Beyond Her Control And She Beats Them

Both Bella and Katniss must leave their families at crucial points in their stories, and the differences both of them leaving their lives is twofold—the reasons why they leave and what they expect to get out of said leaving. Katniss does not have a choice to leave her home and family— Bella does. As central to the first book in the series (our focus for this discussion) Katniss is forced to leave District 12, Prim, Gale, and her mother because of powers far beyond her control—the Games themselves, the Capitol at large, and the system that's been in place since before she was born all make her not leaving impossible. Again, Katniss does not have a choice, and that's a central element of the first two books in the series.

Bella, however, does have a choice. While 10 I suspect that should Bella herself weigh in on the topic, she'd tell us that she didn't, that she was compelled by a fated, otherworldly love that left her unable to live without Edward. That's bunk. No healthy relationship involves one party leaving family, friends, and home and also changing the very make-up of their existence for another partner. I'm sorry, Edward, it's not your fault that you're a vampire, but come the hell on. Bella *does* have a choice, and she makes it and carries it out completely (and then Meyer hedges her bets and allows Bella's old life to merge with her new one pretty quickly, but that's a topic for another day).

But just what does Katniss expect to get out of her leaving? Well, in being forced to leave so that she can participate in a televised battle to the death, she doesn't expect much. But despite the odds not being "ever in her favor," Katniss is fueled by a desire to win (not just to *win*, but to *survive*) so that she can get home to her family and, when circumstances change, she's also driven by the belief that she can also save Peeta and deliver him home as well. Pardon my French, but those are some pretty fucking awesome expectations. What does Bella desire from her total life abandonment? That she can become a mythical beast and live with her boring boyfriend forever. Great. Really top-notch stuff. Very inspirational.

And while both Bella and Katniss get things they want out of their leaving – Bella gets to be a vampire, Katniss gets to go home—Katniss's perceived resolution is much more satisfying and compelling. Despite stacked odds and an evil system, she has persevered and won (though her win is obviously tinged with pain, regret, and suffering), and she has accomplished something bigger and better than herself.

Bella simply triumphs over a specific and ultimately short-lived pain that she's asked for, and asked for with only selfish intentions. Her victory is only worth celebrating if you're convinced that the culmination of an abusive and immature relationship is worth celebrating.

The Hunger Games Presents A Bigger World and Worldview With Real World Applications

The world of *Twilight* is, ostensibly, our current world with a secret underworld that Bella happens to discover through Edward and Jacob. It's not a particularly original or imaginative world creation, and the fact that the vast majority of the series' action (save for jaunts to Italy and the honeymoon on Isle Esme) takes place in a tiny town in Washington makes the whole story feel small. Smaller still? While Bella, Edward, and Jacob's entanglements eventually lead to a big ol' battle between vampires and werewolves, the impact on the rest of the world is, well, nil. What's the worst that could happen? The Cullens and the wolves lose and the Volturi continue on with status quo that, again, effects in an incredibly limited segment of the population? Snooze. Small world, small worldview, little real world application.

15   But *The Hunger Games*? It's much larger. Collins's series presents a big, original (relative to *Twilight*; even I don't think Collins has flipped the switch on dystopian futures), fully-formed, imaginative, and well-crafted world that comes with its very own worldview (read: bleak). While one of my major problems with the series is

that we never learn about the rest of the world (though it's safe to assume that most everything else has been wiped out, or at least reduced to a state without the sort of technology needed to reach other lands—i.e. even something as basic as boats), there is still more than enough detail in what we do learn about.

Collins has imagined a future that feels real and possible, as hard to take as that may be, and one that is ruled by the influence of current things—reality television in particular. Could what happens in *The Hunger Games* happen before what happens in *Twilight*? Yes, and that's infinitely more terrifying and more engaging. Love stories are all well and good, but the reach of Bella and Edward is slim at best—Katniss, the Capitol, and the Games consume whole continents.

The Concept of Bucking Societal Norms and Starting Revolutions

Let's break this down—Bella's big break from typical societal norms is that she becomes a vampire for love. While that's certainly a big change for Bella, it doesn't matter much to anyone else. Her turn does eventually affect others, leading to that big battle between the "good" vampires and werewolves against all those evil vampires, but again, what does that mean for everyone else on the planet? Not much. Bella and Edward start a revolution of sorts by marrying and conceiving of a half human/half vampire child who surpasses even her talented vampire family, but that doesn't mean a whole hell of a lot to the vast majority of the world—you know, the humans. Sure, they bring down the Volturi, but *again*, who cares?

On the other side of the coin, Katniss has spent most of her life busting through what's expected of her—leading her family, leaving District 12 to hunt and gather, volunteering in place of her sister Prim, and eventually helping to usher in a revolution that changes all of Panem. While Katniss's revolutionary activity is but just a piece of the whole puzzle, and she's initially seen as just a figurehead of the movement, she eventually blossoms into one of its most important leaders—both intellectually and physically.

Her final act during battle in *Mockingjay* is perhaps the biggest revolutionary act in all of *The Hunger Games*—and it's one that changes the lives of every man, woman, and child in Panem—and for the better.

Katniss Everdeen Is a Better Hero Than Bella Swan—Hands Down

20   Let's see here—Katniss doesn't need a man to complete her identity, she's capable of saving herself from forces far beyond her control, she's honed real-world skills that can feed and protect her, she finds true love without having to compromise herself and her ideals, and she kickstarts a revolution that aims to better the lives of most of the people who live in her country. And Bella falls in love with a mythical monster and abandons her life, loved ones, and identity to be with him. But, hey, her vampire transformation process goes by swiftly because she's got special mind powers! You make the choice.

A CLOSER LOOK AT
Why *The Hunger Games* Isn't *Twilight* (and Why That's a Good Thing)

1. Erland uses several points to compare and contrast these two series of novels and movies. List those major points.

2. Fold a sheet of paper lengthwise into two columns. In one column, list all the features that Erland identifies that make *The Hunger Games* and *Twilight* similar. Then, in the second column, list all the differences that Erland mentions.

3. After her comparison of *The Hunger Games* and *Twilight*, Erland clearly favors the character of Katniss over the character of Bella. What are some of her reasons for favoring Katniss, and how do these reasons influence her understanding of these two series of movies?

IDEAS FOR
Arguing

1. Imagine you are writing a pitch (a brief proposal) for a new movie. You want to compare it favorably to highly successful movies like *The Hunger Games* or *Twilight*. Yet you also want it to be unique. Write a one-page pitch for your new movie, describing the plot, the major characters, and the settings. In your pitch, compare your movie to one of these blockbuster movies, but also clarify how your movie is different.

2. One of the problems with "Why *The Hunger Games* Isn't *Twilight*" is that, despite their superficial similarities, *The Hunger Games* and *Twilight* come from two different genres. *The Hunger Games* is a science fiction adventure. *Twilight* is a fantasy romance. Choose one of these two movies. Then write a comparison in which you compare it to a movie in its genre.

Causal Analyses—Arguing through Causes and Effects

7 CHAPTER

IN THIS CHAPTER, YOU WILL LEARN—

7.1 How causal analyses are both generative and persuasive arguments

7.2 Strategies for inventing the content of a causal analysis by exploring causes and effects

7.3 How to organize a causal analysis so it delivers information in a straightforward way

7.4 Methods for using style and design to engage with the audience

The purpose of a causal analysis is to explain why people behave a particular way, why something happened, or why something is changing in the world around us. For example, let's say you are interested in figuring out why college students get tattoos (Figure 7.1). If you ask a person with a tattoo, he or she might say something like, "It just seemed cool, and I always wanted one." But you suspect there are deeper reasons people make a lifelong decision to ink themselves. A causal analysis is a good way to find some answers.

7.1 How causal analyses are both generative and persuasive arguments

Causal analyses have both generative and persuasive elements. They are generative because you and others can use them to collaboratively explore the causes and effects that are driving changes in our world. In your college courses, your professors will ask you and others to explore and discuss the motivations behind social movements, historical events, economic and political trends, and natural phenomena. In your career, you will work on team projects that explore business trends, solve crimes, explain human behavior, and describe changes in the environment. Most jobs involve figuring out why changes are happening so the company or organization can respond to those changes. Causal analyses written in the workplace are often called white papers, briefings, reports, marketing studies, trend analyses, and research reports.

Causal analyses are also persuasive because you need to demonstrate in a convincing way that you have identified the causes behind something while explaining

Quick View

Generative   **Persuasive**

Generative Argument—Causal analyses are often produced in teams, especially in the workplace, because people need to work together to explore and explain the causes behind changes and trends. How issues are framed and the narratives we use can greatly influence how people think about and react to important issues.

Persuasive Argument—Causal analyses are also persuasive because usually more than one explanation for a behavior or event is possible. So you need to prove that you have identified the root causes of the change or trend, while explaining its effects.

Genre Patterns

There are many ways to organize a causal analysis. You should adjust these patterns to fit the specific needs of your argument.

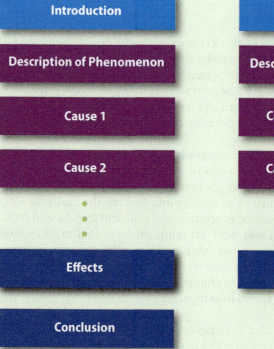

Introduction	**Introduction**
Description of Phenomenon	**Description of Phenomenon**
Cause 1	**Cause 1 and Its Effects**
Cause 2	**Cause 2 and Its Effects**
Effects	**Conclusion**
Conclusion	

FIGURE 7.1 Using a Causal Analysis to Explore a Trend Causal analyses are often used to explain why people do what they do.

the real and potential effects of that change. Usually, more than a few reasons are available to explain why something changed or is changing. In a persuasive way, your goal is to prove to your audience that you have uncovered the root causes behind these changes and that you understand their effects. In some cases, you may need to persuade your audience to take action.

When writing a causal analysis, you are essentially investigating *why* something happens and exploring the potential effects of that change.

Inventing the Content of Your Causal Analysis

7.2 Strategies for inventing the content of a causal analysis by exploring causes and effects

The key question in a causal analysis is "why?" as in, "Why did this happen?" After all, if you want to understand what happened in the past or what is happening right now, you first need to understand *why* it happened or is happening. You need to know what caused or is causing it.

Using a Concept Map to Investigate Causes

A helpful tool for investigating causes is a concept map. To create a concept map, write your subject (an event, behavior, accident, trend, incident) in the center of a piece of paper or your screen (Figure 7.2).

Then do the following:

1. **Write down two to five major causes around your subject and circle them.** You may need to make some educated guesses about these causes, which you can verify or eliminate later. At this point, guesswork is fine.

A Concept Map
That Explores
Causes
When using a
concept map to
explore causes,
first choose two
to five major
causes. Then
choose two to
five minor causes
for each major
cause.

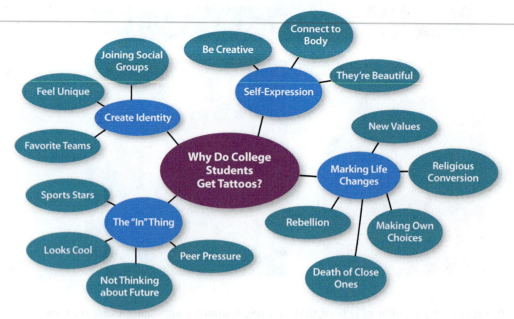

2. **Ask yourself, "What has changed recently that is causing this to happen?"** Pay attention to what is changing about your subject, especially what has changed recently. Usually, if you pay attention to whatever is changing, you will be able to better understand what is causing that change.

3. **Write down two to five minor causes for each major cause.** Analyze each major cause separately, exploring its causes. In other words, identify the minor causes that are beneath each major cause.

4. **Draw connections between causes.** If causes seem related, draw lines to connect them. These connections may help you identify larger causes or relationships among causes that may not seem related.

5. **Use your concept map to identify how the issue is framed.** A concept map will help you identify how the issue is being framed in our culture. Look closely at how people tend to frame this subject through their choice of words and the conclusions they draw from the evidence.

6. **Figure out your angle.** A concept map will help you find a new angle on your topic. An angle is a unique perspective that you can use to explore and discuss your topic. Sometimes, it helps to ask yourself, "What is new or what has happened recently that makes this topic especially interesting right now?"

For example, the concept map shown in Figure 7.2 analyzes why some college students get tattoos. The person who created this map put the subject "Why do college students get tattoos?" in the middle of her screen and then wrote a few major causes around it. As she looked for other major causes, she asked herself, "What has changed recently that is causing college students to get inked?" Then, analyzing each major cause separately, she filled in all the possible minor causes she could think of.

She can also use her concept map to identify common frames or narratives through which people talk about tattoos. Specifically, though tattoos are not uncommon, in American culture they are still framed as edgy symbols of outsider status. Meanwhile, people with tattoos often use narratives to explain why they decided to put particular symbols and pictures permanently on their bodies.

Researching Your Subject

Now you need to do some research to find out whether the ideas in the concept map can be supported with facts and other evidence from sources. A concept map like the one in Figure 7.2 will only help you identify *possible* causes. You need to do research to determine whether these causes actually exist.

Explore with electronic sources—Start entering key words from your concept map into an Internet search engine, such as Bing, Google, or Yahoo. The search engine will help you find websites, blogs, and other electronic sources on your subject. Some of these sources will be more reliable than others. To learn how to determine if an Internet source is reliable, turn to Chapter 16, "Developing Your Research Process."

Explore with print sources—At your college's library or its website, find books and articles that analyze and explain your topic. You can locate these sources through the catalog on your library's website. Then, find them at the library or download them electronically. Or you could use Google Scholar to find academic articles and books online.

Explore with empirical sources—You can interview an expert, create a survey, or conduct field observations to better understand the topic you are investigating. More than likely, a professor, researcher, or staff member on your college campus knows something about your topic. He or she might be a good person to contact for an interview.

While doing research, you will probably discover facts and data that confirm many of the ideas in your concept map. Your research might also help you cross out some of the ideas in your map that lack support.

Since causal analyses tend to be more generative than persuasive, you should pay special attention to any narratives or uses of identification and negotiation to explain behavior or events. Collect any stories told by the people involved, and look for ways they identify themselves with others and negotiate conflicts among themselves.

Note: As you are researching your topic, collect any images on your topic that you find particularly interesting. Photographs or drawings are especially helpful for illustrating the causes and effects of a trend, event, or phenomenon.

MOVES for Arguing

Trying to explain why something happened? Here are some moves that will help you:

The major causes of _____ are _____ and _____.

This happened because_____ changed, which forced _____ to change, too.

In reality, _____ is just a symptom of deeper causes, such as _____, _____, and _____.

People often assume _____ is caused by _____, but it is really caused by _____ and _____.

The effects of this problem are due to a couple different causes, which include _____ and _____.

You cannot fully understand why _____ happens until you understand the underlying reasons why it is happening.

7.3 How to organize a causal analysis so it delivers information in a straightforward way

Organizing and Drafting Your Causal Analysis

With your initial research behind you, you're ready to begin drafting your causal analysis. A typical causal analysis has an introduction, a description of the phenomenon being analyzed, an analysis of its causes and their effects, and a conclusion. The diagrams in the QuickView on page 128 offer a couple patterns you can follow or modify.

Introduction: Identifying Your Topic and Stating Your Main Point

A good introduction for a causal analysis usually includes some or all of the following six moves:

Begin with a grabber or lead—Up front, your introduction should catch your audience's attention with an interesting quote, a scene setter, a compelling statement, an anecdote, or a startling statistic.

State your topic—You should identify your topic (i.e., the subject of your causal analysis) as soon as possible if your grabber or lead didn't do so already.

Identify your purpose—Somewhere in your introduction, it should be clear that you are analyzing the causes and effects of your subject. You don't need a direct statement, such as "I will analyze the causes of the tattoo trend," but you want your audience to know up front what you are trying to achieve.

State your main point or thesis—A causal analysis's thesis will typically claim something is happening due to one or more causes. Here's where you can reveal your angle.

> *Weak Thesis:* Getting a tattoo in college is no longer distinctive or radical.

> *Stronger Thesis:* In this age of social networking and mobile technology, people often feel isolated and their world feels unstable. Getting a tattoo is a way to feel connected to others while making a statement that feels permanent.

Offer background information on the Provide—Provide some historical background on your subject or include information related to your subject that your audience will find familiar.

Stress the importance of your topic—Indicate why this subject is important to your audience—or should be important.

Here's an example introduction for a causal analysis:

Getting inked in college may seem trendy and chic, but it's hardly a new thing. In fact, young people have been getting tattoos as a rite of passage into adulthood for thousands of years (Gilbert, p. 11). Tattoos have been found on ancient Egyptian mummies, as well on Ötzi, the mummified "iceman" found in the Alps who was frozen around 3300 BC ("History," par. 2). In America, tattooing has an especially interesting history, because this form of art was brought to our continent by British sailors who visited the Pacific Islands in the 1700s (Demello, p. 45). For Pacific Islanders, tattoos were symbols of status as well as a way to protect themselves from earthly and spiritual enemies. When British sailors visited the Pacific Islands, especially Tahiti, they began getting tattoos because they liked their decorative features. They brought the concept of tattooing back to the American colonies.

Grabber and Topic

Background information

Getting a tattoo while in college, however, is still something relatively new. Until recently, tattoos were considered low class, a step or two below the white-collar aspirations of a typical college graduate. So why has tattooing become so common among college students that it's almost a cliché to get one? In this age of social networking and mobile technology, people often feel isolated and their world feels unstable. Getting a tattoo is a way to feel connected to others while making a statement that feels permanent.

Stresses importance

Purpose

Thesis statement

As you begin drafting your introduction, you might find it helpful to write one or two sentences for each of these six introductory moves. Then revise them into one or two paragraphs that will form the opening of your argument. Your introduction doesn't need to make all these moves, nor do you need to make them in a specific order. Minimally, your topic, purpose, and main point (thesis statement or question) should be clear to the audience.

Body: Describing the Event or Phenomenon

The body of your causal analysis should begin by thoroughly describing the event or phenomenon you are exploring. When describing your subject, use sensory details and narratives where appropriate to illustrate what you are talking about. You want your audience to visualize what you are analyzing.

For example, let's continue with the topic of college students and tattoos. Your first challenge is to describe the phenomenon:

> In American culture, getting inked has always been associated with freedom, independence, and being an outsider. At the beginning of the twentieth century, tattooing was primarily associated with circus sideshows (the "tattooed lady"), criminals, and prostitutes (Osterud). Tattooing moved into the working-class mainstream after World War II when young American sailors from the Pacific theater came home with tattoos on their arms. In the 1960s, tattooing became common among counterculture groups like hippies, biker gangs, and so-called Jesus freaks. Then, in the later 1990s, tattoos became common among college students as tattooing methods became more artistic, more refined, and less painful (DeJesus, 2011). Getting a tattoo was no longer viewed as something only lower-class people would do.

> Today, spotting a college student with one or more tattoos is hardly unique. A woman studying at Starbucks has a dragon tattoo draped across her shoulders. Some guy in your world history class has Scooby Doo permanently enshrined on his calf. One of your friends has a butterfly tattoo on her abdomen that is only revealed when she is wearing low-riding jeans or a bathing suit. In fact, recent surveys report that 36 percent of college-age people have tattoos (Pew 2006; Laumann & Derick 2006). Most of these tattoos are small, usually placed on upper arms, shoulders, calves, and ankles where they can be covered up. Some college students go further, displaying tattoo "sleeves" that cover their entire arms or shoulders. Meanwhile, others have elaborate drawings that cover their chests or decorate their necks. College athletes, especially in basketball and football, emulate professional athletes with a variety of inked images on their bodies.

In these two paragraphs, the writer has provided an overview of the trend she is analyzing. The sources she uses help her tie her discussion to a larger historical conversation about tattoos.

The body of the causal analysis might also be a good place to insert a table or graph that illustrates the trends you are talking about. Figure 7.3 shows how charts and graphs can be used to present data and illustrate trends.

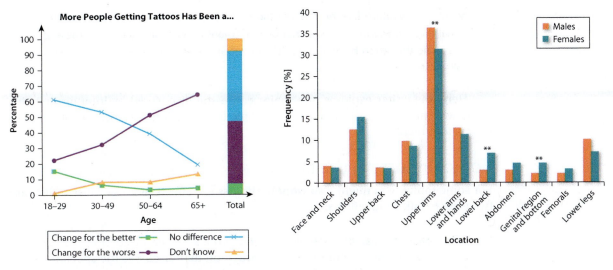

FIGURE 7.3 Using Charts and Graphs to Illustrate Trends
Charts and graphs can help you illustrate trends and present data.

Body: Exploring and Explaining the Causes

After you have described your subject, you can analyze its causes. For most subjects, you should identify the two to five major causes up front:

> Everyone has his or her own reasons for getting a tattoo, but in my interviews with college students, four main causes seemed to emerge: (a) expressing themselves, (b) establishing their unique identity, (c) marking major life changes, and (d) creating a permanent statement of some kind.

Then explore each of these causes separately, giving a paragraph or two to each one. Here is a discussion of one of these causes.

Creating a Unique Identity

Using tattoos to create a unique identity seems especially strong among college students. This isn't surprising. After all, leaving home, family, and friends is a major life-altering event. Most young people are eager to go to college, but this new life and new freedom can feel overwhelming.

My interviews with three students offered some insight into this reason for getting a tattoo. "Lisa," a second-year marketing major, explained that putting a tattoo of a unicorn on her shoulder helped her connect with new social groups. Her tattoo gave her something to talk about with other people, and she felt her unicorn was an outward sign of her personality. Her tattoo became a symbol of her new life at college. "Juan," a civil engineering major, had a scroll tattoo put on his forearm that lists the names of his four best friends from high school. His "crew" all went to different colleges, but he wanted to remember that they would be friends forever. "Sally," an English major, knew her mother wouldn't like the chain tattoo she put around her arm, but she wanted to signal that she was able to make her own decisions as an adult. All three of these students said the tattoo helped them fit in better as they formed their new identities as college students and as adults.

Here, the writer explores one major cause she discovered by interviewing students who have tattoos. She uses the details from her interviewees to support her overall argument.

Body: Discussing the Effects

For some topics, you might also want to discuss the effects of these causes. Here are two ways to talk about effects:

After each cause, discuss its specific effects—After discussing a major cause, add a couple sentences or a paragraph that discusses the specific effects of that cause. For example:

> Interestingly, college students' desire to express their unique identity may cause complications in their future, especially when seeking a job. Some employers view a tattoo as a signal that the applicant has made questionable choices in the past or perhaps doesn't want to fit into the corporate culture (Varenik). For this reason, employment counselors often recommend that students only get tattoos that can be covered up in professional situations. That said, it's hard to anticipate all the types of professional situations that might arise. For example, a corporate retreat to a beach resort might reveal some odd tattooing decisions made in college.

Discuss all the effects at one time—After you have explored and explained all the causes of your subject, you can briefly discuss the two to five major effects in one place.

> Getting a tattoo in college can have some interesting effects, both positive and negative. While at college, tattoos tend to have the desired positive effects. They signal independence and express creativity. They are something to talk about at parties. And they usually succeed in irritating parents and other adults.
>
> After college, though, tattoos have other effects. Let's be honest, the decision to get a forearm SpongeBob tattoo is being made by a 19-year-old who will someday be a 45-year-old. That old tat won't seem quite so cool when SpongeBob is long forgotten. Plus, over the years, tattoos tend to blur and fade with exposure to the sun, making them look more like mustard and ketchup stains than body art. Even more problematic, though, will be the changes that happen naturally with age. Even the fittest people tend to fill out as they age, which can make those tattoos stretch and morph into strange new shapes.

Perhaps most important, though, tattoos may just be another fad. Ten years from now, so-called body art might be viewed with the same humor as parachute pants and mullet haircuts. The difference, of course, is that out-of-fashion clothes can be given away to Goodwill, and you can get a new hairstyle. But those old tattoos will still be there.

In these paragraphs, the writer discusses the major effects of the tattooing trend. She also explains how the causes could lead to unintended effects.

Conclusion: Restating Your Main Point and Looking to the Future

The conclusion of a causal analysis is usually brief. You can use some or all of the following concluding moves to round off your argument:

Signal that you are concluding—Use a heading or transition to indicate that you are wrapping up your argument.

Restate your main point (thesis)—With emphasis, restate your main point or thesis.

Stress the importance of your subject—One last time, explain why this issue is important to your audience.

Look to the future—Discuss briefly the future of this issue.

Avoid adding new ideas or evidence in your conclusion. Instead, your goal is to drive home your main point (your thesis) and leave your audience thinking about the future of this issue.

Using Style and Design in Your Causal Analysis

7.4 Methods for using style and design to engage with the audience

Your causal analysis' style and design depend on your topic, your audience, and the places where your argument will be read or heard. If your topic is exciting, dramatic, or humorous, you will want to choose an energetic or upbeat style and design. If your topic is serious or straightforward, a plainer style would be more appropriate.

Choosing Your Style

Here are some techniques for improving the style of your causal analysis.

Use sensory details that help the audience see and feel your topic—Add details about color, texture, sound, smell, and taste.

Put causes, as much as possible, in the subjects of your sentences—The causes, not the effects, are "doing" something, so put them in the subjects of your sentences. This will create a sense of movement and give your writing energy.

Keep sentences breathing length—It's tempting to use long sentences that connect causes to effects. Make sure those sentences are short enough to read out loud in one breath.

Cut the fat—You're going to be tempted to say more than necessary about your subject. Trim down your argument by focusing on causes and effects. Give your audience the need-to-know information, not everything.

Designing Your Look

Since causal analyses typically explain real-world experiences and happenings, you should look for opportunities to support your argument with photographs and graphics.

Add photographs—If your topic is something you can photograph yourself, go grab a few images (Figure 7.4). Even pictures taken with your phone will add a visual element to your argument. Otherwise, search for photographs on the Internet. *Caution: Most photos on the Internet are owned by someone. If you want to use a photo for a non-educational purpose including posting your argument on the Internet, you will need to ask permission from the owner.*

Create a graph or chart—Causal analyses often describe trends that can be illustrated with a line graph or bar chart (see Figure 7.3 on page 135). Other kinds of charts may be helpful for illustrating your points.

Use headings to highlight causes—Your headings should allow the readers to quickly scan your causal analysis to identify the causes you are discussing.

Choose fonts that reflect your topic—If your topic is modern or trendy, you might choose a modern or chic font for headings, such as Futura or Optima. If your topic is academic or solemn, perhaps a more conservative font like Times or Garamond might be more appropriate.

The appropriate style and design depend on your topic, your audience, and the places your argument will be read or seen. How your writing sounds and looks will set the tone and mindset from which your audience will experience your argument.

Getting Inked: The Real Reasons College Students Get Tattoos

Getting inked in college may seem trendy and chic, but it's hardly a new thing. In fact, young people have been getting tattoos as a rite of passage into adulthood for thousands of years (Gilbert, p. 11). Tattoos have been found on ancient Egyptian mummies, as well on Otzi, the mummified "iceman" found in the Alps who was frozen around 3300 BC ("History," par. 2). In America, tattooing has an especially interesting history, because this phenomenon was brought to our continent by British sailors who visited the Pacific Islands in the 1700s (Demello, p. 45). Pacific Islanders believed tattoos were a symbol of status, as well as a way to protect themselves from earthly and spiritual enemies. When British sailors visited the Pacific Islands, especially Tahiti, they began getting tattoos because they liked their decorative features. They brought the concept of tattooing back to the American colonies.

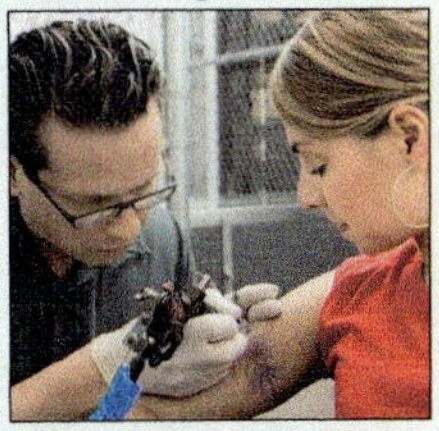

> The photograph is embedded in the text, adding color while supporting the written text.

Visiting a tattoo parlor while in college, however, is still something relatively new. Until recently, tattoos were considered rather working class, a step below the white-collar aspirations of a typical college graduate. So, why has tattooing become so common among college students that it's almost a cliché to get one? In this age of social networking and mobile technology, people often feel isolated and they yearn for permanence. Getting a tattoo is a way to feel connected to others, while making a statement that feels permanent.

A History of Tattooing

> Headings help the readers see the structure of the text.

In contemporary American culture, getting inked has always been associated with freedom, independence, and living on the fringes. At the beginning of the 20th Century, tattooing was primarily associated with circus sideshows (the "tattooed lady"), criminals, and prostitutes (Osterud). Tattooing moved into the working class mainstream after World War II when young American sailors from the Pacific theater came home with tattoos on their arms. In the 1960s, tattooing became common among counterculture groups like hippies, biker gangs, and so-called Jesus freaks. Then, in the later 1990s, Tattoos became more common among college students as tattooing methods became more artistic, refined, and less painful (DeJesus 2011). Getting a tattoo was no longer viewed as something only lower-class people would do.

FIGURE 7.4 Using Photographs and Headings in Your Causal Analysis
A photograph is a good way to illustrate your topic for your readers, especially if you can show a picture of a cause.

All right. Let's get working on that causal analysis. Here are the basics:

1 A causal analysis explores why something happens by paying attention to its causes and effects.

2 A concept map is a good tool for identifying the two to five major causes of your subject.

3 As you identify the causes, keep asking yourself, "What has changed recently that is causing this to happen?"

4 When you have finished identifying the major and minor causes of your subject, look for an angle that gives you a unique perspective on this issue.

5 Research is critical to support your analysis of causes. Look for information in electronic, print, and empirical sources.

6 As you collect information, you should also look for visuals that will support or help explain your topic, its causes, and its effects.

7 In your introduction, grab the readers' attention and state your topic, purpose, and main point clearly.

8 The body of your causal analysis should describe your subject, explore and explain its causes, and discuss its effects.

9 The conclusion for your causal analysis should restate your main point (with emphasis) and discuss the future of this subject.

10 Where appropriate, turn data into charts and graphs that will enhance the written text and make your information easier to access.

1. With a group in your class, create a list of five weird things that have happened in your lives as college students. Then pick two of these things and create a concept map that identifies the two to five causes of these events.

2. Choose a historical event with your group. Separately, create concept maps that tease out all the possible causes that might have led up to this event. You can use an Internet search engine to gather information. Each person's concept map should have anywhere from ten to twenty items. Ask each person to highlight the two to five major causes that seem most important. Compare your concept map with those of others in your group.

3. Choose an important event in your life. This event could be a tragic moment or a moment when something great happened to you. For five minutes, freewrite about that event, concentrating on its effects on your life. How did this moment change you or lead to where you are right now? How did it make you a different person? After you are finished freewriting, highlight the two to five major effects of that moment. Choose one of them and freewrite for another three minutes, discussing how this major effect also caused further changes in your life and perhaps changed the lives of others.

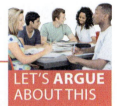

1. People often debate the causes of the American Civil War. Most people believe that the Civil War was primarily about ending slavery. Others will argue that the Civil War was about states' rights and whether the federal government had the right to impose laws on the states. Using the Internet, explore the different sides of this debate by paying attention to what each side says about the causes of the Civil War. Identify the places where the sides agree and highlight places where they disagree. Write a brief causal analysis in which you explain how both sides view the issue differently.

2. The evolution vs. intelligent design debate flares up every few years. The arguments don't change much, and each side makes the same points round after round. When you look at the argument, though, you will notice that both sides often agree on important issues. They are usually just framing those issues in different ways, which leads to different conclusions. Study this debate and identify the frames that both sides tend to use. Write a causal analysis in which you explain how both sides frame this issue differently and therefore come to opposite conclusions.

3. Imagine you and a team of students have been asked to help make your campus a safer place. Using causal analysis, explore some of the causes behind one kind of unsafe behavior on your campus, such as car or bike accidents, unhealthy eating, violence at night, abuse of alcohol or drugs, or sexual harassment. With your team, develop a causal analysis presentation in which you explain the reasons this unsafe behavior happens at your campus. Then offer some suggestions for addressing those causes. As a group, present your findings to your class preferably with PowerPoint, Keynote, Prezi, or another kind of presentation software.

141

In this causal analysis, college student Hemang Sharma discusses why Americans, especially young Americans, are not actively participating in religion. He offers a few interesting trends in American society that explain this demographic shift; however, he doesn't offer much factual support for his claims. As you read, ask yourself whether you agree with the causes he mentions in his analysis.

Religiously Yours

Hemang Sharma

A Pew survey shows that now one in five Americans dissociate themselves from any religion, bringing the infidel heathen population to its highest headcount ever. This includes people that are part of American Atheists, the largest group of nonbelievers who work to spread religious skepticism. It can also include agnostics—people who believe in God but shun organized religion completely, or people who simply do not care.

One may ask, what happened? How has our "One nation under God" experienced an increase in people who don't buy into religion? How does a group with little to no representation in the government, any big lobbying sector or giant corporate backing gather enough followers that now comprise a significant following? There can only be one answer—people started thinking critically.

People have started to see religion as divisive, unnecessary and void of answers. They are fed up by the rules and restrictions of religion. Mormon beliefs banned blacks from entering heaven, theologically, until just about 40 years ago, except for as a slave, which isn't really a heaven when you think about it. Scientology offers you an entire planet as part of postmarital bliss if you are a true believer. Catholicism doesn't allow birth control, thus causing remorse in people indulging in pleasure seeking. Telling AIDS victims to not use condoms, as the Pope did in 2009, has life-and-death consequences. Steaks are a big nono if you're Hindu. Islam doesn't allow bacon, beer, masturbation or premarital sex, thus being inherently against everything us Americans love. Almost all religions persecute gays and women, branding them as unequal. Almost all religions dictate their followers as superior beings to those who don't worship the same god.

It is the absolutism of religion that alienates people. Praying certain times, doing certain things, living life a certain way—Americans don't like being told what to do. People may be open to the idea of a god, but the complications of religions can turn many believers into people who say, "I'm out".

Dr. Richard Dawkins, Sam Harris, the late Christopher Hitchens and Bill Maher can be credited as The Four Horsemen. These men inspired many to take a leap of faith, quite literally. These men, especially in the last decade, have criticized organized religion through television, documentaries, books, debates, densely attended lectures, critical reasoning and even scientific expertise. Dawkins, a man who lectures on the recently discovered "missing link" in evolution, just seems more impressive than religious leaders who claim they know what happens when you die. Or men who claim that promiscuous women and homosexuals cause natural disasters.

In the last five years, the nonreligious population has seen a 33 percent growth, placing 33 million Americans in a robust category of their own. These people were, and still are, often discredited by the popular media, the right wing, churches, mosques and their powerful representation, courtesy of our elected officials who solemnly swear by God. Rep. Pete Stark, D-Calif., remains the only openly atheist elected official in the U.S. Congress.

This week, science, curiosity, and willingness led an Austrian man to jump from space, touching 700-plus mph and landing safely on his feet. And religion helped justify the attack of a girl who wanted other girls to go to school. With the world on the brink of religion-inspired terrorism and men who simply would ignite the world in flame without thinking twice in the name of God, I think it is great news that people are becoming secular or nonbelievers. The majority may call them infidels. I call them rationalists.

A CLOSER LOOK AT
Religiously Yours

1. In this causal analysis, Sharma identifies a few major causes for this shift in American culture. Find those causes and discuss them with your group. Do you agree with the causes he identifies? Are there other causes you might have added? Would you reject any of his causes?

2. One weakness of this argument is that Sharma doesn't make a distinction between atheism and nonpracticing believers. Surveys estimate that only 5 percent of Americans consider themselves atheists, meaning a vast majority of Americans believe in some kind of god. Find at least three places where Sharma blurs the distinction between atheists and people who are nonpracticing believers.

3. Sharma's voice and tone in this argument are clear and strong. Identify two stylistic techniques he is using to strengthen and clarify the voice and tone in this causal analysis.

IDEAS FOR
Arguing

1. Toward the end of this article, Sharma contrasts science with religion. Write a critique in which you argue whether science and religion are compatible in contemporary society. If you believe they are compatible, mention some ways in which science and religion can work hand in hand.

2. Choose another trend in American society (e.g., obesity, social networking, gay rights, political polarization) and write an analysis that explains its causes. As much as possible, relate your causal analysis to the place you live or people who are college age.

Why Working-Class People Vote Conservative

JONATHAN HAIDT

*In this causal analysis, Jonathan Haidt tries to explain American politics to people
in the United Kingdom, where "conservative" means something different than in the
United States. He uses his causal analysis to warn British and American liberals that they
misunderstand why people consider themselves conservatives. Pay attention to how he
debunks some of the usual assumption liberals hold about working-class conservatives.*

Why on Earth would a working-class person ever vote for a conservative candidate? This question has obsessed the American left since Ronald Reagan first captured the votes of so many union members, farmers, urban Catholics and other relatively powerless people—the so-called "Reagan Democrats". Isn't the Republican party the party of big business? Don't the Democrats stand up for the little guy, and try to redistribute the wealth downwards?

Many commentators on the left have embraced some version of the duping hypothesis: the Republican party dupes people into voting against their economic interests by triggering outrage on cultural issues. "Vote for us and we'll protect the American flag!" say the Republicans. "We'll make English the official language of the United States! And most importantly, we'll prevent gay people from threatening your marriage when they … marry! Along the way we'll cut taxes on the rich, cut benefits for the poor, and allow industries to dump their waste into your drinking water, but never mind that. Only we can protect you from gay, Spanish-speaking flag-burners!"

One of the most robust findings in social psychology is that people find ways to believe whatever they want to believe. And the left really want to believe the duping hypothesis. It absolves them from blame and protects them

from the need to look in the mirror or figure out what they stand for in the 21st century.

Here's a more painful but ultimately constructive diagnosis, from the point of view of moral psychology: politics at the national level is more like religion than it is like shopping. It's more about a moral vision that unifies a nation and calls it to greatness than it is about self-interest or specific policies. In most countries, the right tends to see that more clearly than the left. In America, the Republicans did the hard work of drafting their moral vision in the 1970s, and Ronald Reagan was their eloquent spokesman. Patriotism, social order, strong families, personal responsibility (not government safety nets) and free enterprise. Those are values, not government programmes.

The Democrats, in contrast, have tried to win voters' hearts by promising to protect or expand programmes for elderly people, young people, students, poor people and the middle class. Vote for us and we'll use government to take care of everyone! But most Americans don't want to live in a nation based primarily on caring. That's what families are for.

One reason the left has such difficulty forging a lasting connection with voters is that the right has a built-in advantage—conservatives have a broader moral palate than the liberals (as we call leftists in the US). Think about it this way:

5

our tongues have taste buds that are responsive to five classes of chemicals, which we perceive as sweet, sour, salty, bitter, and savoury. Sweetness is generally the most appealing of the five tastes, but when it comes to a serious meal, most people want more than that.

In the same way, you can think of the moral mind as being like a tongue that is sensitive to a variety of moral flavours. In my research with colleagues at YourMorals.org, we have identified six moral concerns as the best candidates for being the innate "taste buds" of the moral sense: care/harm, fairness/cheating, liberty/oppression, loyalty/betrayal, authority/subversion, and sanctity/degradation. Across many kinds of surveys, in the UK as well as in the USA, we find that people who self-identify as being on the left score higher on questions about care/harm. For example, how much would someone have to pay you to kick a dog in the head? Nobody wants to do this, but liberals say they would require more money than conservatives to cause harm to an innocent creature.

But on matters relating to group loyalty, respect for authority and sanctity (treating things as sacred and untouchable, not only in the context of religion), it sometimes seems that liberals lack the moral taste buds, or at least, their moral "cuisine" makes less use of them. For example, according to our data, if you want to hire someone to criticise your nation on a radio show in another nation (loyalty), give the finger to his boss (authority), or sign a piece of paper stating one's willingness to sell his soul (sanctity), you can save a lot of money by posting a sign: "Conservatives need not apply."

In America, it is these three moral foundations that underlie most of the "cultural" issues that, according to duping theorists, are used to distract voters from their self-interest. But are voters really voting against their self-interest when they vote for candidates who share their values? Loyalty, respect for authority and some degree of sanctification create a more binding social order that places some limits on individualism and egoism. As marriage rates plummet,

and globalisation and rising diversity erode the sense of common heritage within each nation, a lot of voters in many western nations find themselves hungering for conservative moral cuisine.

Despite being in the wake of a financial crisis that—if the duping theorists were correct—should have buried the cultural issues and pulled most voters to the left, we are finding in America and many European nations a stronger shift to the right. When people fear the collapse of their society, they want order and national greatness, not a more nurturing government. [10]

Even on the two moral taste buds that both sides claim—fairness and liberty—the right can often out-cook the left. The left typically thinks of equality as being central to fairness, and leftists are extremely sensitive about gross inequalities of outcome—particularly when they correspond along racial or ethnic lines. But the broader meaning of fairness is really proportionality—are people getting rewarded in proportion to the work they put into a common project? Equality of outcomes is only seen as fair by most people in the special case in which everyone has made equal contributions. The conservative media (such as the *Daily Mail*, or *Fox News* in the US) are much more sensitive to the presence of slackers and benefit cheats. They are very effective at stirring up outrage at the government for condoning cheating.

Similarly for liberty. Americans and Britons all love liberty, yet when liberty and care conflict, the left is more likely to choose care. This is the crux of the US's monumental battle over Obama's healthcare plan. Can the federal government compel some people to buy a product (health insurance) in order to make a plan work that extends care to 30 million other people? The derogatory term "nanny state" is rarely used against the right (pastygate being perhaps an exception). Conservatives are more cautious about infringing on individual liberties (e.g., of gun owners in the US and small businessmen) in order to protect vulnerable populations (such as children, animals and immigrants).

In sum, the left has a tendency to place caring for the weak, sick and vulnerable above all other moral concerns. It is admirable and necessary that some political party stands up for victims of injustice, racism or bad luck. But in focusing so much on the needy, the left often fails to address—and sometimes violates—other moral needs, hopes and concerns. When working-class people vote conservative, as most do in the US, they are not voting against their self-interest; they are voting for their moral interest. They are voting for the party that serves to them a more satisfying moral cuisine. The left in the UK and USA should think hard about their recipe for success in the 21st century.

A CLOSER LOOK AT
Why Working Class People Vote Conservative

1. Identify five reasons Haidt believes working-class Americans tend to vote for conservative candidates and support conservative policies. Discuss these five reasons with your group. Do you agree with Haidt's analysis? Which causes would you challenge and what causes might you add?

2. Haidt faults liberals for misunderstanding why working-class Americans tend to be conservative. According to Haidt, what are some of the mistaken views that liberals tend to hold about conservative voters?

3. Haidt believes that liberals will find themselves on the losing end of elections if they don't make changes to their political approach. What are some of the weaknesses he identifies in liberal tendencies? Do you agree with his views?

IDEAS FOR
Arguing

1. Imagine you are going to offer advice to liberals who are concerned about working-class Americans voting for conservatives. Write a proposal (see Chapter 14) in which you discuss the problems with traditional liberal perspectives and offer a way of becoming more attractive to working-class voters.

2. Do research on political parties in another country, such as Canada, Japan, or the United Kingdom. Write a causal analysis to an American audience that explains why their voters tend to divide along different lines than voters in the United States. Also, discuss ways in which conservative voters and liberal voters are similar to their counterparts in the United States.

8

Visual Essays— Arguing by Showing and Telling

IN THIS CHAPTER, YOU WILL LEARN—

8.1 Three types of visual essays: slide shows, poster presentations, and visual narratives

8.2 How to invent the content of a visual essay

8.3 Strategies for organizing and drafting a visual essay

8.4 Techniques for developing a specific tone and attractive design

8.1 Three types of visual essays: slide shows, poster presentations, and visual narratives

Visual essays follow the adage that "it's better to show than to tell." The purpose of a visual essay is to use photographs, drawings, graphs, tables, and illustrations to argue for a specific point. Some common types of visual essays include the following:

Slide show—a series of images that illustrates a particular issue. The images in the slide show are usually accompanied by comments or captions that build an overall argument. Slide shows are often used to generate new ideas, present information, and develop a common understanding of an issue.

Poster presentation—a collection of images and written text that are placed on a poster or posterboard to explain a specific research topic. Poster presentations are widely used to exhibit research in the sciences, but they are becoming common in all fields (Figure 8.1). Poster presentations are useful for generating conversations and persuading people to understand issues from new perspectives.

FIGURE 8.1 Poster Presentations as Visual Arguments
Poster presentations are becoming a common form of visual argument in science, medical, and other fields.

Visual narrative—the use of sequential images to illustrate and explain a historical event or something that happened recently. Visual narratives can be especially useful for framing or reframing issues by displaying visual evidence. For example, lawyers often use visual narratives to reconstruct crimes. Scientists use them to explain natural phenomena.

Today, with the design capabilities of computers, visual essays are becoming more important than ever in college and the workplace. In college, you will be regularly asked to create slide shows, poster presentations, and visual narratives about a variety of topics (Figure 8.1). In your career, you will use visual displays to generate new ideas, present results, and persuade clients. And, as our society becomes more globalized and intercultural, the ability to argue through images will become ever more important.

Learning how to create visual essays will also help you improve your use of photography, graphics, and other images in your written arguments and presentations. These arguments are fun to make, while giving you a powerful way to get your point across to your audience.

Inventing the Content of Your Visual Essay

8.2 How to invent the content of a visual essay

Visual essays typically include a series of images, such as photographs, drawings, graphs, charts, and so on. So you should begin by creating and collecting the images you need. Good planning will save you time by helping you invent the content you need.

Quick View

Generative

Persuasive

Generative Argument—Visual essays are primarily generative, helping you and others use images to collaborate on new ideas and approaches. Images can be used to frame or reframe issues, help people identify with others, and reconstruct events as narratives.

Persuasive Argument—Visual essays can also be persuasive, usually in an indirect way. If organized properly, images can illustrate arguments that are hard to make in written or spoken forms. A single image can be persuasive, and a series of images can create patterns that lead to specific conclusions.

Genre Patterns

Visual essays can follow one of these three patterns, depending on your topic and the purpose of your argument.

Slide Show	Narrative	Research Display
Introduction	**Introduction**	**Introduction**
Image 1 with Commentary	**Image that Sets Scene**	**Methodology**
Image 2 with Commentary	**Image with Complication**	**Results of Research**
Image 3 with Commentary	**Images that Show Evaluation of Complication**	**Discussion of Results**
Image 4 with Commentary	**Image that Shows Resolution**	**Implications of Research**
Conclusion	**Conclusion**	**Conclusion**

Use Storyboards to Sketch Out Your Ideas

Storyboards are used by movie producers and designers to sketch out their ideas. Making a storyboard is like drawing a comic strip or creating a comic book (Figure 8.2).

The easiest way to draw a storyboard is to fold a regular sheet of paper into four panels. Then, in each of the panels, sketch out the images or scenes you will need. Under each panel, write a comment or caption that describes what the panel shows.

At this point, don't worry about drawing the storyboards in a "correct" order. You will probably end up moving them around anyway. Designers also draw storyboards on post-it notes, which they can stick on a wall. That way, they can try out various ways to organize the visual argument.

You can also create storyboards with presentation software like PowerPoint, Keynote, or Prezi. For each panel, make a slide with a title and comment. Your presentation software's "Slide Sorter" then allows you to move slides around to find the best arrangement.

How to Make Friends in College

FIGURE 8.2 A Storyboard
You can use a storyboard to sketch out your visual essay.

Make Your Own Photos or Graphics

After finishing your storyboard, it's time to start creating and collecting images for your visual essay. You can begin by creating your own photographs with your mobile phone or a digital camera. You can also make your own illustrations, graphs, or charts with drawing software like Adobe Illustrator, Corel Draw, or Inkscape.

Photographs—Visit the places and people you are writing about and take some pictures. Then download these photographs to your computer and "Insert" them into your visual essay. If you don't have a mobile phone or a digital camera, the campus library or audio-visual center at your college or university may have a camera you can borrow.

Illustrations, graphs, and charts—A variety of software programs can help you create professional-looking graphs and charts. Also, most word processors, like Word, WordPerfect, and OpenOffice, are bundled with spreadsheet or drawing programs that you can use to make graphs and charts.

Scanning—You can use a scanner to make digital images of documents and artifacts. Anything flat can be scanned to create an image. Scanned images can then be inserted into a document or presentation.

In Chapter 21, Designing Arguments, you'll find helpful strategies for taking great photographs and making graphs and charts. If you need some help, turn to that chapter now.

Find the Images You Need

The Internet is also a treasure trove of images that you can use for educational purposes. To find material for your visual essay, click on the "Images" button in an Internet search engine, like Google or Bing. Then, in the search line, type in key words that describe the kinds of photographs and other images you are looking for. The search engine should bring up a wide variety of images related to your topic. You can then drag these images to your computer's desktop, or you can save them to a folder on your hard drive.

Keep in mind that images from the Internet are almost always owned by others. You can use them without permission, if you are using these images for educational purposes and you aren't putting them on the Internet. However—and this is very important—if you plan to use your visual essay in any noneducational way, you will need to obtain permission from the owners to use the photos, graphs, or charts you take from the Internet. Also, if you want to put your visual essay on the Internet (even for educational purposes), you will need to ask permission to include any images that you don't own yourself.

To receive permission, you should send e-mails to the people who own the images. Often, the owner's name is on the webpage where you found the image you want to use. Tell that person or organization how you want to use the image and where it will appear. If the owner replies and gives you permission to use the image, that's usually enough. However, if the owner doesn't answer or says no, then you cannot use it for noneducational purposes or put it on the Internet.

Images you find on U.S. government websites are usually considered "fair use," which means you can use them without asking permission.

To avoid problems with permissions, you might look for images that are covered by a *Creative Commons* license. A Creative Commons license gives people permission to use images without asking, if they are using them in a way acceptable to the owner. For more information on Creative Commons, go to creativecommons.org.

Do Background Research on the Images You Collected

You should always research the backgrounds of any photographs, illustrations, graphs, or charts that you include in your visual essay. Your research will help you fully understand the context of the images by exploring their history and any backstories behind them.

Electronic sources—Images on the Web almost always have contextual information around them. In other words, make sure you look at the factual details that are included with the images. Then run searches on those details. Learn about the people and places shown. If you are researching the context of a graph or chart, explore how the data or facts were collected and look for other graphics that present similar or contrasting information.

Print sources—You can also collect images through print sources, many of which aren't available through the Internet. Your college library has books, newspapers, magazines, and documents in which images can be found.

Empirical sources—You might set up an experiment that observes how other people react to or interpret the images you have chosen. People often respond to photos, graphs, and other images in ways that you wouldn't expect. What are their impressions? What do they see that you didn't see? You can also ask experts, including professors, to help you better understand what a particular image means.

Research will help you come up with new ways to explore your subject. So look for any opportunities to find new material or unexpected stories.

MOVES for Arguing

A visual essay usually includes written comments (e.g., captions) that explain the images. Here are some common moves in the comments or captions:

When you first see _____, you have the impression that _____.

In this picture of _____, we see a good example of _____.

Not all _____ are like _____. As shown here, some _____ have unique characteristics, such as _____ and _____.

As shown in Figure X, we see how _____ changes when _____ changes.

Both _____ and _____ seem similar at first glance. But, when you put them side by side, as shown here, you begin to notice some important differences.

These images demonstrate that _____ is significant right now and that it will be even more significant as _____ continues to happen.

8.3 Strategies for organizing and drafting a visual essay

Organizing and Drafting Your Visual Essay

The organization of your visual essay depends on what kind of argument you want to make. In the Quickview on page 150 of this chapter, you can see models of three different types of visual essays. Each kind of visual essay calls for a different organizational pattern.

Introduction: Starting with a Title Slide and Opening Slide

In most ways, a visual essay's introduction is similar to introductions of written arguments. However, the written text in your visual essay needs to be more concise, and you will use visuals to make many of the typical introductory moves.

Usually, a visual essay will start with a *title slide*, which identifies the topic of the visual essay and perhaps your main point. The title slide is followed by an *opening* slide that states your main point (thesis), offers background information, and stresses the importance of the topic (Figure 8.3). Here are some common opening moves that are made in the title and opening slides:

Use an interesting title to grab the audience—Your title will be one of the most prominent features of your visual essay, so make sure it stands out visually. Also, your title might use a play on words to spark your audience's imagination.

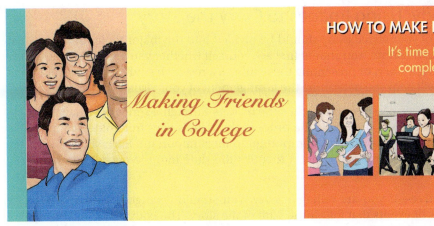
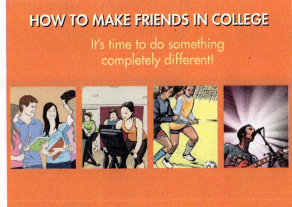

FIGURE 8.3 Title Slide and Opening Slide
Your title slide and opening slide work together as an introduction to your visual essay.

Identify your topic—Your title slide should clearly identify your topic. You might also include one or more images on the title slide to give a quick visual understanding of your topic.

Signal your purpose—Visual essays rarely state their purpose directly, but your purpose should be clear to the audience on the title slide or the opening slide.

State your main point or thesis—Your main point could appear in the subtitle on the title slide, or you could state your main point somewhere on the opening slide. In some situations, you might use a thesis question, which will then be answered in the concluding slide of the visual essay. *If you are creating a research display*, your main point should be spelled out directly for the audience.

> *Weak Thesis:* Making friends in college can be difficult.

> *Stronger Thesis:* College students may have dozens of Facebook friends and numerous Twitter followers, but my research demonstrates that these kinds of social networking tools often make it difficult for students to form friendships in college that are meaningful and lasting.

Provide background information—Images are usually the best way to build a quick overall understanding of your subject, so include a few images in your title and opening slides that illustrate your topic. In some situations, you could use written text on the opening slide to provide background information.

Stress the importance of your topic—Again, images are probably the best way to stress the importance of your topic to your audience. Your essay's first images should pull your audience into the argument.

You can make these opening moves in just about any order.

The Body: Using Images to Carry the Story

The body of your visual essay should be divided into the major topics or scenes that you want to illustrate. You should first ask yourself whether you are organizing a slide show, telling a story, or presenting the results of a research study. Your answer to that question will help you determine the arrangement of your visuals.

Slide show—A slide show walks the readers through a series of visuals on a common topic. Generally, the order of the visuals goes from oldest to most recent, or it goes from least important to most important. Each slide should include a comment or caption that ties the slide into the overall argument that you are making.

Narrative—If you are telling a story, you should arrange the images into scenes or events that follow the path of the story. The body of a typical story will include five major moves:

1. Set a scene

2. Introduce a complication

3. Show how people evaluated the complication

4. Show how the complication was resolved

5. Show what was learned through the experience

You can devote more than one slide to each of these moves. Each slide should include a comment or caption that explains what is being illustrated.

Research display—If you are presenting the results of your research, the body of your visual essay should include six major moves:

1. State your research question and hypothesis

2. Explain your research methods

3. Provide the results of the research

4. Analyze and discuss the results

5. Discuss the implications of the research

6. Suggest future opportunities for research on the topic

In some cases, you may want to include a brief *literature review* before your research methods that summarizes your sources. A literature review might also appear as an "appendix" at the end of the display. Minimally, most research displays should include a bibliographic list of references or works cited at the end of the presentation.

Conclusion: State or Show Your Main Point

The conclusion of your visual essay usually requires only one or two slides. You want to keep your conclusion brief and to the point so your audience will remember your main point.

The visuals and written text you choose for your conclusion should do four things:

Clearly signal that you are concluding—In your final slides, it should be obvious that you are concluding your visual essay. You can signal the conclusion with the title of a concluding slide. Or you can use phrases like "Overall," "In conclusion," or "To sum up" in your written comments to indicate that you are wrapping up.

Highlight your main point or thesis—Clearly illustrate or state the main point or thesis of your visual essay.

Stress the importance of your topic—The visuals in the conclusion should show why this issue is important to the audience. Explain or illustrate why they should care.

Look to the future—If you have a visual that illustrates the future of the issue, you could feature it on the final slide of your visual essay. If you don't have this kind of visual, then spend some time in your written comments discussing the future of this issue. What might happen? How will the lives or beliefs of people be influenced by your topic?

Again, your conclusion should be brief, perhaps one or two slides. You have only a couple minutes at most to bring your argument to a close.

Style and Design: Showing and Telling

8.4 Techniques for developing a specific tone and attractive design

In a visual essay, the words often play a supportive role to the images, but style is still important. You will be using fewer words, so you need to choose them wisely. Meanwhile, your visual essay's design needs to create an appropriate setting for the images. Good style and an attractive design will enhance the way your text sounds and looks to the audience.

Creating a Specific Tone with Words

As you draft and revise the written part of the text, you should keep in mind that people usually scan visual essays instead of studying them closely. As a result, your writing style should make the argument easy to understand and establish a clear voice.

Set a specific tone—You can use clusters of associated words and phrases to establish a specific tone for your subject. Think of one adjective that describes the tone you want your audience to hear as they experience your visual essay (e.g., excited, concerned, weird). Then use a concept map or brainstorming list to generate clusters of words and phrases that express that tone. You can weave these words into your visual essay to create the tone you want.

Keep sentences brief—Your visual essay's sentences should be short enough to be spoken out loud in one breath. Your audiences will be reading quickly and scanning your argument. Your sentences should be a little shorter than usual.

Focus on answers to the Five-W and How questions—When looking at images, your audience will be curious about the who, what, where, when, why, and how of each one. In the comments or captions, you should make sure those answers are easy to find.

Designing for Impact, Consistency, and Attractiveness

The images may be the centerpiece of a visual essay, but you want to also create an overall visual design that will make an impact on the audience (Figure 8.4). A consistent and attractive design will draw the audience to your argument and help them find the information they need.

Chapter 21, "Designing Arguments," offers five principles that you can use to create and edit the setting for your visual essay:

Balance—Each slide should look balanced from left to right and top to bottom. Imagine the slide is balanced on the point of a pencil. Whenever you add something to the left, make sure it is balanced with something on the right. Something added to the top should be balanced with something on the bottom.

Alignment—Pay attention to how visual elements in each slide align vertically and horizontally. Align photographs and other graphics that are meant to be seen together or compared.

Grouping—If items are close together on a slide, your audience will visually "group" them together. So if items are related put them near each other on the slide. If you don't want something grouped with something else, don't put them near each other.

Consistency—Be consistent with visual elements, such as titles, fonts, lists, colors, and lines. The design of your slides should be similar and consistent so the audience isn't forced to figure out a new design with each slide.

Contrast—You can use contrasting sizes and colors to make your visual essay "pop" for the readers. Try using bigger font sizes. Try using colors that reflect your subject and stand out. In some situations, like the example shown in Figure 8.4, a conscious choice of black and white can stand out, too.

If you are using presentation software to create your visual essay, you can choose from several presentation templates. You can modify these templates by changing their color palette to reflect the subject or tone of your visual essay.

TREES

A PHOTO ESSAY BY

CHRISTIAN STEPIEN

FOREST IN FOG
There is so much emotion packed into a foggy scene, especially when trees are involved. It turns an ordinary scene into one that is dream like.

WHITE PINES AND CLOUDS
On a summer walk through Meadowvale Village, I nabbed this image. It was the perfect contrast!

A TREE FENCE
I made this photograph on the way home from Caledon. I drove past the scene, debated if I should go back and make the shot, and about a kilometre down the road I decided, "Yep, I'm going back".

FIGURE 8.4 Setting a Consistent Tone and Look
In this visual essay, the author combines images and words to set a consistent tone. The black-and-white photography is used to create a distinguished and somber tone.

Haven't created a visual essay before? Here are the basics to help you get started:

1 A visual essay features a combination of images and graphics that are supported by written text.

2 Visual essays can take many forms. Some of the most common are the *slide show*, the *poster presentation*, and the *visual narrative*.

3 Storyboarding is a useful way to sketch out your visual essay and identify the kinds of images you will need.

4 The Internet is a good place to find images for your visual essay. You can also take your own pictures with a digital camera or your mobile phone.

5 If you are exhibiting your visual essay in a nonacademic setting (e.g., Internet or public display), you will need to have permission to use any images or graphics that are not owned by you.

6 Using a scanner is also a good way to make digital versions of artifacts that you want to show in your visual essay.

7 You should do research with electronic, print, and empirical sources to understand the background of the images you choose and how people react to them.

8 A visual essay typically has an introduction, body, and conclusion, just like other arguments.

9 The style of your written text should reflect the tone you are trying to set with the images you choose.

10 You can use font choices, color, and page layout to establish a consistent look for your visual essay.

1. Have each member of your group bring in an unusual photograph taken from the Internet or from a personal collection. Let the other members in the group look at each photograph without knowing the image's background. Discuss what each photograph means. Then the person who brought the photograph should explain the background. How does knowing the context of the photograph change its meaning?

2. With your group, use Internet search engines to find examples of the three types of visual essays (slide show, narrative, research display) discussed in this chapter. Do these visual essays demonstrate the strategies discussed in this chapter? What are some other strategies you might add to the ones mentioned in this chapter?

3. Choose a topic that interests you. Type your topic into an Internet search engine and click on the "Images" button. You should see a series of images that are related to your topic. Drag the first ten images to your computer's desktop or hard drive. Then, using presentation software like PowerPoint, create a slide show that uses these images to make a specific point. You can reorder the images to fit the point you are trying to make. Present your slide show to your group and talk about what kind of argument you made with this somewhat random collection of images.

1. With a group, choose a topic that is interesting to all of you. Then have each member of the group collect five photographs, illustrations, and graphics about that topic. Using presentation software, such as PowerPoint, Keynote, or Prezi, turn your group's images into a slide show visual essay. Your argument should have a main point of some kind.

2. Find a visual essay on the Internet. Write a critique of the visual essay in which you highlight the rhetorical decisions made by the author. Pay special attention to the content, organization, style, and design of the text. Also, pay attention to how the author anticipated her or his audience and the context of the visual essay. Do you think the author achieved her or his purpose? Which aspects were especially effective, and which could use some tweaking?

3. Attend an event on your campus that you can photograph with a digital camera or mobile phone. Take a series of photographs at the event. Then create a narrative visual essay by putting those images together. What is the "conflict" that happened at the event? How did people evaluate and resolve the conflict? What do you think people learned from the experience? Hint: The conflict doesn't need to be something wrong or bad. It simply needs to be something that caused change.

ONE STUDENT'S WORK

In this visual essay, student Deepak Atyam describes his summer INSPIRE internships at NASA's Jet Propulsion Laboratory (JPL). The INSPIRE internships allow students interested in space, science, engineering, technology, and math to work with NASA scientists and engineers on research and projects. Atyam eventually went on to the University of California-San Diego to study engineering. Pay attention to how he uses both text and photos to explain what happened those two summers at NASA.

My Summer at JPL

Deepak Atyam

Interning at NASA's Jet Propulsion Laboratory at the age of 17 was amazing. It was the summer of 2010 and I had just finished my junior year in high school. I was tasked with working on the radar for the Mars Science Laboratory's Curiosity rover. The Mars Science Laboratory rover, scheduled to launch Nov. 25, 2011, will go to Mars to assess if a local area of land is suitable for life or if life existed in the past.

My project was to create an Environmental Control System, or ECS, using a jet fuel tank to house the radar for the Curiosity rover. The ECS purged liquid nitrogen to cool the electronics that were controlling the radars' components in the fuel tank.

This system was mounted and tested on an F/A-18 fighter jet in June 2011. It was crazy for me to fathom that some of the brightest minds alive were using a structure that I engineered to complete their tasks. It's just a remarkable feeling when you know you've accomplished something so unique.

After I finished my first great internship at JPL, I continued my high school education. It was a painstakingly long wait before I was able to come back to the place where dreams become a reality. Because of the work I had accomplished as well as my achievements in school I was invited back to JPL to work during the summer of 2011.

The program that brought me to JPL then and now is called INSPIRE, or Interdisciplinary National Science Project Incorporating Research and Education Experience. INSPIRE is a national NASA program that offers high school students the opportunity to experience what it is like to be an engineer or scientist at NASA.

This time around, I worked on a project in a different spectrum from my norm. I was working in a section of a department called Team X. Team X develops rapid mission concepts for engineers and large organizations to formulate budget costs, material predictions and orbit calculations for space missions. Team X pulled in 11 interns, undergrads and high school students to complete a mission development project.

Our initial goal was to create a database that contained information about past, present and future launch vehicles, instruments, spacecraft and cubesats (miniaturized satellites used for space research). After we compiled that information, we were then asked to formulate an entire mission concept from the data we collected so that we could see how well the database actually worked.

During the third week of my internship, I looked for extra work to satisfy my engineering mind and was presented with two different choices: drive rovers around the Mars Yard—a simulated Mars environment—or wire up the Mars 2018 field-test robot. I chose both.

I worked with a fellow intern to do a majority of tests with the engineering model of the Mars Exploration Rover as well as the mobility skeleton of the Curiosity rover, called Scarecrow.

Scarecrow has no instruments or brain, only wheels that exert the same pressure on Earth as they would on Mars to simulate driving on the Red Planet. Our job was to measure how much each rover slipped on the different gradient terrain at variable inclines.

We mounted three GPS units that were able to measure yaw, pitch and roll of the rovers and we learned how to operate the rovers using command lines.

I don't think any other students anywhere in the world had the opportunity to drive engineering models of rovers in simulated environments as part of their internships. I was really lucky to have been offered this project.

These past two years at JPL have been absolutely incredible. I never thought I would be able to do something like this as an undergraduate in college let alone in high school. It was incredible to see the feats of engineering that all of the workers at JPL created. From the mission concept designs at Team X to field test work with the Mechanical Department, nothing ever ceased to awe me.

I am now a freshman studying Aerospace Engineering at the University of California San Diego (UCSD). My experiences at JPL helped me to form a team at UCSD, in collaboration with San Diego State University, to build liquid fueled rockets. I am now leading the production of one of the stages of a two-stage rocket as a freshman.

Working at JPL helped me hone my leadership skills as well as gain a tremendous amount of engineering knowledge I know I would not have been able to gain elsewhere. I couldn't have asked for better experiences as a high school student, but now that I'm in college I hope to go back to JPL for another successful summer. I honestly don't know what I will be working on next summer but I know that with my background of knowledge, whatever I work on will be an awesome engineering task!

A CLOSER LOOK AT
My Summer at JPL

1. In this visual essay, Deepak Atyam uses plenty of detail to describe his experiences at NASA. Find three examples of where he usual his sight to tell his story. Find two examples where he uses details that use his non-visual senses.

2. This visual essay follows a narrative pattern. With your group, discuss how Atyam's ordering of the photographs tells a story.

3. Atyam's voice comes through clearly in the written portion of his argument. With your group, locate five places where his voice seems especially strong. If you were to choose one word that describes the tone of this essay, what would that word be? Then, use this word to explore the photographs he includes. How do the photographs also reflect this tone?

IDEAS FOR
Argument

1. Write a commentary (Chapter 12) in which you argue for or against a new requirement that all students at your college or university should do an internship or travel internationally with a class. Explore the strengths and problems with this kind of requirement.

2. This visual essay originally appeared on the NASA website. Besides telling Atyam's story, it is also designed to publicize NASA's IMPACT program. Write a brief rhetorical analysis (Chapter 4) in which you explain why this kind of student-written visual essay can be more effective than other ways of advertising the program.

Mongolia: Children and the "Dzud"

UNICEF

This visual essay from UNICEF describes the hardships of Mongolian children trapped in a "dzud," which is an extreme weather crisis of snow and frigid weather. Watch how the photos and the text work together to explain the situation to the audience. Also, note how images are used to make the argument is subtle but still powerful.

May 2010: Nineteen of Mongolia's 21 provinces continue to face emergency conditions, caused by heavy snow and extreme cold—a weather crisis called a "dzud" that is unique to the country. The toll on children includes increased food insecurity and poverty and rising child mortality rates. Five-year-old Uralbai, in Khovd Province, is one of these children.

In February, temperatures fell to minus-50 degrees Celsius, and snow impeded access to food, fuel, sanitation and basic medical care. Livestock, a primary source of income, died from hunger and exposure.

Rural areas continue to suffer, even as spring arrives. Over 7.5 million livestock have perished, threatening soil pollution and disease. Lacking alternatives, horses feed on tree bark in Bulgan District.

Herders—80 per cent of the rural population—still struggle to buy food and fuel. Uralbai's family eats a meal of bread and tea, all they can afford after most of their animals died and feed costs tripled.

Snow and lack of paved roads have made many poor, rural areas inaccessible to aid. A doctor makes a house call at a 'ger', a traditional felt tent. He had to leave his car and travel the final kilometre on foot.

He examines a four-month-old baby in Bulgan District. The month of March saw a 35-40 per cent spike in under-five child mortality in some dzud-affected areas. Most of these children died of preventable diseases.

At the height of the dzud, UNICEF joined the Government and other UN agencies to deliver core supplies and services for children. A school employee in Bulgan sorts incoming items.

A UNICEF worker delivers supplies in Altai District. Some 22,000 children, housed in school dormitories during the academic year, needed assistance as heating systems failed and food supplies dwindled.

UNICEF has provided food, fuel, blankets, boots, hygiene supplies, and recreation kits to dormitories in multiple districts. In Uyench, children participate in a UNICEF-led hand-washing lesson.

Anticipating longer-term needs, UNICEF also distributed nutrition supplements and medical supplies to health facilities in 133 districts. A student calls her mother from a crowded Uyench dorm room.

Other assistance includes training for staff at over 400 schools to provide psychosocial support to affected children and families. Children attend a second-grade class in Uyench.

Despite substantial losses affecting more than half a million people, herding remains a valued and critical way of life for much of the country. Children tend goats in Bulgan District.

And poverty and hardship will continue growing long after the snow melts. So UNICEF and other UN emergency support also continue. After school, a first-grade student walks several kilometres to reach her home.

A CLOSER LOOK AT
"Mongolia: Children and the 'Dzud'"

1. In this visual essay, what are some of the basic necessities that the people of Mongolia, especially children, struggle to obtain?

2. What are some strategies UNICEF is using to provide aid to the people of Mongolia? What are some of the needs that are still going unmet in the Mongolian population, especially among children?

3. The Mongolian way of life is very traditional in many ways. As shown in this visual essay, how does this traditional way of life conflict with modern ways of life? What are some ways in which traditional ways and modern ways of life can work together?

IDEAS FOR
Arguing

1. Choose one of the photos in this visual essay. Write a description of the photograph using as much detail as you can. Try to describe the photograph for someone who has not seen it or perhaps cannot see it.

2. Create your own visual essay that documents some aspect of your own life. You might take photographs of an activity or an event. You might explore a place that is important to you. Then write captions that explain these photographs to an audience. Your visual essay should state a thesis or main point in words and intensify that point with images.

9 Narrative Arguments— Arguing with Stories

IN THIS CHAPTER, YOU WILL LEARN—

9.1 How narrative arguments are used in college and the workplace

9.2 How to use freewriting to invent the content of a narrative argument

9.3 Strategies for organizing and drafting narratives

9.4 Ways to use style and design to enhance narrative arguments

9.1 How narrative arguments are used in college and the workplace

Telling a story is often the best way to make an argument. You can use narrative arguments to discuss your experiences or describe a historical or current event. You can also use narrative arguments to share your values and explain how you look at the world. Narrative is one of the most compelling forms of argument because humans enjoy listening to stories.

In this chapter, you will learn primarily about *factual narratives*, which are based on real events that happened to you or someone else. Other kinds of narratives exist, such as fiction, poetry, drama, fables, allegories, myths, or parables. Some scholars correctly claim that these fictional narratives could be viewed as arguments, too. Factual narratives, however, will be the focus of this chapter.

Narrative arguments are common in both college and the workplace. In college, your history and political science professors will ask you to use narratives to describe and argue about historical and current events. Your anthropology, psychology, and sociology professors will ask you to describe and interpret the behavior of people. Even professors in the hard sciences and engineering will occasionally ask you to "tell the story" of a scientific discovery or the invention of a new technology. These are all narrative arguments.

In the workplace, narrative arguments are common in fields like law, medicine, journalism, marketing, science, politics, and business. Lawyers use narratives to make opening and closing statements in court cases. Advertising firms develop *marketing narratives* that connect customers' lives to specific products and services (Figure 9.1). Journalists and historians use narratives to explain important events. Scientists use narratives to describe experiments, natural phenomena, and human activities.

FIGURE 9.1
Narratives in Marketing
This scene is from Chipotle's "The Scarecrow" advertisement, which went viral on the Internet. It used a narrative to argue for sustainable farming.

Narratives are powerful because they allow your audience to *interpret* what the story means while they identify with the people in the story. Your audience will weigh your story's events and characters against their own experiences. This makes narrative arguments more personal and intense.

Inventing the Content of Your Narrative Argument

9.2 How to use freewriting to invent the content of a narrative argument

Sometimes the best way to invent the content of your narrative is to simply tell the story as far as you know it. Then, with your basic story on the screen or page, you can look for details and factual information to fill in your understanding of the event.

Use Freewriting to Release Your Creativity

Freewriting is an especially good way to get those creative juices flowing. Put your fingers on the keyboard or grab a pen and piece of paper. Then do the following:

1. **Freewrite continuously for five minutes, telling your version of the story—**At this point, don't worry about getting the facts straight or even putting the story's events in the right order. Just write down whatever comes to mind. Write freely for five minutes without stopping. You might turn off or darken your screen to help you resist the temptation to revise. Just keep typing.

*QUICK*View

Generative   **Persuasive**

Generative Argument—Narratives are generative because they invite the audience to identify with the people in the story. They are also useful for challenging or reinforcing existing cultural frames. A narrative argument is a good way to build understanding and consensus around an issue.

Persuasive Argument—Narratives are also persuasive in a subtle but powerful way. In situations in which reasoning might not work, a good story can often illustrate how real people experience the world or react to crises and challenges.

Genre Pattern

A narrative argument tends to follow the pattern shown here. You can alter this pattern to fit the needs of your argument.

Set Scene

Complication

Evaluation

Resolution

Lesson or Call to Action

2. **Analyze your freewrite to discover the complication at the center of the story**—The complication is the key moment at which something changed or a problem started. Ask yourself what happened that made the event exciting, scary, funny, or troubling. What event, change, or problem caused the characters in your story to react? Highlight that moment in your freewrite.

3. **Do another five-minute freewrite in which you explore your characters' reactions to the complication**—Spend five more minutes freewriting about how people reacted to the complication. How were their lives changed? What lessons were learned? Your second freewrite will help you figure out why the event was important.

4. **Figure out your narrative's main point or thesis**—All stories have a point. Usually, the main point was a lesson learned. In your narrative argument, you may or may not state this main point explicitly, but you need to clearly understand what the story means to you and what you want it to mean to your audience.

Do Some Research

To really make your narrative argument powerful, you need to do some additional research to deepen your understanding of what happened and why.

Explore electronic sources—Using a search engine, look for sources that also describe the event and explain its meaning. If you are telling a narrative about a current or historical event, for example, you can collect additional details to fill out or clarify your own version. If you are telling a personal story about yourself or others, you should find sources that help you understand human behavior. These sources will allow you to better explain why your characters, including yourself, behaved the way they did.

Explore print sources—You can also find print sources at your campus library. If your event was described in newspapers or magazines, you can use the online Readers Guide or Google Scholar to locate print-based articles and descriptions of the event. Meanwhile, books and journal articles may offer you greater detail and scholarly analyses of the event.

Explore with empirical methods—If possible, you should visit the actual place where your story happened. You can also explore this place through a "street view" like the ones available in Google Maps. Doing so will help you fill in more details about the scene. You can also interview people, including experts, about what happened. Maybe locals or experts can offer you perspectives on the event that are different from your own.

Your freewriting and your research should work together. Freewriting will give you a general sense of what happened and what people learned from it. Your research will then fill in many of your story's details and help you understand it from different perspectives.

MOVES for Arguing

We tell stories all the time, but you probably haven't thought much about how stories are structured. Here are some typical moves for telling stories.

_____ was stuck or unable to go further. He or she continued to struggle and fall short until _____ happened, which allowed _____ to happen.

_____ was being pursued or challenged by _____. After one or two escapes, _____ succeeded because _____ happened.

_____ wanted to be or look like _____. She or he imitated _____ until _____ happened, which resulted in _____.

_____ wanted to do _____ but was too small, young, scared, or weak. Then _____ grew in some way, which allowed him/her/it to do it.

_____ switched places with _____. As a result, both gained new insights into the other's life, and together they learned _____.

_____ wanted (or didn't want) to do _____. The realities of the situation, however, forced her or him to change, which resulted in a transformation of some kind.

9.3 Strategies for organizing and drafting narratives

Organizing and Drafting Your Narrative Argument

The traditional "narrative pattern" is shown in the QuickView diagram on page 174. Most narrative arguments use an organizational pattern similar to this one. Of course, this pattern is not a formula to be followed mechanically, but it is helpful to start drafting your argument with this pattern in mind.

Here's how to organize and draft the sections of a typical narrative.

Set the Scene: Describe the Who, Where, What, and When

Most narrative arguments start out by setting the scene and introducing the main characters. Use rich detail to describe the place the story happened while describing what people were doing.

Last semester, a couple of my girlfriends and I decided to go to Mixers, a sports bar and grill near campus. We're typical college students. My friend, Meghan, is athletic, quiet, and pretty, and my roommate, Laura, is tall and always energetic. We always watch out for each other when we go out.

Mixers is a popular, trendy place that attracts sports-minded college students. It's a great place to meet guys, even though the music is usually a bit too loud. The food is always good, and they let in under-aged college students, like us, for lunch and dinner as long as we stay on the "family" side away from the bar. It's an open secret that if you order a meal, you can order a margarita or daiquiri a bit later without getting checked for ID.

Everything at Mixers that day seemed normal. We ate diner. We ordered soft drinks. Then, when it looked safe, we ordered a round of daiquiris. The server didn't check our IDs, and within a few minutes she was serving us blue, red, and orange drinks in tall glasses with slices of lime perched on the rims. The daiquiris didn't seem too strong, which was typical. The drinks at Mixers are usually weak.

Most narrative arguments don't have a main claim or thesis in the introduction. Instead, you should concentrate on setting the scene for the audience.

Introduce a Complication: Disrupt the Scene

Your audience knows something is going to happen. Otherwise, your narrative argument wouldn't be a story worth telling. The complication disrupts the scene in some way.

Soon, my head started to feel foggy and I was a bit dizzy. I was having trouble staying focused. The world felt like it was moving in slow motion. I looked over at the usually energetic Laura and saw she was staring quietly out into the distance. On the other side of the table, Meghan looked like she was going to fall asleep with her head slightly tilted to the side. She looked exhausted.

I said, "Wow, these are some pretty strong daiquiris."

Laura shook out of her stupor and said, "Yeah, I shouldn't be drunk. I haven't even had half of mine, yet." Meghan was still sitting there, spaced out. My head was spinning and the music sounded muffled.

Not all complications are as dramatic as this one, but your goal is to describe how the original scene was disrupted in some way.

Evaluate the Complication: The Characters React

After the complication, give your characters some time to react and "evaluate" what happened. You characters should consider the different pathways available to them.

"Something's wrong," I said, starting to feel a bit panicked. My heart was racing and I began sweating. I looked around. A couple of the guys at the bar were watching us and seemed to be laughing to themselves. When they saw me looking at them, they turned away, acting like they were watching one of the televisions.

"Laura, we need to get out of here. Look at Meghan." Meghan's eyes were almost closed. I reached over to prod her. She startled awake and then slipped back into a zombie-like state.

Laura said, "I need to go to the bathroom before we leave." I told her I would get the bill.

Our server, a middle-aged woman, came by, and I asked her for the bill. She seemed a bit appalled with us. I know how this situation must have looked. It was only 6:30 in the evening, and we already looked like we were sloppy drunk. Thinking back, I now realize we should have asked the server for help, but I was embarrassed and confused. All I knew was that we needed to get out of there.

Resolve the Complication: The Characters Figure It Out

Most narrative arguments lead up to a moment at which the characters figure things out or take some kind of action that resolves the problem. This moment is sometimes called the "climax." But you shouldn't feel like this moment needs to be exciting or thrilling. Instead, this moment is usually the point at which one or more of the characters change in a significant way or makes an important realization.

I paid the bill, but Laura hadn't come back yet. I decided Meghan couldn't be left alone, and yet I was afraid something had happened to Laura. So, I pulled Meghan up. She and I stumbled to the bathroom, which was near the front door. I looked around for help, but those guys at the bar were watching us with knowing smiles on their face. Others were ignoring us. I'm sure we looked like just a couple more drunk college students.

We found Laura outside the bathroom, talking absently to one of the guys from the bar. I told her we needed to go—now. The guy moved over to stand in her way. He started to tell her she should stay. I put on as angry a face as I could muster, and I said loudly, "No. We're going. Come on, Laura!" Fortunately, Laura followed us out the door, and the guy didn't try to stop us.

For an hour, we sat on a bench a couple blocks from Mixers trying to gather our thoughts. Then, my head began to clear and I called a taxi. Laura and I were wiped out for the rest of the evening. Meghan fell asleep as soon as we made it to our dorm floor. We thought about going to the Student Health Center but we were afraid they might report us to the authorities or to our parents.

The resolution doesn't need to resolve *everything*. It's the moment at which the characters figure out how to deal with the complication.

Offer a Lesson or a Call to Action: Explain What the Story Means

Narrative arguments often end with an explanation of what the story means. Here is where you can make your main point or state your thesis.

The next day, I mentioned what happened to the RA on our dorm floor. She told me we had been roofied and that other girls have had similar experiences at Mixers. A roofie, which is really the sedative Flunitrazepam, can be easily slipped into drinks. It's often called the "date rape" drug because it puts people into a zombie-like state and can cause amnesia. Victims often wake up to find that they were sexually assaulted but can't remember who did it or what happened.

Roofies come in a pill form that can be crushed into a powder. The powder dissolves quickly, and it's almost impossible to detect in drinks. Those guys at the bar probably slipped the drug into our daiquiris before the server brought them over. I'm convinced their buddy outside the bathroom hitting on Laura was taking advantage of the situation. That's probably his usual move.

The RA said we were lucky because she heard rumors that a college student who had been roofied was once assaulted not far from Mixers. She encouraged us to report what had happened. Unfortunately, we didn't make a report because we were afraid to admit we were drinking under age. Now, I realize that we were wrong not to report this crime—and it was a crime—because other women have probably been ruffied since then.

Roofies are a serious problem, and our university should take action against their use. All people, but especially women, should know about this drug and its symptoms. Meanwhile, our campus Student Health Center should make it clear that any students who might have been ruffied will have a safe haven there without fear of being reported.

In the meantime, I'm hoping this story, which I am sending to Mixers, the people in my dorm, the Dean of Students, and the police will raise awareness and help others avoid being drugged and assaulted.

Narrative arguments often end with a stated or unstated lesson. In a generative narrative argument, you might decide to forego a lesson or call to action, allowing your audience to figure out the meaning of your story themselves. In a persuasive narrative argument, you can state your point directly and include a call to action based on the story.

Style and Design in Narrative Arguments

9.4 Ways to use style and design to enhance narrative arguments

Because narrative arguments are stories, they often rely on stylistic techniques and images to clarify ideas and enhance the experience for the readers.

Use plenty of sensory detail—Details will bring your story to life. So use all five of your senses to describe the scenes, characters, and important objects. Include visual details about color, shapes, sizes, and movements. Then use your other senses to include any sounds, tastes, smells, and textures that help illustrate the scenes or describe the characters.

Use active voice—Active voice rather than passive voice is one of the best ways to inject energy into your narrative. In other words, put the "doers" in the subjects of your sentences.

Passive—In early October 1781, the British forces that were under the command of Cornwallis were surrounded and besieged by Washington's troops.

The doer
Active—In early October 1781, <u>Washington's troops</u> surrounded and besieged the British forces that were under the command of Cornwallis.

Passive—The levee was breeched by the floodwaters at 2:00 a.m., forcing us to flee in the middle of the night.

The doer
Active—The <u>floodwaters</u> breached the levee at 2:00 a.m., forcing us to flee in the middle of the night.

Avoid clichés—Clichés and other trite expressions, such as "chomping at the bit," "dead as a doornail," or "walking on eggshells," are common when people tell stories verbally. In writing, however, these hackneyed phrases sound tired and stale. So convert these clichés into regular prose.

Cliché—All through high school, playing sports was <u>never my cup of tea</u>, but I kept busy playing bass guitar and fronting the Skull Monkeys, a punk band.

Regular Prose—All through high school, playing sports never interested me, but I kept busy playing bass guitar and fronting the Skull Monkeys, a punk band.

Vary sentence length to increase or decrease the pace—If you are telling an action-filled story, use brief sentences to increase the pace of the story. If the story is slower paced, use longer sentences to slow the pace down.

Use dialogue to reveal insights about characters—Dialogue is a good way to reveal new insights into the story and illustrate how characters interact with each other. Generally, you should use dialogue as a way to illustrate moments in which characters figure something out about the complication or about themselves.

Designing an Attractive Document

The design of your narrative depends on your argument's purpose and the medium in which it will be published. Here are some design elements that you might consider:

Include photographs—If your story is based on your own experiences, you might include some photographs that show the people, objects, and places mentioned in your narrative argument (Figure 9.2). If your story is historical, you can find photos on the Internet that illustrate what you are describing. Digital photos can be inserted directly into your document. Non-digital images can be scanned and then inserted.

Make the text look attractive—Your audience won't be interested in your document if it looks boring. You can choose a font that distinguishes your headings from the regular text. You can also put your story into a two-column or three-column format, like a magazine.

Add in video or audio—To make your story even more engaging, you might add in video or audio clips that would enhance the story. For example, you

 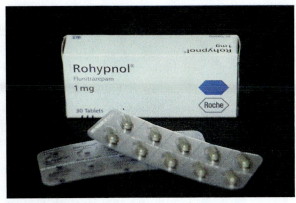

FIGURE 9.2 Use Photographs to Add a Visual Aspect to Your Narrative
Photos, such as these pictures of "roofies" offer a good way to illustrate an aspect of your narrative argument.

could include interviews with people who know something about your subject. Or you can find preexisting video or audio about your topic that can be linked to your document. YouTube, Hulu, or other video sharing sites might be good places to look for this kind of material.

Publish your narrative argument online—Depending on your topic, a variety of political, historical, or cultural websites might publish your narrative argument (Figure 9.3). You can try publishing in online magazines, like *Creative Nonfiction*, *Brevity*, or *Fourth Genre*.

Increasingly, images and design are becoming more important in narrative arguments. Audiences expect texts to be more visual and illustrate important points, so you may need to use visuals to enhance your narrative argument.

FIGURE 9.3
Publish Your Narrative Argument Online
Several websites will publish your narrative argument. *Fourth Genre*, shown here, is a popular website for nonfiction narratives.

Ready to argue through a story? Here are the basics of this chapter:

1 Narrative is one of the most effective ways to argue because people use their own experiences to interpret what the story means, which can make the argument more personal and intense.

2 There are two main kinds of narrative arguments: factual narratives and fictional narratives.

3 Narrative arguments tend to follow a consistent pattern: set the scene, introduce a complication, evaluate the complication, resolve the complication, offer a lesson or call to action.

4 When setting the scene, introduce the characters and explain where they are and when the events happened.

5 The complication in your narrative should disrupt the characters' lives in some way.

6 The characters should then evaluate the complication and resolve it in a way that seems reasonable to the readers.

7 Most narrative arguments end with a lesson or moral that the readers can take away from the text. In some cases, especially when the lesson is obvious, the story will not offer a lesson at the end.

8 You can play with the narrative pattern, but you need to do so consciously. If you rearrange the order of events, make sure you are doing so for a good reason.

9 The style of your narrative will be stronger if you use plenty of detail and write in active voice.

10 When designing your narrative, use photographs and other images to help the audience visualize the story you are trying to tell and the places you are describing.

1. Find two or three factual narratives on the Internet. They don't need to be arguments in an obvious way. Instead, you just need to find nonfiction stories. Then, with your group, study these narratives as arguments. What point do you think the authors want to make?

2. Each year, it seems as though a popular memoir is exposed as a fake. James Frey's book, *A Million Little Pieces* (2003), which was an Oprah's Book Club selection, for example, had many fabricated elements about Frey's recovery from drug addiction. He was called onto her show to be publicly chastised for misleading his readers. That said, the book was still gripping and engaging. Do you think there is a clear line between factual narratives and fictional narratives? With your group, discuss how much "creative license" authors should have when telling their own stories.

3. Think of something funny or strange that happened to you and tell your story to your group, who should pay attention to how you set the scene, introduce a complication, evaluate that complication, and resolve it. When you are finished, explain what you learned from the experience.

1. Remember an event in your life that changed you in a significant way. Describe that event in narrative form. Set the scene and introduce the complication. Then describe how you and others evaluated and resolved the complication. Explain what you learned from the event. Then write a one-page *nonnarrative* version of this argument that uses reasoning and examples to persuade your audience to draw the same conclusions as your narrative version. What are the differences between the narrative and nonnarrative forms for argument? Which one do you find more effective? Write a one-page response to your instructor in which you describe these differences.

2. Find a narrative argument on the Internet or in a print source. Analyze it by looking closely at its content, organization, style, and design. What kinds of facts and other information did the author choose to include? Does the narrative follow the traditional narrative pattern? If not, why does it deviate from the pattern? What tone does the narrative use, and how did the author achieve that tone? Did the author add in any visual elements to enhance the story? Write an analysis of this narrative argument for your class, explaining what you noticed in the narrative argument and whether you found the author's use of narrative effective or not.

3. Find a historical event described in two different sources, preferably two very different sources. For example, you could find the same event described on both conservative and progressive websites. Or you could study how a historical event was described originally in the news and how it is being described today in history textbooks. Compare and contrast how these different sources narrate the same event. Write an analysis for your teacher in which you compare and contrast the two versions.

In this narrative argument, Savannah Hoskins, a student at Purdue University, uses a narrative frame to examine a highly abstract set of questions—"What is art, and what is it for?" Notice how she uses narrative, metaphor, and other strategies to draw readers into her argument and encourage them to listen carefully to her perspective.

The Importance of Wildwood Flower

Savannah Hoskins

Recently an old friend came into town and we decided to catch up over coffee and scones at a local café. My friend, a native New Yorker who had come back to the Midwest to visit his old college stomping grounds, came from a wealthy, well-educated family. He spent his adolescence in a Manhattan brownstone, raised by a successful lawyer and psychologist who brought up their three children with a strong work ethic and no-nonsense worldview. As a result, my friend became a sharp-edged, highly driven young man who put little stock in anything that did not progress him toward his goals. Still, despite our differences, we enjoyed each other's company, in part because we both enjoy a good caffeine-infused argument. So, when the topic of the importance of artistic expression came up, I should not have been surprised when his views strongly contrasted with my own. "I don't see how anyone can possibly argue for the importance of art in schools," he said. "It is completely sending the wrong message. Art is not essential to anyone. It's a luxury for people who can afford it. What the poor need is to put down their instruments and paintbrushes and spend their time in training for a real job." At the time, I simply raised my jaw off the floor and chuckled at the predictability of my former classmate. A few days later, however, his comments still weighed heavily on my mind, forcing me to examine the role art has played in my own family.

My parents are both Appalachian, having grown up in an impoverished mountain region of Alabama called Sand Mountain. Much of my childhood was spent on I-65, in frequent trips back and forth from Alabama to Indiana to visit grandparents, aunts and uncles. After my parents divorced, Mama and I moved around a lot, even moving back to Alabama for a short time. Frequent moves meant I was always the new kid. Desperate to fit in, I became more and more aware of my differences. Not only had I acquired my parent's Southern twang, but also a plethora of expressions that were a part of a Southern dialect completely foreign to my Midwest counterparts. In high school, I began to come into my own, but I must admit I worked hard to get rid of the accent that my Mother chose to embrace. While Mama considered the accent and 'all things Southern' to be a part of a cherished heritage, I blamed my Southern roots for my social failure, and, while I secretly loved my family and their quirky ways, I vowed that I would be as different as I possibly could from the poor, twangy Southerners on the mountain.

One of my most prominent memories from these trips is my grandparents' Music Night. Once a month, my grandparents and their friends get together to play old time music. They alternate homes, congregating with instruments and covered dishes for a night of music, food, and laughter. The group includes a retired factory worker, a teacher, a student from the local community college, a pharmacist, a truck driver, and an elderly clock-maker who built his own upright bass fiddle. A dozen or so musicians sit in a circle, playing their dulcimers, banjos, mandolins, fiddles, guitars, and the occasional flat-top box or harmonica. My Grandaddy plays anything with a string, but his favorite is the 'music box.' The Tennessee Music Box is an example of Appalachian ingenuity. It doesn't look like much; it's not curved and graceful like a fiddle and it lacks the intricacies of the mandolin, but this flat box, when strummed or plucked, produces a rich, full tone.

Mountain music has its roots in the story-song tradition. Expert pickers and novices play together and take compliments with humility and self-deprecating humor. The most seasoned musician will say, "I play a bit." The player who is not recognized in any other facet of his life is afforded a time to shine when they come together with others who share their love of music.

5   I must admit that, as a child, I bought into the stereotype that Appalachian music is "simple" and "country," so I wasn't particularly impressed that my grandparents always scheduled Music Night around our visits. In the living room, the men sat in a circle, each picking and plucking away with focus and determination, their instruments filling the house with the uneven and staggering sound of Bluegrass. The guitar's incessant strumming set the pace with a harmonious twang while the fiddle strings sang, gliding over and around the guitar's acoustic lead. The mandolin pinched my ears as the banjo picker's fingers danced haphazardly along the strings. Throw in the dulcimers, harmonicas and a flat-top box, and the sound was enough to startle my untrained ear.

As the musicians were mostly men, I usually found my way to the kitchen with the wives, listening to their banter about church or their most successful batch of biscuits, along with a little good-natured complaining about their husbands. As a child, I was bored stiff. In between songs, I would hear the men erupt with laughter and compliment each other on how they had improved since the last music night. I would sit in the corner and pout, playing some video game on my Game Boy and rolling my eyes, while my mother shot me pleading looks from across the room, begging me to be civil. Finally, one year I asked Thelma, the wife of a quiet banjo picker named Ray, why they did this every month instead of doing something *fun*. She smiled a nearly toothless smile and let out a chortle that caused me to shyly smile at my own question.

"You think this isn't fun?" she asked, sweetly grinning, as though she knew a secret that I didn't know.

"Well, um…not really. Why don't you guys go see a movie or something?"

"Oh, sweet pea, I haven't been to a picture show in years! When you live like we do, you learn to make your own fun."

"What do you mean?" I asked.

"Well, Ray works long hours at the paper mill pretty much every   10
day, seeing as we can't afford for him to retire, and these old feet just
ain't what they used to be, so I had to give up working at the shirt
factory. I take care of the house and watch the grandbabies. The only
break we really get is this music night. Oh, it just means the world to
Ray to be able to sit down, relax, and play music with his friends. He's
good! Did you hear him? Hey, Ray! Play 'Wildwood Flower' for this
young'un! Why, just look at him grinnin' in there!" She looked over
at her husband for a moment, watching him play, and her lips curled
up into a crooked smile. I was thirteen when I asked Ms. Thelma that
question, but I have never forgotten her answer—or the way she looked
with love at her husband.

Though we didn't have a lot of money growing up, my mother
worked hard to make sure I never missed out. For me, seeing a movie
with my friends, going to see a play in Chicago with my father, or even
having store bought presents under the tree at Christmas never seemed
like a big deal. In fact, it was a luxury I took for granted. I realize now
that my friend wasn't completely wrong. Art, the kind one sees in fancy
New York galleries, may well be a luxury reserved for those who can
afford to own it or have the luxury of time or proximity to museums
to enjoy the beauty it brings to our lives. But art is more than that. For
Appalachian people trapped in the cycle of poverty, shelter and food
are important, but art and creative expression are essential, providing
joy, solace, and dignity, as well as bringing people together in a sense
of community. Not just the kind of art you see in a gallery, but things
like music, story-telling, quilting, carving, and dancing are passed from
generation to generation and revered as a part of the Appalachian
identity and resourcefulness. Skills used for survival by early settlers
were polished and refined into art forms that foster a sense of cultural
pride and individual accomplishment. Thanks to the arts, Appalachian
families are kept warm on cold winter nights by quilts pieced together
from pieces of worn-out clothing and feed sacks, toys are carved, or
"whittled," and dolls made from corn husks or cotton-stuffed feed sacks.

There are many images and stereotypes associated with Appalachia, but nothing exemplifies Appalachian culture more than the home-grown, individual artistry of its people. Artistic expression serves a valuable purpose, not just for those whose art is appreciated by society or "marketable." The personal value of art lies in the process, not the product.

Art and creativity bring people together, creating an avenue for building relationships and helping individuals from different backgrounds to feel a part of community. Time set aside for creating becomes time spent getting to know other people. A simple night of sweet, old time music can feed the soul of those lucky enough to be involved.

A CLOSER LOOK AT
The Importance of Wildwood Flower

1. How does Hoskins set the scene of this narrative? How is the opening scene used as a frame for the rest of her story?

2. Describe the level of detail Hoskins demonstrates in the narrative. What senses does she use to describe the scene?

3. Discuss three ways in which this narrative argument is generative. How it is persuasive? Do you think it leans towards one side over another? Why?

IDEAS FOR
Arguing

1. Choose an event from your life to write a narrative about. Freewrite about it for five minutes. Then re-write the event in a different mood. For example, if you were reflective in your original freewrite, write the second one in a humorous or somber tone. In an e-mail to your instructor, share your two free-writes and reflect on the differences between the two. Did the change of mood alter the angle of the narrative?

2. Think back to a conversation you had with a friend in which you both took different sides. Create a concept map or freewrite about the topic to explore why you felt the way you did (and possibly why your friend felt differently). Write a narrative argument in which you use a story or stories to explain both sides of the issue.

Workers

RICHARD RODRIGUEZ

In this narrative argument, Richard Rodriguez provides a rich and detailed description of his experiences doing physical labor during a college summer break. Notice how Rodriguez provides rich narrative and descriptive detail to invite his readers to identify with him and with other people in the story, but he does not offer an explicit argumentative point, leaving his readers to figure out the meaning of the story.

It was at Stanford, one day near the end of my senior year, that a friend told me about a summer construction job he knew was available. I was quickly alert. Desire uncoiled within me. My friend said that he knew I had been looking for summer employment. He knew I needed some money. Almost apologetically he explained: It was something I probably wouldn't be interested in, but a friend of his, a contractor, needed someone for the summer to do menial jobs. There would be lots of shoveling and raking and sweeping. Nothing too hard. But nothing more interesting either. Still, the pay would be good. Did I want it? Or did I know someone who did?

I did. Yes, I said, surprised to hear myself say it.

In the weeks following, friends cautioned that I had no idea how hard physical labor really is. ("You only *think* you know what it is like to shovel for eight hours straight.") Their objections seemed to me challenges. They resolved the issue. I became happy with my plan. I decided, however, not to tell my parents. I wouldn't tell my mother because I could guess her worried reaction. I would tell my father only after the summer was over, when I could announce that, after all, I did know what "real work" is like.

The day I met the contractor (a Princeton graduate, it turned out), he asked me whether I had done any physical labor before. "In high school, during the summer," I lied. And although he seemed to regard me with skepticism, he decided to give me a try. Several days later, expectant, I arrived at my first construction site. I would take off my shirt to the sun. And at last grasp desired sensation. No longer afraid. At last become like a *bracero*. "We need those tree stumps out of here by tomorrow," the contractor said. I started to work.

I labored with excitement that first morning—and all the days after. The work was harder than I could have expected. But it was never as tedious as my friends had warned me it would be. There was too much physical pleasure in the labor. Especially early in the day, I would be most alert to the sensations of movement and straining. Beginning around seven each morning (when the air was still damp but the scent of weeds and dry earth anticipated the heat of the sun), I would feel my body resist the first thrusts of the shovel. My arms, tightened by sleep, would gradually loosen; after only several minutes, sweat would gather in beads on my forehead and then—a short while later—I would feel my chest silky with sweat in the breeze. I would return to my work. A nervous spark of pain would fly up my arm and settle to burn like an ember in the thick of my shoulder. An hour, two passed. Three. My whole body would assume regular movements; my shoveling would be described by identical, even movements. Even later in the day, my enthusiasm for primitive sensation would survive the heat and the dust and the insects pricking my back. I would strain wildly for sensation as the day came to a close. At three-thirty, quitting time, I would stand upright and slowly let my head fall back, luxuriating in the feeling of tightness relieved.

Some of the men working nearby would watch me and laugh. Two or three of the older men took the trouble to teach me the right way to use a pick, the correct way to shovel. "You're doing it wrong, too fucking hard," one man scolded. Then proceeded to show me—what persons who work with their bodies all their lives quickly learn—the most economical way to use one's body in labor.

"Don't make your back do so much work," he instructed. I stood impatiently listening, half listening, vaguely watching, then noticed his work-thickened fingers clutching the shovel. I was annoyed. I wanted to tell him that I enjoyed shoveling the wrong way. And I didn't want to learn the right way. I wasn't afraid of back pain. I liked the way my body felt sore at the end of the day.

I was about to, but, as it turned out, I didn't say a thing. Rather it was at that moment I realized that I was fooling myself if I expected a few weeks of labor to gain me admission to the world of the laborer. I would not learn in three months what my father had meant by "real work." I was not bound to this job; I could imagine its rapid conclusion. For me the sensations were to be feared. Fatigue took a different toll on their bodies—and minds.

It was, I know, a simple insight. But it was with this realization that I took my first step that summer toward realizing something even more important about the "worker." In the company of carpenters, electricians, plumbers, and painters at lunch, I would often sit quietly, observant. I was not shy in such company. I felt easy, pleased by the knowledge that I was casually accepted, my presence taken for granted by men (exotics) who worked with their hands. Some days the younger men would talk and talk about sex, and they would howl at women who drove by in cars. Other days the talk at lunchtime was subdued; men gathered in separate groups. It depended on who was around. There were rough, good-natured workers. Others were quiet. The more I remember that summer, the more I realize that there was no single type of worker. I am embarrassed to say I had not expected such diversity. I certainly had not expected to meet, for example, a plumber who was an abstract painter in his off hours and admired the work of Mark Rothko. Nor did I expect to meet so many workers with college diplomas. (They were the ones who were not surprised that I intended to enter graduate school in the fall.) I suppose what I really want to say here is painfully obvious, but I must say it nevertheless: The men of that summer were middle-class Americans. They certainly didn't constitute an oppressed society. Carefully completing their work sheets; talking about the fortunes of local football teams; planning Las Vegas vacations; comparing the gas mileage of various makes of campers—they were not *los pobres* my mother had spoken about.

On two occasions, the contractor hired a 10 group of Mexican aliens. They were employed to cut down some trees and haul off debris. In all, there were six men of varying age. The youngest in his late twenties; the oldest (his father?) perhaps sixty years old. They came and they left in a single old truck. Anonymous men. They were never introduced to the other men at the site. Immediately upon their arrival, they would follow the contractor's directions, start working—rarely resting—seemingly driven by a fatalistic sense that work which had to be done was best done as quickly as possible.

I watched them sometimes. Perhaps they watched me. The only time I saw them pay me much notice was one day at lunchtime when I was laughing with the other men. The Mexicans sat apart when they ate, just as they worked by themselves. Quiet. I rarely heard them say much to each other. All I could hear were their voices calling out sharply to one another, giving directions. Otherwise, when they stood briefly resting, they talked among themselves in voices too hard to overhear.

The contractor knew enough Spanish, and the Mexicans—or at least the oldest of them, their spokesman—seemed to know enough English to communicate. But because I was around, the contractor decided one day to make me his translator. (He assumed I could speak Spanish.) I did what I was told. Shyly I went over to tell the Mexicans that the *patrón* wanted them to do something else before they left for the day. As I started to speak, I was afraid with my old fear that I would be unable to pronounce the Spanish words. But it was a simple instruction I had to convey. I could say it in phrases.

The dark sweating faces turned toward me as I spoke. They stopped their work to hear me. Each nodded in response. I stood there. I wanted to say something more. But what could I say in Spanish, even if I could have pronounced the words right? Perhaps I just wanted to engage them in small talk, to be assured of their confidence, our familiarity. I thought for a moment to ask them where in Mexico they were from. Something like that. And maybe I wanted to tell them (a lie, if need be) that my parents were from the same part of Mexico.

I stood there.

15   Their faces watched me. The eyes of the man directly in front of me moved slowly over my shoulder, and I turned to follow his glance toward el patron some distance away. For a moment I felt swept up by that glance into the Mexicans' company. But then I heard one of them returning to work. And then the others went back to work. I left them without saying anything more.

When they had finished, the contractor went over to pay them in cash. (He later told me that he paid them collectively—"for the job," though he wouldn't tell me their wages.

He said something quickly about the good rate of exchange "in their own country.") I can still hear the loudly confident voice he used with the Mexicans. It was the sound of the *gringo* I had heard as a very young boy. And I can still hear the quiet, indistinct sounds of the Mexican, the oldest, who replied. At hearing that voice I was sad for the Mexicans. Depressed by their vulnerability. Angry at myself. The adventure of the summer seemed suddenly ludicrous. I would not shorten the distance I felt from *los pobres* with a few weeks of physical labor. I would not become like them. They were different from me.

After that summer, a great deal—and not very much really—changed in my life. The curse of physical shame was broken by the sun; I was no longer ashamed of my body. No longer would I deny myself the pleasing sensations of my maleness. During those years when middle-class black Americans began to assert with pride, "Black is beautiful," I was able to regard my complexion without shame. I am today darker than I ever was as a boy. I have taken up the middle-class sport of long-distance running. Nearly every day now I run ten or fifteen miles, barely clothed, my skin exposed to the California winter rain and wind or the summer sun of late afternoon. The torso, the soccer player's calves and thighs, the arms of the twenty-year-old I never was, I possess now in my thirties. I study the youthful parody shape in the mirror: the stomach lipped tight by muscle; the shoulders rounded by chin-ups; the arms veined strong. This man. A man. I meet him. He laughs to see me, what I have become.

The dandy. I wear double-breasted Italian suits and custom-made English shoes. I resemble no one so much as my father—the man pictured in those honeymoon photos. At that point in life when he abandoned the dandy's posture, I assume it. At the point when my parents would not consider going on vacation, I register at the Hotel Carlyle in New York and the Plaza Athenée in Paris. I am as taken by the symbols of leisure and wealth as they were. For my parents, however, those symbols became taunts, reminders of all they could not achieve in one lifetime. For me those same symbols are reassuring reminders of public success. I tempt vulgarity to be reassured. I am filled with the gaudy delight, the monstrous grace of the nouveau riche.

In recent years I have had occasion to lecture in ghetto high schools. There I see students of remarkable style and physical grace. (One can see more dandies in such schools than one ever will find in middle-class high schools.) There is not the look of casual assurance I saw students at Stanford display. Ghetto girls mimic high-fashion models. Their dresses are of bold, forceful color; their figures elegant, long; the stance theatrical. Boys wear shirts that grip at their overdeveloped muscular bodies. (Against a powerless future, they engage images of strength.) Bad nutrition does not yet tell. Great disappointment, fatal to youth, awaits them still. For the moment, movements in school hallways are dancelike, a procession of postures in a sexual masque. Watching them, I feel a kind of envy. I wonder how different my adolescence would have been had I been free. . . . But no, it is my parents I see—their optimism during those years when they were entertained by Italian grand opera.

20   The registration clerk in London wonders if I have just been to Switzerland. And the man who carries my luggage in New York guesses the Caribbean. My complexion becomes a mark of my leisure. Yet no one would regard my complexion the same way if I entered such hotels through the service entrance. That is only to say that my complexion assumes its significance from the context of my life. My skin, in itself, means nothing. I stress the point because I know there are people who would label me "disadvantaged" because of my color. They make the same mistake I made as a boy, when I thought a disadvantaged life was circumscribed by particular occupations. That summer I worked in the sun may have made

me physically indistinguishable from the Mexicans working nearby. (My skin was actually darker because, unlike them, I worked without wearing a shirt. By late August my hands were probably as tough as theirs.) But I was not one of *los pobres*. What made me different from them was an attitude of *mind*, my imagination of myself.

I do not blame my mother for warning me away from the sun when I was young. In a world where her brother had become an old man in his twenties because he was dark, my complexion was something to worry about. "Don't run in the sun," she warns me today. I run. In the end, my father was right—though perhaps he did not know how right or why—to say that I would never know what real work is. I will never know what he felt at his last factory job. If tomorrow I worked at some kind of factory, it would go differently for me. My long education would favor me. I could act as a public person—able to defend my interests, to unionize, to petition, to speak up—to challenge and demand. (I will never know what real work is.) I will never know what the Mexicans knew, gathering their shovels and ladders and saws.

Their silence stays with me now. The wages those Mexicans received for their labor were only a measure of their disadvantaged condition. Their silence is more telling. They lack a public identity. They remain profoundly alien. Persons apart. People lacking a union obviously, people without grounds. They depend upon the relative good will or fairness of their employers each day. For such people, lacking a better alternative, it is not such an unreasonable risk.

Their silence stays with me. I have taken these many words to describe its impact. Only: the quiet. Something uncanny about it. Its compliance. Vulnerability. Pathos. As I heard their truck rumbling away, I shuddered, my face mirrored with sweat. I had finally come face to face with *los pobres*.

A CLOSER LOOK AT
Workers

1. This narrative follows an organization similar to the one described in the Quick View diagram at the beginning of this chapter. Where in this narrative can you find the five narrative strategies? How does Rodriguez alter this pattern to keep readers interested?

2. Good narrative arguments invite readers to identify with their characters and experience their values on a deeper level. What are Rodriguez's values? Do you share them?

3. What exactly is the complication that Rodriguez faces? How fully does he resolve that complication? How does he invite us to experience the difficulty of resolving the conflict at the heart of his narrative argument?

IDEAS FOR
Arguing

1. Rodriguez describes his interactions with two groups of workers. The "middle class" laborers share many of Rodriguez's values. The Mexican immigrants, *los pobres*, are very different, but he suggests that his interactions with them lead to insights and a change in his perspective. Write a narrative argument about a job or experience in which you worked alongside people that were different from you. What insights did you gain from that experience? How did that experience change you?

2. Rodriguez does not explicitly state a thesis but instead invites us to identify with him and the other people he describes. He allows us to interpret the story. Write a rhetorical analysis of "Workers" that describes the purpose you think Rodriguez is trying to achieve. Explain how he uses framing, identification, and narration to achieve his goals.

10 Reviews— Arguing about Performance

IN THIS CHAPTER, YOU WILL LEARN—

10.1 How reviews are used to assess products, services, performances, and projects

10.2 Techniques for inventing the content of a review

10.3 Strategies for properly organizing a review in familiar patterns

10.4 How to match a review's style and design to the needs of the audience and the situations in which they will experience the argument

10.1 How reviews are used to assess products, services, performances, and projects

You probably look up reviews on a weekly if not daily basis. When you want to know whether a movie is worth watching, you check out the reviews on RottenTomatoes.com or in your campus newspaper. If you're thinking about buying a product, you check the consumer reviews on Amazon.com or in *Consumer Reports.* In college and your career, you will regularly write reviews of people, products, services, performances, and projects (Figure 10.1).

A review is an argument about performance or quality. When writing a review, you should attempt to analyze the subject as impartially as possible, praising its strengths and pointing out any deficiencies. A well-written review highlights the positives while mentioning areas for improvement.

Reviews can be generative or persuasive. In the workplace, for example, *performance reviews* are usually generative because they are used to evaluate employees and improve projects. Their main objective is to help everyone involved to discuss what is going well and what could be improved. *Published reviews* tend to be persuasive, such as movie reviews and product reviews on consumer websites or in newspapers. These published reviews argue whether something (e.g., movie, restaurant, video game, car, concert) is worth a customer's time and money.

QUICK View

Generative

Persuasive

Generative Argument—Reviews written for the workplace and some college courses tend to be generative because they are used to discuss how well an employee or a project is progressing. These kinds of reviews are usually open ended, highlighting strengths and offering suggestions for improvement.

Persuasive Argument—Reviews written for the public tend to be persuasive because they argue whether someone or something was effective. These reviews typically measure quality and determine whether the subject is worthy of a patron's time and money.

Genre Patterns

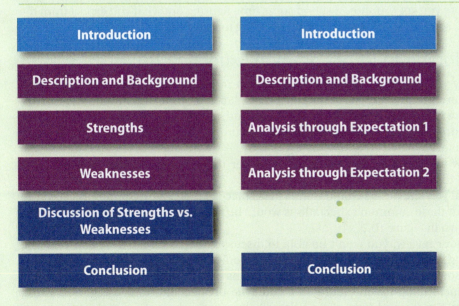

Introduction	Introduction
Description and Background	Description and Background
Strengths	Analysis through Expectation 1
Weaknesses	Analysis through Expectation 2
Discussion of Strengths vs. Weaknesses	
Conclusion	Conclusion

Reviews can follow a variety of patterns, including the two shown here. The pattern on the left is helpful for comparing and contrasting pros and cons. The one on the right focuses on whether the subject is meeting expectations.

FIGURE 10.1 Writing a Review
Performance reviews in the workplace tend to be generative, while published reviews tend to be persuasive.

10.2 Techniques for inventing the content of a review

Inventing the Content of Your Review

Let's state the obvious. To write a review of something, you will need to experience it. But before you go, you should spend some time figuring out what you expect from the product, service, or performance you are going to experience.

Developing a List of Common Expectations

Let's say you are going to review of a new pizza place that just opened near campus. There are probably a variety of pizza places in your area. Some are chains, like Pizza Hut, Dominos, or Papa Johns, and others are locally owned pizza restaurants. Some pizza restaurants have inside dining while others only offer takeout and delivery.

How are you going to determine whether this new pizza place is worth your readers' time and money? You should begin by figuring out some *common expectations* that you and others would want a pizza place to meet. Perhaps the easiest way to figure out these common expectations would be to make a brainstorming list like the one shown in Figure 10.2.

In your review, you won't be able to discuss in depth all the items on your list. Marching your audience through a long list would be boring and ultimately not that useful. So you should group these smaller items into larger categories. For example, the brainstorming list in Figure 10.2 could be divided into four categories: *Crust, Toppings, Service*, and *Value*. Then, describe your expectations for each of these categories.

Crust—The pizza crust should be firm and chewy. It should offer a reliable platform for the pizza toppings without becoming flimsy or soggy. The crust can be thick

> Chewy and firm crust
> Crust can't be too doughy or soggy
> Real mozzarella cheese
> Lots of cheese
> Cheese baked slightly brown and bubbly
> Flavorful sauce but not too spicy
> Fresh toppings
> Not too oily on top
> Friendly serving staff
> Quick delivery
> Large pizza for under $15
> Cheap drinks and free refills
> All the standard toppings
> A few unique toppings that others don't have
> Different kinds of crust available
> Fun restaurant atmosphere
> Progressive music, not Italian-sounding elevator stuff

FIGURE 10.2
Brainstorming a List of Common Expectations
It's helpful to start listing what you or others would expect from the person or thing you are reviewing.

or thin, but it needs to complement the flavor of the pizza, not dominate it with a bready taste.

Toppings—The ingredients must be as fresh as possible. The sauce should be made with fresh tomatoes, not canned. The cheese should be high-quality mozzarella, freshly grated at the restaurant. Any meat toppings should be flavorful and not too greasy. Vegetable toppings should be sliced fresh in the restaurant. A selection of common toppings is expected (e.g., pepperoni, sausage, ham, peppers, onions), but a truly noteworthy pizza place should also offer some toppings that are unexpected (e.g., BBQ chicken, pulled pork, broccoli, green chile, potatoes).

Service—Any interactions with employees—at the counter, at the table, or at my front door—should be friendly and prompt. The people working at the restaurant should enjoy making, serving, and delivering pizza. They should be concerned about keeping their hands and their workspace clean, because making pizza is unavoidably a hands-on process.

Value—The cost needs to be affordable to college students. That means less than $15 for a large pizza. Drinks should be inexpensive (with free refills). Extras, such as breadsticks, cheesebread, dessert pizza, and dipping sauces, should be available at low cost to sweeten the deals.

These categories are the common expectations through which you will review your subject. Of course, these common expectations are not scientific or even based on factual evidence. Instead, they describe your opinion and what you assume other people believe. By explaining these common expectations, you give your audience a good idea of what you expect from your subject.

Researching the Background of Your Subject

The more you know about your subject before experiencing it, the better you will be able to critique or assess it fairly. Good research will give you the background information you need.

Electronic sources—Running Internet searches is a good way to gather background information on your subject. You may even find other reviews of your subject. Keep in mind that other reviewers will also express their opinions, so try to gather facts while not letting other reviewers sway your own views too much.

Print sources—Newspapers and magazines are often good places to collect information on your subject, because reviews are usually about local places or new products. Books are less helpful, but you might find historical facts or discussions of industrial trends that could be helpful.

Empirical sources—Experiencing your subject is the best way to collect empirical evidence. You might also interview experts or conduct surveys to gain a sense of what people expect.

Most reviews are based on personal likes and dislikes, so background research tends to be light. You want to gather enough information to give you a solid sense of your subject and what people expect from it.

Experiencing Your Subject

Here's the fun part: Go experience your subject. If you're critiquing a new pizza place, go there for lunch or dinner. If you are reviewing a concert or other performance, go see it. If you are reviewing a new video game, play it.

However—and here's the key to writing a good review—you should experience your subject on two levels. The first level is how you would normally experience your subject. Eat the pizza. Watch the concert. Play the video game. The second level involves stepping back from the experience and taking note of how you and others are reacting to your subject.

Sometimes it helps to make a *two-column observation* of your subject (Figure 10.3). Fold a piece of paper in half. On the left half, write down everything you see, hear, smell, taste, and feel as you experience your subject. Take special note of anything that is moving or changing. The items on this side of the paper are those "first-level" experiences.

Then flip the folded sheet of paper over. On the right side of the sheet, write your "second-level" reactions to what you are experiencing, both positive and negative. Here is where you need to step back from your subject, trying to view your experience with some distance. You are basically trying to figure out *why* you and others are reacting in particular ways to your subject.

When you unfold your two-column observation, you will have a detailed description of what happened as you experienced your subject.

Of course, sometimes you cannot take notes while you are experiencing your subject. If that's the case, you should write down comments as soon as possible after the experience is over.

FIGURE 10.3 Experiencing Your Subject on Two Levels
When experiencing your subject, take notes about your reactions. Then step back and reflect on your reactions.

MOVES for Arguing

Here are some helpful moves that you can use to review someone or something.

_____ has many strengths, including _____, _____, and _____.

_____ could be improved by changing _____, _____, and _____.

Knowing the backstory behind _____ helps explain why _____ might not have turned out the way people expected.

When people go to _____, they usually expect _____, _____, and _____.

_____ exceeded/didn't meet our expectations because _____, _____, and _____ happened instead.

When weighing the pros and cons of _____, overall I found the experience to be _____.

In the future, I will think differently about _____, and I will be expecting _____, _____, and _____.

10.3 Strategies for properly organizing a review in familiar patterns

Organizing and Drafting Your Review

People read reviews all the time, so your audience will have specific expectations about how that information should be organized. The QuickView on page 195 offers a couple patterns you might consider using.

Introduction: Identify Your Subject and Purpose

Your review's introduction should identify your topic, purpose, and main point (thesis) while grabbing the audience's attention, offering background information, and stressing the importance of the subject.

Grab the Audience's Attention—Use a grabber to bring the audience into the argument. In a movie review, for example, you could describe the opening scene of the movie. *Note: A grabber is probably not appropriate for workplace reviews.*

Identify Your Topic—Clearly identify your subject by name if your grabber didn't do so already. Naming your subject in the introduction is important, because your audience may not see it in the title.

Indicate Your Purpose—Reviews almost never contain an overt purpose statement, such as "My purpose is to review..." However, in your introduction, you want to make sure it's clear to the audience that you are reviewing your subject.

State Your Main Point (Thesis)—A review's introduction will often include an open-ended thesis or question thesis:

An open-ended or question thesis is a good way to save your final main point for the conclusion of the review.

Open-Ended Thesis—The new Mike's Pizza on University Row has been getting rave reviews, but as a self-confessed pizza snob from Chicago, I needed to try the place myself.

Question Thesis—With all the well-established pizza places in this college town, can a new upstart like Mike's Pizza carve out its own niche?

A straightforward main point states the thesis of your argument.

Thesis—Compared to most college town pizza places, the new Mike's Pizza is already one of the best, but there is still room for improvement.

Offer Background Information—Tell your audience some details about the history and setting of your subject.

Stress the Importance of Your Topic—Explain or indicate why your audience should care about this person, product, service, performance, or project.

Body: Summarize, Then Criticize

Don't just tell your audience what you liked or didn't like about your subject. You first need to summarize or describe your subject. Otherwise, readers who have not experienced it won't be able to envision what you are talking about.

> Mike's Pizza is nestled into a corner shop on the Broward Hill Mall. When you walk through the door, the smell and feel of warm pizza and sausage take over your senses. The place is kind of grungy looking, in a good way. The inside is painted black and gold with graffiti, symbols, and quotes covering the walls. About twenty tables with chairs are scattered around the dining area. The pizza-making stations are behind a large counter. There, white-aproned chefs are busy tossing dough and spreading cheese and toppings. The red glow of the pizza oven warms the room.

Once you have described your subject, you can write about what you liked and disliked. Some reviewers like to talk about all the subject's strengths first and then all the weaknesses. Others like to organize this section by handling each common expectation separately, discussing strengths and weaknesses together.

> For me, the crust makes or breaks the whole pizza experience. If the crust is flimsy, doughy, or oily, it doesn't matter how good the toppings taste. It doesn't matter if the Pope flew in from Italy to serve the pizza to me at my table. A good crust needs to be chewy with a slightly crispy puffed edge. Mike's Pizza almost gets there. The pizza crust was firm. It bent slightly when I picked up a slice. But the crust was just a bit too oily and puffy. I could faintly taste the vegetable oil, and one side of the pizza had a brown air bubble in the crust. Despite the flavorful toppings, I still felt something was missing because the crust wasn't doing its part. The pizza tasted good, but the subpar crust kept it from tasting great.

In the paragraph above, for example, the author starts out by describing her expectations for the crust and then discussing whether the crust itself met those expectations.

Conclusion: Give Them Your Overall Assessment

In your conclusion, you should tell your readers your overall opinion about your experience.

Re-state Your Main Point (Thesis)—Sum up your overall reaction to your subject, preferably in one sentence.

Look to the Future—Predict whether the subject of your review will be a success. Will others enjoy it? Will you go back in the future?

Keep your conclusion brief. Once you have stated your overall point (your thesis) and looked to the future, you should finish up. Don't rehash your comments in the body or add new information.

10.4 How to match a review's style and design to the needs of the audience and . the situations in which they will experience the argument

Developing a Style and Design: Find Your Voice

The style and design of your review depends on your subject, your audience, and the situations in which your audience will experience your argument.

Use Style to Establish Your Voice

Your voice is your most obvious expression of who you are as a reviewer and what you think of your subject. While drafting and revising, think about the emotions you want your voice to convey to your audience.

Create a concept map that expresses your voice—In the center of a screen or a piece of paper, put the word that best describes your emotional reaction to your subject. Add words and phrases to the screen or sheet of paper that associate with that word (Figure 10.4). When used in your review, these well-chosen words will help you establish your voice by developing a theme that runs through the review.

Get into character—Sometimes it helps to imagine you are a well-respected critic who just happens to be reviewing the local pizza place, the new movie release, a performance in town, or an opening at the local gallery. Getting into this kind of character will help you write with a critical, confident, and independent voice.

Be descriptive with plenty of color and sensory detail—As the author, you are responsible for experiencing the product or service in the place of your audience. Describe it in rich detail by describing sights, smells, tastes, sounds, and textures. Color is especially important. These sensory details will help you deepen the experience for your audience while adding depth and richness to your voice.

FIGURE 10.4
Using a Concept Map to Explore Your Voice
Creating a concept map is a good way to develop your voice in a review. Using words and phrases that express how you feel about your subject will help you create a specific tone in your writing.

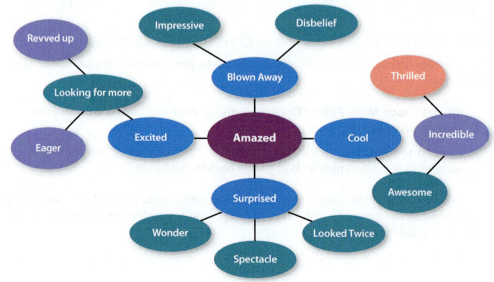

Use Design to Help Your Readers Visualize Your Subject

The more your audience can imagine or see your subject in their minds, the more likely they are to accept your review. That's why putting visuals in your review can be especially helpful.

Take photographs—If you are in a situation in which you can take photographs of your subject, you might use your mobile phone or digital camera to capture a few images. Of course, don't take pictures if you might disrupt the performance or interrupt people doing their jobs. If available, though, images of food, people, services, and locations would help your audience understand what you experienced.

Find images in press materials—Theaters, galleries, and product manufacturers often make professional photographs available to the public, especially the news media. Look on their websites for "Press" or "Media" materials. These photographs can usually be used without asking for permission.

Get images from the Internet—Photographs or visuals that depict to your subject are often available on the Internet (Figure 10.5). *Note: If you use your review for a nonacademic purpose, including posting it on the Internet, you will need to ask permission from the images' owners to include them.*

Match the document design of the publication—If you are writing for a specific publication or medium (the campus newspaper, an entertainment blog, an arts website, or an online magazine), you should try to match the formatting of the publication.

Keep in mind that images should be used to *support* the written text, not replace it. For example, you shouldn't refer your audience to an image without explaining it or interpreting what it shows. Your audience may draw a different conclusion than you expected.

Just want the basics?
Here's what this chapter is about:

1 A review is an analytical critique or detailed assessment of a person, product, service, performance, or project.

2 The goal of a review is to explain why something was effective or not—that is, whether it met your expectations.

3 When reviewing something, you first need to figure out the *common expectations* that you and others would have for your subject.

4 Try to respond to your subject on two levels: as someone experiencing it in a typical way and as someone who is stepping back to review the experience.

5 You might use an open-ended thesis or question thesis in your introduction to focus the review while not giving away the ending.

6 In the body of your review, first summarize your subject. Then analyze it.

7 Your review's conclusions should clearly state your overall assessment of the item you are reviewing.

8 The style of your review depends on your voice. Think about your emotional reaction to your subject. Then reflect that emotion in your voice.

9 To enhance your style, be descriptive with plenty of color and sensory detail.

10 Images, especially photographs, will help your audience imagine or see what you experienced.

1. Think of the music concerts you have attended in the past. With your group, make a list of *common expectations* that you would have for a music concert. Then boil your list down to three to five common expectations that everyone in your group can agree to.

2. Find a movie review on the Internet that you can share with your group. Analyze the content, organization, style, and design of the review. What kinds of information did the author choose to include? Pay special attention to the voice. How does the author succeed or not succeed in establishing her or his voice? Does the voice reflect the emotion the author felt when experiencing the subject? Present your critique of this review to your class.

3. Think of a time when you were disappointed or dissatisfied about a product, service, performance, or project. Make a concept map in which you describe your feelings of disappointment or dissatisfaction. Then compare your map with concept maps from others in your group. What similar things were mentioned by you and your group members? What are some differences?

1. Make a list of five movies that you personally like but you know others generally do not like. Think about the expectations you have for movies like the ones on your list. Then think about the common expectations that other people, in general, have for movies. Choose one of the movies and write a review in which you explain why you like it.

2. With a partner, make a list of local restaurants at which you like to eat. Then make a list of restaurants at which you don't like to eat. Then identify a restaurant that you and your partner disagree about. Separately, you and your partner should make brainstorming lists that identify what you like about that restaurant and a list that describes what you don't like about it. With your lists, debate with your partner about the strengths and weaknesses of the restaurant in front of your group. As you compare experiences, try to figure out what common expectations you share with your partner and where your common expectations differ.

3. Find a show on television that you normally would not watch. Before watching an episode, look for background information on the show. Try to figure out why the show appeals to some kinds of people and why someone like you probably wouldn't want to watch it. Develop a list of common expectations that fit the target audience of this television show. Then watch the show. As you experience it, pay attention to how you experience the show as opposed to how someone in its target audience would experience the show. Write a review in which you explain why the show is effective for some kinds of people, even though it's not effective for you. Where possible, avoid stereotyping the target audience, especially in any way that might seem prejudicial or intolerant.

In this review, student Blair Anthony Robertson offers a rave review of her favorite pizza place. Notice how she provides rich sensory details and uses a friendly, conversational style to show why she thinks this is the best place to go for a great meal.

Dining Review: Masullo Up with the Best Pizza

Blair Robertson

Many folks who love great pizza spend a good portion of their adult lives obsessing over it— searching for it, traveling near and far to eat it and, ultimately, compiling a list of their favorites. These aficionados sift through details obvious and obscure, asking what exactly has to happen to make a great pizza. The water? The dough? The temperature of the oven? Maybe the cheese? The passion of the chef? A touch of magic? When and if they find their way to Masullo Pizza in Sacramento's Land Park neighborhood, their search may well have reached new heights. To taste the pizzas that come out of the 800-degree wood-burning oven here—blistered and charred and bubbling—is to confront a mix of art and science and, surely, a touch of the unexplained.

Masullo is the work of Robert Masullo, who opened this humble but stylish pizza place four years ago, delighting customers with how good the pies were and how serious he was about his craft. He continued to watch and test and study and tweak, until he was turning excellent pies into awe-inspiring pies.

These days Masullo's reputation is rippling beyond the boundaries of the neighborhood, the city, even the state. Recently, Chris Bianco, the Bronx-born, trash-talking pizza demigod, declared Masullo one of the very best practitioners in the high-stakes religion known as Neapolitan pizza-making.

One night a few years back, everything seemed perfect—the dough looked and felt perfect, the timing of the orders was perfect, the vibe in the room was just so—and Masullo knew he was making pizza at its highest level. He wrote on the Masullo Facebook page, "See Naples and die." Translation: It doesn't get any better than this.

That's not hype or braggadocio. We dropped by on several occasions   5 recently to work our way through the assortment of pizzas on the menu, some with sauce, some without. We came away with a simple answer to explain this kind of greatness: Though there is certainly magic, there are no tricks.

At Masullo, it is all about time-honored techniques, old-fashioned values, quality ingredients, attention to detail, high standards and hard work.

The pizzas were so good, the flavors and textures so enthralling— from the crust to the sauce to the little cubes of premium bacon or the medallions of spicy sausage—I can recall the experience weeks later as if I had just polished off a slice moments ago.

It is impossible to pick a favorite. For unadorned simplicity, try the Margherita—tomato sauce, mozzarella, basil. For meaty and spicy, dig into the sausage with a sprinkling of red chili flakes. We almost bypassed the "American" pie with pepperoni, perhaps from memories of too many salty, dreadful pepperoni pizzas from years ago. The pies without sauce, too, were excellent, including the "Jacqueline," which features thin slices of potato and thick, meaty pieces of bacon.

OK, maybe the pepperoni was the best of the best. When I bit into it, there was a sudden, soothing quality, a silky, creamy mouthfeel I found amazing. "See Naples and die." We have eaten pizza at some of the great Neapolitan-style joints in the country, from Delfina in San Francisco to Motorino and Luzzo's in New York City. Masullo is in the big leagues.

I asked the chef about the mouthfeel of his pizza. He talked about the extra virgin olive oil, which is made in small batches by Frate Sole in Woodland. Four years ago, he would drizzle the oil onto the pizza after it came out of the oven. One day, he baked a pie with the olive oil applied beforehand. And there was magic.

10   Where to begin with how all this pizza supremacy is achieved? With the wood for the oven? Each log is split with an ax out back so the size and shape are precisely what the oven needs in terms of heat and burn time. It takes longer to do it this way, but it's the right way. With the starter (also known as sourdough starter or natural leaven)? Stored in a small wine fridge set at 62 to 64 degrees, it is mixed, or fed, each day with flour and water until it bubbles up and doubles in size. It's the life of the dough, the foundation of the next batch. This starter contains natural—not commercial—yeast and is a key component of the crust's flavor, texture and character. It takes longer to make dough this way, but it's the right way.

Then there's the flour used for the dough. It remains a work in progress, even as good as the crust already is. Right now, it's a blend of "00" flour imported from Italy and premium artisan bread flour milled in the Bay Area by a company called Giusto's.

The starter is fed in the evening. The next morning, Masullo mixes the dough, which is then stored in refrigeration for two days, at which time the flavor builds and the dough develops character. In other words, you don't just whip together a batch of dough. We tried to order pizza one night and were told they were out of dough. It's just the way it is in the old-fashioned world of artisan pizza.

The crust is crucial. Though it is largely considered, as Masullo describes it, "a neutral device to carry other flavors," the crust is what distinguishes great pizza from good pizza. Here, it is thin and soft, but with a heft or pull to it as you chew. You'll see telltale air pockets throughout. You'll notice bits of char. The crust blisters the way a good sourdough crust does. You can taste a hint of salt. You can smell the earthiness of the wheat flour.

It is well known by now that Italians eat this style of pizza with a knife and fork. Early on, some Masullo customers balked at the thinness, the softness, the sogginess, of the pies. They wondered why there was so little cheese, and just a smattering of pepperoni or sausage. In this country, we have a certain amount of baggage when it comes to pizza, things we learned during the age of instant coffee, TV dinners and fast food. But Masullo returns us to a time when things were not so rushed, so instant, so easy. It is an excellent place, a revelation and, in the best of ways, the end of the road for those in search of greatness.

A CLOSER LOOK AT
Dining Review: Masullo Up with the Best Pizza

1. How does the article follow the genre pattern described in this chapter? In what ways does this review bend or stretch the genre?

2. How does the list of common expectations in the article compare with that listed in Figure 10.2 of the chapter?

3. Describe the style and voice Robertson uses in the article. How do both enhance the level of detail within the piece? How does he use his senses to better describe Masullo to his audience?

IDEAS FOR
Arguing

1. Choose a product to review that a new college student would need to buy (for example, a laptop) and generate a brainstorming list that identifies your common expectations. In an e-mail to your instructor, describe how you would approach your review of the chosen product based on your brainstorming list.

2. Go to RottenTomatoes.com on the Internet and select a recently released movie. Find a positive review and a negative review of the movie and write a comparison argument (Chapter 6) that compares and contrasts their content, style, voice, and angles. Are they working from the same common list of expectations? Looking closely at their arguments, why do you think these two reviewers came to different conclusions?

The Passion of David Bazan

JESSICA HOPPER

When popular entertainers or other cultural idols change their message, they might disappoint many of their fans who have identified closely with their attitudes and beliefs. In this review of the Christian musician David Bazan, Jessica Hopper describes his change and his fans' reactions. As you read, notice how Hopper weaves empirical research (interviewing Bazan and interpreting song lyrics) into this review to tell the story.

"People used to compare him to Jesus," says a back-stage manager as David Bazan walks off-stage, guitar in hand. "But not so much anymore."

It's Thursday, July 2, and Bazan has just finished his set at Cornerstone, the annual Christian music festival held on a farm near Bushnell, Illinois. He hasn't betrayed his crowd the way Dylan did when he went electric—this is something very different. The kids filling the 1,500-capacity tent know their Jesus from their Judas. There was a time when Bazan's fans believed he was speaking, or rather singing, the Word. Not so much anymore.

As front man for Pedro the Lion, the band he led from 1995 till 2005, Bazan was Christian indie rock's first big crossover star, predating Sufjan by nearly a decade and paving the way for the music's success outside the praise circuit. But as he straddled the secular and spiritual worlds, Bazan began to struggle with his faith. Unable to banish from his mind the possibility that the God he'd loved and prayed to his whole life didn't exist, he started drinking heavily. In '05, the last time he played Cornerstone, he was booted off the grounds for being shitfaced, a milk jug full of vodka in his hand. (The festival is officially dry.)

I worked as Bazan's publicist from 2000 till 2004. When I ran into him in April—we were on a panel together at the Calvin College Festival of Faith & Music in Grand Rapids—I hadn't seen him or talked to him in five and a half years. The first thing he said to me was "I'm not sure if you know this, but my relationship with Christ has changed pretty dramatically in the last few years."

He went on to explain that since 2004 he's been flitting between atheist, skeptic, and agnostic, and that lately he's hovering around agnostic—he can't flat-out deny the presence of God in the world, but he doesn't exactly believe in him either.

Pedro the Lion won a lot of secular fans in part because Bazan's lyrics—keen examinations of faith, set to fuzzed-out guitar hooks—have a through-a-glass-darkly quality, acknowledging the imperfection of human understanding rather than insisting on the obviousness of an absolute truth. As the post-9/11 culture wars began to heat up, Pedro the Lion albums took a turn toward the parabolic: an outraged Bazan churned out artful songs about what befalls the righteous and the folly of those who believe God is on their side.

Bazan's relationship with the divine started out pretty uncomplicated, though. Raised outside Seattle in the Pentecostal church where his father was the music director, he hewed closely to Christian orthodoxy, attended Bible college, and married at 23. Now 33, he didn't do a lot of thinking about politics until the 1999 WTO protests. "Growing up, Christianity didn't feel oppressive for the most part, because it was filtered through my parents. They were and are so sincere, and I saw in them a really pure expression of unconditional love and service," he says. "Once I stepped away, I could see the oppression of it."

Bazan's *Curse Your Branches*, due September 1 on Barsuk, is a visceral accounting of what happened after that. It's a harrowing breakup record—except he's dumping God, Jesus, and the evangelical life. It's his first full-length solo album and also his most autobiographical effort: its drunken narratives, spasms of spiritual dissonance, and family tensions are all scenes from the recent past.

Bazan says he tried to Band-Aid his loss of faith and the painful end of Pedro the Lion with about 18 months of "intense" drinking. "If I didn't have responsibilities, if I wasn't watching [my daughter] Ellanor, I had a deep drive to get blacked out," he says. But as he made peace with where he found himself, the compulsion to get obliterated began to wane. On *Curse Your Branches,* Bazan sometimes directs the blame and indignation at himself, other times at Jesus and the faith. He's mourning what he's lost, and he knows there's no going back.

10 "All fallen leaves should curse their branches / For not letting them decide where they should fall / And not letting them refuse to fall at all," he sings on the title track, with more than a touch of fuck-you in his voice. On "When We Fell," backed by a galloping beat and Wilson-boys harmonies, he calls faith a curse put on him by God: "If my mother cries when I tell her what I discovered / Then I hope she remembers she told me to follow my heart / And if you bully her like you've done me with fear of damnation / Then I hope she can see you for what you are."

The album closer, "In Stitches," may be the best song Bazan's ever written. It's the most emotionally bare piece on the album and as close as he comes to a complete thesis:

This brown liquor wets my tongue
My fingers find the stitches
Firmly back and forth they run
I need no other memory
Of the bits of me I left

When all this lethal drinking
Is hopefully to forget
About you

He follows it with an even more devastating verse, confessing that his efforts to erase God have failed:

I might as well admit it
Like I've even got a choice
The crew have killed the captain
But they still can hear his voice
A shadow on the water
A whisper in the wind
On long walks my with daughter
Who is lately full of questions
About you
About you

The second "about you" comes in late, in a 15 keening falsetto, and those two words carry his entire tangle of feelings—anger, desire, confusion, grief.

Since the jug-of-vodka incident, Bazan has kept a pretty low profile, doing a couple modest solo tours and releasing an EP of raw-sounding songs on Barsuk. Pedro the Lion was a reliable paycheck—most of its albums sold in the neighborhood of 50,000 copies, and the group toured regularly, drawing 400 to 600 people a night. His most recent tour couldn't have been more different: Bazan doesn't have a road band put together yet for his solo stuff, but he couldn't afford to wait for Curse Your Branches to come out. So he found another way to keep in touch with his most devoted fans, booking 60 solo shows in houses and other noncommercial spaces. He played intimate acoustic sets to maybe 40 people each night, at $20 a ticket, and took questions between songs—some of them, unsurprisingly, about the tough spiritual questions his new material raises.

Despite his outspokenness on those questions, he was invited back to Cornerstone for the first time this year.

"I know David has a long history of being a seeker and trying to navigate through his faith. Cornerstone is open to that," says John Herrin, the festival's director. "We welcome plenty of musicians who may not identify themselves as Christians but are artists with an ongoing connection to faith. . . . We're glad to have him back. We don't give up on people; we don't give up on the kids here who are seeking, trying to figure out what they don't believe and what they do. This festival was built on patience."

At Cornerstone, where I catch up with him behind the fair-food midway, Bazan laughs when I suggest that he's there trying to save the Christians. "I am. I am really invested, because I came up in it and I love a lot of evangelical Christians—I care what happens with the movement," he says. "The last 30 years of it have been hijacked; the boomer evangelicals, they were seduced in the most embarrassing and scandalous way into a social, political, and economical posture that is the antithesis of Jesus's teaching."

20   With *Curse Your Branches* and in his recent shows, he's inverting the usual call to witness: "You might be the only Christian they ever meet." He's the doubter's witness, and he might be the only agnostic some of these Christian kids ever really listen to.

When I talk to some of those kids in the merch tent the day after Bazan's set, many of them seem to be trying to spin the new songs, straining to categorize them as Christian so they can justify continuing to listen to them. One fan says it's good that Bazan is singing about the perils of sin, "particularly sexual sin." Another interprets the songs as a witness of addiction, the testimony of the stumbling man.

Cultural critic and progressive Christian author David Dark, who since 2003 has become one of Bazan's closest friends, claims that Bazan's skepticism and anger are in line with biblical tradition. "I doubt this is what your average Cornerstone attendee means, but when David is addressing his idea of his God, the one that he fears exists but refuses to believe in, when he is telling him, 'If this is the situation with us and you, then fuck you—the people who love you, I hope they see you for who you are,' when he's doing that, he is at his most biblical. If we are referring to the deep strains of complaint and prayers and tirades against conceptions of God in the Bible—yes, then in that way he's in your Christian tradition. But I disagree that he's an advocate for the biblical."

When I tell Bazan that there are kids at Cornerstone resisting the clear message of his songs, he's surprised. "That someone could listen to what I was saying and think that I was saying it apologetically—like, in a way that characterizes [doubt] as the wrong posture—bums me out, but that's pretty high-concept given how I'm presenting this stuff. So I have to hand it to someone who can keep on spinning what is so clearly something else." He pauses for a long moment, then adds, "I don't want to be that misunderstood."

During the two days I follow Bazan and his fans around the Cornerstone campus, though, it becomes clear that he isn't really misunderstood at all. Everyone knows what he's singing about—what's happening is that his listeners are taking great pains to sidestep the obvious. "Well, his songs have always been controversial," one says, but when asked to pinpoint the source of the controversy suggests it's because he swears—nothing about not believing in hell or not taking the Bible as God's word. Bazan's agnosticism is the elephant in the merch tent.

Fans rhapsodize about Bazan's work: they   25 love his honesty, they love how they can relate to him, how he's not proselytizing, how he's speaking truth—but they don't tend to delve into what exactly that truth might be. Brice Evans, a 24-year-old from Harrisburg, Illinois, who came to Cornerstone specifically to see Bazan's set, dances artfully around it. "He's showing a side of Christianity that no other band shows," Evans says. "He's trying to get a message across that's more than that."

It's hard to say if anybody is conscious of the irony: the "side of Christianity" Bazan sings about is disenfranchisement from it.

"I think with *Curse Your Branches* David expands the space of the talk-about-able," says Dark. "It's not confessional in the sense that he's down on himself and trying to confess something to God in hopes of being forgiven. I think that's what crowds are trying to make of him, but they're going to have a tougher time when they get the record."

Bazan is known for his dialogues with fans, and during his set he's affable, taking questions from the crowd. Tonight's audience, openly anxious and awed, keeps it light at first: "Would you rather be a werewolf or a vampire?" Then he opens with the new album's lead track, "Hard to Be," a sobering song with an especially hard-hitting second verse:

Wait just a minute/
  You expect me to believe
That all this misbehaving
Grew from one enchanted tree?
And helpless to fight it
We should all be satisfied
With this magical explanation
For why the living die
And why it's hard to be
Hard to be, hard to be
A decent human being?

30   By the time he finishes those lines I can see half a dozen people crying; a woman near me is trembling and sobbing. Others have their heads in their hands. Many look stunned, but no one leaves. When the song ends, the applause is thunderous.

After Bazan plays a cover of Leonard Cohen's "Hallelujah," reinstating the sacrilegious verses left out of the best-known versions, someone shouts, "How's your soul?" Bazan looks up from tuning his guitar and says, "My soul? Oh, it's fine." This elicits an "Amen, brother!" from the back of the tent.

Following Bazan's set a throng of fans—kids, young women with babies on their hips, a handful of youth pastors—queues up around the side of the stage to talk to him. Some kids want hugs and ask geeked-out questions, but just as many attempt to feel him out in a sly way. "I really wished you had played 'Lullaby,'"

says one kid, naming a very early Pedro the Lion song that's probably the most worshipful in Bazan's catalog. A few gently bait him, referring to scripture the way gang members throw signs, eager for a response that will reveal where Bazan is really at.

During discussions like this Bazan doesn't usually get into the subtle barometric fluctuations in his relationship with Jesus, but that still leaves room for plenty of postshow theological talk. "This process feels necessary and natural for these people," he says. "They're in a precarious situation—maybe I am too. To maintain their particular posture, they have to figure out: Do they need to get distance from me, or is it just safe enough to listen to? I empathize as people are trying to gauge, 'Is this guy an atheist? Because I heard he was.'"

Bazan has chosen sides, but old ideas linger. "Some time ago, we were discussing [the Pedro the Lion song] 'Foregone Conclusions,'" Dark says. "I told him I was impressed with the lines 'You were too busy steering conversation toward the Lord / To hear the voice of the Spirit / Begging you to shut the fuck up / You thought it must be the devil / Trying to make you go astray / Besides it could not have been the Lord / Because you don't believe He talks that way.' I thought, what a liberating word for people who've been shoved around by all manner of brainwash. But also Dave's doing something even more subtle, as many interpret the unforgivable sin to be blasphemy against the Holy Spirit—confusing the voice of God for the voice of the devil—so there's a whole 'nother level of theological devastation going on in the song.

"When I brought it up, he laughed and told 35 me he still worries about going to hell for that one. He knows that it's horribly funny that he feels that way, but he won't lie by saying he's entirely over it. He's both 100 percent sincere and 100 percent ironically detached. He's haunted even as he pushes forward, saying what he feels even though he half fears doing so will be cosmically costly for him."

After a long few years in the wilderness, Bazan seems happy—though he's still parsing out his beliefs, he's visibly relieved to be out and open about where he's not at. "It's more comfortable for me to be agnostic," he says. "There's less internal tension by far—that's even with me duking it out with my perception of who God is on a pretty regular basis, and having a lot of uncertainty on that level. For now, just being is enough. Whether things happen naturally, completely outside an author, or whether the dynamics of earth and people are that way because God created them—or however you want to credit it—if you look around and pay attention and observe, there is enough right here to know how to act, to know how to live, to be at peace with one another.

"Because I grew up believing in hell and reckoning, there is a voice in me that says, 'That might not cut it with the man upstairs,' but I think that that has to be enough. For me it is enough."

A CLOSER LOOK
The Passion of David Bazan

1. Why do you think Bazan's fans felt "betrayed" by his change of message in 2005? In your view, are their feelings justified? Point to specific places in the article to back up your conclusions.

2. Most reviews are persuasive rather than generative, because they announce a specific assessment of the product, service, or performance. Here Hopper chooses instead to explain how Bazan has changed, providing ample lyrics and Bazan's own statements to illustrate the origins of Bazan's change and how that change comes out in his music. Why do you think she chooses not to overtly announce her assessment, and how does this choice affect the success of her review?

3. The title of this piece uses the word "passion," which has a special meaning in Christian teachings. In what ways does this article describe Bazan's passion in both the usual sense (intense emotion and enthusiasm) but also the Christian sense (suffering, in particular Jesus Christ's suffering at the crucifixion)?

IDEAS FOR
Arguing

1. Choose an entertainer you have identified with and create a visual essay that describes that person's "journey" and message. You can make a slide show, poster, or visual narrative to illustrate that journey by including images, sound, and words.

2. Write a rhetorical analysis of "The Passion of David Bazan." First, you will need to figure out what you think is Hopper's overall purpose. Is she trying to persuade her readers to some point, or is she trying instead to urge her readers to thoughtfully consider an idea? Pay particular attention to the way Hopper uses framing and narration.

Evaluations— Arguing about Value

CHAPTER 11

IN THIS CHAPTER, YOU WILL LEARN—

11.1 How evaluations are arguments that assess value and quality

11.2 Techniques for inventing the content of an evaluation, including a set of criteria

11.3 Strategies for organizing the content of an evaluation

11.4 Ways to use plain style and basic design to create an impartial tone and look

E valuations are used to assess the value and quality of a product, service, project, or employee. These arguments are similar to reviews, but they are different in some key ways. First, an evaluation uses a defined *set of criteria* to determine objectively whether something or someone has accomplished specific goals. Second, an evaluation is often used to give others feedback about their strengths and areas where they can improve. Both evaluations and reviews are used to argue about quality, but reviews are more opinion based while evaluations are more objective. Evaluations are used to measure value.

11.1 Evaluations are arguments that assess value and quality.

In print and online, you can read numerous evaluations of mobile phones, cars, televisions, vacation spots, and local businesses and services (Figure 11.1). For instance, if you were trying to decide which mobile phone to buy, you would likely check out the evaluations published by trusted sources like *Consumer Reports* or *PC Magazine*. These evaluations assess the quality and features of each product against a consistent set of criteria and help you decide which phone is best for you.

Evaluations are both generative and persuasive. They are generative because you and others will need to collaborate to figure out how to determine quality and

Performance Factors

	Poor	Good	Excellent
Quality of Work	☐	☐	☑
Quantity of Work	☐	☐	☑
Dependability	☐	☑	☐
Communication Skills	☐	☐	☑
Supervision	☐	☐	☑
Leadership Skills	☐	☐	☑
Initiative	☐	☐	☐
Cooperation	☐	☐	☐
Relations	☐	☐	☐
Adaptability	☐	☐	☐
Versatility	☐	☐	☐

FIGURE 11.1 Evaluations Help People Make Decisions about Value
Evaluations are used to measure the value of products, services, projects, and people.

measure your subject's value. When used as generative arguments, evaluations are often written by teams. Evaluations can also be also persuasive. You will at times need to persuade your audience that you have properly determined whether a product or service is worth buying, whether a project is accomplishing its goals, or whether an employee is doing a good job.

In college, your professors will ask you to write evaluations to assess the quality of projects, products, and processes. They will ask you to develop criteria for measuring the value of something, and then you will need to discuss its merits and shortcomings.

In your career, you will use evaluations to recommend whether your company or organization should purchase a product or use a service. As a manager, you will write detailed evaluations of projects and the employees who work for you. Likewise, your supervisors will write evaluations about you and your projects.

11.2 Techniques for inventing the content of an evaluation, including a set of criteria

Inventing the Content of Your Evaluation

When writing an evaluation, your primary goal is to offer an impartial assessment of your subject in a way that minimizes your personal bias and feelings. Being impartial means using a set of criteria developed in advance to make an independent assessment of a product, service, project, or person. Keep in mind that any criteria you choose will have some bias. Nevertheless, you can identify and limit your biases while gaining a critical perspective on your subject.

QUICK View

Generative

Persuasive

Generative Argument—Evaluations are generative because they rely on a set of criteria that were often developed collaboratively. The evaluation's criteria frame how people measure value, so these standards are often negotiated before an evaluation is written.

Persuasive Argument—Evaluations rely on reasoning *(logos)* as they define an objective set of standards to measure value in a logical way. Authority *(ethos)* is also an important component of an evaluation because the audience needs to trust the objectivity and experience of the evaluator.

Genre Patterns

These patterns suggest two ways to organize an evaluation. You should alter these patterns to fit the specific needs of your evaluation.

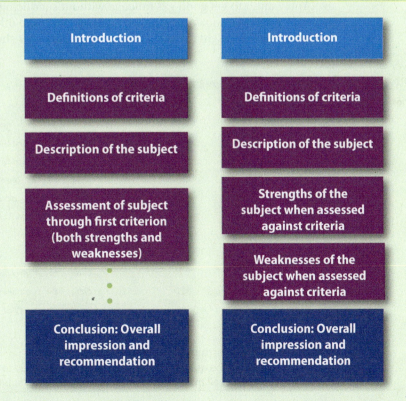

217

FIGURE 11.2 How Would You Evaluate This Car?
An evaluation of a product, like a car, needs to rely on more than an opinion or how someone feels about it. An evaluation should be based on a defined set of criteria.

Develop a Set of Criteria

As you begin inventing the content of your evaluation, use brainstorm a list of the qualities you would expect your subject to have. For example, let's say you want to evaluate this year's Mini Cooper Clubman (Figure 11.2). What are the qualities you would expect this kind of car to have?

Of course, you probably want a sporty car like this one to be quick and responsive. You want it to get good gas mileage without sacrificing fun. And, let's be honest, you want a car that looks good and stands out from the other cars on the road. Your brainstorming list might include some or all of the items shown in Figure 11.3.

Things I would expect in a car	
Cool appearance	Available options
Suitable engine	Good gas mileage
Reliability	Available accessories
Good crash-test results	Low maintenance costs
Visibility on the road	Can carry at least 4 passengers
Smooth lines	Can carry my stuff
Stop quickly	Roof rack available
Reasonable price	Safety
Minimal engine noise	Air bags
Good performance	Side crash support
Good acceleration	Stability systems
Comfortable interior	Traction control
Easy-to-read instrument panel	

FIGURE 11.3 Brainstorming for Criteria
Brainstorming a list of the qualities you value most is a good way to start figuring out the criteria for your evaluation. List all the qualities you would expect your subject to have.

This brainstorming list is a good start, but it's too long to be useful as a set of criteria. After all, if you wrote individually about each of these qualities, your evaluation would become tiresome for your audience. Moreover, this list implies that critical items, like safety, are equivalent to less-critical items, like a roof rack.

To avoid these problems, you should sort these items into a list of three to seven major categories, which will eventually become your evaluation criteria. For example, here are five categories based on the list in Figure 11.3:

Exterior appeal—cool look, smooth lines, attractive colors, available accessories, distinctive appearance, roof rack

Performance—good acceleration, handles well, stops quickly, reliable traction control, stability system

Interior comfort—minimal engine noise, easy-to-use controls, readable dials, legroom, headroom, space for passengers, comfortable seats

Expenses—affordable list price, good gas mileage, low maintenance costs, affordable accessories, low repair costs, warranty

Safety—safety features, airbags, crumple zones

Keep in mind that different audiences will value some items more than others. Choose your major criteria with your audience's needs and values in mind.

Research: Define Your Set of Criteria

You now need to *define* what you mean by these specific criteria. That way your audience will know what you mean by words like "performance" and "interior comfort."

For example, to evaluate a car, you could define your criteria by researching sites like the Insurance Institute for Highway Safety (IIHS) or the National Highway Traffic Safety Administration (NHTSA). Car magazines would also be helpful to determine what a buyer should expect regarding costs, visual appeal, and comfort.

As you do your research, look for both quantitative and qualitative attributes to help assess your subject.

Quantitative attributes—Quantitative items allow you to compare numbers, such as sticker price, gas mileage, and years of warranty coverage.

Qualitative attributes—Qualitative items involve aspects that cannot be measured, such as the car's physical attractiveness or its interior comfort.

Your research should give you a good idea about what kinds of measurable and nonmeasurable qualities you expect in the product, service, project, or person you are evaluating.

Research: Gather Evidence on Your Subject

With your criteria identified and defined, you can now collect information on the subject of your evaluation. The strongest evaluations are ones that are built on a combination of online, print, and empirical sources.

Electronic sources—Use Internet search engines to gather evidence and discover what others have written about your subject. On the Internet, find the facts and data you need to determine whether your subject measures up against your criteria.

Print sources—Most products and services have been critiqued in popular and trade magazines that are available at your library or online. Magazines that specialize in your subject's area, such as *Bicycling* for bicycles or *Outside* for camping equipment, can be especially helpful.

Empirical sources—Examine and interact with your subject directly. If you are evaluating a car, for example, go out and take a test drive. Bring a checklist along that helps you rate the car according to your criteria. If you are evaluating a service, try it out and keep notes about how well that service worked. You can also experiment on your subject, if appropriate.

After you have gathered your evidence, triangulate your sources to determine the reliability of the information they offer. Triangulation is discussed in Chapter 16 on "Developing Your Research Process."

MOVES for Arguing

Here are some helpful moves that you can use as you draft your evaluation.

If you're looking for a _____, you want it to have these qualities. First, it should be able to _____. Second, it should be _____. And finally, a good _____ should _____.

The _____ has excellent _____ because it scores well against these criteria.

The _____ falls short of expectations in the areas of _____ and _____.

If _____ is important to you, you'll be impressed with (be disappointed by) the _____ of this product.

While I found the _____ only mediocre with respect to its _____, I was impressed that _____ is truly exceptional.

Overall, the _____ is _____. It measures up well against its competitors in the following ways: _____, _____, and _____.

11.3 Strategies for organizing the content of an evaluation

Organizing and Drafting Your Evaluation

Evaluations usually follow straightforward organizational patterns, as shown in the QuickView on page 217. They typically define a set of criteria and then use those criteria to evaluate the product, service, project, or person.

Introduction

Your evaluation's introduction should make some or all of the following moves:

Grab your audience's attention—If a grabber is appropriate, you could ask an intriguing question, tell an anecdote, or make an intriguing statement. For example,

> Have you ever wondered whether a typical college graduate can afford a sporty car that can also haul a load of stuff?

> Like many people, I fell in love with the Cooper Mini the first time I saw one. I was walking down Michigan Avenue in Chicago and a cherry-red Mini zipped by with a British flag painted on top. I was hooked.

Identify your topic—Tell your audience exactly what you are evaluating. Make sure you name and define your subject early in the introduction.

Identify your purpose—If needed, you can be blunt about your purpose. Go ahead and tell your audience that you are evaluating your subject.

State your main point (thesis)—Your main point expresses your overall assessment of your subject. The main point is often stated directly in the introduction:

> **Weak thesis**—The Cooper Mini Clubman is a good car.

> **Better thesis**—For an average college graduate, the Cooper Mini Clubman can be a bit costly up front, but its attractive appearance, spacious interior, and solid safety record make this car both practical and fun.

Some evaluations, especially in magazines, use a question thesis in the introduction. Then, the conclusion reveals an overall assessment.

Offer background information—Give your audience a basic understanding of your subject and why you are evaluating it. Information about the *who, what, where, when, why,* and *how* of the subject can be useful.

Stress the importance of the topic—Explain audience why your subject and your evaluation is important to them. You don't need to be direct ("The Cooper Mini Clubman is important to you because..."), but you can mention that a practical first car is an important choice for a college graduate.

A solid introduction sets the stage for the detailed comments that will appear in the body of the introduction.

Definitions of Criteria

Define your criteria by establishing guidelines that will help you and your audience determine if your subject is measuring up to specific standards. For example, here are definitions of the criteria one student developed for evaluating whether a Mini Cooper Clubman would be a good car for a recent college graduate:

External appeal—Let's be honest. A recent college graduate wants a first car to look cool and turn some heads. It needs to stand out. People in their twenties want to drive cars that look unique and distinctive, because the days of minivans and other grocery getters will arrive soon enough. The car's body should have smooth lines and interesting curves. Colors should be bold: red, dark blue, lime green, or bright yellow. And the buyer should be able to accessorize the car with sport kits, alloy wheels, spoilers, and other personalizing features.

Performance—It's too early in life to settle for a car that just gets from Point A to Point B. A new graduate's car needs to have some zip. It needs to accelerate to 60 mph in less than 10 seconds. It needs to be able to handle downtown commuter traffic with good stability, reliable traction, and controlled stops that avoid skidding.

Interior comfort—Most young people are willing to give up some comfort for an attractive interior. But they shouldn't need to sacrifice easy-to-use controls and readable dials. Any car, even a sporty one, should have ample headroom and legroom for the driver and his or her friends. For a recent college graduate, road trips are expected, so the car needs to be able to hold at least three passengers with gear. The cabin should also be fairly quiet. The engine noise should not drown out conversations with friends.

Expenses—After college, money will be tight with student loans to pay off and lots of other stuff to buy. So the car can't be a cash sinkhole. A first car needs to cost something in the $25,000 range (or less). It will need high gas mileage (at least 30 mpg), and the maintenance costs will need to be less than a few hundred per year. The warranty is especially important for a young car buyer. The car needs to give at least three years of full coverage to cover any breakdowns. Any new car should be reliable, meaning minimal repairs, for at least six years.

Safety—New college graduates have a lot to live for, so the car needs to be safe. These days, airbags and antilock brakes are mostly standard. The car should receive at least a "Good" rating in front and side crash protection from the Insurance Institute for Highway Safety (IIHS). The car should be visible enough to be seen from a distance and from another car's side and rear windows.

Criteria usually include a blend of quantitative and qualitative standards to describe what is considered good or bad by the evaluator.

Description of the Subject

Now that you have defined your criteria, it is time to offer a full description of your subject. First provide an overall description of how your subject looks. Then divide your subject into its major parts and describe each of these parts separately.

At this point, your description should be as impartial as possible. Save any evaluative comments or opinions for later.

> The Mini Cooper Clubman looks like the more common standard Mini, but the Clubman is somewhat larger in size. It still has that sporty, retro, all-too-British look with round headlamps, a snub nose, and wheels that seem a little too big for its body. The body itself is a sleekly rounded box with a chrome grill and an additional set of lights in the front that makes it look ready for a road rally. The Clubman is 3.2 inches wider in stance than the standard Mini, and it is about 10 inches longer. That makes the Clubman a little roomier, with enough headroom to make even a six-foot-plus driver comfortable. There is also more space for your gear. The cabin features 9.2 cubic feet of cargo space with the rear seats up and a spacious 32.8 cubic feet with the seats down.
>
> According to the Mini Cooper USA website, the Clubman has a 1.6L 16-valve engine that gives it 121 horsepower. The basic model has a 6-speed manual transmission, but an automatic is also available. The car gets 35 mpg on the highway and 27 mpg in town. It can reach 60 mph in 8.9 seconds, and it has a top speed of 126 mph.
>
> The Clubman comes with many of the safety features that are becoming standard on cars today. It has antilock brakes with cornering brake and dynamic stability control. The car has a six-airbag system with front and side airbags for the driver and passengers. Its 4-foot, 8.1-inch height makes it more visible than most comparable sports cars its size.
>
> The Clubman's suggested retail price is $21,400, and it comes with a four-year/50,000-mile limited warranty with full maintenance for three years or 50,000 miles. J. D. Power, a customer service survey company, regularly gives the Clubman high marks for reliability (Edmunds, "Reliability").

In this description, the car has been divided into four major areas: exterior, engine, safety features, and costs. Each of these features is then described in some depth.

Assessment of the Subject

You are ready to make some judgments about your subject. Evaluations tend to follow one of two paths at this point:

Criterion-by-criterion pattern—You can address each criterion separately, discussing the subject's strengths and weaknesses. (See the QuickView's left diagram on page 217.)

Strengths-and-weaknesses pattern—You can first discuss all of the subject's strengths according to your criteria. Afterward, you can discuss the subject's weaknesses (See the QuickView's right diagram on page 217.)

The criterion-by-criterion evaluation is probably better for longer evaluations, because this pattern will allow you to balance your positive comments with your negative critiques. The strengths-and-weaknesses pattern works well for smaller evaluations.

Here is an example of a strengths-and-weaknesses discussion of the Mini Cooper Clubman addressing the criterion "external appearance."

External Appearance: Very Good

On the plus side, the appearance of the Mini Cooper Clubman still turns heads, though the larger body takes away some of the sporty look of the original Minis. The Clubman still has that boxy but nicely rounded look that stands out from other cars. Its colors are playfully bright, and the chrome in front makes it look retro. There are many accessories available, like sport packages, striping, grill ornaments, and British flag mirrors and roof, to make it even more distinctive. Let's be honest—this car looks fun to drive. It's the kind of car that your friends will beg you to take to the store. It's the kind of car that gets looks from people you might want to meet.

The downside of the larger Clubman is that it looks less agile than the original. Most people immediately sense the larger size of the Clubman, which makes it seem bulkier than the standard Mini. It's kind of like seeing one of your old friends who has recently gained a little weight. The car still looks good, but it doesn't appear as nimble and quick as a typical sports car.

Here, both the strengths and weaknesses are discussed. Notice how these comments are based on the defined criterion offered earlier. This direct connection between each criterion and your comments will make your evaluation sound objective to your audience.

Conclusion

Your audience will expect the conclusion to wrap up with an overall assessment of the subject (your main point or thesis). You may have already stated your overall assessment in the introduction. If so, you should state it again here with more emphasis. If you didn't state your overall assessment in the introduction, you need to state it directly in the conclusion.

The Mini Cooper Clubman is a great car, and we recommend it for any new college graduate who has landed a decent job. The Clubman features good performance, and it is reasonably priced. It also has the additional space required for the college grad who occasionally needs to cram friends or a pile of stuff into a car. Your minivan days may be ahead of you, so now is the time to buy a car like this one.

A good conclusion briefly states the main point of the evaluation. Then it stresses the importance of the subject and offers a "look to the future." The conclusion should be as short and concise as possible. No new information should be introduced at this point in the evaluation.

Style and Design in Evaluations

11.4 Ways to use plain style and basic design to create an impartial tone and look

The style and design of an evaluation should reflect the purpose of the evaluation and the places where it will be read. Workplace evaluations tend to be plain and analytical, making them sound and look impartial. Evaluations in popular venues, like magazines or consumer websites, often have a more distinctive voice and design.

Using Style to Sound Objective

Plain style doesn't mean a flat, boring tone. It means the sentences tend to be simple and straightforward. Meanwhile, the paragraphs should make direct claims and provide support for those claims.

Keep Sentences Simple and Active—Badly written evaluations often sound stuffy and convoluted because their authors want to share too much technical information with the audience, or they rely too heavily on the passive voice. Simpler sentences put doers in the subject slot and use active verbs.

Don't Sound Too Technical—Your words and phrases should be written at a level your audience can understand. This text sounds too technical:

The 1.6L 16-valve alloy engine with a 6-speed Gertrag transmission employs a transverse engine design with fully variable valve lift and timing to improve responsiveness and capacity in variable driving conditions.

Phrases like "transverse engine design" and "variable valve lift and timing" are engineering gobbledygook to most people. So unless your readers are automotive engineers or sports car enthusiasts, you should simplify the sentence by removing some of the technical jargon.

The engineers who designed the Mini Cooper Clubman decided to use a powerful 1.6L 16-valve engine that quickly responds to the driver's wishes.

This simpler sentence still tells the audience what they need to know without all the technical information that they don't need.

Avoid Clichés—Evaluations occasionally devolve into strings of clichés because the author wants to sound like an insider who knows the lingo of the field.

The Clubman has the ponies to gitty up and go, and its brakes allow you to stop on a dime. Get ready for whistles from people on the street, because this little spitfire is ready to turn heads and leave the competition in the dust.

The occasional cliché is fine, but strings of clichés like the ones in this example become tiresome and irritating to the audience. Here's a revision of the sentence:

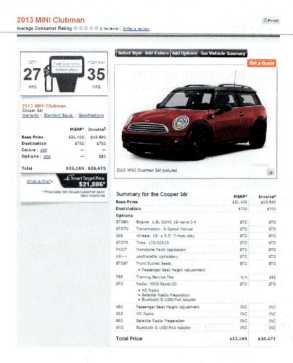

FIGURE 11.4 Using a Table to Highlight Strengths and Weaknesses
This table from Cars.com website gives the audience a quick overview of the technical aspects of the car.

The Clubman's engine and brakes work together well, giving the car excellent acceleration and the ability to stop quickly. The Clubman is a car that people will notice on the street, and it has the power and agility to leave other sports cars behind.

Using Design to Illustrate

Good design will help your audience visualize your subject and quickly find the information they need.

Use Photographs and Graphics—To give your audience an image of your subject, find a photograph on the Internet or take a photograph with your mobile phone.

Tables and graphs are also widely used in evaluations. Cars.com, a website that offers evaluations of cars, uses tables like the one shown in Figure 11.4 to give readers a quick overview of the strengths and weaknesses of each vehicle.

Add Headings—Good headings become access points through which the audience can enter the argument. Headings forecast each section's content. Headings should draw the audience into the text, tempting them to delve into each section.

Boring, Flat Headings	Descriptive, Lively Headings
Description	Introducing the Mini Cooper
Criteria	The Benchmarks for Success
External Appearance	A Pleasure to See
Interior Comfort	Snug but Comfortable
Expenses	Affordable and Reliable
Safety	Surprisingly Safe
Conclusion	Bottom Line: A Real Winner

Your headings can even offer a quick snapshot of your evaluation. The lively headings shown here, for example, give a sense of how the evaluator felt about the car.

Ready to start evaluating something?
Here are the basics:

1 An evaluation uses a defined set of criteria to objectively measure the quality of someone's work or the value of something.

2 In the workplace, evaluations are critical because they help people understand the merits and shortcomings of products, services, projects, and employees.

3 When inventing the content of an evaluation, you need to identify three to seven criteria that both you and your audience would agree are important.

4 You should define each of your criteria so your audience knows what you consider acceptable and not acceptable for each criterion.

5 Solid research on your subject is necessary for you to fully assess the product, service, or person you are evaluating.

6 The typical organization of an evaluation includes an introduction, definitions of criteria, description of the subject, assessment of the subject, and a conclusion.

7 The style of an evaluation is typically plain and straightforward, using simple, active sentences while avoiding excessive clichés.

8 Keep your audience's level of technical expertise in mind so you don't overwhelm them with technical jargon.

9 The visual design of an evaluation often uses photographs and graphics to illustrate the subject and its parts.

10 Evaluations are designed to be read quickly, so descriptive headings should be included that help the audience locate important information.

1. With a group, list ten products that you might be interested in evaluating. What kinds of products did your group list? Did these items share any common characteristics? Discuss why you would be interested in writing or reading an evaluation of these specific products. Why might you seek out an evaluation of these products before purchasing them?

2. Working in a group or by yourself, choose a specific product or service and develop two different sets of criteria, each set appropriate for a different audience. Analyze the first audience by describing its expectations, values, and attitudes. Brainstorm a list of criteria for that audience. Then analyze the second audience. Have some fun with this. Choose an audience with completely different expectations, values, and attitudes. How did the switch to a different audience change your set of criteria? With your group, discuss why a change in audience often leads to a change in evaluation criteria.

3. Imagine that your university is tossing out its grading system. Now students will be evaluated similarly to the way companies evaluate employees. This kind of evaluation, the administration argues, will give better feedback to students and provide potential employers and graduate schools with a better sense of each student's strengths and abilities. What criteria could be used in this new evaluation system for students? Would you prefer a system like this one? Discuss its strengths and limitations with your group.

1. Find an evaluation on the Internet for a product or service that interests you. Write a one- to two-page critique of that evaluation. What are its strengths and weaknesses? Were the criteria defined? Did the evaluation include enough facts to show how the author came up with his or her overall conclusion? What kinds of information were not included in the evaluation that you might have found useful? Write an analysis of this evaluation for your instructor, highlighting its strengths and weaknesses.

2. Post a rebuttal of an evaluation on the Internet for a product you like or dislike. Find its customer reviews on a website like Amazon.com. Choose one of the reviews and write a rebuttal of it. Use a brief list of criteria to demonstrate why the original review was off the mark. Post your rebuttal and e-mail your instructor a link to it.

3. Write an evaluation for a household product you own (e.g., a blender, toaster, portable media player, popcorn popper). Define a set of specific criteria and then evaluate your subject according to expectations that you and your readers share. Explain to your audience why you are giving your subject a positive or negative evaluation.

In this evaluation, student Danielle Cordaro describes the process she and friends followed for deciding which trip to take during spring break. Cordaro briefly defines her criteria early in the evaluation. Then, watch how she uses these criteria to assess the pros and cons of each location.

How We Ended Up in Louisville: An Evaluation of Spring Break Options

Danielle Cordaro

My junior year in high school, I went to Cancun for spring break. My senior year I went to Miami, Florida. Of course, my parents paid for everything. But now that I'm in college, my parents are off the hook. They figure that paying for my tuition fulfills all their parental duties. So last year I had to figure out how to go on spring break and still have fun on a college student's budget. I work part time at Western Michigan's library, so I did have some money—exactly $606.76. Some of our friends were planning on going to exotic places like Jamaica or the Virgin Islands, but the remaining five of us were in the same boat in terms of funds. We decided to sit down and decide what we wanted out of our spring vacation.

I was surprised to find out that our priorities and preferences had changed since high school. Most of us weren't really looking for a big party; we just wanted to get away from school and relax. We decided on a few key criteria. First, we wanted to go somewhere that provided a good mix of activity and relaxation time for five days and six nights. Second, lodging and food could not cost us more than $60 per person per night. Finally, we agreed to use no more than one tank of gas each way to get to and from our destination. That meant that, in our most fuel-efficient car, we could go a maximum of 360 miles from Kalamazoo, Michigan.

Weighing Our Options

Looking at a map, I came up with three possible places to go, which included South Haven, Michigan, Chicago, and Louisville. Then I used my criteria to weigh the pros and cons of each one.

Option 1: Cabining in South Haven, Michigan

Pros: South Haven is only about an hour's drive from Kalamazoo. Right on Lake Michigan, it's a hopping place for college students during the summer months. In the spring, before the water is warm enough to swim in, it's a bit more subdued. The upside about visiting in spring is there are not too many tourists around, which makes activities out in nature more peaceful. South Haven has miles of hiking trails along the shores of Lake Michigan, as well as canoeing, fishing, and horseback riding. There's shopping in the downtown area and a few inexpensive good restaurants. Other plusses include the accommodations. One nice thing about vacationing in Michigan in the middle of April is that it is considered the "off-season." For $200 I found a luxury cabin with accommodations for five people. The cabin included a hot tub outside, a whirlpool bath inside, and a large flat-screen HDTV.

5   **Cons:** There isn't much to do in town, and not many other college students would be around. A few restaurants and bars would be open during the off-season, but they aren't too exciting. Going to South Haven would mean having to make our own fun. So we might find ourselves hanging out in our "luxury cabin" bored out of our minds. You can only hang out in the hot tub and watch that flat-screen HDTV so much before wanting to get out and see some people.

Option 2: Living Large in Chicago

Pros: Chicago is an exciting city with a lot to do. The shopping on Michigan Avenue is legendary. Inexpensive, more educational activities include the Museum of Contemporary Art, the Shedd Aquarium, and the Field Museum. If we wanted to pamper ourselves, we could go to a day spa. One great thing about Chicago is the inexpensive public transportation. If we planned things right, we could avoid cabs and take the elevated train pretty much everywhere, including to the surrounding suburbs, for a few dollars. The restaurants in Chicago are also fantastic, as well as the nightlife. There was no way we could get bored in Chicago—as long as our money held out.

Cons: Chicago is expensive. Parking alone can cost up to twenty dollars a day, even at your own hotel. Good food and adequate lodging are also expensive with meals and hotel running about $80 per person per day. Even at that price, the accommodations wouldn't be luxurious. I was able to find a room in our budget, but one of us would have to sleep on a rollaway cot.

Option 3: Living Ritzy and Spelunking in Kentucky

Pros: Louisville is farther from Kalamazoo than South Haven or   10
Chicago, but offers some of the appeal of both. Downtown Louisville has a lot of character and cute shops, though it's not as ritzy as Chicago. Another nice thing is that there are a lot of interesting things to do that don't involve expensive activities like shopping. Just outside the city are historic landmarks from the pre–Civil War era, as well as hiking and other outside activities. There are even some underground caves you can hike through in Mammoth Park. Best of all, Louisville is a lot less expensive than Chicago. I was able to find two much nicer rooms in Louisville for the price of one in Chicago. Louisville also has some great restaurants that, again, were about half the price of those in Chicago. Food and hotel would be about $50 a day per person, which was well within our budget.

Cons: All right, telling your friends you're going to Louisville for Spring Break is not going to get many oohs and aahs. One of my Cancun-bound friends asked me, "Are you visiting your grandma or something?" We would also need to spend more on gas to make this trip happen. We would need to top off the tank on the way to and from Louisville. Driving down to Mammoth Cave would add more cost.

Drum Roll Please: Our Decision

After a lot of consideration, we decided to go to Louisville. All of us had been to both Chicago and South Haven, but none of us had ever been to Louisville. The trip was great. We spent three days in Louisville just hanging out downtown and enjoying the great shopping and restaurants. The hotel was excellent, too. We had a pool, a hot tub, and a workout room. The last two days we spent in the Mammoth cave area. We stayed at a nice inexpensive bed and breakfast and explored during the day. It wasn't the kind of vacation my friends had in Jamaica on their parents' dime, but it was nice to find out we could put together a trip on a budget, stick to it, and have a pretty good time in the process.

A CLOSER LOOK AT
How We Ended Up in Louisville

1. Where does Cordaro list and define the criteria she will use to evaluate her various options? Are these criteria specific enough for her argument? Are these the criteria you would use when evaluating your own vacation or break options?

2. Evaluations should sound as objective as possible, but they should also be lively and engaging. What stylistic strategies does Cordaro use to make her evaluation enjoyable to read? What other features might she have added to make the evaluation even more engaging?

3. If you were going to add one or two graphics to the evaluation, what would you include? Images, such as photographs of each of the options, are obvious possibilities. What other images would draw readers in and help them evaluate these options for themselves?

IDEAS FOR
Arguing

1. Choose a vacation or entertainment-related experience you've had recently and write a commentary (Chapter 12) that explores an issue, whether serious or somewhat trivial, that was raised during this experience.

2. Write a rich description of an entertainment or vacation spot you know fairly well. It could be a local place or some far-off place you have visited. If it's local, do some empirical research and experience it again. Use plain style mixed with rich sensory details and metaphors to bring your subject to life. Consider adding images and other design features to your text to help readers experience the place for themselves.

iPhone 5 Review

TIM STEVENS

In this evaluation, which appeared on the website Engadget.com, Tim Stevens examines the features and performance of the then-just-released iPhone 5. As you read, notice how Stevens organizes the evaluation under a specific set of criteria, which he calls "benchmarks."

Thinner. Lighter. Faster. Simpler. The moment the iPhone 5 was unveiled we knew that it was checking off all the right boxes, folding in all the improvements and refinements people have been demanding over the past year—yet plenty of folks still went to their respective social networks to type out their bitter disappointment. iPhone upgrade ennui seemed to be sweeping the nation, a sentiment that appeared to quickly dissipate when it came time for people to vote with their wallets.

The iPhone 5 is here—or will be soon, anyway—and it's every bit the device that people were asking for when the iPhone 4S came out. Its new design has less mass yet leaves room for a larger display and LTE wireless, all while increasing battery life. In nearly every respect, this is an upgrade over the 4S that came before, though it arrives almost a year later than many had hoped. Is it too late to keep pace with the rapidly iterating Android offerings, or is it so good it was worth waiting for? The answer lies below.

Hardware

Apple introduced the iPhone 5 to the world by elevating it from a hidden pylon, rising from the floor and literally sitting on a pedestal for the world to admire while precisely focused lights made the thing gleam like a jewel. Clearly, the company is confident that it's knocked it out of the park again, and we have to agree. But, that new design isn't perfect—not quite a grand slam, if you'll allow us to continue the metaphor.

The iPhone 5 is a clear evolution of the stark, industrial design introduced two years ago with the iPhone 4. That collection of square edges and raw materials was a huge contrast to everything else the company was producing and, frankly, everything else on the market. It was like an artifact from another dimension where ergonomics lost out to purity of vision, and Apple saw no reason to compromise that purity for the 4S nor, as it turns out, for the 5.

Visually, much has stayed the same, but the biggest change is impossible to see. Pick up the iPhone 5 and you're immediately struck by the reduction in weight. At 112 grams it's 20 percent lighter than the 4S, a figure that doesn't seem like it would make much of an impact. It does—so much so that it's the lightness, not the bigger display or the thinness, that nearly everybody praises when first getting a chance to hold the iPhone 5 in their own hands.

Meanwhile, the changes in dimensions are surprisingly difficult to detect. That's largely thanks to the iPhone 5 being exactly as wide as the 4 and 4S that came before. This continuity of proportions on the x axis brings familiarity, while a slight increase on the y axis adds functionality. The iPhone 5 measures 4.87 x 2.31 x 0.3 inches (124 x 59 x 7.6mm), making it about a third of an inch (nearly 1cm) taller than before.

Since all the extra room happens outside of your grip you hardly notice it, and this also shifts the phone's center of mass away from the center of your hand, which we think helps augment the perception of lightness.

The new height makes room for that 4-inch, 1,136 x 640 display—the most progressive change by a long shot. Steve Jobs famously said that the 3.5-inch screen size is the "sweet spot" and, frankly, it was about time Apple added a little more sugar. The new height results in a phone with more usable space and better presentation for HD content (the iPhone is finally 16:9). Yet, it's still easy to use with one hand. Each corner is comfortably reachable by thumbs of nearly all sizes.

That reachability is also helped by the decrease in thickness: 7.6mm, down from 9.3mm on the iPhone 4S. It isn't the world's thinnest smartphone that Apple claimed it was (the original Droid RAZR is thinner, among others), but this is still an impressively svelte device.

An all-new aluminum construction extends around the back, which is either anodized black or left raw depending on whether you opt for the darker or lighter of the two offerings. The white phone is bright and clean-looking; the black, dark and menacing. We'll let you draw conclusions about personality based on color preference, but we will say that the black surface seems to suck up fingerprints that are difficult to clean. Even so, we're glad the all-glass back has been retired, though traces of it remain: two slivers of the stuff punctuate the top and bottom of the back sides. These glossy bands break up the matte uniformity, but help boost antenna performance.

10 That said, the antennas still comprise the rim of the device, thinner now and the gap between them filled with a material whose color matches the body—yet more evidence of the design team's attention to detail. These are the same sort of dynamically reconfiguring antennas used on the 4S and, as with that phone, we weren't able to death grip our way into any sort of signal issues.

The face of the device is still fashioned out of glass (no surprise there) and while Apple wouldn't confirm whether that front is indeed the sort of primate-proof silica produced by Corning, we'd hazard a guess that it is. With the metal back now sitting flush to the chamfered edge of the device, the slightly elevated glass surface gives the profile view of the phone a bit of unfortunate asymmetry—it's now thicker on top than on the bottom.

But that elevated glass does mean your finger doesn't hit any rough edges or unfortunate surfaces when tracing the edges of the panel. The front-facing FaceTime HD camera now sits centered, directly above the earpiece. The Home button, meanwhile, has moved a fraction of a millimeter down and its resistance feels slightly different than that on the 4S, a touch more progressive with a more definitive detent. Hopefully the internal mechanism will prove more durable over time.

The position and design of the other buttons is likewise largely unchanged from the 4S, with the discrete, circular volume up and down buttons on the left just below the (slightly thinner) toggle switch. The headphone jack now moves to the bottom, a change that will cause some to modify their well-established pocket-retrieval mannerisms. But, as users of the iPod touch will tell you, having that jack on the bottom feels quite natural, and we agree. This is a good move.

The phone's speakers are also positioned on the bottom, playing out through a series of 26 holes that flank another major change in the iPhone 5: the Lightning connector.

Lightning

Goodbye, venerable Dock connector. Hello, 15 Lightning. For nearly 10 years the 30-pin Dock connector has been ubiquitous, sprouting out of accessories small and large, but ever since iPods started getting thinner we all knew its days were numbered. The giant, clunky connector is a painful legacy of an earlier time that needs to be removed from the ecosystem and, with the iPhone 5, Apple decided it was time to rip off the Band-Aid. Indeed the Dock connector must go and we won't miss it, but Lightning doesn't always feel like a confident step forward.

First, the good: the Lightning connector is infinitely easier to connect. It slots in nicely and does so regardless of orientation, plugging in right-side-up or upside-down. We were able to drive it home without looking the first time, and every time thereafter. (If only the same could be said for the USB connector on the other side.) It's also small, seems infinitely more durable than its flimsy-feeling elder and even stronger than micro-USB alternatives.

Superficially, it's hitting all the right marks, but Lightning comes up short in a number of important areas. It is, of course, incompatible with the roughly 350 million billion iPhone and iPod accessories currently on the market—a problem mostly rectified by a $30 adapter. But, that's not a perfect solution, as even that won't support iPod Out, the specification used in some cars (most notably BMW and Mini) to enable in-dash control of an iPod or iPhone.

That's an admittedly low number of users left with no way forward, as the adapter will provide the power and analog audio that the vast majority of docks and accessories (and cars) in the world need, but it's still disappointing to see those automotive users, owners of some of the most expensive iPod docks on the planet, left out in the cold.

More problematic is the speed of this new connector. Lightning's name comes as a cheeky play on the Thunderbolt connector, yet Lightning is, at least for now, wholly independent from that standard. In fact, the implementation that comes with the iPhone 5 is based on USB 2.0, meaning that theoretical maximum data transfer rates are no faster than what came before. In practice, though, we were surprised to actually find a tangible difference between the two phones.

20   To test this we lined up an iPhone 4S next to an iPhone 5 and ran both through a number of syncs with large files. Pulling 5.5GB of data from iTunes to the iPhone 4S took five minutes and six seconds on average. Syncing those same files to the iPhone 5 took three minutes and 57 seconds on average. So, nearly 20 percent faster, but we're not sure how much of this is due to the new connector and how much can be attributed to faster internals in the phone itself.

We confirmed with Apple that the iPhone 5 itself only supports USB 2.0, so a faster interconnect on the other end wouldn't help anything (and it's unclear whether the internal storage could consume data more quickly if it were there), but there's nothing stopping the company from expanding the Lightning standard to work with Thunderbolt or USB 3.0 in the future. For now, at least, the new connector remains confusingly at odds with Apple's own next-generation and similarly named data interconnect. That's no problem if you're using one of the many and myriad wireless ways to pull content directly onto the device (hello, iCloud), but if you're still pushing your media over a cable from your main iTunes library, it's still going to take awhile.

Internals

The heart of the iPhone 5 is the new A6 processor, a chip that Apple wasn't too keen to describe other than it being "twice as fast" as the last-gen A5 and "22 percent smaller." Thankfully, we have ways—namely, Geekbench, which identifies this as a dual-core 1.05GHz processor paired with 1GB of RAM.

Why not tell this up front? It's clear the folks in Cupertino are sick of people trying to draw conclusions based on core count and gigahertz goals, so they're just sitting this one out. Apple isn't alone, with Intel emphasizing names like Core i5 and Core i7 over raw clock speeds, and Qualcomm and NVIDIA using iterative designations like S4 and Tegra 3 for their respective processors. Still, none have gone so far as to stop publishing key specifications altogether.

Maybe they should. We've long since departed from a time when clock speed or core count could be directly correlated with performance across CPU architectures and, with Apple constructing its own, custom SoC for the A6, that's doubly true. Why, the dual-core A5 chip in the iPhone 4S shows as 800MHz, so looking purely at numbers this new phone should only be 25 percent faster, not twice as fast. We'll put that to the test a little later.

25   For storage you have a choice of 16, 32 or 64GB models priced (on contract) at $199, $299 and $399. Unsurprisingly, storage is not expandable, but hey, dig that iCloud.

Apple has also greatly improved the iPhone's wireless connectivity options, with the addition of LTE being the biggest talking point. Across the regional variants that will be sold around the world, 700MHz AWS bands for LTE for AT&T in the US are supported, plus Rogers, Bell and Telus in Canada and various carriers in Europe and Asia using bands 1, 3 and 5. Meanwhile, a CDMA version handles Verizon and Sprint LTE in the US plus KDDI in Japan using Bands 1, 3, 5, 13 and 25.

That's a lot of spectrum to cover—and we haven't even broached the GSM/EDGE, UMTS/HSPA+, DC-HSDPA support in the GSM model, nor the CDMA EV-DO Rev. A and Rev. B support in the other. What remains to be seen is just what will be open and what will be locked by the various carriers and whether international LTE *compatibility* truly means international LTE *usability*. That, in the short term, seems unlikely—at the very least until the new nano-SIM standard becomes a little more available.

The choice of CDMA vs. GSM will likely come down to which carrier you're on, and which carrier you'd *like* to be on. In the US, it's naturally AT&T offering the GSM model, Sprint and Verizon with CDMA. Beyond the availability of bands, an important distinction is the ability to do simultaneous voice and data. None of the iPhone 5 models can handle Voice over LTE, so when doing voice calling the phone falls back to either GSM or CDMA, and CDMA doesn't support simultaneous voice and data. So, if you

absolutely need to talk and surf at the same time, you're stuck on AT&T in the US.

On top of all that is an expanded selection of WiFi connectivity options. The iPhone 5 adds 802.11a support to complete the set of a/b/g/n compatibility. That connectivity is now dual-band as well, so you can step up out of the crowded 2.4GHz into the clear air at 5GHz. Bluetooth 4.0, GPS and GLONASS support all return. Looking to get directions up the Road of Bones? You're covered here.

Display

The iPhone 5 uses a new 4-inch display that   30
provides a half-inch of additional diagonal extent compared to those iPhones that have come before. Massive difference? Absolutely not, but it does give the phone enough surface area to stay competitive without sizing it beyond the thumb reach of your average consumer. In fact, its four corners seem just as attainable as before, helped by Apple shifting the display down just a few millimeters to get it closer to the center of your hand.

But we've talked enough about how it works in the hand. How does it look? Fantastic, frankly. The iPhone 4S already has one of the best displays on the market with regard to things like pixel density, brightness and contrast, and the iPhone 5 brings that up another notch—and not just because it has an additional 176 rows of pixels. Putting both under the microscope, indeed, shows the same basic subpixel structure.

If there was one complaint about the 4S display it's that it suffered from a somewhat greenish hue. The 5 fixes that—if anything, extending just a smidgen to the warm side, but displaying imagery that's much more chromatically neutral than before. The phone also moves up to full sRGB coverage, meaning it can accurately represent every color provided by that spectrum, a claim to fame few smartphones can match.

Apple also promises fewer layers sandwiched between the subpixels and the surface of the glass, the idea being greater contrast when you're outside. Sure enough, the iPhone 5 is a great device for using out in direct sunlight, though to be fair it's a minor improvement over the 4S, which likewise doesn't fear the sun.

Cameras

The iSight camera here is basically unchanged from the 4S. The overall mechanism has been pared down a bit to fit within the tight confines of the iPhone 5, and the protective bit of glass on the outside has been replaced with a 6mm disc of crystal sapphire for durability, which we rather regrettably did not have a chance to put through a torture test.

35   So, that means we have an 8-megapixel, backside-illuminated sensor shooting through a five-element, f/2.4 lens. And, with the bigger screen, we now have a larger shutter release button, which is slightly easier to tap by big thumbs.

Image quality is still among the best out there for a cameraphone, unimproved but quite impressive in varying conditions. What has improved, though, is the speed. Tap that big ol' thumb as quick as you can and the iPhone 5 will keep up, whereas the iPhone 4S eventually fell behind. It's at least on par with the Galaxy Nexus, which also has a ridiculously quick shooter.

So, while the camera on the back is minimally improved, the one on the front is a big step forward. Replacing the VGA FaceTime camera is a 1.2-megapixel FaceTime HD unit capable of capturing 720p video. Resolution is obviously massively increased, but so too is overall image quality, with far more accurate color reproduction. Of course, whether or not you actually *want* a higher-quality front-facing camera depends on just how much time you spend putting your face on before getting your FaceTime on.

New with iOS 6 is Panorama mode, where you can tap one button and just sweep the phone around to create a massive image. Resulting files are something like 11,000 x 2,500, with the exact resolution varying based on how smoothly you panned from left to right. If you wander up or down the display will warn you to keep in line, and you'll want to, as every time you stray you're effectively cropping the resulting image.

The file is captured in one seamless motion and the final product is almost always free of the sort of glitches and visual aberrations typically found in these self-stitching panoramas. That said, it isn't totally error-free. We took one panorama inside the New Museum in New York City, a room full of thin black lines against a white background. It's about as tough a test as Panorama mode will ever see and indeed you can make out some slight glitches in those lines, but in normal cityscapes and country scenes we struggled to find signs of artifacting. The results are almost always very impressive.

Video capture remains the same on the   40 rear-facing camera—1080p30 maximum and offering bright contrast and colors plus the same digital image stabilization that we saw before, which results in reasonably smooth shots even when you, yourself, aren't so smooth.

Performance and Battery Life

Two times faster? Twice the graphics performance? Better battery life? Actually, yes. The iPhone 5 over-delivers on all those promises. Running the Geekbench test suite on the iPhone 4S gave us an average score of 634. The iPhone 5 netted an average of 1,628. That's more than twice as fast and, while you won't necessarily see such huge increases in day-to-day usage, apps do load noticeably quicker, HDR images are processed in half the time and tasks like video rendering in iMovie are equally expedient.

SunSpider scores average at 924ms, which is more than twice as fast as the 2,200ms the iPhone 4S manages and still quite a bit quicker than the 1,400ms scored by the Galaxy S III and the 1,700ms managed by the HTC One X. More important than numbers, web pages load very quickly, snapping into view as fast as your data plan can shovel the bits into Safari and, once there, smoothly reacting to your gestures.

Naturally, we'd be telling just half the story if we only talked performance. There's an important question that's left: what kind of battery life can you expect? Power is nothing without longevity and, shockingly, the iPhone 5 copes amazingly well. In a day of heavy usage with LTE, GPS and WiFi all enabled, we managed 14 hours and 18 minutes before the phone succumbed to the elements.

On our standard battery rundown test, in which we loop a video with LTE and WiFi enabled and social accounts pinging at regular intervals, the iPhone 5 managed a hugely impressive 11 hours and 15 minutes. That's just 10 minutes shy of the Motorola Droid RAZR Maxx.

45   When it comes to wireless performance, the iPhone 5 didn't disappoint either. We tested a CDMA variant on Verizon's network, going between 3G and 4G connectivity as we traveled about this great nation. Overall, the iPhone 5 did an excellent job at finding and keeping signals, and call quality is quite good. Callers came through loud and clear and said we sounded great as well—though most of the time we sadly couldn't tell them what we were calling them on. Data transmission speeds were at or above comparable Android LTE devices held nearby, usually in the 10-20 Mbps range both up and down.

Software

The iPhone ships with Apple's latest mobile operating system, and for our full take on that we'll direct you toward our full iOS 6 review. But, let's discuss a few things that are particularly applicable to smartphones. It's the new Maps app that will have the biggest impact on most users, and in general we found Maps beautiful and fast, a smooth and very aesthetically pleasing way to get from place to place.

But, it isn't nearly as comprehensive as Google's offerings on Android. The biggest drawback is the unfortunate lack of public transportation directions. If you haven't quite mastered New York City's subway system, you won't get any help from your iPhone 5. Curiously, the app offers to give you public transportation directions, but should you choose that option it pops you straight into the App Store with a search for "Routing Apps." Right now, there are zero results.

It also lacks the detailed layering that you can apply in Google Maps and Google Navigation, showing you whatever you want to see. Maps will list some important POIs—mostly gas stations and convenience shops—but if you want to see all Mexican restaurants on your route you'll have to dig deeper. Finally, while Maps does show traffic, we never saw it give a warning about traffic along a route currently being navigated. That's important information for road trippers.

Passbook is similarly incomplete. This is Apple dipping its toes into the virtual wallet space, providing the ability for companies to write custom apps that will slot in here and provide access to things like movie tickets and value cards. But, as few major players have pledged to deploy their services here, this serves as a framework for something that will be cool rather than something that actually is right now. We're expecting good things.

The new Shared Photo Streams feature, 50 however, is a welcome addition. Here you can select a few pictures from your roll, or indeed a new picture you just snapped, and share it with one or more friends—or post it in the public for all to see. New photos added to the stream popped up within about 30 seconds and, while it isn't quite as seamless and fun as Google+ Events, it's a nice way to share photos with friends.

In general, iOS 6 has seen some nice nips and tucks where it needed it. iCloud integration is tighter, Safari is better and the overall experience is more polished. But, it isn't a major step forward in any regard. Suffice to say, conservative iPhone users won't have to worry about anyone moving their cheese, but if you didn't like iOS before, you still won't today.

Wrap-Up

The iPhone 5 is a significant improvement over the iPhone 4S in nearly every regard, and in those areas that didn't see an upgrade over its predecessor—camera, storage capacity—one could make a strong case that the iPhone 4S was already ahead of the curve. Every area, that is, except for the OS. If anything, it's the operating system here that's beginning to feel a bit dated and beginning to show its age.

Still, the iPhone 5 absolutely shines. Pick your benchmark and you'll find Apple's thin new weapon sitting at or near the top. Will it convince you to give up your Android or Windows Phone ways and join the iOS side? Maybe, maybe not. Will it wow you? Hold it in your hand—you might be surprised. For the iOS faithful this is a no-brainer upgrade. This is without a doubt the best iPhone yet. This is a hallmark of design. This is the one you've been waiting for.

A CLOSER LOOK AT
iPhone 5 Review

1. The QuickView of evaluations at the beginning of this chapter shows two basic organizational patterns for evaluations. Which of these patterns does this evaluation follow? Why is this pattern the most appropriate one for this topic?

2. Evaluations are usually considered more objective sounding than reviews because evaluations offer specific criteria that readers would agree are important for judging the quality of the subject. What are the criteria Stevens lists, and do you agree that these are the most important criteria for judging a smart phone? What other criteria would readers find important?

3. Stevens includes a great amount of technical terminology in this evaluation. Do you think that he goes too far or not far enough? In other words, is the technical level about right for an audience considering buying a new iPhone?

IDEAS FOR
Arguing

1. Imagine that you work for an organization or company that wants to purchase smart phones for all its members, all of whom must use the exact same model. Write a proposal (Chapter 14) in which you recommend purchasing a certain model. Be sure to explain why this model is best suited toward this specific organization/company and its members.

2. Write a narrative argument (Chapter 9) that explores a current issue involving technology and whether it is beneficial or harmful. Recounting the experiences of yourself or others, grab your readers' attention by first setting the scene, and then introduce a complication that you or others faced. At the end of your narrative argument, be sure that your story offers a lesson or a call to action.

12 Commentaries— Arguing about Current Issues and Events

12.1 How commentaries allow you to express your opinion on current issues and events

Writing a commentary is a great way to figure out what you believe while expressing your opinions. In college, your professors will ask you to write commentaries that argue about current issues and events (Figure 12.1). In the workplace, you will write commentaries that discuss how technological shifts, economic trends, and events will affect your company, organization, and industry.

Your commentaries will be based on your opinions. Of course, you will need to thoroughly research your topics, but your primary objective is to express what *you* believe and support your views with good reasons. As a result, commentaries tend to be more persuasive than generative. You are telling your audience your opinion and trying to win them over to your side. Nevertheless, you need to be aware of how generative forms of argument, such as identity, framing, and cultural narratives, can affect how people understand issues and how they react to events. You may find yourself using generative methods to negotiate with your audience, especially when overt attempts to persuade them might not work.

FIGURE 12.1 Commenting on Current Issues and Events
Commentaries respond to current issues and events.

Commentaries are usually written about issues and events that are open to interpretation, such as politics, religion, civil rights, ethics, fashion, and the arts. People have legitimate differences of opinion on these kinds of issues. Commentaries are arguments that help people discuss their differences in an opinionated and well-reasoned way. As a result, when reading your commentary, your audience will be primarily interested in *what* you believe and *why* you believe it.

Inventing the Content of Your Commentary

12.2 Strategies for inventing the content of a commentary

When writing a commentary, you are typically responding to events or issues that are important right now. Much of the content of your commentary will be based on stories in the media that are still developing.

Choosing a Topic and Figuring Out a New Angle

When writing a commentary, you should choose a topic that is currently in the news. Then, find a new angle on that topic.

Find a current topic

To find a topic, you might look at the major stories on news websites, such as CNN, New York Times, Fox News, or Reuters. If you want to write about a local issue, the newspaper or local television news would be a good place to find an interesting topic.

Your topic should be narrow and specific. A common mistake is to choose a topic that is too broad, such as racism, the legalization of drugs, or some other complex social issue. Instead, narrow your topic to something you can handle in a short commentary. Posing your topic as a question is a good way to narrow it.

Racism—Should a new video game that uses racist slurs and themes be boycotted by gamers?

QUICK View

Generative   Persuasive

Generative Argument—Commentaries have some generative elements. You can use identification, framing, and narrative to build a sense of understanding and consensus with the audience, especially when they are unlikely to agree with your argument.

Persuasive Argument—Commentaries are persuasive in nature, which means you will need to use good reasoning, appeals to authority, and appropriate emotional appeals to support and, if possible, prove your side of the argument.

Genre Pattern

> **Introduction**
>
> **Explain the Current Event or Issue**
>
> **Support for Your Argument**
>
> **Support for Your Argument**
>
> •
> •
> •
>
> **Clarification of Your Argument**
>
> **Conclusion**

The commentary is a flexible genre, so the pattern shown here offers only one common way to organize your argument. You should adjust this pattern to fit the needs of your subject, purpose, audience, and the context.

Legalizing drugs—Should marijuana be legalized for terminal cancer patients?

Space exploration—Should we be investing more in our space program to detect dangerous asteroids that might hit the Earth?

These kinds of questions will help you narrow down your topic to something you can manage.

Come up with a new angle

Completely new topics are rare, but there are always new angles on existing topics. For example, issues like racism, drug legalization, and space exploration are not new topics. And yet we are still arguing about them. Why? Usually, an event brings these issues back into the public eye (e.g., a violent act, a protest, a court case, an election). These events give the public a chance to reevaluate and re-argue positions on these issues.

To find a new angle on an existing topic, ask yourself, "What has happened recently or what has changed that makes this topic particularly interesting right now?" For example,

New angle on racism—The recent release of *Vietnam Vengeance*, a video game that relies heavily on racial stereotypes, dialogue, and slurs, has caused concern about the effects of racist content on the young people who play these games.

New angle on legalizing drugs—Recent news stories have show that "medical" marijuana is being abused by people who are not really sick, but at least one group, terminal cancer patients, has greatly benefited from recent changes in drug laws.

New angle on space exploration—The recent explosion of a previously un-detected 10-ton meteorite over Russia was the wake-up call we needed to invest more in space exploration.

Your angle puts a new spin on your topic by reacting to something that has happened recently or changed.

Figuring Out What You Believe

To help you explore what you believe, you can create what is called a *credo statement* (Figure 12.2). The word "credo" is the Latin word for "I believe." The purpose of a credo statement is to compel you to state and analyze your core beliefs. Here are four prompts to help you write a credo statement about your topic.

I believe…

Freewrite about your topic for two minutes, starting with a sentence that completes the phrase, "I believe…" While freewriting, your goal is to identify one of your core beliefs that doesn't change easily. When you run out of ideas, start another sentence with the phrase, "I believe…" and start writing again.

My assumptions are…

Look closely at your "I believe…" statement. Circle or highlight the two or three *assumptions* that explain why you believe what you believe. Then spend a couple more minutes freewriting about why you hold these assumptions. As you write,

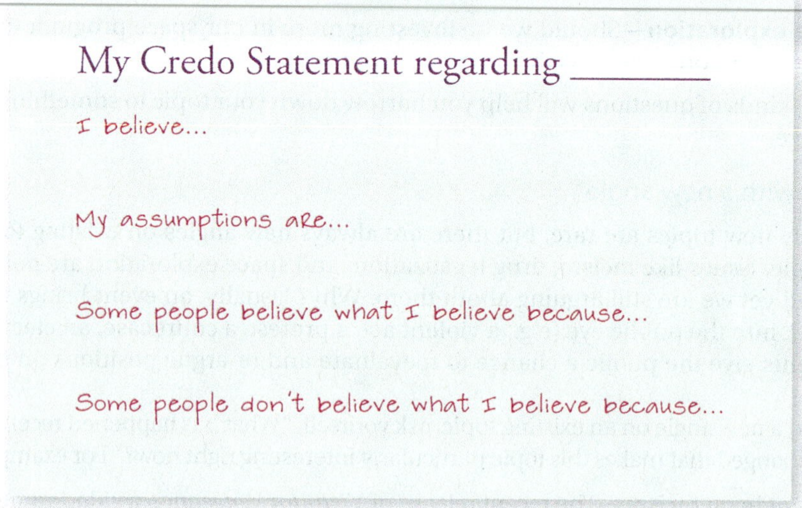

My Credo Statement regarding _____

I believe...

My assumptions are...

Some people believe what I believe because...

Some people don't believe what I believe because...

FIGURE 12.2 A Credo Statement A credo statement can help you sort out what you believe and why you believe it.

think about how your upbringing, culture, family, or experiences have formed your core belief.

Some people believe what I believe because…

Spend two minutes freewriting about why you think others hold this same core belief and therefore agree with you. Again, think about how their cultures, families, or experiences have led them to believe the same thing as you.

Some people don't believe what I believe because…

Spend two minutes freewriting about why you think some people *don't* hold this core belief. You need to be fair at this point. Don't write down statements like, "They're morons" or "They're crazy." You want to figure out why some people hold a different core belief than you. Think about how their various experiences and backgrounds have led them to accept a different core belief than you.

When you are finished with your credo statement, you should look closely at how you will support your argument. As discussed in Chapter 3, persuasive arguments tend to be built on reasoning (*logos*), appeals to authority (*ethos*), and appeals to emotion (*pathos*). Go through your credo statement to look for all three of these kinds of proofs.

Researching Your Topic

Your opinion alone is not going to persuade people to agree with you. Instead, you need to do research on your topic to support your views and anticipate counterarguments.

Electronic sources—Run Internet searches on your topic. You should look for sources that both agree and disagree with your opinion, so you can see all sides of the issue.

Print sources—Depending on your topic, print sources like magazines and newspapers can be especially helpful. Magazines and newspapers tend to report on current events and issues, so they will usually offer an up-to-date understanding of your topic. Books can be helpful for collecting background information on your topic but usually won't contain the most recent facts or events.

Empirical sources—Discover other people's opinions by interviewing, surveying, or observing others. Ask others if they agree with your opinion. You will find that some people do and some don't. Try to figure out how their different core beliefs lead them to hold different opinions than you do.

When researching your subject, you need to do more than locate sources that already agree with your opinion. Opposing arguments will help you better define and defend your own position.

MOVES for Arguing

Here are some helpful moves you can use when writing about current issues and events.

Generally speaking, I believe _____ is the best way to understand what happened.

I'm really not concerned about _____, but I do believe that _____ is something we should address now rather than later.

When _____ happened before, we responded by doing _____, which was (or was not) the best way to handle it.

You bring up some good points and I understand where you are coming from, but our best path right now is _____.

I may not be completely right about this issue, but _____ is what I believe and I believe we should do _____.

Others may believe _____, and I respect their opinions, but I have a different point of view based on my own experiences.

12.3 Techniques
for organizing and
drafting a commentary

Organizing and Drafting Your Commentary

The commentary is a flexible genre, so there are numerous ways to organize this kind of argument. The QuickView on page 242 illustrates a pattern that will help you begin drafting. You should alter this pattern to fit your specific topic, purpose, audience, and context.

Introduction

Your commentary's introduction should include some or all of the following moves:

Grab your audience's attention—A commentary needs to catch the audience's attention. A variety of grabbers are available, including asking a question, telling an interesting anecdote, offering a startling statistic or an intriguing quote, or addressing the readers as "you." You might also try using dialogue. For example,

> Recently, I overheard a couple guys from my fraternity laughing about "wasting gooks." As an Asian American, I hadn't heard that slur used in public for a long time. The word "gook" seemed like a relic from the Vietnam era. So I leaned in to hear more. One of the guys said, "So I ran into the village and starting shooting as many gooks as I could." The other guy laughed, "It's amazing how many dinks you can waste when you earn enough points to get the AK-47." That's when I figured out that they were talking about the new video game, *Vietnam Vengeance,* which was released last week. What surprised me, though, was their casual use of long-dormant racial slurs for Southeast Asians. These kinds of racial slurs are becoming more common in single-shooter video games.

Identify your topic—If your grabber didn't identify your topic, then you might need to be more explicit after the grabber is finished.

Identify your purpose—The purpose of your commentary should be obvious to the audience somewhere in your introduction. Occasionally commentaries will reveal their purpose outright: "In this paper, I will demonstrate…" If you don't want to state your purpose directly, make sure your purpose is otherwise clear to your audience.

State your main point (thesis)—Commentaries are persuasive, so your main point should be stated somewhere in the introduction, typically at the end. That way, your audience will know what you are trying to prove.

> **Weak Thesis:** Racism is a problem in some video games.

> **Better Thesis:** Racism should be fought in all its forms, which is why gamers should not buy video games that have racist language and themes.

Offer background information—Provide the audience with enough background information to connect with your topic. Historical information is helpful, or you can offer some background details to define or explain your topic.

Stress the importance of the topic—In most cases, the importance of your commentary's topic should be obvious to your audience. But if you're writing about something that might not be familiar, tell them why this issue is something they should care about.

Your introduction doesn't need to make all of these moves, nor do you need to make them in this order. Minimally, you should identify your topic, purpose, and main point.

The Body: Making Your Case

The body of your commentary will typically have three parts: explain the current event or issue, support your side of the argument, and clarify your position.

Explain the current event or issue—Before you argue for your opinion, you need to give your audience some basic information about your topic. Start out by explaining what happened and who was involved. Tell your audience where and when it happened, and describe how it happened. As much as possible, you want to present the facts in a straightforward way. Sometimes it helps to use the Five-W and How questions to sort out and explain the current situation:

What happened? Who was involved? Where did it happen? When did it happen? Why did it happen? How did it happen?

Support your position—Use good evidence and reasoning to support your argument.

Racist themes in video games, despite the video game industry's claims to the contrary, have profound effects on how players view people from other cultures. A 2008 study, for example, found that gamers were more likely to respond to violent stimuli after playing games with black characters than after playing games with white characters (Melinda, Burgess, Dill, Sterner, Burgess, & Brown). In a collection of essays on violent video games, researcher Nate Garrelts (2005) states, "the prevailing theory among violence researchers is that video games teach players violent social scripts that may be reenacted in the world outside the game" (p. 12). The majority of this research has explored racially charged stereotypes of blacks and Hispanics in these games, but it's not too difficult to see that Asian characters portrayed as enemies or villains could shape the way gamers perceive Asian people. Video games already lack diversity, overwhelmingly using white protagonists to battle against enemies or villains who are often not white. So when the "us" is usually represented by a white male and the "them" is routinely nonwhite, gamers adopt a racial social script that tells them who is heroic and who are the bad guys.

Evidence from sources (*ethos*)

Reasoning (*logos*)

Reasoning (*logos*)

In a college-length commentary, each major point in the body will likely receive one or two paragraphs of coverage. In a workplace commentary, each major point may receive three or more paragraphs of coverage.

Clarify your position—A clarification typically shows your audience that you are aware of the complexities of the issue and that your position is open to change in the future:

As an American citizen who values my constitutional rights, especially the right to free speech, I realize offensive forms of speech are protected. In fact, I agree that people have the right to use racist language. I am also aware that some of this racist language could be considered historically accurate because soldiers did use those slurs during the Vietnam War. Clearly, racism has been and will continue to be part of any culture, especially in wartime, and it's not something that will go away because some video game designers changed how their characters express themselves. Nevertheless, video games have more impact than most media, due to their repetition of violent social scripts and their appeal to young people.

The intent of a clarification paragraph is to deflect claims that you are being too one sided or too simplistic.

The Conclusion

The conclusion of your commentary should be brief. Here are the moves you can make to wrap up your commentary:

Signal you are concluding—Use a heading, transitional phrase, or transitional sentence to signal your conclusion. Doing so will wake up your audience and prepare them to consider your main point.

Restate your main point (with more emphasis)—Now it's time to drive home your main point or thesis. In your conclusion, restate the point you made in the introduction's thesis but express it in different words. Commentary writers will often look for a way to add more emphasis or energy to their concluding thesis statement.

Look to the future—In one or two sentences, describe the future of this issue to the audience. In most cases, you want to describe a positive future that will come about because people made good choices about this issue. Occasionally, though, commentary writers will put their audience on notice by describing a less desirable future if people don't take action.

Here is an example conclusion for a commentary:

In the end, those of us who enjoy video games can make a difference on this issue. Racism may still exist in American culture, but that doesn't mean we shouldn't stop racism whenever it crawls out from under its rock. Gamers who want to fight racism should avoid buying games like *Vietnam Vengeance* that trade on racist slurs, stereotypes, and themes. That way, in the future, everyone can enjoy video games, leaving behind the culture of racism that once went with them.

The brevity of the conclusion brings this argument to a decisive ending.

Style and Design

Commentaries are persuasive documents, so you should use style and design to attract, entertain, and move your audience.

Use Persuasive Style Techniques to Add Visuality and Energy

You have often been told to "show, don't just tell." This advice is especially important when writing a commentary because these arguments discuss significant events and issues. You want to be as visual as possible.

Use the senses to describe events

Where possible, describe scenes and people with sensory information. In other words, "show" what something looked or felt like by adding color, sound, taste, smell, and texture. You want your audience to be able to experience your subject through your words.

Use metaphors, similes, and analogies

You can also use metaphors, similes, and analogies to enhance your commentary. These stylistic devices can be used to create images in the minds of the audience by comparing something unfamiliar to something the audience understands:

> **Metaphor**—The video game *Vietnam Vengeance* is a minefield of hate speech.

> **Simile**—A large meteoroid strike, such as the one that exploded over Siberia in 1908, would be as powerful as a modern-day nuclear warhead.

> **Analogy**—For many cancer patients, using medical marijuana to soothe pain is about as unexciting as taking Tylenol for a headache.

These visual elements will also make your argument more persuasive.

Get into character

If you want your audience to be excited about your subject, then imagine you are excited. Get into character and write about your subject with that mindset. If you want them to be angry, you should imagine you are angry. Getting into character will help you be less inhibited about adding emotion to your writing.

Use Design to Help the Audience See Your Perspective

You can also use design and images to clarify your message and enhance the persuasiveness of your argument.

Use descriptive headings

One way to set a tone both stylistically and visually is to use descriptive headings. You should avoid using stale headings such as *Current Issue, Support, Clarification,* and *Conclusion.* Instead, use descriptive headings like these:

Racism: Hiding in Plain Sight in Video Games

The Effects of Slurs and Stereotypes

The Effects of Racial Violence

The Fine Line of Free Speech

Conclusion: Leaving Racism Behind

Headings have two benefits. First, they highlight the major topics of your commentary for your audience, so people can easily locate the information they need. And, second, headings provide helpful transitions between major sections in your argument. They allow you to move smoothly from one section to the next.

Use images to support your argument

People believe what they can see. To support your opinion, you should search for images that illustrate the events and issues you are discussing. For example, using an image such as the one in Figure 12.3 would help your audience better understand the effects of a meteor strike. You can take images off the Internet if you are using them for strictly academic purposes (and not putting them elsewhere on the Internet). However, if you want to put your commentary on the Internet or publish it in print form, you will need to receive permission from the owner of the image.

FIGURE 12.3
Using Images to Support Your Commentary Adding an image is an effective way to show your audience what you are discussing in your commentary.

All right, let's write that commentary. Here is what you need to know:

1 Commentaries allow you to express your opinion on a variety of current issues and events.

2 The basis of a commentary is your opinion, because your main purpose is to express what *you* believe.

3 You should narrow your topic to something you can handle in a brief argument.

4 Completely new topics for commentaries are rare, but there are always new angles available on existing topics.

5 To find your angle, ask yourself what has happened recently or changed that makes this topic especially interesting right now.

6 To help you discover what you believe and why, a credo statement will allow you to explain what you believe, identify your assumptions, and explain why others agree or disagree with you.

7 In your introduction, you should use a grabber to capture your audience's attention.

8 The body of your commentary should explain the current event or issue and offer three to five reasons why you believe what you believe.

9 Your commentary's conclusion should be brief, and your main point (thesis) should be obvious to your readers·

10 The style and design of your commentary should capture your voice while making your argument attractive and easy to understand.

1. Ask each member of your group to list three issues that are currently in the news. Then have each person write down an answer to the question "What is new about this issue or what has changed recently?" Ask each person to share his or her list. What issues did members of your group have in common? What issues did other group members list that were different from yours?

2. In this chapter, you learned about using a credo statement to figure out what you believe and why you believe it. A credo statement includes four prompts: "I believe...," "My assumptions are...," "Some people believe what I believe because...," and "Some people don't believe what I believe because...." Choose a topic that interests you. Then use freewriting to generate your own credo statement on this issue. Share the results of your freewriting with your group.

3. Surely, you have met someone who gets angry or frustrated when expressing his or her opinion. With your group, brainstorm a list of reasons you believe some people struggle to express their beliefs. Then think of one time when you were frustrated and had trouble expressing your opinion. Describe this experience to your group, and explain why you thought you struggled to express your opinion in a clear, persuasive way.

LET'S **ARGUE**
ABOUT THIS

1. Find a commentary published in a newspaper, print magazine, or online magazine. Look closely at the content and organization of the commentary. What kinds of information did the author include to support his or her opinion? How did he or she arrange the information to support the commentary's main point or thesis? Write a rhetorical analysis (see Chapter 4) of this commentary, explaining why you thought it was effective or not.

2. Choose an issue that you care deeply about. State in one word how you feel about that issue. Are you excited, angry, concerned, or surprised? Use your one word as a focal point, and freewrite for five minutes. Then underline the key words in your freewrite. How do these words reflect how you feel about this issue? Write an e-mail to your instructor in which you explain how your key words and the words that associate with it can be used to create your voice in a commentary.

3. Imagine you have been asked to write a weekly column for your campus newspaper. The topics are up to you, but you need to come up with something new each week. Make a list of ten topics that you would be personally interested in writing about. Then choose one of these topics. Think of a new angle on this topic. Use a credo statement to figure out what you already believe about this subject and why. Then write an article-length commentary on this subject.

O N E   S T U D E N T ' S   W O R K

In this commentary, Mpaza Kapembwa uses a personal experience to provide a fresh angle on a current and contentious issue, affirmative action. Kapembwa wrote this commentary while attending Williams College, which is a highly selective liberal arts school in western Massachusetts. The article appeared in USA Today College.

Affirmative Action Creates False Stigmas

Mpaza Kapembwa

This year, the Supreme Court will hear another affirmative action college admissions case. It seems like this policy is challenged in the courts each year.

As a beneficiary of this policy, I am at odds as to whether it needs to be upheld or not. While affirmative action has helped minorities have access to higher education, it also creates stigmas. Supreme Court Justice Clarence Thomas, an opponent to affirmative action, says many employers never took him very seriously despite having a Yale Law degree because they assumed he got in just because of affirmative action.

I have faced similar assumptions.

Someone told me I was lucky because it was easier for me to get into Williams College because I am a minority. He went on to say that because I am African, writing the admissions essay must have been a piece of cake since I have such a great story. He must have thought I didn't understand what he was saying, so he went on: "If there are two students who are both highly qualified and one is white and the other a minority student, the minority will get in." I knew our conversation was headed toward affirmative action so in a moment of weakness, I chose not to engage in that conversation. I had just gotten here. The last thing I wanted was to start questioning whether I truly belonged at Williams.

As much as I disagree with these assumptions, I do understand why   5
someone would think it is easier for minorities to get into top schools.
Being a minority is often associated with being socially disadvantaged.
Being African means coming from one of the poorest places on the planet.
Together, these qualities make the recipe for one sad application essay that
will woo the admissions officers and give those applicants an advantage
over a white student who grew up in a privileged family. Besides, people
might ask, what can someone who was brought up in an advantaged family
write about?

I had a chance to observe an admissions officer reading applications
and it's not as simple as minority students get preference. There are a lot
of factors that go into it. Each application is read for 20 minutes and then
passed on to one or two more officers. If one factor really stood out more
than the others, then why spend an hour on each application?

Apart from the obvious, Williams tries to make the campus diverse so
as to reflect the demographics of the United States. Thus another important
factor in admissions is judging students according to where they come from.
It's unfortunate that, in some cases, both white and minority applicants
come from poor school systems and rough environments. If all students
were to be judged by the same standard, any college would be doing itself
a disservice. It would be judging apples and oranges on the same scale.
A student who comes from a public school with a graduation rate of 50%
cannot be judged on the same scale as a student who comes from a private
school with a 95% graduation rate.

Some might assume that minority applicants will write a sad essay
about every instance of unfair treatment they have encountered in their
lives. While some students have faced more challenges than others, we
have all gone through difficult times. Suffering is relative. We all have a
sad story to tell—that's why having a sad story doesn't give anyone an
advantage. The most important thing is not what or who you lost, but
how that made you a better person or helped you change the lives of
others.

Sad stories will definitely get you some sympathy, but not admission to a top college. College admissions officers are every student's best friends. They won't let any applicant in unless they are fully convinced they will be able to survive in an academically challenging environment. They know that if any student is ill-qualified and admitted because of a single factor, that student will be miserable.

10   Anyone who thinks they don't have an interesting story because they come from privilege is selling themselves short. If it were up to me, everyone here would write a memoir. At Williams alone, there are more than 2,000 stories that we could learn from and every story is interesting and worth listening to.

Last April, I had the privilege to meet the CEO of the Coca-Cola Company, Muhtar Kent. He told me, "If you can have the humility to talk to me, you should do the same to the person in the street because we all have important stories."

We are Williams because we are not one story or one experience. We are Williams because we all have an important story to tell. We are Williams because we are all uniquely different.

A CLOSER LOOK AT
Affirmative Action Creates False Stigmas

1. Examine Kapembwa's introductory paragraphs closely. How well do they grab readers' attention, identify the topic and purpose, and state the thesis? What else might the author have done to strengthen these aspects of the commentary?

2. Commentaries tend to be more persuasive than generative, but Kapembwa uses a variety of generative strategies (identification, framing, cultural narratives) to negotiate with readers and draw them in. Identify where these strategies are used and discuss whether they help or hurt the effectiveness of this commentary for this topic.

3. Is the main point (thesis) clearly stated? If so, where is it stated? If not, write down what you feel is the main claim.

IDEAS FOR
Arguing

1. Go to *USA Today College* or another website on the Internet and find other opinion pieces written by students on the topic of affirmative action. Select the piece that you find most interesting and write a comparison argument (Chapter 6) that compares Kapembwa's commentary with the one you found. For instance, how do they compare in terms of the use of persuasive and generative strategies? Which is more compelling? Which is more thought provoking?

2. Write a research paper or research report (Chapter 15) on the topic of affirmative action or some other current issue in higher educations (grading, Internet-based courses, tuition costs, etc.). In addition to using print and electronic research sources, try to give your work a local angle by doing empirical research, such as surveys, interviews, and even personal experiences.

Is It Really the End of Men?

ERIKA CHRISTAKIS AND NICHOLAS A. CHRISTAKIS

In this commentary, the authors examine a recent book, The End of Men, *which "argues that changes in the new world economy have dramatically shifted gender roles." Notice how the authors agree and disagree with the book and use this opportunity to offer a new perspective on an issue that has been debated, as they point out, since ancient times.*

It's a story as old as Aristophanes' Lysistrata, the trope of a gender reversal that puts "women on top," but in a new book that's getting lots of attention, a journalist is trying to prove that this fiction has become a reality. In *The End of Men: And the Rise of Women*, Hanna Rosin argues that changes in the world economy have dramatically shifted gender roles. Women have adapted more skillfully to the new socioeconomic landscape by doggedly pursuing self-improvement opportunities, rebranding as the economy requires it, and above all possessing the kind of 21st century work attributes—such as strong communication skills, collaborative leadership and flexibility—that are nudging out the brawny, stuck-in-amber guys. Rock steadiness, long a cherished masculine trait, is about as useful in our fleet-footed economy as a flint arrowhead. Life favors the adapters, and it turns out they're more likely to be women.

Rosin is a gifted storyteller with a talent for ferreting out volumes of illustrative data, and she paints a compelling picture of the ways women are ascendant: women comprise the majority of undergraduate and graduate students on campuses nationwide and are outstripping men for professional degrees; newly employed single women are actually making more money than single men; women seem to have more ambition and a better ability to plan for the future. Moreover, as women gain more financial and cultural power, rates of teen pregnancy, violence and other bad outcomes have dropped. (There may be too much of a good thing: alarmingly, Rosin points to evidence that women may themselves become more violent toward men as they assume the cultural profile of traditional manhood.)

She's even sanguine about college hookup culture, claiming that young women are pretty happy with the crude status quo; they don't want to make any commitments that would jeopardize their career prospects and are willing to forgo what one forlorn undergraduate described as "someone to take me for a frozen yogurt" to avoid being trapped by an early marriage. We ourselves aren't so sure about this point since, from our perspective, the decline of college dating (which hasn't led automatically to marriage since the 1950s, by the way) denies both young women and men an opportunity to practice relationship skills they'll need in order to find long-term partners later. And it's hard to imagine why anyone tolerates the strikingly retro imbalance of sexual satisfaction (to wit: ability to reach orgasm) that accompanies casual hookup culture.

5   But while *The End of Men* captures a profound change in our cultural zeitgeist, one still has to wonder: Why are the relations between men and women still portrayed as a zero-sum game? Why do we need to establish who is winning and losing the war? So much of the coverage of gender issues—indeed the book's cover title itself—pits women and men against one another. In this way, Rosin, who mainly eschews biological explanations for gender differences, still cleaves to a binary characterization of men and women: when one is up, the other must be down. But history suggests that society is better served, and not only economically, when we see men and women engaged in cooperation rather than pitched battle.

When we see one sex as "on top," it makes it harder to recognize the downsides. American women are clearly having their "moment," but, as Rosin notes, their higher powers have resulted in bigger anxieties and more unhappiness than 40 years ago. That's a bitter pill for feminism. Rosin attributes the problem to women's inability to cede authority and delegate household responsibilities to their partners, but that explanation assumes they even have partners. We know that many women are single mothers, in precarious financial straits trying to keep their families afloat without a glimpse of any kind of man in the picture. They have achieved a new sense of autonomy, Rosin notes, that has undoubtedly contributed to declining levels of sexual violence. But they're hardly the fierce amazons we'd like to imagine.

Even the relatively equal and reportedly strong marriages of the educated class—the stable unions where financial and family responsibilities are traded off over the course of a marriage—show some chinks: experts put estimates of sexless marriages as high as 15% to 20%.

There is something else inescapable with this kind of dichotomy: if it is O.K. for women to be seen as superior in some regards, it's also O.K. for men to be seen as superior in others. That's not an argument about how women and men are "meant" to be, innately or in some ultimate, unchanging sense. But surely we can be honest with ourselves about what we see in front of us at a given moment in time, whether we are talking about rates of murder or rates of admission to graduate engineering programs. Former Harvard president Larry Summers was excoriated for his hypotheses about women and science and mathematics (mainly by people who had not carefully read his remarks), but one wonders if Summers had said something positive about women rather than men whether his remarks would have been noted at all. A world in which men and women are seen in opposition means that whenever we say a nice thing about one gender, we must be saying something bad about the other. But that is not the sort of world that helps us address complex problems, and it's not the sort of world most of us would want to inhabit.

A CLOSER LOOK AT
Is It Really the End of Men?

1. What are the major causes for the shift in gender roles that the authors of this commentary and Rosin say has occurred?

2. Use the "agreeing while disagreeing" move to sum up the authors' stance toward *Is It Really the End of Men*: "Although Christakis and Christakis agree with Rosin's argument that

_____, they take issue with the way that Rosin suggests _____."

3. Judging from your experience, in what ways have gender roles been shifting? In what ways have those shifts been beneficial and in what ways harmful? Finally, who has benefitted and who has been harmed by these shifts?

IDEAS FOR
Arguing

1. "Is It Really the End of Men?" is a commentary, but it is also a refutation (Chapter 13). On the Internet, find a commentary or other opinion piece that you disagree with and write a rebuttal-commentary. Be sure to summarize the article accurately and thoroughly. Like Christakis and Christakis, you should offer one or two new insights about the issue.

2. Write a causal analysis (Chapter 7) that explores the reasons for the recent changes in gender roles. According to the authors, Rosin identifies the changes in the worldwide economy as a major cause. In your opinion, what other factors have brought about these shifts?

Refutation— Arguing the Opposing Side

CHAPTER 13

IN THIS CHAPTER, YOU WILL LEARN—

13.1 How to constructively disagree with an argument using two kinds of refutation: rebuttals and counterarguments

13.2 Methods for analyzing an opposing position to identify places where you can agree and disagree

13.3 Strategies for rebutting opposing positions and for offering counterarguments

13.4 Ways to use style and design to build understanding and persuade others

Refutations are arguments that counter other points of view. When you come across an opinion that you believe is inaccurate, misinformed, or just plain wrong, you can use a refutation to figure out why you disagree with it and persuade others to your side.

There are two kinds of refutation:

Rebuttal—A rebuttal focuses almost completely on the opposing argument, trying to disprove, correct, or undermine it by directly challenging its evidence, reasoning, and tone.

Counterargument—A counterargument responds to another's argument by challenging its weaknesses and offering a different perspective or alternative approach.

13.1 How to constructively disagree with an argument using two kinds of refutation: rebuttals and counterarguments

Refutations are primarily persuasive forms of argument, but they have their generative qualities. In the generative mode, you should use conversations to better understand all sides of the issue, while paying attention to how others frame issues or identify with one side or the other of the debate. In persuasive mode, you will need to convince the audience with good evidence, reasoning (*logos*), appeals to authority (*ethos*), and emotional appeals (*pathos*).

In college, your professors will ask you to write arguments for or against assertions made by public figures, politicians, experts, and even other students. Refutations are assigned in argument-based courses like political science, education, the humanities, prelaw, and some human sciences.

Refutation is equally important in the workplace (Figure 13.1). Lawyers and legislators regularly refute or counter the arguments of others. Refutations are also important in business, science, medicine, and education as leaders in these fields work out new strategies, pathways, and plans. Refutation gives you the ability to highlight those limitations tactfully while figuring out or laying the groundwork for your own views.

FIGURE 13.1 Using Refutation to Examine Issues and Arguments
Refutations can help you counter the positions of those you oppose but also think through issues with the people you work with.

13.2 Methods for analyzing an opposing position to identify places where you can agree and disagree

Inventing the Content of Your Refutation

When disagreeing with someone else, you need to do more than simply state a strong opinion or announce your opposing view. To refute an opposing point of view, you need to begin with good evidence and solid reasoning.

Let's say you have found an argument you disagree with. Read the argument a couple times so you are familiar with its major points and evidence. Then, you can use the Believing and Doubting Game to analyze the argument closely.

QUICK View

Generative

Persuasive

Generative Argument—Refutations can play a role in generative argument. By challenging others' positions, you reveal limitations and explain how to alter and improve their positions. When used properly, refutation helps people develop stronger arguments.

Persuasive Argument—Refutations are used to persuade the audience that an argument is unsound and explain why. By pointing out weaknesses in reasoning (*logos*), appeals to authority (*ethos*), and emotional appeals (*pathos*), you can persuade the audience that they too should disagree. A counterargument uses a rebuttal as the springboard for presenting an alternate position.

Genre Patterns

These patterns for a rebuttal and counterargument are suggestions. Refutation arguments can be organized in a variety of ways.

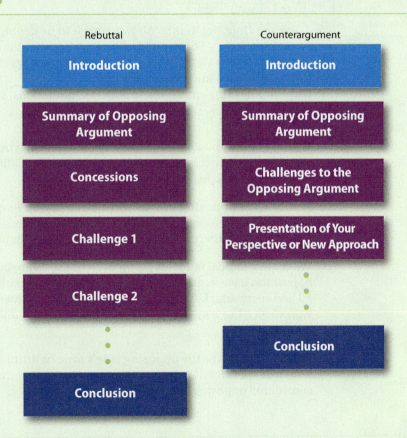

Rebuttal

- Introduction
- Summary of Opposing Argument
- Concessions
- Challenge 1
- Challenge 2
- Conclusion

Counterargument

- Introduction
- Summary of Opposing Argument
- Challenges to the Opposing Argument
- Presentation of Your Perspective or New Approach
- Conclusion

Step One: Play the Believing Game— Where Do We Agree?

Identifying places where you agree with the opposing view might seem like a strange way to start. But by first figuring out where you agree, you can better understand why you disagree.

Start out by playing the Believing Game, which you learned about in Chapter 4 on critical reading. Pretend you are completely convinced by the opposing argument. What are its strengths? What points does the argument make that most people would agree with? Why exactly is this argument persuasive to its supporters? Make a list of two or three reasons why a "believer" would accept this argument.

This kind of "believing" analysis is important. You will sharpen your understanding of your own views as you figure out why others believe differently. And, eventually, when drafting your refutation you can demonstrate your goodwill to the audience by identifying places of agreement or acknowledging that others have strong feelings about the issue. Doing so shows the audience that your response is reasonable and fair, making them more open to considering your side of the argument.

Step Two: Play the Doubting Game—Where Do We Disagree?

Now, play the Doubting Game. Allow yourself to be deeply skeptical about the argument you are refuting. Focus on identifying the major points on which you disagree. More than likely, you won't need to refute all of these opposing points, so choose the two to five issues that are most significant.

Use the following questions to look for limitations and flaws in the opposing argument:

- **Where is the opposing side factually incorrect?** If you can show that the opposing argument is based on inaccurate or misleading facts or data, you can challenge its conclusions facts.

- **Where is the opposing side using weak or flawed reasoning?** Look for places where the opposition is using *if… then*, *either…or*, and *cause and effect* statements in which there are unstated or questionable assumptions.

- **Where are logical fallacies being used in the opposing argument?** Does the opposition base its case on logical fallacies, such as straw-man arguments or ad hominem attacks? Pointing out a logical fallacy doesn't prove the opposing view wrong, but it's a good way to show that the argument is questionable or doubtful.

- **Can you challenge the opposing side's tone or attitude?** If the opposition's tone is aloof, sarcastic, or flippant, you can point out that they have not seriously considered opposing views.

- **Can you question the opposing side's authority on this issue?** Perhaps you can challenge the authority of the sources they use. Are these sources using evidence that is based on something more than opinion? Are the opposition's sources reliable?

- **Can you draw attention to the opposition's financial interests?** You can point out that the opposition believes what they believe because they stand to gain financially (or perhaps avoid losses).

As you play the Doubting Game you should look for weaknesses from all these areas. When you draft your refutation, however, you should only mention the most significant ones. Too many will be tiresome and make you appear overly combative.

Step Three: Do Your Research—Where Is the Evidence?

If you want your refutation to successfully influence your audience, you need to thoroughly research the issues involved. You need facts, data, examples, quotes, and other evidence to challenge the opposing view and support your own understanding.

Electronic sources—Internet searches will turn up a wealth of credible and not-so-credible sources of information. You might find reports available at policy institutes (aka "think tanks") to be especially helpful. Some of the more reliable think tanks include the Brookings Institution (www.brookings.edu), the Pew Research Center (www.pewresearch.org), and the American Enterprise Institute (www.aei.org). The U.S. federal government also offers a wealth of statistics and information on just about any topic.

Print sources—Use the online catalog at your university library to find books and articles about your subject (Figure 13.2). You should pay special attention to newspapers and magazines because they will often give you the most recent information about your issue. Books will help you find facts that are usually considered established and less controversial.

Empirical sources—Interview experts at your university or in your community. More than likely, someone on your college campus or in your community is an expert on the subject you are discussing. That person may help you identify the places people disagree about a specific issue and help you understand why. With some subjects, you might be able to make field observations. Or, you could create a survey to sample the opinions of others.

Again, without solid evidence you are not going to be able to support your argument or challenge the opposing argument. Collect a variety of sources, not just the ones that agree with you. Then you will be able to triangulate your sources to develop

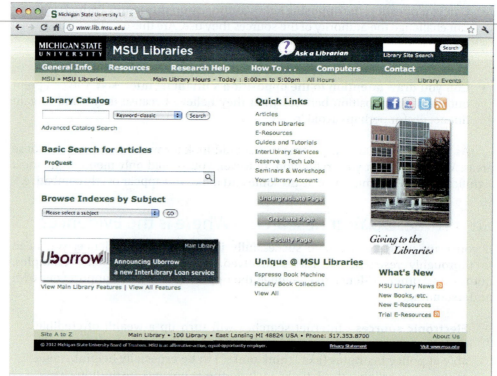

FIGURE 13.2 Your Campus Library's Website
Your campus library has a wealth of easy-to-access print documents. Finding sources is as simple as going to your library's website.

your best argument. Also, while collecting sources, make sure you keep track of them so you can cite them properly.

Step 4: Synthesis—Where Do We Go from Here?

The Believing and Doubting Game usually ends with a "synthesis" phase that can help you figure out the basis of your own argument. More than likely, you still disagree with the argument you are refuting. At this point, however, you should have a better sense of why the opposing side believes what they believe and why you believe what you believe. Your research should have also provided you more evidence to challenge the other side and support your side.

As you work toward a synthesis, it's important to understand that most points of view, even ones you strongly disagree with, have some merit. In other words, it's very rare that someone is completely wrong. So you should look for places you can agree with the other side or at least acknowledge that they have valid reasons for reaching conclusions that conflict with yours.

Meanwhile, if you want to write a counterargument, not just a rebuttal, you should come up with better way forward. Here is where your generative argument skills will be useful. Pay special attention to how the other side is framing the issue or using identity to influence the audience. Then figure out how you can reframe the issue in a different but positive way. Try to use identity to appeal to your audience's values and experiences, demonstrating that your ideas are the best way forward.

MOVES for Arguing

Have you ever been arguing with someone, and they say something you believe is just wrong or wrong headed? Yet when you open your mouth to respond, you have trouble explaining why you disagree? Here are some moves that will help you:

The author has not acknowledged three important points, which shows he/she does not fully understand the issue. First, _____. Second, _____. Third, _____.

When you look closely at the other side's reasoning, you see that their assumptions are _____, _____, and _____, which do not logically lead to their conclusions.

The other side may sound appealing, but they are assuming _____, which is not true.

The other side believes that _____ causes _____, but actually _____ has been proven to be caused by _____.

The other side wants you to believe we must choose between _____ or _____. In reality, we can have both. For instance, we can _____.....

My opponent is arguing that the costs outweigh the benefits. As a matter of fact, we can have _____ and _____ for much less than you would expect.

As a _____, my opponent may understand _____, but he/she doesn't have the background or experience to understand _____.

Although _____ makes the important point that _____, he/she fails to understand that _____.

The other side's tone, which is _____, shows that they are not serious about this issue or they think others will understand it.

Of course the opposition believes _____, because they will gain _____ and _____ if we accept their views on this issue.

13.3 Strategies for rebutting opposing positions and for offering counterarguments

Organizing and Drafting Your Refutation

Refutations can be organized in a variety of ways, two of which are shown in the Quick-View on page 261. As you sketch out an outline, first think about the purpose of your argument. Specifically, you need to decide whether you are rebutting the opposing argument (i.e. directly challenging and undermining it) or offering a counterargument (i.e. highlighting weaknesses in the other position and offering a better way forward).

Like almost any argument, your refutation should have an introduction, body, and conclusion.

Introduction: Set the Stage

You might find it helpful to think of your refutation as a debate on a stage. Imagine you are on a stage with the author of the argument you are refuting. Your introduction needs to set the framework for your position.

Grab the audience's attention—Use a question, compelling statement, or anecdote to capture the audience's attention. Your grabber will often name the topic under debate and stress its importance.

Identify your topic—If your grabber didn't do so already, name your topic and define its scope. Tell your audience what issue you are arguing about. In some cases, you might narrow the scope of the argument by identifying the issues you are not arguing about.

State your purpose—If you writing a rebuttal argument, tell your audience that you will be challenging the opposing argument's major points. If you are offering a counterargument, indicate to your audience that you will be pointing out the limitations of the opposing side and presenting an alternative way to understand and respond to the issue.

State your main point (thesis)—State your main argument (thesis) in positive terms. Tell your audience what you will be proving.

> *Weak Thesis:* Deporting illegal immigrants won't work.

> *Stronger Thesis:* Like it or not, illegal immigrants have become important members of our society, and we need to find constructive ways to provide them pathways to citizenship and help them assimilate.

Provide background information—Offer details on the argument you are refuting, including the author, its title, and where it appeared. You can also provide some historical information on your topic or explain what has recently brought the issue to light.

Stress the importance of the topic—Clearly, the issue being discussed is important to both or all sides. Briefly, explain what is at stake for all sides and the audience.

These introductory moves can be made in a variety of different arrangements. Minimally, you should tell your audience your topic, purpose, and main point. The other moves are helpful for setting the stage for the argument.

Body: Identify the Points of Contention

The body of your refutation should clearly identify the points of contention that you are rebutting or countering. Then, if you are offering a counterargument, you can present your own views or steer the discussion a different way.

Summarize the opposing views objectively

The body of your refutation will likely begin with a summary of the opposing position. You should summarize the other side's argument in a fair, reasonable, and complete way. If you appear to be too biased or to be slanting the argument too much, your audience will question whether your proofs are trustworthy. Instead, summarize the opposing position fairly and objectively, reviewing their major two to five points.

Make any necessary concessions

Then concede any points from the opposing position that you agree with. It's rare that one side of an argument is completely wrong. If you concede one or two points, you will show your audience that you are searching for common ground. Usually, a couple sentences or a paragraph of concessions is enough in a college-level refutation.

Challenge the opposing argument

Spend some time challenging the opposing argument's major points with solid evidence, reasoning, appeals to authority, and emotional appeals. You might want to question the simpler points first and challenge the more complex points later. Spend at least one paragraph on each of the opposing side's major points.

Present your different perspective or new approach (for counterarguments)

If you are offering a counterargument, you should now offer an alternative way to understand the issue or present a better way forward. You have already shown why the opposing position's arguments aren't acceptable. Now you have the opportunity to put forward your own ideas. Usually, this part of a refutation is not long or elaborate. Primarily, you want to reframe the discussion by offering a different perspective or new approach that alters how your audience thinks about the issue. Back up your claims with solid evidence, reasoning, appeals to authority, and emotional appeals.

Conclusion

Your conclusion should bring the debate back to the beginning. Here is where you press home your main point (thesis) with emphasis. A conclusion will typically make up to four moves:

Signal that you are concluding—Use a heading, transitional phrase, or transitional sentence to signal that you are bringing your argument to an end.

Restate your main point (thesis)—As in the introduction, your best strategy is to state your main point, or thesis, in positive terms. Stay positive and constructive here and throughout your conclusion.

Restress the importance of the subject—Tell the audience what is at stake. Explain briefly why this issue is important to all sides.

Look to the future—Often, refutations end with a look to the future. In one or two sentences, explain where you see this issue going. If possible, end the argument on a positive or at least a hopeful note.

In your conclusion, don't argue further against the opposing side or bring up new issues that weren't discussed in the body of the argument. Keep your conclusion brief (one or two paragraphs) and positive. You want your main point to be the highlight of the conclusion.

13.4 Ways to use style and design to build understanding and persuade others

Using Style and Design in Refutations

Choose a style and design that is appropriate to your audience and the situations in which they will consider your refutation.

Using a Plain, Objective Style

The most effective style for a refutation is usually a plain, objective style with perhaps a hint of irritation. Since you are already challenging the opposing side's views, your argument will already feel contentious to the audience. A calm discussion of the issues demonstrates to your audience that you are being reasonable.

Keep your tone simple and straightforward—Your refutation should rely on solid facts and use good reasoning to make your case. Avoid exaggeration or sarcasm and limit your use of emotional adjectives. For example, if you call your opposition "ridiculous," "outrageous," or "silly," you will sound partisan, extreme, or dismissive. Instead, use an objective tone to make your argument sound more measured and reasonable than the opposition's argument.

Use concessive transitions to signal goodwill—An effective way to build goodwill with your audience is to use *concessive transitions* in which you agree with the opposing side in introductory phrases. These transitions include *while, though, although, despite, whereas,* and *even though.*

> **Although** illegal immigration has some economic benefits, Reynolds is correct when he suggests that simply ignoring this issue is no long possible.

> **Even though** Howards is correct that the elephants in zoos are well cared for, these large warm-weather animals suffer terribly during the winter in northern climates.

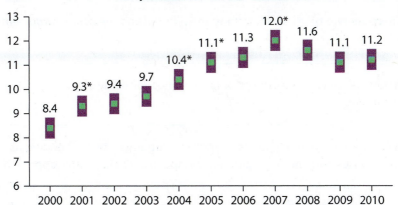

Estimates of the U.S. Unauthorized Immigrant Population, 2000–2010 (*millions*)

Notes: Bars indicate low and high points of the estimated 90% confidence interval. The symbol * indicates the change from the previous year is statistically significant.

FIGURE 13.3
Illustrating a Point with a Graph
A graph is often a good way to visually refute someone else's argument. People trust what they can see.

> **While** I agree with the Democrats that creating jobs is important, borrowing more money from places like China and Saudi Arabia only pushes America's financial problems onto the next generation.

By agreeing on some issues or acknowledging a few points, you aren't weakening your argument. Instead, you are signaling places where both sides might reach common ground. You are also demonstrating to your audience that you are being reasonable.

Using Graphics to Illustrate Your Points

People tend to believe what they see. If you can "show" your audience that the other side is wrong, your refutation will be much more effective. Specifically, a graph, table, or image can drive home a point and make it memorable.

Use graphs and charts to illustrate trends—Graphs and charts are especially helpful for showing how an issue has changed over time (Figure 13.3). You can use graphed data to illustrate trends or even demonstrate that commonly held views are not true or that the facts have changed.

Add images—Photographs, too, are useful for showing the audience the limitations of the opposing argument and supporting your own. If you can offer an image that illustrates an accurate version of the truth, you can cast doubt on the opposing side while supporting your own views.

In your written text, tell your audience how each graphic fits in with your argument and what they should notice about the graphic. Your captions can repeat a point you made in the written text or even restate a key claim.

Ready to get started on your refutation? Here's what you need to know.

1 There are two types of refutations: the *rebuttal* and the *counterargument*.

2 A rebuttal disproves, corrects, or undermines someone else's argument.

3 A counterargument responds to another's argument by challenging its weaknesses and offering a different perspective or alternative approach.

4 When inventing, analyze your opponent's position, identifying two to five major points that you would like to argue against.

5 Identify one or two places at which you can agree with the opposition or concede a point.

6 Explain specifically why you believe the opposition is wrong, using facts and reasoning to back up your claims.

7 As you organize and draft your refutation, make sure you explain the other side objectively and fairly.

8 The best style for a refutation is an objective tone with a hint of irritation.

9 Use illustrations and graphics to demonstrate visually how the opposition is wrong.

10 Don't rely on emotional arguments to refute your opposition. Your argument needs to be reasonable and calm. You should demonstrate goodwill.

1. With your group, find three refutations with an Internet search engine. You might use the keyword "rebuttal" to help you find good ones. Then compare and contrast these refutations. Which ones did you find most persuasive? As a group, write a brief analysis in which you discuss the content, organization, style, and design of the refutations.

2. Find a rebuttal on YouTube or a similar video site, and show it to your group. How are public refutations handled differently than written refutations? Did the speaker seem nervous? What other kinds of emotions did she or he show? What would be some of the advantages and disadvantages of delivering a refutation as a speech rather than in writing? Present your findings to your class.

3. Think back on your own life. Do you remember a moment when you wish you had a great comeback against another argument? Do you remember not speaking up when someone said something you disagreed with? How could you have handled this disagreement differently? Tell your group what you would have done differently.

1. Find an argument in the public sphere that you disagree with. Go through the refutation process described in this chapter. First, analyze the opposing viewpoint. Second, identify places you agree with the opposing viewpoint. Third, identify points on which you disagree. Then do some research on the Internet and write a one-page rebuttal or counterargument. In a reflection to your instructor, discuss how you would expand your argument and describe your position's strengths and weaknesses.

2. Find an argument that you agree with (the stronger your beliefs, the better). Now turn the tables and write a one-page rebuttal or counterargument to that argument. This is going to be difficult, because you are basically making an argument *against* a position you believe in. Your goal, however, is to identify the potential soft spots in your own beliefs. In an e-mail to your instructor, explain the strengths and the weaknesses of your original beliefs. Then explain how you might counter the opposition's argument now that you have seen the argument from the other side.

3. Find two opposing articles that are strongly for and against using Wikipedia as a source for college research papers. Write an analysis in which you explore both sides of the argument. Which side do you think makes the best argument? Does each side properly refute the other's arguments? Which side better anticipates the arguments against its position, making its position harder to challenge? Write a refutation that offers a counterargument against both of these positions and uses the best ideas from each side.

In this rebuttal paper, written for a first-year-writing course at Pennsylvania State University, Angela Moore argues against a pro-capital punishment article published by the Heritage Foundation, a conservative-learning think tank. Notice how Moore uses research to back up her claims against the original argument.

Against Capital Punishment

Angela Moore

Your hands and feet are restricted by bracelets and ankle wear you did not choose for style or comfort. You are read a document, and escorted into a room with no more decor than a gas station bathroom; there is a gurney with restraints attached, an intravenous, and a clear wall in which a small audience sits, watching you intently like a pathetic rat in an experiment. You are scared because you know you've done nothing wrong; you are innocent and your death sentence is about to be carried out via the cocktail of drugs found in the intravenous with your name on it.

Unfortunately, this is a reality for some, particularly 23 proven-innocent souls who have suffered the death penalty since the year 1900 (Radelet, 1990). However, even with these shocking and grave circumstances well known, there are many people in America who are still in favor of capital punishment, or the death penalty. One such person is David B. Muhlhausen, author of a 2007 article entitled "The Death Penalty Deters Crime and Saves Lives," which can be found on the website of The Heritage Foundation, a conservatively based organization. In his article, Muhlhausen discusses the reasons why the death penalty should not be abolished. However, his claims do not hold; they stand on unstable and debatable ground. The death penalty should indeed be abolished for many reasons including, but not limited to lack of deterrence, an accepted logic of retribution, a possibility for error as seen in the opening sequence, and the fact that the death penalty violates a citizen's right to not be subjected to cruel and unusual punishment, as stated in the Bill of Rights.

Those who oppose the death penalty do however hold some of the same, basic principles shared by those who are against capital punishment. For example, it is reasonable to state that most, if not all of Americans would like their friends and family, along with themselves, to live in a safe environment in which one is not on guard for their life all hours of the day. So too, it can be securely said that most believe that wrongdoers or criminals should be punished for their acts of lawlessness. Even further, it is safe to say that the punishment should certainly fit the crime that has been committed. Discrepancy only occurs when defining and determining what punishment, namely the death penalty, is appropriate in cases dealing with the most heinous of crimes, such as rape and/or murder. The arguments made by Muhlhausen in his article, "The Death Penalty Deters Crime and Saves Lives," are exactly what the title of his article reads. However, these two motives are both inaccurate and lacking.

First of all, capital punishment does not deter future crime, and certainly not previous crime. Arguments in favor of the death penalty, such as the ones in the article previously stated, have claimed that due to the harshness of punishment by death, criminals will and do refrain from committing a lawless act. This is simply not the case, however. In a study done by the *New York Times*, it was found that the homicide rate in states with capital punishment was actually higher, some 48 percent, than their no-option-of-death-penalty counterparts (Bonner & Fessenden, 2000). The point can also be made that murders are almost always committed in sudden fits of passion, and therefore no consideration is given to the consequences of the action.

Muhlhausen's claim that the death penalty saves lives also falls through.   5
In reality, instating capital punishment may actually damage quality of life through the acceptance of the logic of retribution. If taken literally, we would not only have to execute the harshest of criminals, but also make their punishment fit the crime they committed; we would have to rape

rapists, and murder serial killers over and over again (Bedau, 2012). Also, when this logic is accepted, so too is the old saying "an eye for an eye…" In a society in which we are supposed to be thriving, making grand discoveries every day, pushing forward, and creating "change," is this outdated, barbaric logic not showing regression and prehistoric-like tendencies? The finality of the retribution taken on the life of the criminal also begs the question, "where was the possibility for reformation of the individual?"

Beyond the arguments of the article from The Heritage Foundation, one can find flaws within the death penalty such as the possibility of error, namely in putting the wrong person to death for a crime they did not commit, as was previously illustrated. Human error exists in all arenas of life, and the courtroom is no exception. In years past, DNA evidence did not exist, and therefore most evidence leading to a conviction was circumstantial, putting many innocent "criminals" on death row. Since 1973, 142 people in 25 US states have been released from death row with evidence of their innocence, most likely as the result of reexamination and the use of DNA (Death Penalty Information Center). Also, a certain amount of discrimination has landed innocent men on death row. This fact is not created in the minds of anti-death penalty activists. Statistics confirm that between 1930 and 1990, 4,016 persons were executed in the United States and of these, 2,129, or 53 percent, were African American (Bedau). When dealing with a person's life and mortality, the possibility of error should not exist, and if it does, then the medium questioning this right to life must be eliminated.

Lastly, capital punishment violates one of our basic rights outlined in the Constitution of the United States in which the use of "cruel and unusual punishment" is prohibited. Our country was founded on certain principles that set us apart from other nations; principles such as freedom and basic rights are of the upmost importance. Our Constitution goes as far as to include a Bill of Rights, outlining precious rights all humans were designed to have. Six major forms of execution are accepted in our world today. These include lethal injection, the electric chair, hanging, death by firing squad, gas chamber, and stoning. When our country, which prides itself on a fair and democratic outlook, accepts three of these forms of torture (electric chair, lethal injection, and firing squad), how can we be seen as the role models for other industrialized nations? How can other nations look to us for guidance in what fairness is, when most of our allies such as Great Britain and France have abolished the death penalty in law and/or practice, along with 26 other European nations (Bedau)?

All bias aside, when the evidence is laid out plainly, it can be deciphered that capital punishment is indeed a faulty practice that should be abolished in both law and practice. Both sides of the argument can agree that in order to remain a safe nation by the citizen's standard, punishment for wrongdoing is a necessary action that should take place, and it should fit the severity of the crime, to a moral point. Someone's life, whether it is the life of the victim, the perpetrator, or the family of either of the individuals, should never be taken by another human hand. Murder by definition is to kill or slaughter inhumanly or barbarously; whether it's done by a peer, a governmental body, or an establishment the act is wrong.

References

Bedau, H. A. (2012) The case against the death penalty. American Civil Liberties Union. Retrieved from http://www.aclu.org/capital-punishment/case-against-death-penalty

Bonner, R. & Fessenden, F. (2000, September 20) Absence of executions: A special report. *New York Times*. Retreived from http://www.nytimes.com/2000/09/22/us/absence-executions-special-report-states-with-no-death-penalty-share-lower.html?pagewanted=all&src=pm

Death Penalty Information Center (2012) The innocence list. Retrieved from http://www.deathpenaltyinfo.org/innocence-list-those-freed-death-row

Mulhausen, D. B. (2007) The death penalty deters crime and saves lives. The Heritage Foundation. Retrieved from http://www.heritage.org/research/testimony/the-death-penalty-deters-crime-and-saves-lives

Radelet, M. R. (1990) Facing the death penalty: Essays on a cruel and unusual punishment. Philadelphia: Temple.

A CLOSER LOOK AT
Against Capital Punishment

1. Read through this refutation carefully and list the arguments made in the original argument that Moore rebuts. In addition to her rebuttal, what counterarguments does Moore provide?

2. Play the Believing and Doubting Game with Moore's article. First, assume the perspective of someone who agrees wholeheartedly with her refutation, and explain why her rebuttal and counterarguments are compelling. Then assume

the opposite perspective, and give reasons for doubting the soundness of her assertions. In the end, where do you stand on this issue?

3. Go to the original article written by David B. Muhlhausen and published by the Heritage Foundation on the Internet and read it carefully. Does Moore do justice to Muhlhausen's argument? What suggestions could you offer to Moore for improving her refutation?

IDEAS FOR
Arguing

1. Create a visual or multimedia argument about the capital punishment debate. Create a 10- to 15-slide presentation that summarizes both sides of the debate and states your own position. Explain how people who disagree with you understand the issue. Then show your side and explain why you feel your position is stronger. Add photographs and other visuals such as charts and graphs where they are appropriate and strengthen your argument.

2. Write a refutation of Moore's refutation. Where are the weak points in her argument? Where does she fail to represent the pro-capital punishment fairly or completely? Describe which of her claims seem questionable to you and explain why you feel those claims are not sound.

The Atheist Crusade: A Jewish Rebuttal to Richard Dawkins' *The God Delusion*

SARA YOHEVED RIGLER WITH RABBI MOSHE ZELDMAN

In this refutation, the authors explain why they disagree with evolutionary biologist Richard Dawkins's argument that religion has been a major cause of the world's evils. Notice how they take each of Dawkins's arguments quite seriously, summarizing his views and then rebutting them with logic.

Columnist and psychiatrist Theodore Dalrymple, writing in the prestigious "City Journal," discloses the origins of his atheism. He was nine years old and attending prayer assembly in his British school. The headmaster Mr. Clinton commanded the children to keep their eyes shut lest God depart the assembly hall. Young Theodore wanted to test the hypothesis, so he opened his eyes suddenly so as to catch a glimpse of the fleeing God. Instead he saw Mr. Clinton praying with one eye open in order to survey the children. "I quickly concluded," recounts Dalrymple, "that Mr. Clinton did not believe what he said about the need to keep our eyes shut. And if he did not believe that, why should I believe in his God? In such illogical leaps do our beliefs often originate, to be disciplined later in life by elaborate rationalization."

Over the last year and a half, such "elaborate rationalizations" of atheism have spawned a spate of books condemning God, religion, and religious believers. Christopher Hitchens' book, *God is Not Great: How Religion Poisons Everything* reached #1 on the *New York Times* bestseller list in just three weeks. Richard Dawkins' The *God Delusion* has sold over 1.5 million copies and has been translated into 31 languages. It was on the *New York Times* bestseller list for 51 weeks. The BBC produced a two-hour documentary based on the book, entitled, "Religion: The Root of All Evil?"

Many critics have pointed out that the appeal of these books is less in the soundness of their arguments than in the eloquence of their prose. As Bruce DeSilva of the Associated Press wrote: "Hitchens has nothing new to say, although it must be acknowledged that he says it exceptionally well."

The venom of their invective actually turns these proud rationalists into irrational hate-mongers.

5   Five of the six books constituting the neo-atheist crusade can be dismissed as screeds, full of what Theodore Dalrymple describes as "sloppiness and lack of intellectual scruple, with the assumption of certainty where there is none." The venom of their invective against God and religious believers actually turns these proud rationalists into irrational hate-mongers. Witness Sam Harris's declaration in his book *The End of Faith*: "The link between belief and behavior raises the stakes considerably. Some propositions are so dangerous that it may be ethical to kill people for believing them."

Obviously, such a diatribe does not merit a rational rebuttal.

1. The Danger of Religion?

Only *The God Delusion* by Richard Dawkins, a professor of evolutionary biology at Oxford, merits serious discussion. Dawkins advances four basic arguments.

One is that religion is dangerous. His BBC documentary begins with the 9/11 attack on the World Trade Center. He then shows footage of wounded Israelis after a suicide bombing. From this he pans to pictures of Hasidic Jews praying at the Western Wall, and announces, "Religious terrorism is the logical outcome of deeply held faith."

Dawkins's distorted syllogism—that because Muslim terrorists are religious and Muslim terrorists murder, therefore all religious people are potential murderers—is enough to make a freshman student of logic go apoplectic.

10   The obvious rebuttal of Dawkins's allegation that religion causes terrorism, wars, crusades, inquisitions, jihad, etc. is a cursory look at the genocides of the 20th century. An estimated 80,000,000 human beings were murdered in the course of the 20th century (not including war casualties), and they were all murdered by atheists: Hitler, Stalin, Pol Pot, and Mao.

Dawkins writes that this point comes up "after just about every public lecture that I ever give on the subject of religion, and in most of my radio interviews as well." He then devotes seven pages to attempting to prove that Hitler was not an atheist but a Catholic. He sums up this section: "Stalin was probably an atheist and Hitler probably wasn't; but even if they were both atheists, the bottom line of the Stalin/Hitler debating point is very simple. Individual atheists may do evil things but they don't do evil things in the name of atheism."

If Dawkins had asked Stalin or Mao if they were motivated by their ideology, they would certainly have contended that all their policies derived directly from their Communist principles. Even today the Communist regime of China is cutting open live Falon Gong practitioners and removing their vital organs for sale on the lucrative organ transplant market. This atrocity is consistent with their atheistic ideology that regards human beings in exclusively economic terms and denies that human life is sacred because human beings were created "in the image of God." Since Communism is an inherently atheistic system that denies both God and the Divine soul, Dawkins's contention that atheists "don't do evil things in the name of atheism" is blatantly false.

It's like saying medicine is evil because Dr. Josef Mengele committed heinous acts in the name of medical research.

Furthermore, to say that religion is evil because religious people have committed heinous acts in the name of religion is like saying medicine is evil because Dr. Josef Mengele committed heinous acts against the subjects of his Auschwitz experiments in the name of medical research. One can take any constructive enterprise and use it for destructive purposes. This offers no grounds for condemning the enterprise itself.

15   One of the many distortions in which all the neo-atheist books abound is that they rant about the evil byproducts of religion without ever mentioning religion's benefits to every society throughout history. As Theodore Dalrymple observes: "The thinness of the new atheism is evident in its approach to our civilization, which until recently was religious to its core. To regret religion is, in fact, to regret our civilization and its monuments, its achievements, and its legacy."

Dalrymple gives as examples the Cathedral of Chartres and the *Saint Matthew Passion*. Judaism can point to its legacy of Western values. As Ken Spiro demonstrates in his book *World-Perfect*, Judaism has given the world its core values: respect for human life, peace, justice, equality before the law, education, and social responsibility.

Even Oxford University, where Prof. Dawkins enjoys tenure, was founded nine cen-

turies ago by religious Christians, among them the Bishop of Rochester.

2. Science vs. Religion

Dawkins contends that religion and science are irrevocably opposed. He maintains that, unlike science, faith in God is irrational: "Faith demands a positive suspension of critical faculties." The Dawkins dogma states: "Science uses reason and evidence to reach logical conclusions. Religion is about turning untested belief into unshakable truth through the power of institutions and the passage of time."

Dawkins, who was raised in the Church of England, naturally associates religion with irrational beliefs such as the virgin birth and God impregnating a human being to give birth to a God-man. This, however, has nothing to do with Judaism. Just open a page of the Talmud, read Maimonides, or spend one hour learning in a yeshiva, and you will experience Judaism's rigorous argumentation to discern the truth. The primary focus in Judaism is the study of Torah and the development, not the "suspension," of critical faculties.

20   Judaism's perfectly rational belief in God, as enunciated by Maimonides, is that there must be a non-physical, infinite source of the physical, finite universe. As will be shown below, there is no other plausible explanation for how the universe got here.

Einstein understood that the beginning of the universe implies a transcendent force that brought it into being. That's why for so long he clung to his belief in a static universe (one that had always existed, and therefore had no beginning) and resisted the mounting evidence for an expanding universe.

As Lawrence Kelemen in his book *Permission to Believe*, explains the challenge posed by an expanding universe:

> Why would a dot containing all matter
> and energy—a dot that sat quietly for
> an eternity—suddenly explode? The

Law of Inertia insists that objects at rest should remain at rest unless acted upon by an external force. Since all matter and energy would be contained within this dot, there could be nothing outside the dot to get things going—nothing natural, at least. What force could have ignited the initial explosion?

Faced with evidence of an expanding universe discovered by astronomer Vesto Slipher and deduced by mathematicians Willem de Sitter and Alexander Friedman, Einstein refused to accept the inevitable conclusion. "I have not yet fallen into the hands of the priests," was Einstein's famous response to the possibility of an expanding universe. Clearly he understood that an expanding universe must have a non-physical First Cause.

25 Since then, of course, science has proven that the universe is expanding from the original event known as the Big Bang. This reality gives scientific backing to Maimonides' philosophical contention that a supernatural force must have initiated the natural universe.

The respected journal *Astrophysics and Space Science* [issue 269–270 (1999)] states clearly that the Big Bang points to a "transcendent cause of the universe":

> The absolute origin of the universe, of all matter and energy, even of physical space and time themselves, in the Big Bang singularity contradicts the perennial naturalistic assumption that the universe has always existed. One after another, models designed to avert the initial cosmological singularity—the Steady State model, the Oscillating model, Vacuum Fluctuation models—have come and gone. Current quantum gravity models, such as the Hartle-Hawking model and the Vilenkin model, must appeal to the physically unintelligible and metaphysically dubious device of "imaginary time" to avoid the universe's beginning. The

> contingency implied by an absolute beginning ex nihilo points to a transcendent cause of the universe beyond space and time. Philosophical objections to a cause of the universe fail to carry conviction. [pp. 723–740]

In a flippant two and a half pages, Dawkins dismisses Thomas Aquinas' proofs for the existence of God (Maimonides, who preceded Aquinas by two centuries, writes similar arguments). "The five 'proofs' asserted by Thomas Aquinas in the thirteenth century don't prove anything, and are easily—though I hesitate to say so, given his eminence—exposed as vacuous." [p. 100]

Dawkins simply fails to understand the depth of argument of philosophy, and is too arrogant to admit when he's out of his element.

Dawkins's rebuttal of Aquinas would earn 30 him a "D" in any first year philosophy course. A biologist, not a philosopher, Dawkins simply fails to understand the depth of argument of philosophy, and is too arrogant to admit when he's out of his element.

The problem of "First Cause" is the knock-out argument against which Dawkins has no defense. Even if Dawkins, the evolutionary biologist, could prove that human beings evolved out of some primordial soup, evolution still begs the bigger questions: Where did the elements of the primordial soup come from? What caused the first particles to come into being? What caused the Big Bang? How can you believe in a beginning without also believing in a beginner? To these classical challenges to atheism, Dawkins offers no response.

Dawkins's sanguine belief that although scientists have not yet created life, someday in the future they will succeed, suspiciously resembles messianic hopes:

> I shall not be surprised if, within the next few years, chemists report that they have successfully midwifed a new origin of life in the laboratory. Nevertheless it hasn't happened yet, and it is still possible to maintain that

the probability of its happening is, and always was, exceedingly low—although it did happen once! [p. 165]

Of course Dawkins would then have to explain how to do it without having the original chemicals. Dawkins may be able to make a salad, but let's see him create the vegetables.

35 Dawkins's insistence that religion and science contradict each other dismisses with an imperious sweep of the hand an entire body of work written by respected scientists who show that science in fact corroborates the Genesis narrative. Although the bibliography of such books is too lengthy to list here, three excellent examples are: *The Science of God: The Convergence of Scientific and Biblical Wisdom* by M.I.T. physicist Dr. Gerald Schroeder, *The Language of God* by Dr. Francis Collins, Director of the Human Genome Project, who, by the way, grew up as an agnostic, and *There Is a God: How the World's Most Notorious Atheist Changed His Mind* by Anthony Flew and Roy Varghese.

3. Religious Education As Child Abuse

Dawkins's third point is that indoctrinating children with religious teachings is akin to child abuse, because they prevent children from learning to think independently. He writes that terms like "Catholic child" or "Muslim child" should make people flinch.

Dawkins is, in fact, surprisingly tolerant of the sexual abuse of children. He writes: "We live in a time of hysteria about pedophilia ... It is clearly unjust to visit upon all pedophiles a vengeance appropriate to the tiny minority who are also murderers." [p. 354–5] He has, however, zero tolerance for what he considers the far worse crime of raising a child in a particular religion:

Once, in the question time after a lecture in Dublin, I was asked what I thought about the widely publicized cases of sexual abuse by Catholic priests in Ireland. I replied that, horrible as sexual abuse no doubt was,

the damage was arguably less than the long-term psychological damage inflicted by bringing the child up Catholic in the first place. [p. 356]

While it takes a whole book to refute a book, suffice it to say that all parents, whether religious or secular, inculcate their children with their own beliefs. Does Dawkins not raise his children with a prejudice to be pro-democracy? Anticocaine? In the name of intellectual honesty, would he expose his children to every perverse element of society? In the name of intellectual balance, would he permit his children to study Muslim theology in a Saudi mosque for a few months?

4. Darwinian Morality

Dawkins' final point is that human beings 40 don't need religion for morality. In his BBC documentary, as a troop of chimpanzees frolics in the background, he asserts that morality is also the product of evolution.

His explanation is simple: "Morality stems from altruistic genes naturally selected in our evolutionary past." Pointing to the social structures abounding in the animal kingdom, he asserts that "survival of the fittest" favored the evolutionary development of moral traits:

Natural selection favours genes that predispose individuals, in relationships of asymmetric need and opportunity, to give when they can, and to solicit giving when they can't. It also favors tendencies to remember obligations, bear grudges, police exchange relationships and punish cheats who take, but don't give when their turn comes. [pp. 248–9]

Here the title of Dawkins's documentary, "Religion: The Root of All Evil" turns out to be true, although not in the way he intended. Religion is indeed the root of all evil, because without religion there would be no concept of "evil."

And religion is also the root of all good. Simply put, without religion determining an absolute system of values, what makes anything evil or good?

If human beings were nothing but advanced monkeys, as evolutionists would have us believe, the concept of morality would be irrelevant. A lion that devours a kicking and struggling "innocent" zebra is not "evil." She is merely following her instinct, and instincts in the animal kingdom carry no moral value.

Dawkins offers an example: "Vampire bats learn which other individuals of their social group can be relied upon to pay their debts (in regurgitated blood) and which individuals cheat." [p. 248] But is the bat who pays his debts "good" and the bat who cheats "evil"? Of course not.

According to Dawkins, the terrorists flying into the Twin Towers are no different than the lion devouring the zebra.

By taking God out of the picture there is nothing evil about evil. According to Dawkins, the terrorists flying into the Twin Towers are no different than the lion devouring the zebra.

Even in the development of human civilization, social contracts were expedient rather than moral. The Code of Hammurabi, for example, prohibits stealing for the mutual protection of property rights, not because stealing is "evil."

Morality could have been introduced into the world only by God, for no one else has the arbitrary right to declare universal standards of right and wrong. And much of the morality that God ordained is counter-intuitive and goes against instinct.

For example, historian Paul Johnson [*A History of the Jews*, p. 34] has pointed out that, among all the legal codes of the ancient Near East, only the Bible declared that crimes against property are never capital, because the sacredness of human life supersedes property values. The Torah also commands people to release the debts owed to them at the end of every seven years, to return purchased land to its original owner every fifty years, to proactively intercede when another person's life is in danger, and to not carry a grudge or take revenge. (Remember Dawkins's statement, quoted above, that natural selection favors those who "bear grudges.")

In his duel against religion Richard Dawkins chose his weapon: rationality. While he certainly gets points for his eloquent use of the Queen's English and for his cynical wit, in terms of rational argument Dawkins wields a dull sword indeed.

---

[1]Most laughable is Dawkins' attempt to show the strides made in a constantly evolving morality. His "proof" that morality evolves is that a half century ago in England almost everyone was racist, and now almost no one is racist. A half century ago almost everyone was homophobic and now the majority is not. This is the apex of moral evolution in Dawkins' estimation.

But what about the Holocaust? The present genocide in Darfur? The stealing of organs of live Falon Gong practitioners? The sadism that accompanied or accompanies each of these atrocities dramatically refutes any notion of moral evolution. Dawkins's fancied "moral evolution" must mean that human beings are demonstrably less barbaric with the passing of centuries, but in terms of moral level, Rudolph Hoess, the commandant of Auschwitz, had nothing over Genghis Khan.

A CLOSER LOOK AT
The Atheist Crusade

1. This refutation has the features of both a rebuttal and a counterargument. In what ways is it primarily a rebuttal, and in what ways is it also a counterargument? Point to specific places where the authors are rebutting and where they are offering counterarguments.

2. Even in highly persuasive or antagonistic arguments, readers need to be convinced that the other side is being represented fairly. How do Rigler and Zeldman show that they are taking Dawkins's views seriously and representing them fully and fairly?

3. Find three places where the authors challenge Dawkins's logic. Using the section on logical fallacies in Chapter 3 ("Strategy 5: Avoid Fallacies"), identify the logical fallacy that the authors say Dawkins has committed and how they describe his lapses in logic.

IDEAS FOR
Arguing

1. Write a comparison argument (Chapter 6) that describes, compares, and contrasts religious faith with scientific understanding. Do you, like Richard Dawkins, believe that faith is a delusion that is inferior to scientific understanding? Do you believe that science is a also a faith that is in the end a delusion? Or do you, like many other scientists and nonscientists, believe they are just different ways of understanding that sometimes do not overlap?

2. Write a causal analysis (Chapter 7) that explores why some people hold strongly to religious beliefs while others hold just as strongly to atheism or skepticism about religious belief.

Proposals— Arguing about the Future

14

IN THIS CHAPTER, YOU WILL LEARN—

14.1 How proposals are used to solve problems and make plans for the future

14.2 Methods for inventing the content of a proposal

14.3 Techniques for organizing and drafting the sections of a proposal

14.4 Ways to use style and design to make a proposal more visual and persuasive

Let's say you have a good idea. Maybe you want to invent a new product or start a new business. Maybe you want to solve a problem in your community, or you think you know a better way to do something (Figure 14.1). Writing a proposal will help you put your ideas into action.

14.1 How proposals are used to solve problems and make plans for the future

Proposals are arguments about the future. They are used to explain problems and then offer plans for solving those problems. As a result, proposals are some of the most persuasive arguments you can write because their aim is to convince people to say yes to your ideas.

Proposals are common in the workplace, and they are becoming more common in advanced college courses. Increasingly, professors are asking teams of students to be entrepreneurial and write proposals that explain their projects. In the workplace, you will need to collaborate with your colleagues on proposals that describe new ideas, products, and services.

The world around you is always changing and evolving, creating new opportunities and new problems to solve. In college and your career, you will use proposals to manage these changes and argue persuasively for your ideas.

QUICK View

Generative

Persuasive

Generative Argument—Proposals are among the most persuasive forms of argument, but they have their generative qualities also. They are often used as planning documents for teams. Also, proposals should present solutions in ways that benefit everyone involved.

Persuasive Argument—The main purpose of a proposal is to persuade the audience to accept a vision of the future. Proposals use reasoning (*logos*), appeals to authority (*ethos*), and emotional appeals (*pathos*) to persuade the audience to say yes to an idea.

Genre Pattern

Proposals can follow a variety of patterns, but they will usually address the elements shown in this diagram. The Qualifications section usually won't appear in an argument for a college course, but it is important in workplace proposals.

Introduction

Description of the Problem

Plan for Solving the Problem

Qualifications of People Involved

Conclusion: Costs & Benefits

FIGURE 14.1 Using Proposals to Solve Problems
Proposals are written to solve problems by pitching new projects, products, and services.

Inventing the Content of Your Proposal

14.2 Methods for inventing the content of a proposal

The most challenging aspect of writing a proposal is coming up with new ideas. It's easy to point out problems, but it's difficult to fully understand those problems and devise solutions for doing something about them. Fortunately, you can use some powerful planning tools to help you generate the content for your proposal.

Identify the Causes of the Problem

Your first task is to figure out what is causing the problem. A concept map is one of the most useful tools for doing so.

Put the problem you want to solve in the center of your screen or a piece of paper. Then ask yourself, "What are the three to five major causes of this problem?" Write those three to five causes around the problem (Figure 14.2).

Now ask yourself, "What are the three to five minor causes of each major cause?" Write those minor causes around each of the major courses.

Your concept map should give you an overall sense of the problem and what is causing it. Essentially, you are doing a causal analysis to explain why the problem exists.

Identify the Steps in Your Plan

Now that you have a better understanding of the problem and its causes, you can figure out a plan for solving it. Your plan will include a series *steps* or *actions* that will help you reach your plan's main objective.

Again, a concept map can be helpful at this point. Put your solution in the middle of your screen or a sheet of paper. Map out the three to five *major steps* that would be

FIGURE 14.2
Using a Concept Map to Analyze the Problem Drawing a concept map is a good way to better understand the problem and what is causing it.

needed to achieve that solution. Then around each major step write three to five *minor steps* that would be needed to accomplish the major step (Figure 14.3).

Your concept map will help you sketch out a step-by-step plan for solving the problem. Each major step in your map will likely become a major step in your plan. The minor steps will be used to support the major steps. Your concept map will also reveal the reasoning (*logos*) that supports your plan.

FIGURE 14.3
Developing a Plan with a Concept Map You can use a concept map to help you figure out the major and minor steps of your plan.

Identify the Costs and Benefits

With your plan roughed out, you should identify its *costs and benefits*. Start by identifying which steps will cost money or time (Figure 14.4). Then make an estimate of those costs. At this point, you will only be able to form a rough estimate of the costs. That's fine for now. You can figure out the real costs as the proposal nears completion.

After you have roughed out the costs, create another list that identifies the benefits of your proposal (Figure 14.4). Ask yourself, "If this plan were to succeed, what benefits would the audience receive?" You want to help your audience do their own cost-benefits analysis so they can see that the benefits of the project are worth its costs.

Costs (Money and Time)

- Create Safety Task Force (Meet once a week)
- Develop after-dark shuttle ($1,000,000)
- Improve lighting on campus ($2,000,000)
- Establish safety patrols ($10,000)
- Create information network ($500,000)

Benefits of My Plan

- Increase the number of students taking night classes
- Allow students to feel more comfortable studying on campus at night
- Reduce risk and number of assaults on campus
- Improve the reputation of campus in the community
- Help parents feel more secure about sending their kids to our university
- Minimize graffiti and damage caused by loiterers and troublemakers
- Improved production of faculty who want to work on campus after dark
- Make campus a draw for the community to bring in more revenue to local businesses

---

FIGURE 14.4 Making a Rough Estimate of Costs and Benefits
At this point, the costs and benefits of your plan will be rough. Nevertheless, listing them helps you decide whether the benefits are worth the costs.

Researching: Gathering Support

Now that you have mapped out the problem, sketched out your plan, and identified costs and benefits, you are ready to do research on your topic with a combination of electronic, print, and empirical sources.

Electronic sources—The Internet can help you find useful electronic sources, including information about projects similar to the one you are proposing. You can also look for evidence and examples that would support your argument.

MOVES for Arguing

Proposals are some of the most persuasive arguments. Here are some moves to help you get your audience to say yes.

The problem we are trying to solve was caused by _____, _____, and _____.

If we don't do something about this problem, _____, _____, and _____ will happen.

Recently, _____ and _____ have happened, which has opened a unique opportunity for us to do something new.

We are proposing a plan with _____ major steps/phases.

Our team is uniquely qualified to do this project because we are _____ and _____.

The benefits of the project, which include _____, _____, and _____, are worth the cost, which is _____.

If you accept our proposal, you will receive _____, _____, and _____.

Print sources—Newspapers and magazines often provide the most useful print information because proposals tend to be about current or local issues. These print sources will help you deepen your factual understanding of the problem and perhaps gain new insights that you didn't have before.

Empirical sources—On just about any college campus, you can find experts to interview about the problem you are trying to solve. You can use your university's website to find out which faculty or staff members are experts on your topic. Then contact them to set up an appointment, preferably during their office hours.

When researching your topic, you should triangulate your sources to determine whether the evidence you have collected is reliable (See Chapter 16 on Developing Your Research Process).

14.3 Techniques for organizing and drafting the sections of a proposal

Organizing and Drafting Your Proposal

Proposals are typically complex arguments, so they can be a challenge to organize.

You might find it helpful to think of each section in the proposal as a separate document. For example, you can draft the Description of the Problem section as a *causal analysis* that explains the problem, its causes, and its effects. Then you can draft the Plan for Solving the Problem as a *description* in which you explain your plan step by step. When you are finished drafting each section separately, you can put them together and revise the proposal from top to bottom.

The Introduction: Identifying the Problem

A proposal's introduction typically makes up to six moves:

Grab the audience's attention—Use an anecdote, compelling statement, interesting fact, or intriguing question to capture the audience's attention.

Identify your topic—Tell your audience what your proposal is about if your grabber didn't do so already. In other words, clearly identify the problem you are trying to solve.

State your purpose—In one sentence, tell your audience the purpose of your proposal. Often a proposal's purpose is stated directly, using phrasing like the following: "In this proposal, our primary objective is to..."

State your main point (thesis)—Clearly state the result you are seeking so your audience knows exactly what you are asking them to agree to.

> *Weak thesis:* Campus safety needs to be improved at our university.

> *Better thesis:* We are asking you to approve an integrated plan for campus safety that will make this university safer and more competitive. Our safety plan will help us retain top students, improve our university's reputation, and attract top-tier research faculty.

Offer background information—Provide historical information on your topic so your audience has a basic understanding of the problem you are trying to solve. You might talk about how the problem began or what changed to create this problem.

Stress the importance of the topic—Explain briefly why this problem should be important to your audience.

These introductory moves can be made in just about any order, and not all of them are needed. Minimally, you should tell your audience your topic, purpose, and main point.

The Problem Section: Analyzing the Problem's Causes

In the Problem section, you want to explain the problem, its causes, and its effects as clearly as possible. As mentioned before, you might find it helpful to draft this section as a causal analysis that could stand alone.

The opening paragraph for this section will typically make two moves: state the problem and stress its importance.

> Currently, our campus is not considered a safe place at night by students, faculty, and staff. Many people are afraid to be here after dark because they are worried about being assaulted or harassed. As a result, our university is missing opportunities to expand its course offerings, increase research activities, and stage cultural events in the evening.

In the body of this section, you should analyze the causes and effects of the problem, discussing each major cause separately.

Major Cause 1: Lack of Adequate Lighting

The lack of adequate lighting is the primary reason people do not feel safe on campus at night. In our survey of students and faculty, we discovered that 62 percent of women and 34 percent of men will not walk on campus at night alone, specifically because there isn't enough lighting. Sergeant Cal Hoskins, a campus police officer, confirmed that there are too many dark areas on campus where assaults could happen. He said, "The current lighting on campus is not consistent. A pedestrian might be in a well-lit area in one part of the campus, but then they need to cross a dark area to get to the next well-lit area. Those dark areas are problematic." His statement reinforces what we found when we toured campus at night with a map (Figure B). Walking around campus, we marked areas that were "well-lit," "partially lit," and "dark." As shown in Figure B, there are large dark spaces between the islands of well-lit and partially lit areas of campus. There are many "shadow areas" with little or no lighting.

This lack of lighting has both apparent and subtle effects. One obvious effect is that students won't take classes or study on campus at night. Students who don't feel safe walking to class from their dorm room or the parking lot will avoid signing up for classes that are held after dark. As a result, the university misses out on offering revenue-generating classes to resident students and commuter students. A less apparent effect is that students have fewer opportunities to study on campus, join clubs, or simply socialize. In other words, the nighttime activities that help students succeed and value the university are not available because students feel they need to stay in their dorms or housing after dark.

Each major cause would receive this kind of thorough analysis in which the minor causes and the effects are explained to the audience.

The Plan Section: Describing Your Solution

Your next task is to describe your plan for solving the problem. You want to explain step by step *how* you would solve the problem and *why* you would do it that way.

In the opening paragraph of this section, you should briefly identify your solution and tell the audience why your approach makes the most sense. Some proposal writers like to forecast the major steps of their plan by listing them at this point:

To improve security, we are proposing the Campus Night Owls project, an integrated plan for improving the safety of campus. Our plan has four major steps:

- Phase One: Improve campus lighting to create safety corridors.

- Phase Two: Create safety patrols of police and student volunteers.

- Phase Three: Add more nighttime shuttle busses that help people move around campus.

- Phase Four: Develop a safety networking system to keep people informed.

An integrated security system like the Campus Night Owls project would make people safer while improving the university's ability to compete for top students and faculty.

The body paragraphs of this section should describe your plan step by step in detail. Each major step will likely receive one to three paragraphs of coverage.

Phase Four: Develop a Safety Networking System to Keep People Informed

One of the best ways to help people feel more secure is to create a safety networking system that allows them to monitor security issues on campus and to quickly receive information when a security incident occurs. Twitter, Facebook, and a university-wide e-mail listserv would allow the University Police quickly announce a security incident and recommend courses of action. Twitter and Facebook would be especially effective ways to send safety information, because students would receive alerts on their phones. So, if something happens while they are en route to campus or walking across campus, they can take immediate action.

Another way to get information out is to install electronic message boards throughout campus. Usually, these message boards would offer information about campus events and the weather. But, in an emergency situation, they could explain what is happening and offer safety information.

Typically, the final paragraph in your proposal's Plan section will summarize the *deliverables* of the project. Deliverables are the items that the audience will receive if they say yes to the project.

When the Campus Night Owls project is finished, our campus will be much safer because of its integrated security system. We will have lighting corridors for safe walking, security patrols staffed by campus police and students, regular night shuttles that move people around campus, and an information networking system that keeps people informed. With this system in place, we will see an increase in enrollment and other extracurricular activities on campus after dark.

Note: The items in this paragraph will overlap with some of the benefits that will be mentioned later in the conclusion of the proposal. That's fine. The repetition of benefits is helpful and even desirable in a proposal.

The Qualifications Section: Describing Who Will Do the Work

In a workplace proposal, the Plan section is often followed by a Qualifications section that describes *who* will carry out the plan and *why* they are qualified to do the work. In proposals written for college courses, your professors probably won't ask you to include a Qualifications section, but let's talk about how to write one in case you are asked for it.

A typical Qualifications section will offer the following kinds of information:

Description of personnel—Brief bios of the project's management team and descriptions of the workforce of the company or organization.

Description of company or organization—A historical background on the company or organization that will do the work, as well as a description of its facilities and manufacturing capabilities.

Previous experience—Brief descriptions of prior projects that the company or organization has completed.

Depending on the size of the project, the Qualifications section could be long (many pages) or brief (half a page). If your company or organization is familiar to the audience, a brief description of qualifications might be all that's needed. However, your proposal's Qualifications section could run several pages if your company is unfamiliar to the audience or you need to prove the credentials of your management team or organization.

Conclusion: Discussing the Costs and Benefits of the Plan

Proposals tend to conclude with a discussion of the costs and benefits of the plan. In your conclusion, you want to put the costs and benefits side by side so the audience can do a basic cost–benefit analysis. That way, they can decide if the project is worth the time and money.

The conclusion of a proposal will typically make six moves:

Signal the conclusion—Use a heading, transitional phrase, or transitional sentence to signal clearly that you are concluding. Proposals tend to be longer arguments, so you want to alert your audience that you will be making your final points.

Restate your main point (thesis)—Again, tell your audience the main point or thesis of your proposal. Your main point first appeared in the introduction, and you now want to restate it in the conclusion to bring your argument to a close.

State the costs of the plan—In a straightforward way, tell the audience what your project will cost. Don't apologize (e.g., "We're sorry to tell you that..."), and don't use any slick salesperson talk (e.g., "For the low, low price of..."). Just tell them your estimate of the money and time needed to put your plan into action.

Identify the major benefits of the plan—Immediately after the costs, list the major benefits of your plan (usually three to five). Proposal writers will often put these items in a bulleted list so the audience can see exactly what they receive if they agree to the proposal.

Restress the importance of the subject—Briefly, tell the audience again why this project is important. You want them to understand that this matter is important and needs action. If possible, stress the importance in positive terms by highlighting the benefits of saying yes.

Look to the Future—In a few sentences, describe the positive future that will happen if they say yes to your proposal. A positive look to the future leaves the audience with the sense that the future will be better than the present.

These six moves tend to be made in the order listed above, but you can adjust them to fit your subject, audience, and the context of your argument.

Your conclusion should not be too long (one to three paragraphs). Basically, you want to leave the audience with the message, "Here is what you get if you say yes to this proposal, and here is why you will be better off."

Using Style and Design in Proposals

14.4 Ways to use style and design to make a proposal more visual and persuasive

Proposals are persuasive arguments, so your style and design need to reflect the emotions (*pathos*) and energy of your ideas.

Using Persuasive Style

Generally, your proposal's style should be upbeat and action oriented. Attempting to frighten your audience is not a good way to persuade them to agree to your project. Instead, analyze the problem in plain terms and use a positive tone to explain your plan and its benefits.

Use active sentences—Generally, proposals are written in the active voice because you are trying to persuade people to take action. Active voice means putting people in the subjects of sentences and using active verbs to express what they are doing or will do. Where possible, avoid using passive voice.

Use metaphors and similes—Similes and metaphors are useful for explaining new ideas in a visual way. For example, using a simile like "our campus is like maze of shadows" is more visually persuasive than simply saying "our campus is dark." Likewise, you could use a metaphor to call lighted paths "safety corridors" to create a stronger sense of security.

Minimize jargon—When writing a proposal, you might be tempted to rely on technical terminology and acronyms. Your audience, though, may not be experts in area you are discussing. Even in the workplace, decision-makers are often not experts in the field. So you should keep jargon to a minimum and define any specialized terms that the audience might not be familiar with.

Proposals tend to be used in highly competitive and persuasive situations, so you want to make sure your style matches the importance of the problem you are trying to solve.

Designing Your Proposal

The design of your proposal should help the readers find the information they need, and it should make your proposal attractive. Let's be honest. Nobody wants to read a proposal that looks like the one on the left in Figure 14.5. The stale design of this document signals, "This proposal is going to be boring and hard to read." The design on the right, though, signals, "This proposal is forward thinking and you will quickly find the information you need."

Design a look that matches your proposal's tone—If you want your readers to get excited about your ideas, use fonts, titles, and images that reflect that excitement. For example, you could use sans serif typefaces like Arial or Futura in the title and headings. Add in some colorful images and graphs. You could widen one of the margins to create more white space.

Use meaningful, active headings—Your proposal's headings should be active and descriptive, such as "Walking Our Campus at Night: A Maze of Shadows," "Developing Safety Corridors," and "Creating a Safer Tomorrow."

Include relevant graphs and tables—Where possible, put data into charts and create graphs that show trends. These graphs will reinforce the major points in your argument. You can also use tables to organize and present factual information.

Effective style and design are important elements of a persuasive proposal. Your audience is much more likely to agree with your proposal if your style is lively and the design makes the text easy to read and attractive.

Sheila Johnson
Gina Valvano
Thomas Young
English 110

Proposal: Making Campus Safer at Night

At 10:01 pm on November 5th, Jill Franklin was leaving her Marketing 354 class. She braced herself for the frightening walk to her car, which was in the Carson Street parking garage about a quarter mile away. The sun was long gone. The McCallister College campus, which is warm and welcoming during the day, now stood ominously like a maze of shadows. Jill started walking, cautiously looking into the dark areas where anyone could be hiding. A few students were walking on campus, but in the darkness just about anything could happen. Soon, she was walking by herself. As she walked past Agronomy Hall, a man came out from behind a tree and demanded her purse.

If you have ever been on the McCallister campus at night, you know exactly what evening students like Jill are experiencing. Generally, everyone likes to believe that our campus is safe. And yet, according to the University Police, there were three assaults and eight robberies on our campus last year. Almost all of these crimes happened at night when students and faculty were trying to get home after class or after studying at the library.

Of course, the lack of safety is a problem for students and faculty. Even more importantly, though, McCallister University is missing out on opportunities to grow its evening programs that cater to working students. To make campus safer, we are proposing the "Light Campus, New Horizons Initiative," that will make campus a safe place to work and study. By improving campus safety, we believe McCallister University

---

Making Campus Safer at Night

At 10:01 pm on November 5th, Jill Franklin was leaving her Marketing 354 class. She braced herself for the frightening walk to her car, which was in the Carson Street parking garage about a quarter mile away. The sun was long gone. The McCallister College campus, which is warm and welcoming during the day, now stood ominously like a maze of shadows. Jill started walking, cautiously looking into the dark areas where anyone could be hiding. A few students were walking on campus, but in the darkness just about anything could happen. Soon, she was walking by herself. As she walked past Agronomy Hall, a man came out from behind a tree and demanded money.

If you have ever been on the McCallister campus at night, you know exactly what evening students like Jill are experiencing. Generally, everyone likes to believe that our campus is safe. And yet, according to the University Police, there were three assaults and eight robberies on our campus last year. Almost all of these crimes happened at night when students and faculty were trying to get home after class or after studying at the library.

Of course, the lack of safety on campus is a problem for students and faculty. Even more importantly, though, McCallister University is missing out on opportunities to grow its evening programs that cater to working students. To make campus safer, we are proposing the "Light Campus, New Horizons Initiative," that will make campus a safe place to work and study. By improving campus safety, we believe McCallister University will not only make campus safer for students, but we can attract students who would otherwise go to competing community colleges and for-profit universities that are offering classes at night to students who cannot attend them during the day.

Walking Our Campus At Night: A Maze of Shadows

After most faculty and students go home for the day, the class day is just beginning for many other students. Many of these students work during the day, and they are completing their undergraduate degree or they are working on advanced degrees. Many students also need to study on campus because they need access to the library or their residence is not quiet enough to allow

Written by
Sheila Johnson
Gina Valvano
Thomas Young
English 110

FIGURE 14.5 Designing Your Proposal

Readers prefer proposals that look attractive and appear easy to read. The proposal on the right has the same basic content as the one on the left, but it looks much more attractive and readable.

Are you ready to use proposals to persuade? Here are the basics:

1 The purpose of a proposal is to explain a problem and offer a plan or strategy for solving that problem.

2 Proposals are some of the most persuasive arguments you will write because their primary purpose is to convince people to say yes to your ideas.

3 A typical proposal has five sections: Introduction, Description of the Problem, Plan for Solving the Problem, Qualifications, and a Conclusion with costs and benefits.

4 When analyzing the problem, first identify its three to five major causes and then figure out the three to five minor causes behind each major cause.

5 When describing your plan, identify the three to five major steps needed to solve the problem.

6 When describing your qualifications, offer biographical information about the people involved and a description of your organization's facilities, manufacturing abilities, and previous experience.

7 The conclusion of your proposal should highlight the major benefits of the plan while stating the costs.

8 The style and design of your proposal should reflect the enthusiasm you want your audience to feel about your ideas.

9 Your proposal's style should be upbeat and action oriented.

10 The design of your proposal should be attractive and signal to the audience that important information will be easy to find.

1. With your group, make a list of three situations in which people use proposals in their personal lives. For example, one person might "propose" to marry someone else. How are these proposals similar to and different from proposals like the ones described in this chapter?

2. Ask each person in your group to bring a sample proposal found on the Internet. To find proposals, simply type "proposal" and a topic of your choice. Usually, something will come up. Then, have each person use this chapter to analyze his or her proposal. How does each proposal reflect the strategies described in this chapter? What differences do you see? How might you improve the proposals your group found?

3. Have each person in your group bring a common household item to class. Then, using the proposal pattern shown at the beginning of this chapter, try to sell that item to your group. The trick is to figure out what problem your household item solves in their lives. Identify the causes and effects of that problem. Then show step by step how your product solves that problem. Conclude by arguing out the costs and benefits of purchasing the product. (Note: You do not need to describe your qualifications for this exercise—but you might anyway).

1. Find a problem on campus or in your community. Write a brief two-minute proposal in which you explain the problem and offer a solution. End by arguing the costs and benefits of solving the problem that you are describing. This two-minute proposal may be the basis of a larger proposal that you will write for your instructor.

2. In the workplace, people are increasingly being asked to make "elevator pitches" to sell their ideas. An elevator pitch is a short one- to two-minute proposal that briefly explains the problem and offers a solution. Using YouTube or another video-sharing website, find a couple elevator pitch competitions in which people are proposing new ideas. Then write an analysis in which you highlight the strategies that make an elevator pitch effective and the strategies that don't.

3. Find a boring-looking proposal on the Internet, preferably in a format that you can use on your computer (.doc or .docx). Do a design makeover of the proposal to make it more readable and attractive to its audience. Include a title and headings that highlight important sections. Add in photos or graphics where appropriate. Choose typefaces that reflect the tone of the proposal. Then write a one-page reflection in which you explain why you chose to make these specific design changes.

READINGS

ONE STUDENT'S WORK

In this student-written proposal, the authors have addressed a problem they feel institutions and ordinary people need to deal with—high energy costs and the depletion of non-renewable fossil fuels. As you read, notice how they first define the define the problem in terms of its causes and costs, then carefully offer a plan for dealing with the problem, and finally explain why the benefits outweigh the costs. Notice also, how they use common persuasive strategies (ethos, pathos, and logos) to stress the importance of the problem and the benefits of their plan.

Project Helios

Danny Crites, Jacob Field, Fred Garcia,
Joshua Herrera, Stormy Molina

Introduction

Project Helios aims to reduce the carbon footprint of the University of New Mexico (UNM) and reduce its energy costs by re-equipping three buildings with solar power within 6 years. In addition to saving money, with a well-designed public relations strategy, this effort will also create notable awareness of alternative energy sources locally and even across the United States, helping to effect widespread changes in attitudes about solar power.

The United States consumes 21% of the world's energy, even though the country makes up only about 4.5% of the earth's population. On average, New Mexico uses roughly 0.7% of energy in the United States, accounting for 0.13% of the world's energy consumption (U.S. Energy Information Administration, 2010). UNM and its various branches account for a significant percentage of population, land, and energy usage in New Mexico.

By harnessing an alternative energy source that will eventually serve all of UNM, this project will help reduce New Mexico's energy use. Additionally, it will lower energy costs, reducing the amount of funds required by the university from sources such as tuition and grants. Finally, by using well-planned promotional tactics, we will raise awareness of the growing problem of excessive energy consumption. This, in turn, will increase interest in solar technology, thereby inspiring more research on solar energy and advancing the existing technology. These changes will produce lower costs and more reliable and efficient designs in the future.

The Problem: More Consumption, More Costs

In the past two decades, the use of non-renewable fossil fuels—such as petroleum, coal, and natural gas—has increased dramatically. High consumption of these resources has not only aggravated problems such as pollution and carbon dioxide emissions, but it has also increased the cost of these resources on the local, national, and global levels.

Energy Consumption: The United States and New Mexico

5 Energy consumption in the United States is a growing concern, since the country uses a disproportionate percentage of the world's energy. The majority of energy in the United States of America comes from nonrenewable sources such as petroleum (37%), natural gas (24%), and coal (23%) (U.S. Energy Information Administration, 2010). As of 2010, the world's population is over 6.8 billion people, with 309 million people living in the United States (U.S. Census Bureau, 2010). The non-renewable energy resources of this world are being depleted increasingly rapidly.

At this point, it may appear there is enough energy to meet America's needs, but developing countries, such as China and India, have large populations that are growing along with their needs for energy to fuel their residential, industrial, and transportation sectors. When our nation's energy use is evaluated alongside its global peers, it becomes clear that the United States is grossly overusing these limited resources. Meanwhile, the energy needs of other nations are growing quickly. As these trends continue, the nation will either need to compete against growing countries for resources or develop the capacity for utilizing alternative means of energy.

Cost of Energy: New Mexico and the University of New Mexico

The utility needs of UNM, such as water, natural gas, electricity, etc., are provided by Power New Mexico (PNM), New Mexico Gas Company, and UNM's own district energy system. Utilities for UNM's campuses are controlled mainly by UNM's Physical Plant Department. UNM, of course, has little control over rising energy prices. For instance, even with a large amount of natural gas available in New Mexico, the price of the gas has risen 180% in the past ten years (Zumwalt & Vosevich, 2009). Because natural gas is one of the resources used to make electricity, the cost of electricity has also increased.

The University of New Mexico's Albuquerque campuses require considerable energy resources. Four energy-generating facilities on UNM campuses can provide up to 8,300 kilowatts of electricity, 202,000 pounds of steam, and 2,000 gallons of water a minute, which helps control the cost of energy on UNM's campuses. It is estimated that in one year, UNM can consume 130,379,000 kilowatt hours of electricity, 388,572,279 pounds of steam, and 256,669,128 gallons of water.

Although UNM produces roughly 25% of its own energy, the remaining 75% is purchased from PNM (Zumwalt & Vosevich, 2009). This strains UNM's budget. With a total annual budge of about $2 billion a year, UNM currently pays $300 million (about 15%) of its total budget on utilities (University of New Mexico, 2008). Because of PNM's increases in natural gas and water costs, UNM's utility bill will rise substantially, an increase estimated at $30 million for 2010 (Zumwalt & Vosevich, 2009).

Because energy costs drive up tuition and other fees that are paid for by UNM students and the citizens of New Mexico, it is essential that UNM manage these costs while looking for ways to become less dependent on high-cost forms of energy.   10

Project Plan: Harnessing Solar Energy and Talking About It

Project Helios challenges the University of New Mexico to harness alternative and renewable sources of energy, starting with the installation of solar panel systems on Dane Smith Hall, the Student Union Building (SUB), and Popejoy Hall. This will result in two desirable outcomes. First, the University's overall budget and carbon footprint will decrease. Second, it will enhance public awareness about the growing problems associated with using fossil fuels and about the advantages of solar energy. This in turn will result in more widespread interest in and demand for solar energy as well as more solar-technology research and innovation.

To allow UNM and the State of New Mexico achieve these goals, we will purchase solar panel systems, and we will install and integrate them into the buildings. In addition, we will publicize Project Helios and expand the project to other UNM buildings and campuses.

Phase 1: Purchasing Solar Panel Systems

The first phase involves purchasing solar panel systems (Figure 1). First, we will compare the solar technology vendors in the Albuquerque area. Our staff will research the vendors to find reviews and basic information about their solar panel products and related services. We will also conduct interviews with the vendors to obtain estimates and assess the quality of their products and services. The vendors' estimates will be compared with the allotted funding in our budget. A vendor will be chosen after about six to eight weeks of research and discussion. We will then place our orders with the chosen company and work out any logistics needed to bring the solar panels to UNM's main campus.

Phase 2: Installing and Integrating the Systems

The second phase is to install and integrate the solar technology into Dane Smith Hall, the Student Union Building (SUB), and Popejoy Hall. The solar panels will be "on-the-grid," which means that these buildings

FIGURE 1: Solar panel systems like this one are especially effective in sunny places like New Mexico.

will receive energy from the panels as well as PNM. Surplus energy will be sold back to PNM. We will begin integrating Dane Smith Hall, then follow up with the SUB and Popejoy Hall. These three buildings have ample roof space and are used more than others by UNM students, staff, and faculty and by visitors to UNM (Figure 2).

Professional solar technicians will begin the process of installing the solar technology. After the initial setup, UNM has various campus resources that can complete the integration. These resources include the respected and informed minds of the engineering faculty, as well as engineering fellows and students who want to gain experience working with solar technology.   15

Phase 3: Promoting Project Helios with a Public Relations Campaign

By publicizing Project Helios, we can send a positive message not only about renewable energy but also about UNM. We will provide project updates through a website and a printed annual publication. These resources will inform the UNM community and the public about this project, highlighting sustainability and energy cost reduction. These publications will demonstrate how solar technology has resulted in reduced fossil fuel consumption.

Additionally, we will foster dialogue with the community regarding Project Helios and incorporate the ideas of community leaders and activists. This too will stimulate the community's interest in developing a "green"

FIGURE 2: Rooftop solar panels like this one would be ideal for larger UNM buildings.

university. We plan to begin public relations before the purchase of our first solar panel, as good publicity will help to promote awareness. Public relations efforts will continue throughout the project. With each step of purchasing and integrating solar technology at UNM, public awareness will grow.

Phase 4: Expanding Project Helios

The final, long-term goal of Project Helios is to expand solar technology to all of UNM and its satellite and branch campuses, paving the way for more integration after Project Helios is complete. When it has been demonstrated that solar technology actually saves money over the long term, UNM will be in a good position for further integration on the main campus and on branches such as Valencia, Los Alamos, and the West campus. We are confident about the promise of such expansion because solar energy will inevitably become even more affordable and efficient.

Costs and Benefits: Investing in the Future

The costs of this project are far outweighed by its benefits. As explained here, the project is an investment that will easily pay for itself. Just as important, Project Helios is an investment in our students and their futures, as the project provides them with genuine experiential learning about solar technology, an industry that is sure to be a mainstay of the U.S. economy and especially important in sunny New Mexico. By publicizing Project Helios through print and web publications, we will publicize how the project aligns with the goals of the UNM and Albuquerque communities. Public relations efforts will also heighten UNM's national profile as a "green" university, thus attracting prospective students and bringing prestige to the institution.

20   The projected cost of Project Helios is $2,497,905 as shown in Appendix A. The project is divided into three segments each consisting of two years each. We will be requesting funds at the beginning of each two-year period. For Segment 1 we are requesting $759,635. For Segment 2, we will request $832,635. Segment 3 will cost an estimated $905,635.

Segment 1 will cover the installation, insurance, security, and maintenance of the solar panel system on Dane Smith Hall for the first two years. Segment 2 will cover Dane Smith Hall and the SUB for the second two-year segment. Lastly, Segment 3 will cover Dane Smith Hall, the SUB, and Popejoy Hall for the final two years. The cost of insurance and maintenance increases with each segment as more systems are installed and maintained.

The maintenance will be conducted by UNM students under the supervision of UNM faculty with expertise in solar technology and electrical systems. This will help motivate UNM's student body to research alternative energy, and it will also provide students with meaningful on-campus work, which has been shown to increase student engagement.

In addition to the installation, security, and maintenance of the panels, public relations costs accrue in each segment. The yearly advertisements in the *Daily Lobo*, at $300 per segment, will allow us to directly promote the project to the UNM community. One publication will be available every two years, costing $5,000 per segment, and will detail the progress the solar panels have made in lowering the energy costs for the building they are associated with as well as how they helped UNM become more sustainable. These publications will be sent to UNM's administrators, local press, investors in UNM, local, state, and national legislators, and throughout the State of New Mexico.

Conclusion

Thank you for considering our proposal. The problem of fossil-fuel depletion and global warming grows with every light turned on, every computer started up, and every student registering for a class. By integrating solar technology, the University of New Mexico will provide an example that illustrates why investment in renewable energies pays off and why projects like this one are needed.

Project Helios will benefit the university by reducing the energy usage of nonrenewable resources and decreasing the precious revenue dedicated to the utility budget. Additionally, the University will raise awareness and promote research in the field of solar technologies.

This project will advance the technology's efficiency and affordability. When you have finished considering this proposal, you can contact Albuquerque Environmental, Inc. at (505) 555-6347 or at projecthelios@aei.com. We look forward to beginning Project Helios in the near future.

References

American Petroleum Institute. (2009, January 21). Facts about fossil fuels. Retrieved April 6, 2010, from http://www.api.org/classroom/tools/facts-fossil-fuels.cfm

The College Sustainability Report Card. (2009). University of New Mexico. Retrieved April 8, 2010, from http://www.greenreportcard.org/report-card-2009/schools/ university-of-new-mexico

Landry, C. (2010, March 17). February gasoline demand, production rise to record levels. API. Retrieved April 5, 2010, from http://www.api.org/Newsroom/feb-10- record-demand.cfm

National Geographic News. (2007, June 14). Global warming fast facts. Retrieved April 7, 2010, from http://news.nationalgeographic.com/news/pf/73625218.html

PNM. (2009, May 28). New PNM electric rates will be phased in. Retrieved April 10, 2010, from http://www.pnm.com/news/2009/0528_rates_approved.htm

University of New Mexico. (2008). Funding New Mexico's flagship university. Retrieved April 10, 2010, from http://www.unm.edu/annualreport/2008/connect_foundations/ finances.html

U.S. Energy Information Administration. (2010, April 14). U.S. energy facts explained. Retrieved April 17, 2010, from http://tonto.eia.doe.gov/energyexplained/index.cfm?page=us_energy_home

U.S. Department of Energy. (2011, July 25). Buildings Database: Toyota South Campus Office Development. Retrieved July 13, 2013, from https://buildingdata.energy.gov/content/toyota-south-campus-office-development

U.S. Department of Energy. (2010, November 6). Solar Multimedia: Denver Museum of Nature and Science goes solar. Retrieved July 13, 2013, from https://www.eeremultimedia.energy.gov/solar/photographs/denver_museum_nature_and_science_goes_solar

Zumwalt, J. & Vosevich, M. (March, 2009). Utilities at the University of New Mexico. Albuquerque, NM: Physical Plant Department. Retrieved from http:// www.unm.edu/~budget/guidelines/glpresentation/Utilities.pdf

Appendix A: Budget Table

This table shows how the project costs were calculated. The project is divided into three segments.

Budget Item	Description	Cost for Segment 1	Cost for Segment 2	Cost for Segment 3	Total Cost
Solar Panel System	Each system contains all the panels, wires, connections, and installation for one building.	$675,000	$675,000	$675,000	$2,025,000
Insurance	Insurance for the solar panel systems	$60,000 ($1000/month × 60 months for 1 system)	$120,000 ($1000/month × 60 months for 2 systems)	$180,000 ($1000/month × 60 months for 3 systems)	$360,000
Security	A keypad and alarm door lock	$185	$185	$185	$555
Security	A security camera system	$150	$150	$150	$450
Maintenance	One student needed to maintain panels for each building.	$13,000 ($50/week × 260 weeks × 1 student)	$26,000 ($50/week × 260 weeks × 2 students)	$39,000 ($50/week × 260 weeks × 3 students)	$78,000
Advertising	Daily Lobo advertisement once a year	$300 ($60 × 5 years)	$300 ($60 × 5 years)	$300 ($60 × 5 years)	$900
Advertising	Webmaster	$6,000 ($100/month × 60 months)	$6,000 ($100/month × 60 months)	$6,000 ($100/month × 60 months)	$18,000
Advertising	Create and disperse a publication to the UNM community every segment.	$5,000 ($5000/ publication)	$5,000 ($5000/ publication)	$5,000 ($5000/ publication)	$15,000
TOTAL		$759,635	$832,635	$905,635	**$2,497,90**

A CLOSER LOOK AT
Project Helios

1. The authors contend that their proposal offers a variety of benefits. What are those benefits? Which of the benefits do you think is stressed above the others?

2. The authors supplement their proposal's argument with photographs and a table. They also use figure captions that explain the point of each of these visual elements. Explain how these visuals serve as more than just "eye candy" but also clarify and reinforce the main points they want their readers to grasp. What other visuals

can you think of that could help the proposal make its case even more powerfully?

3. Proposals are among the most persuasive of arguments. Readers understand that proposals aim to persuade them to some belief or action. Read the document and identify the places where the author use logical statements and examples (*logos*), appeals to authority and expertise (*ethos*), and emotions (*pathos*) to persuade. Which kinds of appeals are most effective in this proposal?

IDEAS FOR
Arguing

1. Imagine that you work for a firm that wrote the Project Helios proposal and have been tasked with creating a ten- to fifteen-minute presentation that summarizes the proposal. Turn this proposal into a slideshow. Use PowerPoint or other presentation software to create a presentation that includes ten to fifteen slides.

2. Write a counterargument to the Project Helios proposal. Whether you agree or disagree, make an argument highlights its weaknesses and offers a better way to lower energy costs on a college campus.

The End of Poverty

JEFFREY D. SACHS

In this proposal, Columbia University economics professor Jeffrey D. Sachs explains the problem of global poverty and offers a nine-step plan for making a difference. As you read, notice how Sachs frames the problem with narrative and other evidence to motivate his readers into caring about this problem and agreeing with him about the best solution.

We can banish extreme poverty in our generation—yet 8 million people die each year because they are too poor to survive. The tragedy is that with a little help, they could

even thrive. In a bold new book, Jeffrey D. Sachs shows how we can make it happen

It is still midmorning in Malawi when we arrive at a small village, Nthandire, about an hour outside of Lilongwe, the capital. We have come over dirt roads, passing women and children walking barefoot with water jugs, wood for fuel, and other bundles. The midmorning temperature is sweltering. In this subsistence maize-growing region of a poor, landlocked country in southern Africa, families cling to life on an unforgiving terrain. This year has been a lot more difficult than usual because the rains have failed. The crops are withering in the fields that we pass.

If the village were filled with able-bodied men, who could have built rainwater-collecting units on rooftops and in the fields, the situation would not be so dire. But as we arrive in the village, we see no able-bodied young men at all. In fact, older women and dozens of children greet us, but there is not a young man or woman in sight. Where, we ask, are the workers? Out in the fields? The aid worker who has led us to the village shakes his head sadly and says no. Nearly all are dead. The village has been devastated by AIDS.

The presence of death in Nthandire has been overwhelming in recent years. The grandmothers whom we meet are guardians for their orphaned grandchildren. The margin of survival is extraordinarily narrow; sometimes it closes entirely. One woman we meet in front of her mud hut has 15 orphaned grandchildren. Her small farm plot, a little more than an acre in all, would be too small to feed her family even if the rains had been plentiful. The soil nutrients have been depleted so significantly in this part of Malawi that crop yields reach only about a half-ton per acre, about one-third of normal. This year, because of the drought, she will get almost nothing. She reaches into her apron and pulls out a handful of semi-rotten, bug-infested millet, which will be the basis for the gruel she will prepare for the meal that evening. It will be the one meal the children have that day.

5   I ask her about the health of the children. She points to a child of about 4 and says that the girl contracted malaria the week before. The

woman had carried her grandchild on her back for the six miles to the local hospital. When they got there, there was no quinine, the antimalarial medicine, available that day. With the child in high fever, the two were sent home and told to return the next day. In a small miracle, when they returned after another six-mile trek, the quinine had come in, and the child responded to treatment and survived. It was a close call though. More than 1 million African children, and perhaps as many as 3 million, succumb to malaria each year.

As we proceed through the village, I stoop down to ask one of the young girls her name and age. She looks about 7 or 8 but is actually 12, stunted from years of undernutrition. When I ask her what her dreams are for her own life, she says that she wants to be a teacher and that she is prepared to study and work hard to achieve that. I know that her chances of surviving to go on to secondary school and a teachers college are slim under the circumstances.

The plight of Malawi has been rightly described by Carol Bellamy, head of UNICEF, as the perfect storm of human deprivation, one that brings together climatic disaster, impoverishment, the AIDS pandemic and the long-standing burdens of malaria, schistosomiasis and other diseases. In the face of this horrific maelstrom, the world community has so far displayed a fair bit of hand-wringing and even some high-minded rhetoric, but precious little action. It is no good to lecture the dying that they should have done better with their lot in life. Rather it is our task to help them onto the ladder of development, to give them at least a foothold on the bottom rung, from which they can then proceed to climb on their own.

This is a story about ending poverty in our time. It is not a forecast. I am not predicting what will happen, only explaining what can happen. Currently, more than 8 million people around the world die each year because they are too poor to stay alive. Every morning our newspapers could report, "More than 20,000 people perished yesterday of extreme poverty."

How? The poor die in hospital wards that lack drugs, in villages that lack antimalarial bed nets, in houses that lack safe drinking water. They die namelessly, without public comment. Sadly, such stories rarely get written.

Since Sept. 11, 2001, the U.S. has launched a war on terrorism, but it has neglected the deeper causes of global instability. The nearly $500 billion that the U.S. will spend this year on the military will never buy lasting peace if the U.S. continues to spend only one-thirtieth of that, around $16 billion, to address the plight of the poorest of the poor, whose societies are destabilized by extreme poverty. The $16 billion represents 0.15% of U.S. income, just 15¢ on every $100 of our national income. The share devoted to helping the poor has declined for decades and is a tiny fraction of what the U.S. has repeatedly promised, and failed, to give.

10   Yet our generation, in the U.S. and abroad, can choose to end extreme poverty by the year 2025. To do it, we need to adopt a new method, which I call "clinical economics," to underscore the similarities between good development economics and good clinical medicine. In the past quarter-century, the development economics imposed by rich countries on the poorest countries has been too much like medicine in the 18th century, when doctors used leeches to draw blood from their patients, often killing them in the process. Development economics needs an overhaul in order to be much more like modern medicine, a profession of rigor, insight and practicality. The sources of poverty are multidimensional. So are the solutions. In my view, clean water, productive soils and a functioning health-care system are just as relevant to development as foreign exchange rates. The task of ending extreme poverty is a collective one—for you as well as for me. The end of poverty will require a global network of cooperation among people who have never met and who do not necessarily trust one another.

One part of the puzzle is relatively easy. Most people in the world, with a little bit of prodding, would accept the fact that schools, clinics, roads, electricity, ports, soil nutrients, clean water and sanitation are the basic necessities not only for a life of dignity and health but also to make an economy work. They would also accept the fact that the poor may need help to meet their basic needs. But they might be skeptical that the world could pull off any effective way to give that help. If the poor are poor because they are lazy or their governments are corrupt, how could global cooperation help?

Fortunately, these common beliefs are misconceptions—only a small part of the explanation of why the poor are poor. In all corners of the world, the poor face structural challenges that keep them from getting even their first foot on the ladder of development. Most societies with the right ingredients—good harbors, close contacts with the rich world, favorable climates, adequate energy sources and freedom from epidemic disease—have escaped extreme poverty. The world's remaining challenge is not mainly to overcome laziness and corruption, but rather to take on the solvable problems of geographic isolation, disease and natural hazards, and to do so with new arrangements of political responsibility that can get the job done. We need plans, systems, mutual accountability and financing mechanisms. But even before we have all of that apparatus in place—what I call the economic plumbing—we must first understand more concretely what such a strategy means to the people who can be helped.

Nearly half the 6 billion people in the world are poor. As a matter of definition, there are three degrees of poverty: extreme (or absolute) poverty, moderate poverty and relative poverty. Extreme poverty, defined by the World Bank as getting by on an income of less than $1 a day, means that households cannot meet basic needs for survival. They are chronically hungry, unable to get health care, lack safe drinking water and sanitation, cannot afford education for their children and perhaps lack rudimentary shelter—a roof to keep rain out of the hut—and basic articles of clothing, like shoes. We can describe extreme poverty as "the poverty that kills." Unlike moderate or relative poverty, extreme poverty now exists only in developing countries. Moderate poverty, defined as living on $1 to $2 a day, refers to conditions in which basic needs are met, but just barely. Being in relative poverty, defined by a household income level below a given proportion of the national average, means lacking things that the middle class now takes for granted.

The total number of people living in extreme poverty, the World Bank estimates, is 1.1 billion, down from 1.5 billion in 1981. While that is progress, much of the one-sixth of humanity in extreme poverty suffers the ravages of AIDS, drought, isolation and civil wars, and is thereby trapped in a vicious cycle of deprivation and death. Moreover, while the economic boom in East Asia has helped reduce the proportion of the extreme poor in that region from 58% in 1981 to 15% in 2001, and in South Asia from 52% to 31%, the situation is deeply entrenched in Africa, where almost half of the continent's population lives in extreme poverty—a proportion that has actually grown worse over the past two decades as the rest of the world has grown more prosperous.

15   A few centuries ago, vast divides in wealth and poverty around the world did not exist. Just about everybody was poor, with the exception of a very small minority of rulers and large landowners. Life was as difficult in much of Europe as it was in India or China. Your great-great-grandparents were, with very few exceptions, poor and living on a farm. The onset of the Industrial Revolution, supported by a rise in agricultural productivity, unleashed an explosive period of modern economic growth. Both population and per-capita income came unstuck, rising at rates never before imagined. The global population rose more than sixfold in just two centuries, while the world's average per-capita income rose even faster, increasing around ninefold between 1820 and 2000. In today's rich countries, the economic growth was even more astounding. The U.S. per-capita income increased almost 25-fold during this period. In beholding that success, many people embrace faulty social theories of those differences. When a society is economically dominant, it is easy for its members to assume that such dominance reflects a deeper superiority—whether religious, racial, genetic, ethnic, cultural or institutional—rather than an accident of timing or geography.

Such theories justified brutal forms of exploitation of the poor during colonial rule, and they persist even today among those who lack an understanding of what happened and is still happening in the Third World. In fact, the failure of the Third World to grow as rapidly as the First World is the result of a complex mix of factors, some geographical, some historical and some political. Imperial rule often left the conquered regions bereft of education, health care, indigenous political leadership and adequate physical infrastructure. Often, newly independent countries in the post–World War II period made disastrous political choices, such as socialist economic models or a drive for self-sufficiency behind inefficient trade barriers. But perhaps most pertinent today, many regions that got left furthest behind have faced special obstacles and hardships: diseases such as malaria, drought-prone climates in locations not suitable for irrigation, extreme isolation in mountains and landlocked regions, an absence of energy resources such as coal, gas and oil, and other liabilities that have kept these areas outside of the mainstream of global economic growth. Countries ranging from Bolivia to Malawi to Afghanistan face challenges almost unknown in the rich world, challenges that are at first harrowing to contemplate, but on second thought encouraging in the sense that they also lend themselves to practical solutions.

In the past quarter-century, when poor countries have pleaded with the rich world for help, they have been sent to the world money doctor, the International Monetary Fund. For a quarter-century, and changing only very recently, the main IMF prescription has been budgetary belt-tightening for patients much too poor to own belts. IMF-led austerity has frequently resulted in riots, coups and the collapse of public services. Finally, however, that approach is beginning to change.

It has taken me 20 years to understand what good development economics should be, and I am still learning. In my role as director of the U.N. Millennium Project, which has the goal of helping to cut the world's extreme poverty in half by 2015, I spent several eye-opening days with colleagues last July in a group of eight Kenyan villages known as the Sauri sublocation in the Siaya district of Nyanza province. We visited farms, clinics, hospitals and schools. We found a region beset by hunger, AIDS and malaria. The situation is grim, but salvageable.

More than 200 members of the community came to meet with us one afternoon. Hungry, thin and ill, they stayed for 3 1/2 hours, speaking with dignity, eloquence and clarity about their predicament. They are impoverished, but they are capable and resourceful. Though struggling to survive, they are not dispirited but are determined to improve their situation. They know well how they could get back to high ground.

20   The meeting took place on the grounds of a school called the Bar Sauri Primary School, where headmistress Anne Marcelline Omolo shepherds hundreds of schoolchildren through primary education and the travails of daily life. Despite disease, orphanhood and hunger, all 33 of last year's eighth-grade class passed the Kenyan national secondary-school exams. On a Sunday last July, we saw why. On their "day off" from school, this year's class of eighth-graders sat at their desks from 6:30 a.m. until 6 p.m. preparing months in advance for this year's national examinations in November. Unfortunately, many who will pass the exams will be unable to take a position in a secondary school because of lack of money for tuition, uniforms and supplies. Nonetheless, to boost the fortitude of the eighth-graders during the critical examination year, the community provides them with a midday meal, cooked with wood and water the students bring from home. Alas, the community is currently unable to provide midday meals for the younger children, who must fend for themselves.

When our village meeting got under way, I canvassed the group and got very perceptive accounts of the grim situation. Only two of the 200 farmers at the meeting reported using fertilizer at present. Around 25% are using improved fallows with nitrogen-fixing trees, a scientific farming approach developed and introduced into Sauri by the World Agroforestry Center. With this novel technique, villagers grow trees that naturally return nitrogen to the soil by converting it from the atmosphere, thus dramatically improving yields. The new method could be used throughout the village if more money were available for planting the trees alongside their maize crops.

The rest of the community is farming on tiny plots, sometimes no more than one-quarter of an acre, with soils that are so depleted of nutrients and organic matter that even if the rains are good, the households still go hungry. If the rains fail, the households face the risk of death from severe undernutrition. Stunting, meaning low height for one's age, is widespread, a sign of pervasive and chronic undernutrition of the children.

The real shocker came with my follow-up question. How many farmers had used fertilizers in the past? Every hand in the room went up. Farmer after farmer described how the price of fertilizer was now out of reach, and how their current impoverishment left them unable to purchase what they had used in the past.

As the afternoon unfolded, the gravity of the community's predicament became more apparent. I asked how many households were home to one or more orphaned children left behind by the AIDS pandemic. Virtually every hand in the room shot up. I asked how many households were receiving remittances from family members living in Nairobi and other cities. The response was that the only things coming back from the cities were coffins and orphans, not remittances.

I asked how many households had some- 25 body currently suffering from malaria. Around three-fourths of the hands shot up. How many use antimalarial bed nets? Two out of 200 hands went up. How many knew about bed nets? All hands. And how many would like to use bed nets? All hands remained up. The problem, many of the women explained, is that they cannot afford the bed nets, which sell for a few dollars per net, and are too expensive even when partially subsidized by international donor agencies.

A few years back, Sauri's residents cooked with locally collected wood, but the decline in the number of trees has left the area bereft of sufficient fuel. Villagers said that they now buy pieces of fuel wood in Yala or Muhanda, a bundle of seven sticks costing around 30¢. Not only are seven sticks barely enough to cook one meal, but for a lack of 30¢, many villagers had in fact reverted to cooking with cow dung or to eating uncooked meals.

The dying village's isolation is stunning. There are no cars or trucks owned or used within Sauri, and only a handful of villagers said they had ridden in any kind of motorized transport during the past year. Around half of the individuals at the meeting said that they had never made a phone call in their entire lives.

This village could be rescued, but not by itself. Survival depends on addressing a series of specific challenges, all of which can be met with known, proven, reliable and appropriate technologies and interventions. (Thanks to a grant from the Lenfest Foundation in the U.S., the Earth Institute at Columbia University will put some novel ideas to work in Sauri.) Sauri's villages, and impoverished villages like them all over the world, can be set on a path of development at a cost that is tiny for the world but too high for the villages themselves and for the Kenyan government on its own. African safari guides speak of the Big Five animals to watch for on the savannah. The world should speak of the Big Five development interventions that would spell the difference between life and death for the savannah's people. Sauri's Big Five are:

Boosting Agriculture

With fertilizers, cover crops, irrigation and improved seeds, Sauri's farmers could triple their food yields and quickly end chronic hunger. Grain could be protected in locally made storage bins using leaves from the improved fallow species tephrosia, which has insecticide properties.

Improving Basic Health

A village clinic with one doctor and nurse for the 5,000 residents would provide free antimalarial bed nets, effective antimalarial medicines and treatments for HIV/ AIDS opportunistic infections.

Investing in Education

Meals for all the children at the primary school could improve the health of the kids, the quality of education and the attendance at school. Expanded vocational training for the students could teach them the skills of modern farming, computer literacy, basic infrastructure maintenance and carpentry. The village is ready and eager to be empowered by increased information and technical knowledge.

Bringing Power

Electricity could be made available to the villages either via a power line or an off-grid diesel generator. The electricity would power lights and perhaps a computer for the school; pumps for safe well water; power for milling grain, refrigeration and other needs. The villagers emphasized that the students would like to study after sunset but cannot do so without electric lighting.

Providing Clean Water And Sanitation

With enough water points and latrines for the safety of the entire village, women and children would save countless hours of toil each day fetching water. The water could be provided through a combination of protected springs, rainwater harvesting and other basic technologies.

The irony is that the cost of these services for Sauri's 5,000 residents would be very low. My Earth Institute colleagues and I estimated that the combined cost of these improvements, even including the cost of treatment for AIDS, would total only $70 per person per year, or around $350,000 for all of Sauri. The benefits would be astounding. Sooner rather than later, these investments would repay themselves not only in lives saved, children educated and communities preserved, but also in direct commercial returns to the villages and the chance for self-sustaining economic growth.

35   The international donor community should be thinking round-the-clock of one question: How can the Big Five interventions be done on a larger scale in rural areas similar to Sauri? With a population of some 33 million people, of whom two-thirds are in rural areas, Kenya would need annual investments on the order of $1.5 billion for its Sauris, with donors filling most of that financing gap, since the national government is already stretched beyond its means. Instead, donor support for investment in rural Kenya is perhaps $100 million, or a mere one-fifteenth of what is needed. And Kenya's debt service to the rich world is several hundred million dollars per year. Kenya's budget is still being drained by the international community, not bolstered by it. This is all the more remarkable since Kenya is a new and fragile democracy that should be receiving considerable help.

The outside world has pat answers concerning extremely impoverished countries, especially those in Africa. Everything comes back, again and again, to corruption and misrule. Western officials argue that Africa simply needs to behave itself better, to allow market forces to operate without interference by corrupt rulers. Yet the critics of African governance have it wrong. Politics simply can't explain Africa's prolonged economic crisis. The claim that Africa's corruption is the basic source of the problem does not withstand serious scrutiny. During the past decade I witnessed how relatively well-governed countries in Africa, such as Ghana, Malawi, Mali and Senegal, failed to prosper, whereas societies in Asia perceived to have extensive corruption, such as Bangladesh, Indonesia and Pakistan, enjoyed rapid economic growth.

What is the explanation? Every situation of extreme poverty around the world contains some of its own unique causes, which need to be diagnosed just as a doctor would a patient. For example, Africa is burdened with malaria like no other part of the world, simply because it is unlucky in providing the perfect conditions for that disease: high temperatures, plenty of breeding sites and particular species of malaria-transmitting mosquitoes that prefer to bite humans rather than cattle.

Another myth is that the developed world already gives plenty of aid to the world's poor. Former U.S. Secretary of the Treasury Paul O'Neill expressed a common frustration when he remarked about aid for Africa: "We've spent trillions of dollars on these problems and we have damn near nothing to show for it." O'Neill was no foe of foreign aid. Indeed, he wanted to fix the system so that more U.S. aid could be justified. But he was wrong to believe that vast flows of aid to Africa had been squandered. President Bush said in a press conference in April 2004 that as "the greatest power on the face of the earth, we have an obligation to help the spread of freedom. We have an obligation to feed the hungry." Yet how does the U.S. fulfill its obligation? U.S. aid to farmers in poor countries to help them grow more food runs at around $200 million per year, far less than $1 per person per year for the hundreds of millions of people living in subsistence farm households.

From the world as a whole, the amount of aid per African per year is really very small, just $30 per sub-Saharan African in 2002. Of that modest amount, almost $5 was actually for consultants from the donor countries, more than $3 was for emergency aid, about $4 went for servicing Africa's debts and $5 was for debt-relief operations. The rest, about $12, went to Africa. Since the "money down the drain" argument is heard most frequently in the U.S., it's worth looking at the same calculations for U.S. aid alone. In 2002, the U.S. gave $3 per sub-Saharan African. Taking out the parts for U.S. consultants and technical cooperation, food and other emergency aid, administrative costs and debt relief, the aid per African came to the grand total of perhaps 6¢.

40 The U.S. has promised repeatedly over the decades, as a signatory to global agreements like the Monterrey Consensus of 2002, to give a much larger proportion of its annual output, specifically up to 0.7% of GNP, to official development assistance. The U.S.'s failure to follow through has no political fallout domestically, of course, because not one in a million U.S. citizens even knows of statements like the Monterrey Consensus. But we should not underestimate the salience that it has abroad. Spin as we might in the U.S. about our generosity, the poor countries are fully aware of what we are not doing.

The costs of action are a tiny fraction of the costs of inaction. And yet we must carry out these tasks in a context of global inertia, proclivities to war and prejudice, and understandable skepticism around the world that this time can be different from the past. Here are nine steps to the goal:

Commit to The Task

Oxfam and many other leaders in civil society have embraced the goal of Making Poverty History. The world as a whole needs now to embrace the goal.

Adopt A Plan of Action

The U.N.'s Millennium Development Goals, approved by all of the world's governments at the start of the millennium, are the down payment on ending poverty. The MDGs set out specific targets for cutting poverty, hunger, disease and environmental degradation by 2015 and thereby laid the foundation for eliminating extreme poverty by 2025. The rich and poor countries have solemnly agreed to work toward fulfilling the MDGs. The key is to follow through.

Raise The Voice of The Poor

Mahatma Gandhi and Martin Luther King Jr. did not wait for the rich and powerful to come to their rescue. They asserted their call to justice and made their stand in the face of official arrogance and neglect. It is time for the democracies in the poor world—Brazil, India, Nigeria, Senegal, South Africa and dozens of others—to join together to issue the call to action.

Redeem The U.S. Role in The World

The richest and most powerful country, long the leader and inspiration in democratic ideals, is barely participating in global efforts to end poverty and protect the environment, thus undermining its own security. It's time to honor the commitment to give 0.7% of our national income to these crucial goals.

Rescue The Imf and World Bank

They have the experience and technical sophistication to play an important role. They have the internal motivation of a highly professional staff. Yet they have been used like debt-collection agencies for the big creditor countries. It's time to restore their role in helping all 182 of their member countries, not just the rich ones, in the pursuit of enlightened globalization.

Strengthen the U.N.

It is no use blaming the U.N. for the missteps of recent years. Why are U.N. agencies less operational than they should be? Not because of "U.N. bureaucracy," though that exists, but because the powerful countries fear ceding more authority. Yet U.N. specialized agencies have a core role to play in the ending of poverty. It is time to empower the likes of the U.N. Children's Fund (UNICEF), the World Health Organization (WHO), the Food and Agricultural Organization (FAO), and many others to do the job—on the ground, country by country.

Harness Global Science

New technology has led directly to improved standards of living, yet science tends to follow market forces as well as to lead them. It is not surprising that the rich get richer in a continuing cycle of growth while the poorest are often left behind. A special effort should be made by the powerhouses of world science to address the unmet challenges of the poor.

Promote Sustainable Development

Ending extreme poverty can relieve many of the pressures on the environment. When impoverished households are more productive on their farms, for example, they face less pressure to cut down neighboring forests in search of new farmland. Still, even as extreme poverty ends, we must not fuel prosperity with a lack of concern for industrial pollution and the unchecked burning of fossil fuels.

Make A Personal Commitment

50   It all comes back to us. Individuals, working in unison, form and shape societies. The final myth I will debunk here is that politicians are punished by their constituents for supporting actions to help the poor. There is plenty of experience to show that the broad public will accept such measures, especially if they see that the rich within their own societies are asked to meet their fair share of the burden. Great social forces are the mere accumulation of individual actions. Let the future say of our generation that we sent forth mighty currents of hope, and that we worked together to heal the world.

A CLOSER LOOK AT
The End of Poverty

1. This article follows the organization of a proposal fairly closely. Look through the article and identify the places where the following elements are addressed (a) the problem, (b) the author's plan for addressing the problem, and (c) the costs and benefits of his plan. Come up with a lively and descriptive heading for each of these elements.

2. Sachs begins by grabbing the audience's attention with compelling narratives about the lives of poverty-stricken people and his experience with them. What other strategies does he use to convince readers that poverty is an important problem they should care about? In all, how effectively does Sachs allow readers identify with the problem?

3. Sachs's plan for addressing world poverty includes nine steps. In your opinion, which of these steps would be most effective for solving the problem? Which steps are you most skeptical about?

IDEAS FOR
Arguing

1. Choose a problem at your college or in your community that you have experienced or care about. Write a narrative argument (Chapter 9) that would help readers understand the nature and seriousness of the problem. Be sure to set the scene and to introduce, evaluate, and resolve the complication. At the end of your narrative argument, offer a lesson or make a call to action.

2. Write a rhetorical analysis of Sachs's proposal argument. Use one or two of the analytical methods described in Chapter 4 to examine how his argument works and to explain why it is effective or not.

Research Papers and Reports— Arguing with Research

IN THIS CHAPTER, YOU WILL LEARN—

15.1 The purposes of research papers and research reports, as well as their similarities and differences

15.2 How to use research to generate the content of a research paper or report

15.3 Methods for organizing and drafting large arguments

15.4 Strategies for achieving an academic or professional tone in research papers or reports

Research papers and reports are often used as capstone projects for college courses. When professors ask you to do a "research project," they want you to study a topic in depth and use your research to make a thorough argument. They also want you to write in an organized and engaging way, using multiple sources to back up your argument.

The terms "research paper" and "research report" are often used interchangeably, which can cause some confusion. Though similar, these two related genres are distinct in some significant ways:

Research papers—Research papers are common in the humanities, business, law, and the arts. They are often assigned in courses like management, political science, prelaw, history, philosophy, literature, languages, film studies, music, religion, and art history. Research papers are typically used to argue about current issues, business ethics, politics, legal issues, historical events, literary criticism, cultures, and social trends.

FIGURE 15.1 Doing Research in College and Your Career
Research will be important to your success in college and your career.

Research reports—Research reports are common in the sciences, marketing, engineering, economics, and technology. A research report typically includes a section called the "Methodology" or "Methods" in which the researcher explains how the report's evidence was collected, especially any empirical facts, data, and observations. A research report presents research results and discusses those results.

The QuickView on page 317 illustrates some of the key differences between research papers and research reports. They are similar genres, but the differences are important and worth keeping in mind.

Today, employers often rank the ability to do research at the top of desired skills for job applicants. Research allows you and others to make informed decisions and contribute knowledge to your field (Figure 15.1). Your ability to do high-quality research will be critical to your success in college and your career.

15.2 How to use research to generate the content of a research paper or report

Inventing the Content of Your Research Paper or Report

Let's begin by stating the obvious. To write a research paper or report, you need to do a substantial amount of research. The results of your research will then be used to develop a thorough and informed argument.

In Chapter 16, "Developing Your Research Process," a six-step research process is discussed in depth. You should turn to Chapter 16 to help you complete the research phase of this project. For now, let's summarize those six steps, focusing specifically on the needs of a research paper or report.

QUICK View

Generative

Persuasive

Generative Argument—Research papers and reports tend to be more generative than persuasive. Essentially, the purpose of a research project is to synthesize and explain existing evidence so your audience can better understand an important issue.

Persuasive Argument—In some cases, research papers and reports are persuasive arguments, especially when you are using research-based evidence to argue a controversial point or support a specific course of action. Persuasive research papers and reports often conclude with specific recommendations or calls to action.

Genre Patterns

These patterns for research papers and reports are suggestions. You should adjust the organization of your research paper or report to suit your argument's specific topic, purpose, audience, and context.

Research Paper I	Research Paper II	Research Report
Introduction	Introduction	Introduction
Background on Topic	Background on Topic	Research Methodology
Finding 1: Most Important	Finding 1: Time Period 1	Result 1
Finding 2: Next Most Important	Finding 2: Time Period 2	Result 2
Discussion	Discussion	Discussion
Conclusion	Conclusion	Conclusion

Step 1: Define Your Research Question

When starting a research project, you first need to formulate your *research question*. Your research question identifies the basic unknown that you want your research to solve. Here are some example research questions:

Research Question: Will concussion-related lawsuits pose a threat to the existence of college football programs?

Research Question: How was the War of 1812 a critical turning point in the unification of the United States?

Research Question: Why have vampires become such powerful sex symbols in popular novels and movies?

Research Question: Why do guys in college like to cross-dress as women for Halloween?

Step 2: Develop Your Working Thesis (Hypothesis)

When you have figured out your research question, you can then formulate your *working thesis,* or *hypothesis.* Your working thesis states your best answer, at this point, to your research question.

Working Thesis: If current concussion-related lawsuits against professional football are successful, it is only a matter of time before college football programs find themselves threatened by similar lawsuits from former players.

Working Thesis: The War of 1812 was the first time the United States as one nation felt threatened, forcing it to behave like a unified republic and not a federation of states.

Working Thesis: Because vampires are portrayed as seductive, physically strong, and impulsive, they represent the "forbidden mate" that many people secretly fantasize about.

Working Thesis: There are two reasons college males cross-dress on Halloween: (1) for straight males, it is a safe opportunity to step outside traditional gender roles, and (2) for some gay males, it's an opportunity to outwardly express a felt identity in a non-threatening way.

Your working thesis (or hypothesis) is your best guess about where you believe the research question will lead you. However, as you do your research, your working thesis will evolve as you make new discoveries and draw more informed conclusions. Eventually, your working thesis will become the main point (thesis statement) of your research paper or report.

Step 3: Develop Your Research Methodology

Now, you need to figure out how you are going to collect the evidence needed to answer your research question. Your research methodology describes the series of steps you will follow to collect evidence from electronic, print, and empirical sources.

Electronic sources—If your topic involves current events, electronic sources may be your best forms of evidence. You should search for evidence on websites, blogs, and listservs, because these sources often contain the most up-to-date information. Other electronic media can also be useful, such as television and radio broadcasts, podcasts, documentaries, and videos.

Note: Online encyclopedias like Wikipedia can be helpful starting places for your research; however, your instructors probably won't let you use them as citable sources because the authors are unknown and the information can be easily altered.

Print sources—Print sources are typically your most reliable sources. They include books, journal articles, magazine articles, newspaper articles, government publications, and other items that were originally written to appear on paper. You can collect a variety of print sources from libraries, especially your university's library (Figure 15.2). Many print sources, such as newspaper and magazine articles, are also available for viewing and downloading through the Internet.

Empirical sources—You can collect your own evidence with empirical methods, such as field observations, surveys, interviews, experiments, and personal experiences.

FIGURE 15.2 Go to the Library! Your university library is still one of the best sources of evidence for your research project. Don't let a short walk across campus keep you from rounding out your research.

Your research project should draw evidence from all three of these kinds of sources. If you are too reliant on one kind of source, such as electronic sources, you probably won't gain a full understanding of your subject.

Step 4: Triangulate Your Sources

In Chapter 16, you will learn about using the "Research Triangle" to *triangulate* your print, electronic, and empirical sources. Triangulation involves using all three types of sources to compare and corroborate the evidence you collect. Here is triangulation in brief:

- **Three-sided information (reliable):** Reliable evidence is being found in all three types of sources (electronic, print, and empirical).

- **Two-sided information (open to doubt):** Reliable evidence can only be found in two of the three types of sources (e.g., electronic and print only).

- **One-sided information (unreliable):** Key evidence is only being found in one of the three types of sources (e.g., electronic only).

If your research project does not have evidence from all three sides of the Research Triangle, you should find a way to collect evidence from the missing sides.

Step 5: Identify Your Major Findings and Draw Your Conclusions

Your major findings and conclusions are the discoveries and big ideas that your argument will present to your audience.

Major Findings

Use your sources to identify two to five *major findings* about your topic. List them out on your screen. If you have more than five major findings, you should determine whether you can consolidate findings or cross out less important ones. Of course, your research paper can present more than five major findings, but if you have too many "major" findings, your research paper or report will begin to sound tedious to your audience.

Conclusions

Use your major findings to draw two to five *major conclusions* about your research topic. Your conclusions present the big ideas you want your audience to take away from your research. You can have more than five major conclusions, but again you risk making your research paper or report sound tedious to your audience if you discuss too many.

Step 6: Turn Your Working Thesis into a Final Thesis

As you complete your research, you should revise your thesis one last time. Your final thesis will be the main claim or main point that your research paper or research report will prove. This thesis statement will probably appear in both the introduction and conclusion of your argument.

MOVES for Arguing

Research papers and reports can be both generative and persuasive. Here are some common moves they will make.

This issue is important because _____, _____, and _____.

People generally believe _____, but my research shows that _____ is more likely.

My research question was _____, and my hypothesis was _____.

My research methods included _____ major steps.

The results of my research show _____,_____,and _____.

My findings demonstrate that _____,_____, and _____ are likely true.

I recommend that the following actions be taken: _____,_____, and _____.

Organizing and Drafting Your Research Paper or Research Report

The research paper and research report genres are similar in many ways, but they can also differ in content and organization. The QuickView on page 317 illustrates those differences. Let's look at their similarities and differences.

Introduction: Tell Them What You Are Going to Tell Them

The introduction should establish the framework for the rest of the argument. In other words, you are going to "tell the audience what you are going to tell them." Typically, an introduction will make most or all of the following opening moves:

Identify your topic—Clearly identify and define the topic of your research project. Clarify the scope and boundaries of the project by telling the audience what you are writing about and perhaps what you are not writing about.

State your purpose—Using one sentence, tell your audience the purpose of your research project. Your purpose statement should be straightforward so your audience knows what you are trying to achieve.

> In this research paper, I will argue that concussion-related lawsuits pose a significant threat to the existence of many college football programs.

> My aim is to demonstrate that the War of 1812 was an important turning point in the history of the United States because it was the first time Americans felt unified as part of a greater nation, not as citizens of separate states.

> The purpose of my research paper is to show that today's vampire novels and movies appeal to young women because they combine two age-old storylines: the princess narrative with the forbidden mate narrative.

> In this report, I will demonstrate that straight and gay males cross-dress on Halloween for different reasons, even though their behaviors are often the same.

Your purpose statement should be direct because you want your audience to understand exactly what you are trying to achieve.

State your main point (thesis)—Most readers, including your professors, will expect you to state your argument's main point in the introduction. That way, they can evaluate your evidence as they read the body of the text. You should sharpen your thesis down to a clear point.

> **Weak:** Concussions threaten the viability of college football.

> **Better:** Concussion-related lawsuits against professional football will almost certainly be used as a legal basis for filing lawsuits against college football programs.

Weak: The War of 1812 was an important event in American history.

Better: Though mostly forgotten today, the War of 1812 was a turning point in the history of the United States because this war allowed citizens to unite around a common cause and develop a strong sense of national identity.

Weak: Vampire novels are a guilty pleasure for many women.

Better: Vampire novels tap into deep-seated princess and forbidden mate narratives, making them pleasurable reads even in an age when women no longer fantasize about a prince whisking them away.

Weak: College males cross-dress on Halloween for a variety of reasons.

Stronger: Interestingly, my research shows that straight college males cross-dress on Halloween to experience being feminine, while some gay men see the holiday as a safe way to outwardly express a felt identity.

Your main point (thesis) is your big idea (your main conclusion) for the research paper or report.

Provide background information—Briefly, give your audience enough background information about your topic to familiarize them with it. Usually historical information or references to recent events are good ways to give your audience some background on your topic.

Stress the importance of the topic—Explain to your audience why they should pay attention to this particular issue and why it is important.

These introductory moves can be made in just about any order. Most research papers and reports will include all five moves. At a minimum, your introduction should tell your readers your topic, purpose, and main point (thesis).

Background Section (Research Papers Only)

In your Background section, your goal is to give your audience a brief overall understanding of your subject's history. Specifically, you want to explain the *who, what, where, when, why,* and *how* issues that define it.

As you describe the historical background of your subject, you should use quotes from experts and cite your sources. These authoritative sources will strengthen your argument's credibility. They will also help your audience understand where your information came from and who has already written something about your subject.

The Background section is typically organized one of two ways:

Chronological Review

The section walks the audience chronologically through the topic, explaining how it began, what has happened, how people have responded, and where the situation stands at the moment.

Review of the Two or More Sides of the Issue

Usually, one side is explained first and then the other side is explained. Then, the positions are compared and contrasted to show where they agree and disagree.

Research Methodology or Methods Section (Research Reports Only)

In a research report, a Methodology section or Methods section typically follows the introduction. The purpose of a Methodology section is to describe step by step how you completed your research.

Opening

Your Methodology section should start with an opening paragraph (one or two sentences) that offers an overall description of your research methods.

> To test our hypothesis, we used a 10-question survey to confirm or challenge the facts and figures we found in print and electronic sources. Our research methods followed three major steps: (1) develop the survey, (2) circulate the survey on campus, and (3) analyze its results.

Body of the Methodology Section

In a college research report, each major step will usually receive one or two paragraphs of explanation in the body of your Methodology section (Figure 15.3). Explain *how* each major step was completed and *why* you thought each step was needed.

Limitations (Closing)

In the closing of your Methodology section, include a paragraph that identifies any major limitations of your research methods. No research methodology is perfect, so identify places where your findings might be limited due to time, access to information, or financial resources.

The Methodology section for a college-level paper will usually run about four to six paragraphs. You should describe your methods with enough detail to allow someone else to replicate your research methodology.

Findings or Results Section

In your Findings section (also called a Results section), you should describe and explain your three to five major findings separately and in depth. Typically, each major finding will receive one or two paragraphs of coverage. Your major findings can be organized two ways:

- **By importance.** They are arranged from most important to least important.

- **By the order in which they occurred.** They are arranged in the order in which they occured or were discovered.

Support each of your findings by citing the evidence you found while doing your research. Where possible, you should use properly labeled graphs, photographs, or other visuals to illustrate your results.

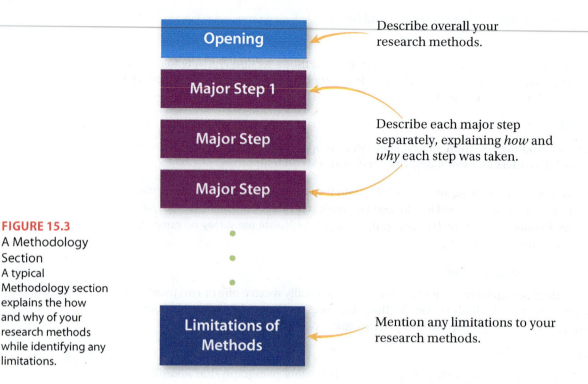

FIGURE 15.3
A Methodology Section
A typical Methodology section explains the how and why of your research methods while identifying any limitations.

Discussion Section

The Discussion section interprets your findings for the audience and states your major conclusions. Revisit your thesis, as well as your purpose and main point. Explain how the findings of your research support the thesis of your argument. You might also account for or explain any findings that don't support your thesis.

The purpose of the Discussion section is to present your two to five major conclusions about your topic. In a college-level research paper or report, this section will usually comprise about two to three paragraphs.

Conclusion/Recommendations

The conclusion should summarize your major ideas, restate your main point with more emphasis, and, if appropriate, make some recommendations. You should not include any new evidence or information at this point.

In your conclusion, make some or all of the following four moves:

Signal clearly that you are concluding—You should use a heading or transitional phrase to signal to the audience that you are concluding the argument. This signal is important, because it will indicate that you are about to restate your main point and offer any recommendations.

Restate your main point (with emphasis)—Use similar but new phrasing to the restate your thesis. Your goal is to show your audience that you have proven what you set out to prove.

Offer two to five recommendations (optional)—Most argumentative research reports and some argumentative research papers offer recommendations. You might place your recommendations in a bulleted list to make them easy to locate.

Look to the future—Research papers and reports often end with a brief look into the future. In a few sentences, explain where you think the issue will go from here. You might also mention future possibilities for research on this topic.

Your conclusion should be relatively brief. A one- or two-paragraph conclusion is usually enough for most college research papers or reports.

References or Works Cited

Beginning on a separate page, you should include a list of your sources in a standard bibliographic style, such as the MLA or APA bibliographic style. For MLA style, you should use the heading "Works Cited." For APA style, your sources should appear under the heading "References." You can turn to Chapters 18 and 19 for more specific information about how to list your sources.

Developing Your Style and Design: Sounding and Looking Professional

15.4 Strategies for achieving an academic or professional tone in research papers or reports

Research papers and reports are formal assignments, so your instructors and supervisors will expect you to use a style and design that is academic and professional.

Style: Make It Plain and Straightforward

Your style should be straightforward and plain, establishing an academic or professional voice. Here are some strategies for writing with an academic or professional style:

Use Plain Sentences

Your sentences should be simple, straightforward, and breathing length. Move the subject of each sentence (i.e., what the sentence is about) to an early position in the sentence. Use active verbs where possible. Try to minimize the number of prepositional phrases, especially chains of prepositional phrases. Also, keep your sentences breathing length to avoid overly complex and convoluted sentences.

Avoid Bureaucratic or Pompous Phrasings

Phrasings like "in lieu of," "regarding," "indeed," "in accordance with," or "pursuant to" sometimes find their way into research papers and reports. These kinds of bureaucratic phrasings make the author sound uncomfortable with the material. A good guideline is to only use words or phrases that you would use in everyday speech.

Define Technical Terms, Jargon, and Acronyms

When you use technical terms or acronyms, offer a sentence definition or parenthetical definition to explain what they mean:

Sentence definition—A concussion is a traumatic brain injury that can lead to temporary problems with balance, attention, decision making, and agility.

Parenthetical definition—Childhood obesity has been linked to type II diabetes, <u>a chronic disease in which the body cannot produce the proper amount of insulin to maintain healthy blood sugar levels.</u>

Technical terms, jargon, and acronyms are useful and appropriate in research papers and reports, but they need to be defined for the audience.

Limit the Use of Passive Voice

The passive voice is fine if used in moderation. However, writers often overuse passive voice in research papers and reports because the ideas are often complex.

Passive—The survey's results <u>were confirmed</u> by our student interviews.

Active—Our student interviews <u>confirmed</u> the survey's results.

Passive—In 1814, the U.S. Capitol Building and White House in Washington, D.C., <u>were captured and burned</u> by British soldiers.

Active—In 1814, British soldiers <u>captured and burned</u> the U.S. Capitol Building and White House in Washington, D.C.

Using passive voice isn't wrong. Passive voice just makes your writing less active and harder to read because it conceals *who* or *what* is doing the action.

Minimize the Use of Nominalizations

A nominalization occurs when the action of the sentence appears as a noun rather than a verb.

Nominalization—This research paper offers a <u>presentation</u> of our findings into football-related concussions and their potential effects on college sports programs.

Revised—This research paper <u>presents</u> our findings into football-related concussions and their potential effects on college sports programs.

Nominalizations are often called "shun" words because they typically end with the suffixes "-tion" or "-sion." In your draft, look for places where you use these shun words. Then, where appropriate, change them into active verbs or adjectives.

Designing Your Research Paper or Report

The design of your research paper or report should highlight the important information that the audience needs, while making the text attractive.

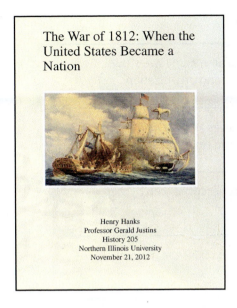

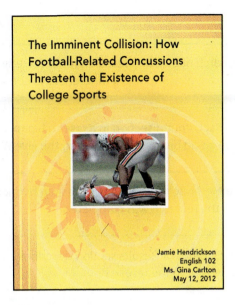

FIGURE 15.4 Cover Pages
A cover page can be used to set a tone for the entire document.

Follow Your Instructor's Formatting Guidelines

Your instructor will likely give you some specific guidelines about how the document or presentation should look (e.g., margins, line spacing, font, headings, header/footer, page numbers, etc.). You should follow those instructions exactly.

Include a Cover Page

The cover page should include the title of the document, your name, your professor's name, the course, and the date (Figure 15.4). You might also include an image to set a specific tone for the document.

Use Headings

Headings give the audience an overall sense of how the information is organized, while helping them locate the information they need. Headings also help you bridge the transitions between larger sections.

Add Visuals to Illustrate Key Points

You can use photographs, tables, graphs, and charts to support or amplify what is in the written text. If you find an idea difficult to describe in writing, perhaps you can find a photograph that illustrates what you mean. If you have data and facts that could be turned into a graph or chart, you can use these kinds of visuals to illustrate trends.

Add a Table of Contents

If your research paper or report is ten pages or longer, you might consider adding a table of contents. Most word processors can quickly generate a table of contents for your document. Use tabs, especially "leader" tabs, to line up the page numbers vertically on the right side of the sheet.

The design of your research paper or report is important. If your document is accessible and visually attractive, your audience will likely spend more time considering your argument.

Ready to write that research paper or report? Here's what you need to know.

1 Research papers and research reports are similar in many ways, but there are also important differences in content and organization.

2 The Background section in a research paper gives an overview of the issue being discussed, answering the Five W and How questions.

3 The Methodology section in a research report describes step by step how the research was completed.

4 The Findings or Results section describes and explains the major findings from the research.

5 The Discussion section interprets the major findings and states your major conclusions about your topic.

6 The style and design of your research paper or report should be academic and professional.

7 Your argument's style should use plain, straightforward sentences while minimizing the use of bureaucratic phrasings, passive voice, and nominalizations.

8 When designing the document, make sure the instructor's formatting guidelines are followed closely.

9 Additional design features like a cover page and headings, even if not required, can set a positive, professional tone for the audience.

10 Visuals, such as graphs, charts, and photographs, can be used to reinforce and illustrate important points in the argument.

1. On the Internet, find a research paper or report that you believe is poorly re-searched. Highlight the places in the text where the author makes claims that are unsupported or seem to be based purely on opinion. As the reader of the docu-ment, how do you feel about this kind of unsupported argument? If you were to disagree with this author's views, where would you challenge his or her points? How might you use research to support an opposing view? Show this article to your group and discuss how its weaknesses undermine its argument.

2. Find one example of a research paper and of a research report, preferably on a similar topic. Compare and contrast the two documents. What are some of the similarities? What are some of the differences? In what fields are research papers, like the one you found, most common? In what fields are research reports most common? With your group, discuss why the authors of these documents chose to write research papers instead of research reports and vice versa.

3. A simple search on the Internet will turn up a variety of websites from which you can buy a research paper. Find a few of these websites and look them over. If you were an instructor, how easy would it be to detect a purchased research paper? What would be some of the telltale signs that a student did not write the paper that was handed in? What would be an appropriate sanction for someone who handed in a research paper that is not their own? Discuss these issues with your group and come up with a policy that you would like your instructor to follow if someone were to buy or copy a research paper.

1. Choose a current topic on which you would like to do some research and con-tribute your viewpoint. Develop a research question about this topic and come up with a working thesis or hypothesis. Try to narrow your topic to something that could be handled in a research paper or research report. Send your topic, research question, and your working thesis to your instructor via e-mail.

2. What kind of evidence (print, electronic, or empirical) do you think is most trustworthy when writing a research project? Does the most appropriate evidence depend on the topic that is being researched, or is one kind of evidence more compelling than the others? In a group of three people, choose three different topics for the group and ask each person to work out the pros and cons of the three kinds of evidence for each topic. Then share the strengths and weaknesses of the three kinds of evidence. As a group, write a briefing (one page) in which you dis-cuss whether you feel some kinds of evidence are more trustworthy than others.

3. Choose a topic, develop a research question, and state a working thesis. Write an out-line of a research paper or research report based on the diagrams in the QuickView Guide at the beginning of this chapter. Then list the moves you would need to make in the introduction and conclusion of the document. Share your outline with your group. Ask each group member to critique the others' research questions, working theses, and outlines. In a written comment to each of your group members, explain their research projects' strengths and what you find most interesting about them. Then offer ideas for improvement. Offer suggestions about the kinds of sources that would be most helpful for supporting each research paper or report.

329

ONE STUDENT'S WORK

In this research paper, student Khizer Amin explores the available research on concussions in ice hockey. Though the paper is specifically about hockey, his evidence and his conclusions can be applied to all contact sports, including football and soccer. As you read his argument, notice how he uses research-based evidence to logically build his argument that concussions are a significant problem in hockey and other contact sports.

Concussions in Ice Hockey: Is it Time to Worry?

Khizer Amin

After receiving two hits to the head in the span of two games, Sidney Crosby, the All-Star center for the Pittsburgh Penguins, was sidelined from hockey in February (Joyce, par. 6). The long and arduous recovery process that ensued garnered continuous questions about when Crosby would return, and upon his return, whether he would be able to regain his high calibre of play. A concussion with consequences of this magnitude is by no means a rare occurrence in sport; in fact, head injuries are the most common cause of death amongst athletes (Cantu, 289). However, Sidney Crosby's reputation as one of the best in the game has pointed the public spotlight on the severity and consequences of concussions and head injury. Since the incident, researchers have seized the opportunity eager to engage the general public in dialogue regarding the issues of aggression and unnecessary physicality in sport.

Definition of Concussion

A concussion is defined by the American Association of Neurological Surgeons (AANS) as, "a clinical syndrome characterized by immediate and transient alteration in brain function, including alteration of mental status and level of consciousness, resulting from mechanical force or trauma" (AANS, par. 2). Immediate symptoms vary from case to case, ranging from a temporary loss of consciousness to amnesia, dizziness, and prolonged confusion (Ropper and Gorson, par. 5).

The generally accepted guidelines for what constitutes a concussion have evolved greatly over recent years as the scientific community has furthered its understanding and knowledge of traumatic brain injuries. In the past, researchers and clinicians characterized loss of consciousness as a necessary and defining symptom of concussions. Furthermore, concussions were not believed to result in long-term debilitations. In contrast to these old beliefs, recent research has found that concussions are a serious risk factor for neurological disorders that may only become apparent years after the original incident (Webbe, 46; Tator, 715).

The development of modern diagnostic techniques has decreased the number of concussions that go undetected and thus untreated. Neurological testing and on-field evaluations for potentially concussed athletes are now more robust and comprehensive. In particular, 'day-after-concussion' examinations are valuable diagnostic tools, since the onset of symptoms may only present themselves at a later time (Casson, Pellman, and Vianno, 236). The injured individual is able to report any changes in mood, appetite, tiredness and sleep patterns. Computerized neuropsychological testing is a recent development that allows athletes, trainers, and parents to monitor cognitive functioning (Lovell, 96). After a concussion, results from this test can be compared to baseline scores (from a test done prior to any injury) to monitor an individual's recovery process.

The Mechanism of Concussion

5   Concussions are generally a functional injury and can often occur without any externally visible impression or contusion to the body (McCrory, et al., 437). They occur when the brain is accelerated into the skull due to some sort of impact or external force. Concussions are caused by a combination of two major types of forces: translational and

rotational (Webbe, 47). Translational forces cause linear accelerations, resulting in stretching and compression of the brain (Meaney and Smith, 21). The collision of the brain against the inner walls of the cranium causes brain tissue damage and elevated intracranial pressure. Conversely, rotational forces cause the brain to accelerate angularly along its mid-vertical axis. This force often results in the shearing of brain tissue and temporary loss of consciousness due to the impact from rotation at the midbrain (Ropper and Gorson, 167). Current evidence suggests that rotational accelerations imparted on the brain are the more severe and important force implicated in the onset of concussions (Webbe, 169).

Concussions in Sport

Concussions are most commonly a result of falling or striking an object or another person (Colantonio, et al. 784). Athletes are prone to such injuries due to the physicality and aggressive behaviour often associated with sport. Amongst individuals 16—34 years of age, a Canadian National Population Health Survey found that 85% of concussions are sport-related (Gordon, Dooley, and Wood, 377). A study in Alberta monitoring the number of emergency department visits due to sport and recreational head injuries reported that ice hockey players accounted for the largest proportion of head injuries, at about 21% (Kelly et al. 79). This may be due to the excessively physical nature of the game, or simply because of the sheer number of participants in the sport, which is after all 'Canada's game'. Other major causes of head injuries were – in order from least to most frequent— cycling, playground activities, soccer, football, and rugby (Kelly et al. 79). It is clear, therefore, that concussions and head injuries are of concern across a variety of sports and activities, and an exploration of both general and activity-specific intervention methods is warranted.

Recent studies have associated concussions in sports with a decline in long-term brain function (de Beaumont et al. 697). Athletes incurring a concussion in early adulthood were found to score lower on neuropsychological testing and suffer from bradykinesia (slowed movement) decades after diagnosis (de Beaumont et al. 705). A link between concussions and the onset of clinical depression in later life has also been made; athletes who have incurred one or two concussions are 1.5 times more likely to suffer from depression in later years (Guskiewicz et al. 906).

Youth athletes are prone to the most negative sequelae of concussions. Concussions can inhibit proper development of the brain resulting in developmental disabilities, severe motor dysfunctions and psychiatric conditions that will burden the child for the entirety of their life (Marchie and Cusimano 124). This is of great concern when considering that 10-12% of Canadian minor league hockey players aged 9-17 report being victims of head injuries each season (126).

Second-impact syndrome is a condition that has gained scientific and media recognition in recent years. Essentially, this refers to incurring a second concussion while an individual is still suffering from the adverse effects of an earlier one (Saunders and Harbaugh 538). It is possible that the two concussions have a compounding effect in terms of the damage caused to the brain. Even a very minor blow to the head after an initial concussion has been associated with sharp increases in intracranial pressure, haemorrhaging, and subsequent death (539). Due to the severity of concussions and the danger of second-impact syndrome, it is important for players, coaches, trainers, and team doctors to follow appropriate return-to-play guidelines.

Increased awareness of the consequences of concussions in sport has   10 prompted many athletes to donate their brains towards concussion research ("Athlete" par. 4). These donations have fuelled much research towards discerning important details about the mechanisms and long-term impacts of concussions. For example, researchers at Boston University recently studied the brain of Rick Martin, a former NHL star. Analysis of Martin's brain revealed that he had chronic traumatic encephalopathy, a disease which leads to cognitive decline and ultimately dementia (Christie par. 1).

Implications on The Culture of Ice Hockey

Concussions in hockey are most often caused by body checking (Warsh et al. 134), a form of physical contact between players, which is legal in the NHL and many minor leagues. However, the newfound dangers of concussions in recent findings has called into question the current culture that exists around aggression and fighting in hockey and other sports (Marchie and Cusimano 125).

Athletes, officials, fans, and the general public often become desensitized to aggression in sport and begin to accept it as part of the game (Fields, Collins, and Comstock 35). In fact, many individuals display elevated levels of aggression while engaged in sports (Boardley and Kavussanu 177), which begs the question of why physical aggression is accepted and legal in athletics but not in other facets of everyday life.

In the past, proponents of physical contact in sports have argued that safety equipment such as helmets and mouth-guards provide ample protection from injuries. While there is evidence of a reduced number of general injuries, there is little scientific evidence demonstrating that current equipment is capable of preventing concussions (McCrory et al. 155; Daneshvar et al. 160). Furthermore, while helmets do indeed reduce the force of impact to the head, there is no evidence that wearing helmets corresponds to a reduced rate of concussions in athletes. As such, there has been a gradual paradigm shift in the scientific community regarding the best means of reducing concussions. Rather than advocating for increased use of safety equipment, there is now an increased focus on changing rules, regulations, and the culture of sport to reduce the number of falls and hits to the head in the first place (McCrory et al. 156; Warsh et al. 140).

The minimum age at which hockey associations should allow participants to body check has become a highly controversial and debated topic in the hockey community. Proponents for lowering the minimum age argue that it allows youth to properly learn and adjust to the techniques behind giving and taking a hit. However, a systematic review exploring the relationship between body checking and injuries found that leagues which permit checking in younger players are associated with higher rates of injuries and fractures (Warsch et al. 140). Based on their findings, the authors recommended that body checking be removed from leagues for younger athletes, with the minimum age for introduction of physical contact being at least 13 years. In line with this, the Ontario Hockey Federation recently introduced new regulations that effectively banned body checking in all house leagues and some select leagues (Lee par. 1).

Conclusion

Concussions are serious injuries with potential serious long-term   15
neurological and psychiatric consequences. Based on current scientific evidence, it is apparent that modifications to the rules surrounding hockey are warranted and could potentially reduce rates of concussion. Imposing greater sanctions on actions such as head hits and checks from behind may help to make Canada's game safer for all participants. Only 1 in every 4000 minor hockey league players will ever fulfill the ultimate dream of playing in the NHL (Marchie and Cusimano, 124). In this light, is it reasonable for our youth to have to–or be allowed to–put their future livelihoods on the line every time they step onto the ice?

Works Cited

"Athlete Brain Donations for Concussion Study Reach 300." *ESPN. com*. 12 Oct. 2010. Web. 16 Oct. 2011.

American Association of Neurological Surgeons [AANS]. "Concussion." *Patient Information*. 2005. Web. 10 Oct. 2011.

Boardley, Ian, and Maria Kavussanu. "Effects of Goal Orientation and Perceived Value of Toughness on Antisocial Behavior in Soccer: The Mediating Role of Moral Disengagement." *Journal of Sport & Exercise Psychology* 32.2 (2010): 176–92. Print.

Cantu, Robert. "Head Injuries in Sport." *British Journal of Sports Medicine* 30.4 (1996): 289–96. Print.

Casson, Ira, Elliot Pellman, and David Viano. "Concussion in Athletes: Information for Team Physicians on the Neurologic Evaluation." *Seminars in Spine Surgery* 22.4 (2010): 234–44. Print.

Christie, James. "Former Sabres Rick Martin Had Brain Disease." *The Globe and Mail.* 5 Oct. 2011. Web. 16 Oct. 2011.

Colantonio, Angela, Christine Saverino, Brandon Zagorski, B. Swaine, John Lewko, Susan Jaglal, and Lee Vernich. "Hospitalizations and Emergency Department Visits for TBI in Ontario." *The Canadian Journal of Neurological Sciences* 37.6 (2010): 783–90. Print.

Daneshvar, Daniel, Christie Baugh, Christopher Nowinski, Ann McKee, Robert Stern, and Robert Cantu. "Helmets and Mouth Guards: The Role of Personal Equipment in Preventing Sport-Related Concussions." *Clinics in Sports Medicine* 30.1 (2011): 145–63. Print.

de Beaumont, Louis, Hugo Théoret, David Mongeon, Julie Messier, Suzanne Leclerc, Sebastian Tremblay, Dave Ellemberg, and Maryse Lassonde. "Brain Function Decline in Healthy Retired Athletes Who Sustained Their Last Sports Concussion in Early Adulthood."*Brain: A Journal of Neurology* 132.3 (2009): 695–708. Print.

Fields, Sarah, Christy Collins, and R. Dawn Comstock. "Violence in Youth Sports: Hazing, Brawling, and Foul Play." *British Journal of Sports Medicine* 44 (2010): 32–7. Print.

Gordon, Kevin, Joseph Dooley, and Ellen Wood. "Descriptive Epidemiology of Concussion." *Pediatric Neurology* 34.5 (2006): 376–78. Print.

Guskiewicz, Kevin, Steven Marshall, Julian Bailes, Michael McCrea, Hernden Harding, Amy Matthews, Johna Mihalik, and Robert Cantu. "Recurrent Concussion and Risk of Depression in Retired Professional Football Players." *Medicine and Science in Sports and Exercise* 39.6 (2007): 903–09. Print.

Joyce, Gare. "Will Sid Ever be the Same?" *Sportsnet Magazine.* 29 Sep. 2011. Web. 11 Oct. 2011.

Kelly, Kaven, H. Lissel, Brian Rowe, JoAnnVincenten, and Don Voaklander. "Sport and Recreation-Related Head Injuries Treated in the Emergency Department." *Clinical Journal of Sport Medicine* 11.2 (2001): 77–81. Print.

Lee, Eddie. "Ontario Hockey Federation Bans Bodychecking in House Leagues." *TheStar.com*. 6 May 2011. Web. 11 Oct. 2011.

Lovell, Mark. "The Management of Sports-Related Concussion: Current Status and Future Trends." *Clinics in Sports Medicine* 28.1 (2009): 95–111. Print.

Marchie, Anthony, and Michael Cusimano. "Bodychecking and Concussions in Ice Hockey: Should Our Youth Pay the Price?" *Canadian Medical Association Journal* 169.2 (2003): 124–28. Print

McCrory, Paul, Willem Meeuwisse, Karen Johnston, Jiri Dvorak, Mark Aubry, Mick Molloy, and Robert Cantu. "Consensus Statement on Concussion in Sport." *The Physician and Sportsmedicine* 37.2 (2009): 141–59. Print.

Meaney, Douglas, and Douglass H. Smith. "Biomechanics of Concussion." *Clinics in Sports Medicine* 30.1 (2011): 19–31. Print.

Ropper Allen, and Kenneth Gorson. "Concussion." *The New England Journal of Medicine* 356.2 (2007): 166–72. Print.

Saunders, Richard, and Robert Harbaugh. "The Second Impact in Catastrophic Contact-Sports Head Trauma." *Journal of the American Medical Association* 252.4 (1984): 538–39. Print.

Tator, Charles. "Brain Injury is a Major Problem in Canada and Annual Incidence is Not Declining." *The Canadian Journal of Neurological Sciences* 37.6 (2010): 714–15. Print.

Warsh, Joel, SAerban Constantin, Andrew Howard, and Alison Macpherson. "A Systematic Review of the Association Between Body Checking and Injury in Youth Ice Hockey." *Clinical Journal of Sport Medicine* 19.2 (2009): 134–44. Print.

Webbe, Frank. "Definition, Physiology, and Severity of Cerebral Concussion." *Sports Neuropsychology: Assessment and Management of Traumatic Brain Injury.* Ed. R. J. Echemendia. New York: Guilford Press, 2006. 45–70. Print.

A CLOSER LOOK AT
Concussions in Hockey

1. Consulting the QuickView at the beginning of this chapter, decide which of the four organizational structures most closely resembles the structure of "Concussions in Hockey." Find three ways in which it doesn't follow the patterns in the QuickView.

2. Does Amin present the research of both sides of the controversy, or does he focus more on one side? How could he make his coverage more balanced?

3. Where exactly does Amin reveal his main point in the introduction and conclusion? Highlight the sentences where the main point appears. Compare these two statements. How are they similar? How are they different?

IDEAS FOR
Arguing

1. Write a refutation of Amin's research paper. You could choose to disagree entirely by pointing out lapses in his logic or challenging his research. Or you could extend his argument into another direction and advance a more compelling main point (thesis) or offer further recommendations.

2. Conduct your own local research project into sports-related concussions. Describe what has been happening recently with this issue and the specific controversies and debates. Conclude with your interpretation of the findings and offer two to five recommendations.

Does TV Help Make Americans Passive and Accepting of Authority?

BRUCE E. LEVINE

In this research-based argument, clinical psychology and social critic Bruce E. Levine argues that while television watching is enjoyable and in some ways benefits society, overall it causes Americans to passively accept the status quo. As you read, notice how he offers a new and interesting angle on this issue by combining research with his own personal observations.

Historically, television viewing has been used by various authorities to quiet potentially disruptive people—from kids to psychiatric inpatients to prison inmates. In 1992, *Newsweek* reported, "Faced with severe overcrowding and limited budgets for rehabilitation and counseling, more and more prison officials are using TV to keep inmates quiet" (Springen & Kantrowitz, par. 1). Joe Corpier, a convicted murderer, was quoted, "If there's a good movie, it's usually pretty quiet through the whole institution." Both public and private-enterprise prisons have recognized that providing inmates with cable television can be a more economical method to keep them quiet and subdued than it would be to hire more guards.

Just as I have not emptied my refrigerator of beer, I have not gotten rid of my television, but I recognize the effects of beer and TV. During some dismal periods of my life, TV has been my "drug of choice," and I've watched thousands of hours of TV sports and escapist crap. When I don't need to take the edge off, I have watched Bill Moyers, *Frontline* and other "good television." But I don't kid myself—the research shows that the more TV of any kind we watch, the more passive most of us become.

American TV Viewing

Sociologist Robert Putnam in Bowling Alone (2000) reported that in 1950, about 10 percent of American homes had television sets, but this had grown to more than 99 percent. Putnam also reported that the number of TVs in the average U.S. household had grown to 2.24 sets, with 66 percent of households having three or more sets; the TV set is turned on in the average U.S. home for seven hours a day; two-thirds of Americans regularly watch TV during dinner; and about 40 percent of Americans' leisure time is spent on television. And Putnam also reported that spouses spend three to four times more time watching television together than they do talking to each other.

In 2009, the Nielsen Company reported that U.S. TV viewing was at an all-time high, the average American viewing television 151 hours per month if one includes the following "three screens": a television set, a laptop/personal computer and a cell phone (Gandossey). This increase, according to Nielson, is part of a long-term trend attributable to not only greater availability of screens, increased variety of different viewing methods, more digital recorders, DVR, and TiVo devices but also a tanking economy creating the need for low-cost diversions. And in 2011, the *New York Times* reported, "Americans watched more television than ever in 2010, according to the Nielsen Company. Total viewing of broadcast networks and basic cable channels rose about

1 percent for the year, to an average of 34 hours per person per week" (Stelter, 2011, par. 3)

In February 2012, the *New York Times* reported that young people were watching slightly less television in 2011 than the record highs in 2010 (Stelter, 2012). In 2011, as compared to 2010, those 25-34 and 12-17 years of age were watching nine minutes less a day, and 18-24 year olds were watching television six fewer minutes a day. Those 35 and older are spending slightly more time watching TV. However, there is some controversy about trends here, as the New York Times also reported: "According to data for the first nine months of 2011, children spent as much time in front of the television set as they did in 2010, and in some cases spent more. But the proportion of live viewing is shrinking while time-shifted viewing is expanding" (par. 13).

Online television viewing is increasingly significant, especially so for young people. In one marketing survey of 1,000 Americans reported in 2010 , 64% of said they watched at least some TV online (O'Dell). Among those younger than 25 in this survey, 83% watched at least some of their TV online, with 23% of this younger group watching "most" of their TV online, and 6% watching "all" of their TV online.

How does the United States compare to the rest of the world in TV viewing? There aren't many cross-national studies, and precise comparisons are difficult because of different measurements and different time periods. NOP World, a market research organization, interviewed more than 30,000 people in 30 countries in a study released in 2005, and reported that the United States was one of the highest TV-viewing nations. NationMaster.com, more than a decade ago, reporting on only the United States, Australia, and 11 European countries, found the following: the United States and the United Kingdom were the highest-viewing nations at 28 hours per week, with the lowest-viewing nations being Finland, Norway, and Sweden at 18 hours per week ("Television," 2012).

The majority of what Americans view on television—whether on the TV, laptop, or smartphone screen—is through channels owned by six corporations: General Electric (NBC, MSNBC,

CNBC, Bravo, and SyFi); Walt Disney (ABC, the Disney Channel, A&E, and Lifetime); Rupert Murdoch's News Corporation (Fox, Fox Business Channel, National Geographic, and FX); Time Warner (CNN, CW, HBO, Cinemax, Cartoon Network, TBS, TNT); Viacom (MTV, Nickelodeon/Nick@Nite, VH1, BET, Comedy Central); and CBS (CBS Television Network, CBS Television Distribution Group, Showtime, and CW, a joint venture with Time Warner). In addition to their television holdings, these media giants have vast holdings in radio, movie studios and publishing.

However, while progressives lament the concentrated corporate control of the media, there is evidence that the mere act of watching TV—regardless of the content—may well have a primary pacifying effect.

How TV Viewing Can Make Us Passive

10 Who among us hasn't spent time watching a show we didn't actually like, or found ourselves flipping through the channels long after we've concluded there isn't anything worth watching?

Jerry Mander is a "reformed sinner" of sorts who left his job in advertising to publish *Four Arguments for the Elimination of Television* in 1978. He explains how viewers are mesmerized by what TV insiders call "technical events"— quick cuts, zoom-ins, zoom-outs, rolls, pans, animation, music, graphics, and voice-overs, all of which lure viewers to continue watching even though they have no interest in the content. TV insiders know that it's these technical events—in which viewers see and hear things that real life does not present—that spellbind people to continue watching.

The "hold on us" of TV technical events, according to Robert Kubey and Mihaly Csikszentmihalyi's 2002 *Scientific American* article "Television Addiction Is No Mere Metaphor," is due to our "orienting response"— our instinctive reaction to any sudden or novel stimulus (p. 51). They report that:

> In 1986 Byron Reeves of Stanford University, Esther Thorson of the University of Missouri and their colleagues began to study whether the simple formal features of television—cuts,

edits, zooms, pans, sudden noises— activate the orienting response, thereby keeping attention on the screen. By watching how brain waves were affected by formal features, the researchers concluded that these stylistic tricks can indeed trigger involuntary responses and "derive their attentional value through the evolutionary significance of detecting movement. . . . It is the form, not the content, of television that is unique." (p. 51)

Kubey and Csikszentmihalyi claim that TV addiction is, at least psychologically, similar to drug addiction. Using their Experience Sampling Method (in which participants carried a beeper and were signaled six to eight times a day at random to report their activity), Kubey and Csikszentmihalyi found that almost immediately after turning on the TV, subjects reported feeling more relaxed, and because this occurs so quickly and the tension returns so rapidly after the TV is turned off, people are conditioned to associate TV viewing with a lack of tension. They concluded:

> Habit-forming drugs work in similar ways. A tranquilizer that leaves the body rapidly is much more likely to cause dependence than one that leaves the body slowly, precisely because the user is more aware that the drug's effects are wearing off. Similarly, viewers' vague learned sense that they will feel less relaxed if they stop viewing may be a significant factor in not turning the set off. (p. 51)

15 Mander (1978) documents research showing that regardless of the programming, viewers' brainwaves slow down, transforming them to a more passive, nonresistant state. In one study that Mander reports comparing brainwave activity in reading versus television watching, it was found the brain's response to reading is more active, unlike the passive response to television— this no matter what the TV content. Comparing the brain effects of TV viewing to reading, Kubey and Csikszentmihalyi report similar EEG results as measured by alpha brain-wave production. Maybe that's why when I view a fantastic Bill

Moyers interview on TV, I can recall almost nothing except that I enjoyed it; this in contrast to how many content specifics I can remember when I read a transcript of a Moyers interview. Kubey and Csikszentmihalyi's survey also revealed that:

> The sense of relaxation ends when the set is turned off, but the feelings of passivity and lowered alertness continue. Survey participants commonly reflect that television has somehow absorbed or sucked out their energy, leaving them depleted. They say they have more difficulty concentrating after viewing than before. In contrast, they rarely indicate such difficulty after reading. (p. 51)

Mander strongly disagrees with the idea that TV is merely a window through which any perception, any argument, or reality may pass. Instead, he claims TV is inherently biased by its technology. For a variety of technical reasons, including TV's need for sharp contrast to maintain interest, Mander explains that authoritarian-based programming is more technically interesting to viewers than democracy-based programming. War and violence may be unpleasant in real life; however, peace and cooperation make for "boring television." And charismatic authority figures are more "interesting" on TV than are ordinary citizens debating issues.

In a truly democratic society, one is gaining knowledge directly through one's own experience with the world, not through the filter of an authority or what Mander calls a mediated experience (p. 55). TV-dominated people ultimately accept others' mediated version of the world rather than discovering their own version based on their own experiences. Robert Keeshan, who played Captain Kangaroo in the long-running children's program, was critical of television—including so-called "good television"—in a manner rarely heard from those who work in it:

20

> When you are spending time in front of the television, you are not doing other things. The young child of three or four years is in the stage of the greatest emotional development that human beings undergo. And we only develop when we experience things, real-life things: a conversation with Mother, touching Father, going places, doing things, relating to others. This kind of experience is critical to a young child, and when the child spends thirty-five hours per week in front of the TV set, it is impossible to have the full range of real-life experience that a young child must have. Even if we had an overabundance of good television programs, it wouldn't solve the problem. (quoted in Mander, p. 265)

Whatever the content of the program, television watching is an isolating experience. Most people are watching alone, but even when watching it with others, they are routinely glued to the TV rather than interacting with one another. TV keeps us indoors, and it keeps us from mixing it up in real life. People who are watching TV are isolated from other people, from the natural world, even from their own thoughts and senses. TV creates isolation, and because it also reduces our awareness of our own feelings, when we start to feel lonely we are tempted to watch more so as to dull the ache of isolation.

Television is a "dream come true" for an authoritarian society. Those with the most money own most of what people see. Fear-based TV programming makes people more afraid and distrustful of one another, which is good for an authoritarian society depending on a "divide and conquer" strategy. Television isolates people so they are not joining together to govern themselves. Viewing television puts one in a brain state that makes it difficult to think critically, and it quiets and subdues a population. And spending one's free time isolated and watching TV interferes with the connection to one's own humanity, and thus makes it easier to accept an authority's version of society and life.

Whether it is in American penitentiaries or homes, TV is a staple of American pacification. When there's no beer in our refrigerators, when our pot hookup has been busted, and when we can't score a psychotropic drug prescription, there is always TV to take off the edge and chill us out.

REFERENCES

Gandossey, T. (2009, February 24). TV viewing at 'all time high,' Nielson says. *CNN.com*. Retrieved from http://edition.cnn.com/2009/SHOWBIZ/TV/02/24/us.video.nielsen/

Kubey, R, Csikszentmihalyi, M. (2002, February 23). Television addition is no mere metaphor. *Scientific American, 286*, 48–55.

Mander, J. (1978). *Four arguments for the elimination of television.* New York: Quill.

O'Dell, J. (2010, April 12). TV viewing's shift to the web [stats]. *Mashable.com*. Retrieved from http://mashable.com/2010/04/12/tv-online/

Springen, K, Kantrowitz, B. (1992, May 31). Hooking up at the big house. *Newsweek Magazine*. Retrieved from http://www.thedailybeast.com

/newsweek/1992/05/31/hooking-up-at-the-big-house.html.

Stelter, B. (2011, January 2). TV viewing continues to edge up. *New York Times*. Retrieved from http://www.nytimes.com/2011/01/03/business/media/03ratings.html?_r=4&amp&

Stelter, B. (2012, February 8). Youths are watching, but less often on TV. *New York Times*. Retrieved from http://www.nytimes.com/2012/02/09/business/media/young-people-are-watching-but-less-often-on-tv.html?

Television viewing (most recent) by country. (2012). *Nationmaster.com*. Retrieved from http://www.nationmaster.com/red/graph/med_tel_vie-media-television-viewing&amp

A CLOSER LOOK AT
Does TV Help Make Americans Passive and Accepting of Authority?

1. Find the places where Levine discusses his own personal interactions with television. How do these brief anecdotes help his readers identify with his position? Do you think these passages strengthen his argument, or do they merely distract readers?

2. According to Levine, why does television viewing make us passive? List the reasons he cites. In what other ways does television make us

passive? On the other hand, in what ways can television empower us and spur us to action?

3. Some people would argue that while Levine shows why television is a significant problem, he fails to offer solutions. What recommendations could he have proposed for reducing the problems associated with television viewing, or for improving television itself? List three to five possible solutions for dealing with this problem.

IDEAS FOR
Arguing

1. Write a factual personal narrative argument (Chapter 9) that supports, extends, or challenges Levine's argument. Explore your own television viewing experiences or explore instead other forms of entertainment, such as Internet social sites, online gaming, movies, or gambling.

2. Choose a television show or other multimedia event (movie, video, podcast, etc.) and write a rhetorical analysis that explains how it causes people to become passive or spurs them toward social action.

The Research
Project

3 PART

RESEARCH can be both fun and rewarding. It's like solving a mystery or exploring a new place.

16 Developing Your Research Process

Students often cringe when a professor asks them to do research for a project. That's too bad, because doing research can be both fun and rewarding. Researching a topic is like solving a mystery or discovering new places. Once you know how to do research quickly and efficiently, you will see that exploring new issues is both challenging and fun. Meanwhile, doing research is easier than ever with computers and mobile devices (Figure 16.1).

Research is the systematic investigation of a topic or issue. The ability to do research will be vital to your success in college and your career. In college, many of your courses will require you to study topics methodically and write arguments that are supported with research-based sources. In the workplace, research is an everyday task that will help you and your colleagues gather information, make informed decisions, and take action. Many employers prominently mention the ability to do research as a critical skill they look for in new employees.

FIGURE 16.1 Doing Research Is Like Solving a Mystery Doing research is challenging and fun. Usually, once you get started, you will find yourself immersed in the project.

Developing Your Research Process

16.1 How to develop your own research process

The best way to do research is to follow a *research process* that fits your personal work habits. Everyone does research a little differently, but here is a model that you can use to develop a research process that works for you:

Step 1: Define your research question.

Step 2: Develop a working thesis or hypothesis.

Step 3: Collect print, electronic, and empirical sources.

Step 4: Triangulate your sources.

Step 5: Identify your major findings.

Step 6: Modify or accept your working thesis/hypothesis.

This six-step research process is loosely based on the scientific method. It is designed to help you pose good questions and test a *working thesis* or *hypothesis* (Figure 16.2). You can modify this process to fit your own work habits and style.

Step 1: Define Your Research Question

To start, you first need to figure out the *research question* you are trying to answer. Defining a research question will help you accomplish two things. First, it will help you sharpen your understanding of your research topic. Second, it will help you develop a new angle on that topic.

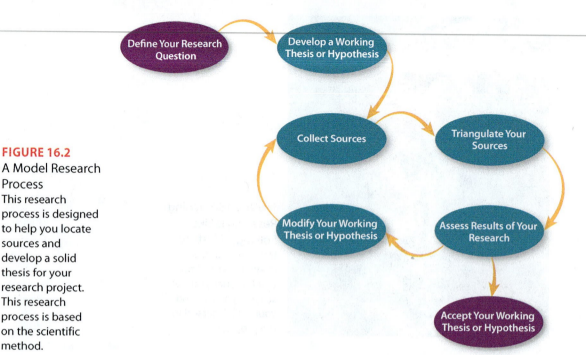

FIGURE 16.2
A Model Research Process
This research process is designed to help you locate sources and develop a solid thesis for your research project. This research process is based on the scientific method.

Here are some example research topics and research questions:

Research Topic: Fashion on a College Campus

Research Question: How can college students dress well on a limited budget?

Research Topic: Slave Narratives in the Pre–Civil War Era

Research Question: How did slave narratives influence and energize the abolition movement before the American Civil War?

Research Topic: Nutrition in high school lunches

Research Question: If offered healthy options along with standard cafeteria food, will high school students make good choices about what to eat?

Each of these research questions sets a direction or angle for the topic. Your research question identifies the topic, angle, and the purpose of your project.

Step 2: Develop a Working Thesis or Hypothesis

Your *working thesis* or *hypothesis* is your best prediction, right now, about how you will answer your research question. Of course, you can't answer the question with certainty at this point—you haven't done any research. However, you can probably take an educated guess about how the research project will likely turn out. By forming a working thesis right now, you can figure out what kinds of evidence will be needed to answer your question.

In one sentence, write down your working thesis. Here are some working theses based on the research questions above:

Working Thesis: Being fashionable at college often means staying with basics that can be used interchangeably (jeans, cotton dresses, high-heeled loafers) while accessorizing with unique items that set the "look" apart (scarves, fedoras, blazers).

Working Thesis: The publication of slave narratives before the American Civil War kept the embers of Northern dissatisfaction with the South glowing, which helped abolitionists spur Northerners to arms when the Confederate states seceded.

Hypothesis: Given healthy options, some high school students will make better dietary choices at school lunch; however, the majority of students will simply continue to choose the high-calorie foods that taste good and are promoted by mass-media advertising.

Your working thesis should be limited to one sentence so you can focus your research project. If you need more than one sentence to state your working thesis, your topic may be too complex or broad to be handled in a college paper.

Step 3. Collect Print, Electronic, and Empirical Sources

Now it's time to collect sources to determine whether your working thesis holds up. You should search for information from three types of sources:

Electronic sources—websites, blogs, listservs, television and radio broadcasts, podcasts, documentaries, and videos. Many of these sources can be located with Internet search engines like Google, Bing, or Yahoo. Some electronic sources not available through the Internet but may be available through your campus library.

Print sources—books, journals, magazines, newspapers, government publications, reference materials, and microform/microfiche. Your campus library's online catalog should help you locate these materials. Otherwise, Google Scholar is a useful tool for finding print sources.

Empirical sources—field observations, surveys, interviews, case studies, experiments, and personal experiences. Empirical sources require you to experience your subject directly by observing it, measuring it, or discussing it with experts.

As you search for information on your topic, you should try to collect material from all three types of sources. A mixture of sources will help you understand your topic from a variety of perspectives.

Step 4: Triangulate Your Sources

Triangulation involves using the Research Triangle to compare and corroborate the evidence you find in online, print, and empirical sources (Figure 16.3). That way, you can determine whether the evidence is reliable. Here is how triangulation works.

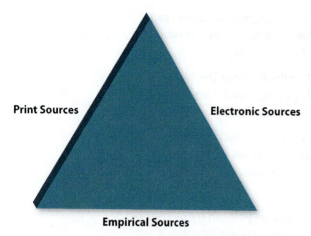

Three-sided information—If you find comparable information from all three sides of the Research Triangle, there is a good chance that the information is reliable.

Two-sided information—If you can gather similar facts from only two sides of the Research Triangle, the information is probably still reliable but open to doubt.

One-sided information—If you can only find evidence from one side of the Research Triangle, then you should question whether the information can be trusted.

FIGURE 16.3 The Research Triangle
When collecting information, you should look for sources on all three sides of the research triangle.

Of course, triangulating your sources with the Research Triangle will not guarantee that your sources are reliable or trustworthy. The "truth" and even the "facts" are usually a bit more slippery than that. Instead, triangulation helps you challenge your sources and look for corroborating evidence in diverse places.

You need to be especially skeptical of sources that seem to be drawing their information from just one common source. A blog, for example, could be drawing its evidence from a magazine article, which took the evidence from an interview. In this kind of situation, triangulation really isn't possible, because you're simply finding the same evidence even though it appears in three different media.

You should also be skeptical of sources that are biased toward one perspective on an issue, especially sources that agree with your own personal opinion. When doing research, your aim is to gain a full understanding of the argument, not just back up what you already believe. So, look for a variety of sources that allow you to see all sides of the issue.

Step 5: Identify Your Major Findings

With your sources collected and triangulated, you are ready to identify the *major findings* of your research.

Ask yourself: What are the two to five most important discoveries I made while doing research? These two to five items are your *major findings*. List them and rank them from most important to least important.

Pushing yourself to choose only two to five major findings might seem a bit artificial, but it has two benefits. First, when you limit yourself to a handful of major findings, you can examine and explain them in depth for your audience. Second, if you identify too many major findings, your audience won't be able to figure out which ones are most important. By focusing on a few major findings, you will highlight them for your audience.

Step 6: Modify or Accept Your Working Thesis

You should now revisit your working thesis. More than likely, your sources revealed some interesting new points of view and evidence that you didn't expect. If so, it's likely you will need to modify your working thesis to fit this new evidence. At this point you have a few options:

- **Revise your working thesis**—You can revise your working thesis and do some additional research to see if it holds up.

- **Accept your revised working thesis**—If you're comfortable with your revised working thesis, you're ready to start organizing and drafting your argument.

- **Abandon your working thesis**—If your working thesis now seems incorrect, you can abandon it and formulate a new working thesis.

The decision to abandon a working thesis is always a difficult choice in research projects, but sometimes your research will reveal that your original working thesis missed the mark. That's fine, and it happens regularly in the sciences. If you are really open to finding the truth (and not just confirming what you previously believed), you should be willing to change your beliefs to fit what your research reveals.

Eventually, you will settle on a working thesis you can back up with research. At this point, your working thesis becomes the main point or final thesis that will be the cornerstone of your argument.

Finding Primary and Secondary Sources

16.2 The differences between primary sources and secondary sources

Researchers often make a distinction between *primary sources* and *secondary sources*.

Primary sources—Primary sources include the artifacts, records, statements, or other items that were created or used by the people directly involved with the subject of the research (Figure 16.4). Primary sources might include personal papers, letters, e-mails, objects, clothing, tools, creative works, music, or quotes from interviews. Primary sources also include any data or statistics that you or others collected from experiments, observations, or other empirical research.

Secondary sources—Secondary sources include the published works of scholars, journalists, experts, and other knowledgeable people who have analyzed, studied, or commented on the subject. For example, secondary sources can include books, journal articles, magazine articles, newspapers, and blogs.

FIGURE 16.4
Primary Sources
Primary sources are typically items that were directly connected in some way with the events and people involved with the topic.

For college papers, most of your research will rely on secondary sources because you will tend to use articles and books to explain and support your views. For many topics, though, you should able to locate primary sources by visiting archives, historic sites, museums, or galleries. Any empirical research you do, such as experiments, surveys, interviews, observations, will also be considered primary sources. You should always look for ways to incorporate at least one primary source in your research.

16.3 How to collect evidence from print, electronic, and empirical sources

Finding Print Sources

Today, the distinctions between print sources and electronic sources are becoming blurred, especially as print sources are increasingly available through the Internet. For the purpose of research, print sources are texts that originally appeared or were designed to appear in a print format, usually on paper.

With today's easy access to the Internet, you might be tempted to bypass print sources altogether. That would be a mistake. After all, the most reliable evidence is often found in books and articles. Moreover, printed information cannot be easily changed from one day to the next, which typically makes it more reliable than electronic sources.

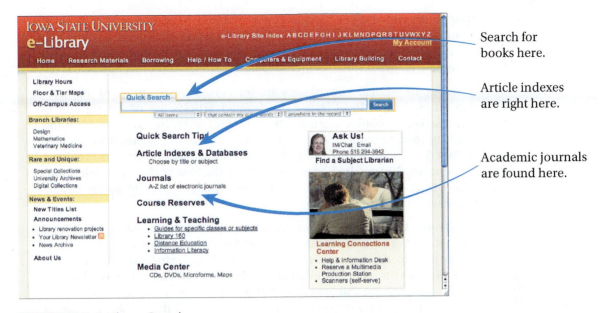

Search for
books here.

Article indexes
are right here.

Academic journals
are found here.

FIGURE 16.5 A Library Portal
Your library's website gives you access to a variety of print and electronic information.

To find print sources, your best approach is to use your campus library's website, which is also sometimes called a "library portal" or "catalog" (Figure 16.5). Your library's website will give you access to online catalogs, search engines, and databases that can help you locate the print sources shelved in the library or available through *interlibrary loan*. Here are the kinds of sources that you should look for:

Books—Books are often considered the most reliable print sources. The time and expense of producing a book usually ensures a level of fact-checking, review, and editing that exceeds other sources. Books, however, are not neutral or unbiased sources of information. Their authors have their own opinions, biases, and agendas, so you still need to read books critically and corroborate the facts you find.

Academic journals—Academic journal articles are written and reviewed by scholars, consultants, and subject-matter experts (SMEs), so they tend to be reliable sources of evidence. On your library's website, look for a link, button, or tab that will allow you to search for articles through *periodical indexes*. Some of the more popular periodical indexes include ArticleFirst, EBSCO-host, LexisNexis, PsychINFO, and IEEE Explore.

Magazines—Magazines offer a variety of articles, which you can find through the *Readers' Guide to Periodical Literature*. The *Readers' Guide* is an online index that is probably available through your library's website.

Your library will also keep recent copies of many magazines in its periodical room or reference room. If you are looking for an article from a past issue, you might go directly to the magazine's website. Some other useful indexes for finding magazine articles include Find Articles, MagPortal, and InfoTrac.

Newspapers—Local newspapers are often your best sources of information on current or local issues. Newspaper articles are not as rigorously fact-checked as books, journals, or even magazines, but they are often the most up-to-date sources of information on breaking stories and popular culture. You can find articles through newspaper indexes, such as ProQuest Newspapers, Chronicling America, LexisNexis, New York Times Index, and EBSCOhost. Then you can go to the newspaper's website to access the article itself.

Government documents—You might be surprised at how many useful documents are available from the federal and state governments. These documents tend to be thoroughly researched and are written in an accessible style. You can find them through government websites, such as The Catalog of U.S. Government Publications. At the state level, you can explore state government websites or you can check the online catalogs at the libraries of larger public universities.

Much of your "library research" can be handled from your computer, phone, tablet, or laptop. Copies of many print items can often be downloaded directly to your computer. Otherwise, a trip to the library will usually take less than an hour.

Two increasingly helpful online sources for print texts are Google Books and Google Scholar. Google Books is an online library that has full or partial copies of many books that might not be available in your library. Plus, Google Books is searchable, allowing you to target specific information in a wide variety of books. Google Scholar is a good way to search for a variety of academic articles that are available on the Internet.

Finding Electronic Sources

Electronic sources are texts that were designed to be viewed on a screen or listened to through an electronic medium. They include sources like websites, blogs, wikis, podcasts, television and radio broadcasts, movies, and documentaries.

Using Internet Search Engines

Your professors will often say something like, "I don't want you to just use the first five results you find through Google, Bing, or Yahoo." Internet search engines are extremely sophisticated and helpful, but they can't do your research for you. You need to be selective about the kinds of electronic sources you use.

Knowing a few search engine tricks can help you better target the information you need. For example, let's say you are doing research on the abuse of energy drinks among college students. You might start by entering a phrase into a search engine:

energy drinks

The search engine, as you would expect, will bring up millions of web pages that refer to this topic. Obviously, you don't have time to look through even a fraction of these sites. Also, most of them don't have useful information that pertains to your project.

What should you do? You need to narrow your search to find the handful of useful web pages among these millions (Figure 16.6). Here are some tricks that will focus your search when using a search engine:

Use exact words—Use exact words that will target the kinds of information you are looking for. Choose words that exactly describe your topic and your angle on that topic.

    effects of energy drinks on college students taking final exams

Use quotation marks—When terms are put in quotation marks, the search engine will only look for pages on which those words appear.

    effects of "energy drinks" on college students taking "final exams"

Use the minus (–) sign—If you are receiving results you don't want, you can use the minus sign (–) to remove topics that you don't need.

    effects of energy drinks on college student final exams –driving –alcohol –obesity

FIGURE 16.6
Narrowing Your Search on a Search Engine
You can use specific keywords and symbols to help you sharpen your search for sources with a search engine. Dogpile, the search engine shown here, is a good alternative to some of the better-known search engines.

Use the plus (+) sign—Using the plus (+) sign will ensure that some topics will be specifically searched for. The plus sign will stress some words over others when web pages are ranked by the search engine.

> effects of +energy drinks on college student final +exams

Use wildcard symbols—Most search engines will allow the use of wildcard symbols (*, %, or ?) that help you fill in words of a phrase, title, or lyric you can't remember.

> "Red Bull * you wings" energy drinks college students

Using specific words, quotation marks, and symbols will help you quickly narrow your search to websites that will be most useful.

Evaluating Information from the Internet

Just about anyone can put up a website that provides so-called "facts." So you need to be critical and even skeptical about the information you find on the Internet.

Research the background of each source—A quick Internet search on each source will usually help you determine whether an author or organization is credible and basing their information on solid facts and reasoning.

Confirm each source's facts—Any source's facts should generally match up with facts in other credible sources. If one source is saying something that seems out of line with other sources, you should be skeptical.

Look out for deceptive websites—Some websites are specifically created to mislead the public about important issues, usually for political reasons. A website might look professional and sophisticated, but it could be peddling junk information.

Follow the money—If the person, organization, or corporation behind the website stands to gain financially, then you should be even more cautious about the information provided. The possibility of financial gain can bias even credible sources.

All sources have some bias, so do some backchecking on each one to determine whether its information is trustworthy.

Using Wikis and Blogs

Your Internet search will turn up potentially useful information stored on wikis and blogs. A helpful guideline for using wikis and blogs is to not rely on them as your main sources of evidence. Instead, they are helpful for figuring out the scope of the issue and understanding the major points of disagreement.

Wikis—Just about any Internet search will turn up information housed on Wikipedia. Some other popular wikis include WikiHow, WikiAnswers, and Wikibooks. The information on these major wikis can give you a good overview of your topic and the issues involved. The main problem with Wikipedia and other wikis is that users are allowed to change the content. So inaccurate or even misleading facts might be placed on a page. Another problem is that the authors of the information are not known; therefore, you have no one to cite as an authority. Wikis are a fine as a starting place for research, but most professors will not allow you to use them as citable sources.

Blogs—Likewise, blogs are rarely acceptable as citable sources of information. They are sometimes authored by experts, but many blogs are just the opinions of people who may or may not know what they are talking about. Treat blogs as you would a wiki. They are good places to figure out what others are saying about your topic, and they can help you identify the issues about which people disagree.

Using Documentaries, Broadcasts, and Podcasts

Some other electronic sources include documentaries, television and radio broadcasts, and podcasts. Many of these sources are available through the Internet or at your local library. A number of helpful documentaries and broadcasts can also be found on Netflix, Hulu, and YouTube. Your university's library may have access to documentaries on DVD or as downloads.

Documentaries—Documentaries are nonfiction films, television programs, or radio broadcasts that document some aspect of reality. They use facts and stories to help people understand places, historical events, and the lives of others through video, images, sounds, and artifacts. Keep in mind that documentaries are opinionated arguments and they should be treated as such. You can draw facts and quotes from them, but you should always remember that the people behind the documentary have a particular point of view that they would like you to accept.

Broadcasts—You can also draw information from television and radio broadcasts. Often, the news media will create special programs or news segments that discuss the topic you are researching. If you missed the program when it was first aired, you can usually find it archived on the source's website. Keep in mind, though, that even the news media, which usually claim to be objective, will have some bias. You should be aware of any bias and look for evidence that corroborates and challenges what you find in a broadcast.

Podcasts—A podcast is an audio or video program that is available for download through the Internet. You can listen to or view podcasts through your mobile phone, portable media player, or computer. Popular places to find podcasts include iTunes, PodcastAlley.com, Podcast.net, Podcast-bunker, and the NPR Podcast Directory. Podcasts tend to be less formal than news broadcasts. Because they are low-budget media, they can be produced quickly and easily. Podcasts can be good sources of information, but before trusting a podcast as a source, you need to check into the background of the people or organization that made it.

Electronic sources have become a regular part of doing research, so using them is fine. However, you should triangulate the information you find in electronic sources with print and empirical sources.

Finding Empirical Sources

Empirical sources of information give you the opportunity to generate your own evidence. You can interview people, do a survey, run an experiment, or conduct field observations. These hands-on experiences help you confirm or challenge the information you are finding in print and electronic sources.

Gathering empirical evidence might seem like a lot of work, but it's not—and it can be fun. You will find it interesting to check whether the factual claims made by others hold up in the real world.

Interviewing People

Interviews are a great way to go behind the facts to explore the views of experts and regular people (Figure 16.7). Plus, interviewing others is a good way to collect quotes that support your argument. Here are some strategies for interviewing people:

FIGURE 16.7
Conducting an Interview
Interviewing an expert is a good way to confirm or challenge what you are finding in secondary sources. Also, interviews are a good way to collect quotes for your argument.

Prepare for the Interview

1. **Do your research.** You need to know as much as possible about your topic before you interview someone about it.

2. **Create a list of three to five fact-based questions.** Your research will probably turn up some facts that you want your interviewee to confirm or challenge.

3. **Create a list of five to ten open-ended questions.** Write down five to ten questions that cannot be answered with a simple "yes" or "no." Your questions should urge the interviewee to offer a detailed explanation or opinion.

4. **Decide how you will record the interview.** Decide whether you want to record the interview as a video or make an audio recording. Or do you want to take written notes? Each of these methods has its pros and cons. For example, audio recording captures the whole conversation, but interviewees are often more guarded about their answers when they are being recorded.

5. **Set up the interview.** The best place to do an interview is at a neutral site, like a classroom, a room in the library, or perhaps a café. The second best place is at the interviewee's office. If necessary, you can do interviews over the phone.

Conduct the Interview

1. **Explain the purpose of your project and how long the interview will take.** Start out by explaining to the interviewee the purpose of your project and how the information from the interview will be used. Also, tell the interviewee how long you expect the interview will take.

2. **Ask permission to record.** If you are recording the interview in any way, ask permission to make the recording. First, ask if recording is all right before you turn on your recorder. Then, once the recorder is on, ask again so you record the interviewee's verbal permission.

3. **Ask your fact-based questions first.** Warm up the interviewee by asking questions that allow him or her to confirm or deny the facts you have already collected.

4. **Ask your open-ended questions next.** Ask the interviewee about his or her opinions, feelings, experiences, and views about the topic.

5. **Ask if he or she would like to provide any other information.** Often people want to tell you things you did not expect or know about. You can wrap up the interview by asking, "Is there anything else you would like to add about this topic?"

6. **Thank the interviewee.** Don't forget to thank the interviewee for his or her time and thoughts.

Follow Up the Interview

1. **Write down everything you remember.** As soon as possible after the interview, describe the interviewee in your notes and fill out any details you couldn't write down during the interview. Do this even if you recorded the interview.

2. **Get your quotes right.** Clarify any direct quotations you collected from your interviewee. If appropriate, you might e-mail your quotes to the interviewee for confirmation.

3. **Back-check the facts.** If the interviewee said something that was new to you or that conflicted with your previous findings, you should use electronic or print sources to back-check the facts. If there is a conflict you cannot resolve, you can send an e-mail to the interviewee to ask for clarification.

4. **Send a thank you note.** Usually an e-mail that thanks your interviewee is sufficient, but some people prefer a card or brief letter of thanks.

Using an Informal Survey

Unless you are majoring in a field that has taught you how to conduct scientific surveys, the surveys you will devise for your arguments will be informal and unscientific. These kinds of "unscientific" surveys are helpful for gaining an overall sense of people's opinions, but they won't give you solid data on which to base conclusions.

Conducting an informal survey is easier than ever. Many free online services, such as SurveyMonkey and Zoomerang, allow you to create and distribute your own surveys. These websites will also collect and tabulate the results for you. Here is how to create a useful, though unscientific, survey:

1. **Identify the population you want to survey.** Some surveys target specific kinds of people (e.g., college students, women from ages 18–22, medical doctors). Others are designed to be filled out by anyone.

2. **Develop your questions.** Create a list of five to ten questions that can be answered quickly. Surveys typically use four basic types of questions: rating scales, multiple choice, numeric open-ended, and open-ended. Figure 16.8 shows examples of all four types.

3. **Check your questions for neutrality.** Make sure your questions are as neutral as possible. Don't influence the people you are surveying by asking biased or slanted questions that fit your own beliefs or an outcome you are seeking.

4. **Distribute the survey.** Ask a number of people to complete your survey, and note the kinds of people who agree to do it. Not everyone will be interested in completing your survey, so remember that your results might reflect the views of specific kinds of people.

5. **Tabulate your results.** When your surveys are returned, convert any quantitative responses into data. If you collected written answers, pull out phrases and quotes that seem to reflect how the people you surveyed felt about your topic.

A critic might point out that your informal survey is not objective and that your results are not statistically valid. That's fine, as long as you are not using your survey to make important decisions or claim you have discovered some kind of truth. Your informal survey will still give you some helpful information about the opinions of others.

Rating Scale

Birth control should be free and easily available to high school students.

Strongly Agree	Agree	Disagree	Strongly Disagree	No Opinion
☐	☐	☐	☐	☐

Multiple Choice

Who gave you the most information about birth control when you were in high school?

☐ Parents   ☐ Sex ed in school

☐ Friends   ☐ Magazines

☐ Brother or sister   ☐ Internet

☐ Television programs   ☐ School nurse or health center

☐ Doctor or nonschool health center   ☐ Other

Numeric Open-Ended

At what age do you think adolescents should be taught about birth control options?

_____

Text Open-Ended

In a brief answer, describe what role you believe schools should have in educating adolescents about birth control options. _____

_____

_____

_____

_____

Doing Field Observations

Field observations are a good way to confirm or challenge whether people, nature, or
animals behave in expected ways (Figure 16.8). Your observations will likely be informal and unscientific. After all, doing a formal scientific observation (ethnography or
case study) typically requires more time than you will have available to write a college
argument. Nevertheless, you can still make useful observations as long as you are
aware of the limitations of your methods. Here are some techniques for doing field
observations.

FIGURE 16.8
Doing Field Observations
Your field observations can help you figure out how people, nature, or animals behave.

1. **Choose an appropriate location (field site).** You want to choose a field site that allows you to see as much as possible while not making it obvious that you are watching and taking notes. People will typically change their behavior if they think someone is watching them.

2. **Take notes in a two-column format.** A good field note technique is to use two columns to record what you see. On the left side, list the people, things, and events you observed. On the right side, write down how you interpret what you observed.

3. **Use the Five W and How questions.** Keep notes about the *who, what, where, when, why,* and *how* elements that you observe. Try to include as much detail as possible.

4. **Use your senses.** Take notes about the things you see, hear, smell, touch, and taste while you are observing.

5. **Pay attention to things that are moving or changing.** Take special note of the things that moved or changed while you were observing and what caused them to do so.

When you are finished taking notes, spend some time interpreting what you observed. Look for patterns in your observations to help you make sense of your field site.

16.4 Strategies for triangulating and evaluating sources

Evaluating Your Sources

All sources are not created equal. Depending on your research project, some of the sources you find will be better and more reliable than others. So you should spend time asking the following five questions of each source:

Question 1: Is This Source Credible?

The credibility of a source depends on who wrote it, who sponsored or published it, and where the facts or data came from. You should conduct some background research on the authors or sponsors of the source. A quick Internet search should turn up biographical information on the people who wrote or produced the information you want to use. Check their credentials and determine whether they have the background to offer reliable evidence.

Then figure out who is sponsoring the research behind the source. Obviously, a person, company, or organization that stands to gain financially will have some bias. So follow the money to determine whether the author or sponsor will gain financially if people accept the evidence provided. There is nothing wrong with a source having a financial incentive, but you should always keep in mind that these incentives will usually create more bias.

Also, look at each source's sources. Where did the author get his or her information? Make sure you can track down where the author collected his or her facts and data. If the sources behind the facts and data aren't cited in some way, then you should be skeptical about whether the information is accurate. Meanwhile, if a source is using empirical methods (surveys, interviews, experiments) to generate data, you should analyze whether those methods were reasonably impartial. Look for any indication that the author used methods that were slanted toward a preferred outcome.

Question 2: Is This Source Accurate?

The accuracy of a source can be hard to determine. Earlier in this chapter, you learned how to triangulate sources. Triangulation helps you figure out whether a source's information is accurate. If a source is presenting facts and data that are significantly out of line with your other sources, you should treat that evidence with added skepticism.

Accuracy might also depend on the tools and methods used to collect the evidence. A more exact experiment or closer observation might yield results that make some sources more accurate or reliable than others.

Question 3: Is This Source Current?

Depending on your topic, the currency of your source might help you determine whether its evidence is still reliable. In quickly evolving fields, such as medicine, technology, or popular culture, even the best sources can be outdated within a couple years. In fields that don't change quickly, such as history, geology, or anthropology, a decades-old source might still be current.

To help you determine whether the source is current, look at the date when it was published. Some sources will have been updated or revised, so pay attention to how often the information has been changed or brought up to date. Electronic sources can be especially problematic for determining currency. A reliable electronic source should give you a clear sense of when the information was originally published and last updated. If you can't find a publication or revision date, then you will need to be extra careful about triangulating the source's evidence with other sources.

Question 4: Does the Source Engage Two or More Sides of the Issue?

A reliable source will usually explain and engage at least two sides of an issue. You should have a clear sense that the author understands and has considered the other sides of the issue. Meanwhile, you should be skeptical of an author who is only telling one side of the story or seems to be unaware that other views may exist.

If a source only offers one side of the issue, the information might still be useful but chances are good the author isn't telling you everything. You should do extra research to determine how others might view the issue differently than the author.

Question 5: Are You Biased for or against the Information in This Source?

Finally, be honest about how your own personal beliefs will influence or bias your understanding of each source. We all believe some things are true and some aren't. You cannot set those biases completely aside. So, as you evaluate each source, ask yourself whether you trust the source because it happens to agree with your own personal views. And if you disagree with a source, ask yourself whether your own biases taint whether you believe the source is reliable or credible.

Collecting evidence for your argument is not difficult and it's fun. This is what you need to know.

1 Developing your own research process is a good way to do better research in a more efficient way.

2 A model research process includes these steps: (1) define a research question, (2) develop a working thesis, (3) collect sources, (4) triangulate sources, (5) identify major findings, and (6) modify or accept your working thesis.

3 Primary sources include artifacts, records, statements, or other items that were created or used by the people directly involved with the issue.

4 Secondary sources include the published works of experts, scholars, journalists, and other knowledgeable people who have analyzed, studied, or commented on the issue.

5 Print sources offer some of the most reliable information available on just about any topic.

6 Electronic sources are items that were designed to be viewed on a screen or listened to through an electronic medium.

7 Empirical sources give you hands-on ways to confirm or challenge the information you find in print and electronic sources.

8 Some common empirical methods for a college argument include interviews, surveys, and field observations.

9 You need to evaluate your sources to determine if they are credible, accurate, current, and balanced.

10 When evaluating a source, you should both "follow the money" to see if financial issues might bias it and figure out whether you are personally biased for or against the source.

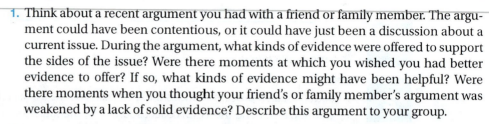

1. Think about a recent argument you had with a friend or family member. The argument could have been contentious, or it could have just been a discussion about a current issue. During the argument, what kinds of evidence were offered to support the sides of the issue? Were there moments at which you wished you had better evidence to offer? If so, what kinds of evidence might have been helpful? Were there moments when you thought your friend's or family member's argument was weakened by a lack of solid evidence? Describe this argument to your group.

2. Using the Internet, find an argument that is well supported with evidence. Then trace that evidence by finding the sources the author uses. Keep tracing the evidence until you find a primary source. Now that you have reached this basic level, do you still think the argument is well supported? If someone were to challenge this argument, how could a close look at the primary sources be used to raise doubts?

3. With your group, choose a contentious issue that is often argued about in our society (gun control, reproductive rights, freedom of speech, etc.). Then ask each member of your group to gather five secondary sources on that topic, including at least two print sources. Compare the sources you found. Whether you agree with the sources or not, did you find their use of evidence effective? According to your group, which side of the argument best used evidence to support its views? Why? What made that use of evidence stronger?

1. Write a brief commentary in which you argue for (or against) the claim that "all the information necessary for a research project can be found through the Internet." In your argument, explain some of the advantages and shortcomings of doing exclusively electronic research. If you are challenging the claim, explain why you think print and empirical sources are still needed, even though it seems that just about everything is on the Internet.

2. A research plan is a step-by-step description of your research methods. For the research project you are working on right now, write up a step-by-step research plan that describes how you will gather print, electronic, and empirical sources that will help you better understand your topic and support your argument. Then put those steps on a calendar and assign completion dates to each one. In an e-mail to your instructor, describe your research plan and explain why you think it offers the most effective way to explore your topic.

3. You are probably working on a paper right now that involves research. Using your campus library's website, locate five possible print sources (two books and three articles) that might offer evidence for your argument. Then, using the Internet, find five possible electronic sources that would also offer useful evidence. Finally, list two ways in which you could generate empirical evidence for your argument. In an e-mail to your instructor, list your ten print and electronic sources using MLA or APA bibliographic style. Then, list your two possible empirical sources.

Crediting, Quoting, Paraphrasing, and Summarizing

17

IN THIS CHAPTER YOU WILL LEARN HOW TO—

17.1 Give credit to a source when you use information exclusive to that source.

17.2 Quote, paraphrase, and summarize your sources.

17.3 Frame quotes, paraphrases, and summaries in your texts.

17.4 Avoid plagiarizing the works and ideas of others.

In Chapter 16, you learned how to collect and triangulate a variety of print, electronic, and empirical sources. Now you will learn how to weave those sources seamlessly into your argument. There are four primary ways you can incorporate sources into your argument:

Crediting—You can credit a source for a specific fact or idea with a *parenthetical citation*. The citation names the source and usually identifies the page number where you found the fact or idea.

Quoting—You can quote keywords, phrases, sentences, and longer passages taken directly from a source to explain or support your argument.

Paraphrasing—You can restate or interpret the ideas of someone else in your own words. A paraphrase makes the ideas easier to understand, and it usually mirrors the source's organization or line of reasoning.

Summarizing—You can use your own words to explain the ideas of someone else while also rearranging those ideas to highlight the issues most important to your argument. A summary, unlike a paraphrase, does *not* mirror the source's organization and line of reasoning.

Crediting, quoting, paraphrasing, and summarizing your sources will help you build your argument on solid evidence. Meanwhile, using sources allows you to join the broader conversation about the issue you are arguing about. When you incorporate your sources properly, your argument will have more authority and will be better supported with facts and reasoning.

This chapter will show you how to incorporate the ideas and words of others into your argument while giving credit to your sources. Chapters 18 and 19 will show you how to cite your sources properly using MLA and APA documentation styles.

17.1 Give credit to a source when you use information exclusive to that source.

Crediting a Source

If you use facts, data, or ideas that are found exclusively in one source, then you should give that source credit with a parenthetical citation. Here are two examples:

> When Hurricane Katrina hit New Orleans, many things went wrong because of the city's incompetent politicians, corrupt government, poverty, and culture of violence (Flannery 310).

Parenthetical Citation →

> As Flannery (2005) points out, many things went wrong when Hurricane Katrina hit New Orleans because of the city's incompetent politicians, corrupt government, poverty, and culture of violence (p. 310).

Parenthetical Citation →

The first example above uses MLA in-text citation style. In this style, the name and page number are usually placed in parentheses at the end of the sentence. The second example uses APA in-text citation style, placing the year after the name of the source and a page number at the end of the sentence. The correct way to use a parenthetical citation depends on how the source is being used. Turn to Chapters 18 ("Using MLA Style") or Chapter 19 ("Using APA Style") to learn how to use these two different in-text citation styles.

There are two benefits to crediting a source with an in-text citation. First, your argument will be stronger because your audience will see where you found your information. Second, you won't be accused of taking or plagiarizing someone else's ideas.

But do you need to cite *everything*? No. You don't need to cite information that is considered common knowledge. Common knowledge includes any facts or ideas that are generally known to most people or can be found in numerous independent sources. For instance, the following items would all be considered common knowledge:

- Ellen DeGeneres is the host of the *Ellen DeGeneres Show*.

- Madison is the capital of Wisconsin.

- The *Declaration of Independence* was signed in 1776.

- The cerebrum is the largest part of the human brain, and it is responsible for most higher functions, such as perception, thought, judgment, and action.

Common knowledge is information that is so widely known that it no longer belongs to anyone. Here's a simple guideline: If you are unsure whether a fact is common knowledge, use a citation.

Using a Quote or Quotation

17.2 Quote, paraphrase, and summarize your sources.

A quotation is the exact use of a word, phrase, sentence, or passage taken directly from the work of another author or speaker. When using someone else's words, you need to copy their words exactly as they appear in the original. Then put quotation marks around those words or set them off as *block quotes*. Here are some guidelines for quoting brief and long passages from a source.

Brief Quotations

A brief quotation takes a word, phrase, or sentence directly from an original source.

Words

If an author uses a word or term in a unique or special way, you can put quotes around the word or term in your own text. After the first time you quote a word or term, you don't need to continue putting it inside quotation marks.

> **Acceptable quotation**—According to Archer and Rahmstorf, two types of climate-related changes could occur, "abrupt transitions" and "smooth transitions" (6).

> **Unacceptable quotation**—According to Archer and Rahmstorf, two types of climate-related changes could occur, abrupt transitions and smooth transitions (6).

Phrases

If you want to use an entire phrase from a source, you need to put quotation marks around it. Then you should weave the quote into one of your sentences, making sure it flows with the rest of your writing.

> **Acceptable quotation**—Robert Henson explains the global warming mechanism in simple terms when he writes, "the more greenhouse gas we add, the more our planet warms" (26).

> **Unacceptable quotation**—Robert Henson explains the global warming mechanism in simple terms by pointing out that the more greenhouse gas we add, the more our planet warms (26).

Sentences

When using an entire sentence from a source, you should use a *signal phrase* (e.g., "As Hoggan argues,") or a colon to indicate the quotation.

> **Acceptable quotation**—James Hoggan highlights an interesting paradox when he points out, "while scientists were growing more convinced about the proof and more concerned about the risks of climate change, members of the general public were drifting into confusion" (22).

Acceptable quotation—"While scientists were growing more convinced about the proof and more concerned about the risks of climate change," James Hoggan points out, "members of the general public were drifting into confusion" (22).

Unacceptable quotation—While scientists were growing more convinced about the proof and more concerned about the risks of climate change, members of the general public were drifting into confusion, according to Hoggan (22).

Acceptable quotation using a colon—James Hoggan points out the following inconsistency: "While scientists were growing more convinced about the proof and more concerned about the risks of climate change, members of the general public were drifting into confusion" (22).

Unacceptable quotation using a colon—James Hoggan points out the following inconsistency: While scientists were growing more convinced about the proof and more concerned about the risks of climate change, members of the general public were drifting into confusion (22).

Long Quotations (Block Quotes)

Occasionally, you may need to quote a passage at length from a source. A quote that is longer than three lines of text in your argument should be formatted as a *block quote*. To create a block quote, you should indent the entire quotation to separate it visually from your regular text. With block quotes, quotation marks should not be used. Meanwhile, the parenthetical citation appears at the end of the quote, *outside* the final punctuation mark.

> Despite these misinformation campaigns, the general public is gradually beginning to accept that climate change is happening. In response, as Hoggan argues, the fossil-fuel industry is changing tactics:
>
> > As the evidence of climate change has become more compelling—as the science has grown more certain and as people have come to recognize the changes occurring before their eyes—a new and more dangerous form of junk scientist has begun to emerge: the nondenier deniers. These are people who put themselves forth as reasonable interpreters of the science, even as allies in the fight to bring climate change to the public's attention. But then they throw in a variety of arguments that undermine the public appetite for action. (*Climate* 118)
>
> These so-called "scientists," who are often merely public relations agents with titles that sound scientific (e.g., "Director of Ecological Analysis"), will usually agree that human-caused climate change is happening. However, they will then attempt to spin the argument by suggesting that climate change may actually have beneficial or minimal effects.

Note: Block quotes should not be used as an easy way to beef up your word count. When writing an argument, you need to do more than string together a series of block quotes with some of your own words holding them together. You should use block quotes occasionally and only when the original source makes a point in a unique way that cannot be paraphrased or summarized.

Paraphrasing and Summarizing

17.3 Frame quotes, paraphrases, and summaries in your texts.

When paraphrasing or summarizing, you are using someone else's ideas but putting them into your own words. Paraphrases and summaries are similar and different in some important ways:

Paraphrase—A paraphrase follows the organization and line of thought of the original source. Often, a paraphrase addresses only a portion of a text, and it is about the same length or a little shorter than the portion in the original text.

Summary—a summary strips out many of the details and examples from the original source and reorganizes the author's main points from most important to least important. A summary usually covers the entire content of the source in a condensed and shorter way.

Figure 17.1 includes a source text that we will be using to discuss paraphrasing and summarizing in this part of the chapter.

It's disgraceful that the media allows such routine distortions in complex system debates like climate change, as if a fact is somehow an "opinion" and all opinions should be aired. If the opinion were that the writer doesn't think the net melting is important enough to build policies to hedge against it—fine, that is an opinion and belongs in the op-ed space. But to allow known falsehoods or misframings of science is not an opinion, just an error or worse. That should in my view be distinguished from real opinions—value judgments on what we should do about it, for example—and a newspaper has a right to demand that such demonstrable factual errors be removed. If a political writer claimed that blacks were better off in the Jim Crow South than now, would that be an "opinion" they would publish in their newspaper? Or that smoking doesn't cause cancer? You get the point.

The question isn't whether reporters, politicians, lawyers, and others or their methods are wrong or that "impartial" scientists are morally superior—but rather the techniques of advocacy-as-usual are suited for a subject like climate change in the public arena. In the advocacy arena, everybody knows the game—spin for the client. But in science, the playing field for public discussions is not level. Any spin on the facts would cause damage to a scientist's reputation—especially young scientists. That is decidedly not true for a status quo defender advocating for client interest. They are rewarded for winning, not for fairly reporting evidence.

Scientists think that advocacy based on a "win for the client" mentality that deliberately selects facts out of context is highly unethical. Unaware of how the advocacy game is played outside the culture of scientific peer review, scientists can stumble into the pitfall of being labeled advocates lobbying for a special interest, even if they had no such intention.

FIGURE 17.1
Source Text
This excerpt from Stephen Schneider's *Science as a Contact Sport* will be used in this chapter to demonstrate paraphrasing and summarizing.

Paraphrasing

The purpose of paraphrasing is to explain and describe a portion of a source's text in your own words. A paraphrase is usually about the same length as or a little shorter than the source material being paraphrased. For example, the writers of the following acceptable and unacceptable paraphrases of the text in Figure 17.1 are trying to explain Schneider's claim that scientific facts are not the same as opinion and that scientists should not be treated as special-interest advocates.

Acceptable Paraphrase

Schneider argues in rather strong terms that journalists need to be more mindful of the differences between "opinion" and "factual evidence" when reporting on climate change (207). Factual evidence includes the data and measurements that prove climate change is happening and that burning fossil fuels is the main cause. Opinion is the debate about what people or governments should do to respond to climate change. He points out that journalists often allow distortions and dishonesties to go uncorrected or unchallenged because they want to appear balanced or fair to both sides of an issue. This "balanced" approach, Schneider suggests, puts climate scientists at a distinct disadvantage. After all, the media is well suited to professional advocates, such as politicians, lawyers, advertisers, and corporate spokespeople, who are paid to "win" for their clients (208). Ethical scientists, quite differently, cannot spin or cherry pick the evidence to advocate for one side or another. As a result, Schneider points out, many scientists mistakenly find themselves being challenged as lobbyists for a special interest, even when they are simply trying to explain their findings and the proven facts of climate change (208).

In this acceptable paraphrase, the writer put the ideas from the source into her own words. When she used exact words from Schneider's book, she placed them inside quotation marks.

Now let's look at a paraphrase that is too close to the original source:

Unacceptable Paraphrase

Schneider writes that it's disgraceful that journalists are not more attentive to the differences between opinion and factual evidence when reporting on climate change (207). Scientific facts are not somehow "opinions" that should be aired like all opinions. Opinions are value judgments on what we should do about climate change. Schneider points out that journalists often allow known falsehoods or misframings of science to go unchallenged because they want to seem balanced or fair to the opinions of both sides. This "balanced" approach, Schneider suggests, puts scientists at a distinct disadvantage because the playing field is not level. After all, the media spotlight is well suited to professional advocates, such as politicians, lawyers, advertisers, and corporate spokespeople, who are rewarded for winning, not reporting the evidence fairly (208). Scientists, quite differently, cannot be ==viewed as deliberately selecting facts out of context== to support one position or another. As a result, Schneider points out, many climate scientists ==stumble into the pitfall of being labeled as advocates lobbying for a special interest==, even when they are simply trying to explain their findings and the proven facts of climate change (208).

The highlighted words and phrases are taken directly from Schneider's argument. Even though the writer explicitly cites the source of these ideas, too many words are lifted directly from the source without quotation or attribution. If the writer felt it was important to use these exact words and phrases, she should have placed them inside quotation marks.

Summarizing

When summarizing someone's work, your goal is to capture the source's main ideas while leaving out most of its details and examples. A summary often goes beyond the source's major points to explain the source's structure—its tone, angle, or purpose, its style, its underlying values, or the persuasive strategies it uses to drive home its points.

Acceptable Paragraph-Length Summary

With a passionate appeal, Schneider brings forward his main argument in Chapter 7, titled "The Media Wars: The Stories Behind Persistent Distortion." He argues that the crucial distinction between scientific evidence and opinion is often distorted in the media, making climate scientists appear to be lobbyists for their own special interests and therefore not objective (207). Journalists, Schneider points out, want to appear balanced and fair, so they will routinely pit climate scientists against professional advocates, like politicians, lawyers, and corporate spokespeople. The problem with these so-called balanced debates is that the climate scientist is trying to explain the facts and data objectively, while the professional advocate is doing everything possible to undermine and spin that evidence to "win for the client" (208). As a result, journalists allow many distortions and misrepresentations to go unchallenged, because they assume fairness means allowing both sides to express their opinions. The flaw with this approach is that the existence of climate change is not an opinion—it's based on scientifically proven evidence (207). The media's "balanced" approach inaccurately implies that climate change is just another opinion.

Notice how this summary prioritizes Schneider's key point by putting it up front. Then the summary reorganizes his ideas by order of importance.

An unacceptable summary like the one below usually relies too much on the wording of the original text, and it often does not prioritize the most important points in the source text.

Unacceptable Summary

Schneider brings forward his main argument in Chapter 7, titled "The Media Wars: The Stories Behind Persistent Distortion." He argues that the line between scientific evidence and opinion is often distorted in the media, allowing environmental scientists to be labeled advocates lobbying for a special interest, even if they had no such intention (207). Journalists want to appear balanced and fair, so they will routinely pit climate change scientists against reporters, politicians, lawyers, and others. The problem with these public discussions is that the playing field is not level because the scientist is trying to explain the facts and data, while the professional advocate is using advocacy-as-usual techniques to undermine and spin that evidence to "win for the client," which scientists believe is highly unethical (208). As a result, journalists allow routine distortions in debates about climate change, because they assume a fact is somehow an "opinion" and that all opinions should be aired (207). The flaw with this approach is that the existence of climate change is not an opinion—it's based on scientifically proven evidence. The media's "balanced" approach inaccurately implies that climate change is just another opinion.

The highlighted phrases in this unacceptable summary show places where the author used almost the same wording as the original text.

Framing Quotes, Paraphrases, and Summaries

Your readers should easily see the boundaries between your ideas and the ideas you are taking from your sources. To help them identify these boundaries, you should use signal phrases and parenthetical citations to *frame* the quotation or ideas you took from an outside source. Then you should connect your source's words and ideas to your overall argument (Figure 17.2). Here is how to do it:

Signal Phrase

A signal phrase indicates where the source material came from. The words "as" and "in" are often at the heart of a signal phrase (e.g., As Hoggan suggests. In Chapter 2 of his *Rough Guide to Climate Change*, Henson argues).

Source Material

Material taken from your source should be separated from your own words with commas, quotation marks, and other punctuation to indicate which words and ideas came directly from the source and which are your own.

Parenthetical Citation

A citation allows readers to find the exact page or website of the source. In MLA or APA documentation style, an in-text citation is used to cite the source. In other documentation styles, you might use a footnote or endnote.

Connection

When you connect the source's ideas to your ideas, you will make it clear how the source material fits in with your own statements and claims.

Figure 17.2 offers a diagram that color codes these features. The following three examples use these colors to highlight signal phrases, source material, citations, and connections.

As Charles Schmidt points out, a gulf is widening between two types of climate change skeptics. The arguments by conservative bloggers, politicians, and pundits, who deny climate change is happening, are increasingly out of line with the arguments of skeptical scientists, who now generally believe that climate change is happening but are unconvinced about its causes and effects ("Closer," 2010, p. A53). As a result, the footing beneath climate change deniers is crumbling away, leaving their arguments sounding increasingly baseless.

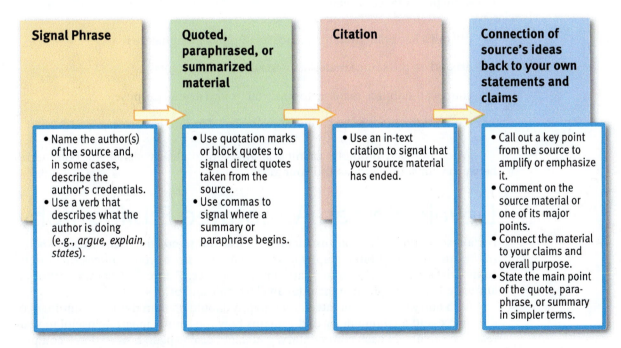

Signal Phrase	Quoted, paraphrased, or summarized material	Citation	Connection of source's ideas back to your own statements and claims
• Name the author(s) of the source and, in some cases, describe the author's credentials. • Use a verb that describes what the author is doing (e.g., *argue*, *explain*, *states*).	• Use quotation marks or block quotes to signal direct quotes taken from the source. • Use commas to signal where a summary or paraphrase begins.	• Use an in-text citation to signal that your source material has ended.	• Call out a key point from the source to amplify or emphasize it. • Comment on the source material or one of its major points. • Connect the material to your claims and overall purpose. • State the main point of the quote, paraphrase, or summary in simpler terms.

FIGURE 17.2 Framing Material from a Source
Material taken from a source should be clearly framed with a signal phrase, a citation, and a connection to your own statements and claims.

For now, though, as Hoffman demonstrates, the quarrel between the climate change "convinced" and climate change "skeptics" still means both sides are talking past each other (p. 3). Consequently, we are currently in a stalemate position, or what Hoffman calls a "logic schism," waiting for the tipping point when the ever-increasing amount of evidence of human-caused climate change finally overcomes the fossil-fuel industry's marketing and political campaigns.

Studies show, however, that getting others to change their minds about climate change is more than a matter of presenting facts and using good reasoning (Moser & Dilling, 2011; Nisbet & Scheufele, 2009). Even when presented with rock-solid evidence, climate skeptics are reluctant to change their minds, because their beliefs have become part of their identity. They fear that changing their minds on an issue like climate change threatens who they are and how they will live their lives.

As shown in this example, each frame begins with a signal phrase. Signal phrases typically rely on an action verb that signals what the author of the source is trying to achieve in the material that is being quoted, paraphrased, or summarized. Figure 17.3 provides a helpful list of verbs you can use to signal quotes, paraphrases, and summaries.

The frame usually ends with a *connection* that shows how the source material fits into your overall discussion or argument. Your connection should do one of the following things for your readers:

- call out a key point from the source to amplify or emphasize it

- expand on the source material or one of its major points

- connect the source material to your claims and overall purpose

- rephrase the main point of the source material in simpler terms

When handled properly, framing allows you to clearly signal the boundaries between your source's ideas and your ideas.

Developing an Annotated Bibliography

For a research project, your instructor may ask you to create an *annotated bibliography*. An annotated bibliography is an alphabetical list of your sources that briefly summarizes and offers commentary on each source. Figure 17.4 shows part of an annotated bibliography that includes an electronic and print source.

Each entry in your annotated bibliography should offer an unbiased summary of the source and a commentary that explains how the source might be useful to your research project. In each commentary, you might also explain how a source complements or contradicts other sources you have collected.

accepts	accuses	acknowledges
adds	admits	advises
agrees	alleges	allows
analyzes	announces	answers
argues	asks	asserts
believes	charges	claims
comments	compares	complains
concedes	concludes	confirms
considers	contends	countercharges
criticizes	declares	demonstrates
denies	describes	disagrees
discusses	disputes	emphasizes
explains	expresses	finds
grants	holds	illustrates
implies	insists	interprets
maintains	notes	objects
observes	offers	point outs
proclaims	proposes	provides
quarrels	reacts	reasons
refutes	rejects	remarks
replies	reports	responds
reveals	shows	states
suggests	supports	thinks
urges	writes	

FIGURE 17.3
Verbs for Signal Phrases
Use verbs like these to introduce quotations, paraphrases, and summaries. You can also use them in signal phrases.

When developing your annotated bibliography, you should follow the bibliographic format you will use in your argument. For example, you could use either MLA or APA documentation styles (see Chapters 18 and 19). That way, when you list your sources in a Works Cited or References list, they will already be in the proper format.

An annotated bibliography is helpful in a few important ways. First, it will help you remember and keep track of your sources. As your research project grows larger and the sources add up, you won't be able to remember the details of each one. The summaries in your annotated bibliography will give you easy-to-access synopses for review. Second, your annotated bibliography will help you think about your sources in depth and figure out how they work together. The act of summarizing each source will allow you to gain a thorough understanding of the public conversation about your topic. Third, your instructor might use your annotated bibliography to help you identify gaps in your research or places where you could expand on interesting issues.

While putting together your annotated bibliography, you should be mindful about the risk of plagiarism. When you take a quote or an idea from a source, make sure you label it properly in your summary. Clearly identify any direct quotes with quotation marks, and write down the pages where specific quotes or ideas were found. If you are copying a large quotation, you should use a block quote in your entry. Being careful about plagiarism is important while making your annotated bibliography, because otherwise you will eventually forget which words and ideas came from your sources and which didn't. You might innocently use them in your work, thinking they were your own.

"2012 Was One of the 10 Warmest Years on Record." NOAAnews.com.
National Oceanic and Atmospheric Administration (NOAA),
6 Aug. 2013. Web. 3 Sep. 2013.

On this webpage, the NOAA summarizes the major findings of its *State of the Climate in 2012* report. Some of the highlights of the report include a) the Arctic continues to warm with sea ice reaching a record low, while the Antarctic sea ice reached a record high, b) sea surface temperatures across the globe are increasing, c) ocean heat content continues to be near record levels, d) the occurrences of cyclones have not seen an increase, and e) the amounts of greenhouse gases continue to climb. The authors write, "Conditions in the Arctic were a major story of 2012, with the region experiencing unprecedented change and breaking several records" (par. 3).

Commentary: This webpage summarizes the eye-opening findings in the full report. Basically, their findings show that climate change is continuing to have a significant effect on the Earth's surface, especially in the Northern Hemisphere. The report confirms the concerns of many of the other sources I have found. However, there are some interesting countertrends such as the increase in Antarctic ice levels. I need to look into that issue further to see what that means.

Weber, Elke and Paul Stern. "Public Understanding of Climate Change in the United States." *American Psychologist* 66.4 (2011): 315-28. Print.

In this article, the authors argue that climate change is an especially difficult issue for the public to understand because there is a "mismatch between people's usual modes of understanding and the task" (317). They point out that much of the problem isn't the public's inability to understand climate change science. Instead, it is "a deficit in trust in the conveyors of climate models and data" (323). They argue that the problem is often an issue of "framing" rather than facts or logic (333).

Commentary: This article explains why there is such a gap between the views of climate scientists and much of the American public. As the authors point out, the resistance to climate change science is often due to a political pre-disposition to not believe the messengers (i.e. climate scientists and environmentalists). Like other articles (Hampton and Smith; Jenkins), these authors seem to be suggesting that re-framing the issue may be the best way forward, not trying to convince people with more facts.

FIGURE 17.4
Excerpt from an Annotated Bibliography In this excerpt from an annotated bibliography, the writer has used MLA documentation style to list her sources. Then, for each source, she offers a summary and a paragraph that comments on how the source relates to her research project.

Avoiding Plagiarism

The Council of Writing Program Administrators defines plagiarism this way:

> In an instructional setting, plagiarism occurs when a writer deliberately uses someone else's language, ideas, or other original (not common-knowledge) material without acknowledging its source (par. 4).

In college, plagiarism is a form of academic dishonesty—the same as cheating on an exam—and it can lead to a failing grade on an assignment or even failure of the class. In the workplace, plagiarism is a form of copyright infringement in which one person illegally takes the ideas or words of someone else without their permission. Copyright infringement can lead to costly lawsuits and the firing of any employee who commits it.

Plagiarism is not always intentional. Sometimes writers forget to copy down their sources in their notes. Sometimes they forget where specific ideas came from. But even if you plagiarize accidentally, you may find yourself in serious trouble with your professors, your university, or your employer. So it is crucial that you understand the kinds of plagiarism and learn how to avoid them.

Academic Dishonesty

The most obvious form of plagiarism occurs when someone hands in work that is not his or her own. Everyone, including your professors, knows about "cheater" websites that sell college papers. Everyone also knows about "borrowing" a friend's or roommate's paper. And everyone knows it's easy to cut and paste a sample paper from the Internet. (If you found it, chances are good your professor will find it, too).

And yet, some students still foolishly try to get away with this kind of academic dishonesty. Your professors aren't that stupid. If you hand in a paper that's not your own, you're being dishonest. When students get caught, they often fail the class, which looks bad on their transcripts and is very difficult to explain to future employers or graduate school admissions committees. Students who intentionally plagiarize might even be expelled. Academic dishonesty is clearly deliberate, and few people will have sympathy for someone who is so obviously cheating.

Ironically, people who buy, download, or copy papers often spend more time and energy finding the paper and worrying about the consequences of getting caught than they would if they just wrote the paper in the first place. Plus, they missed the opportunity to improve their writing and research skills.

Patchwriting

Usually, patchwriting happens when someone cuts and pastes one or more paragraphs from a website or other source and then alters words and sentences to make them look like his or her own. Writing scholar Rebecca Moore Howard defines patchwriting as "copying from a source text and then deleting some words, altering grammatical structures, or plugging in one synonym for another" (xvii).

When done intentionally, patchwriting is clearly a form of academic dishonesty, because the writer is presenting someone else's ideas as his or her own without attribution. Some students have even tried to patchwrite an entire paper. They cut and paste several paragraphs from a variety of sources. Then they add some transitions and a few of their own sentences while altering the words and sentences from the original. As a result, little of the paper is based on their own ideas. This kind of dishonesty, when caught, usually leads to a failing grade on the paper and for the class.

Patchwriting can also happen unintentionally, especially when a writer copies sentences or paragraphs from a source and then forgets the material was taken from somewhere else. The writer might even cite the source, not realizing that the included text is too close to the original. Unfortunately, your professor cannot tell whether you were intentionally being dishonest or just made an honest mistake.

To avoid patchwriting, make sure you carefully identify your sources in your notes. Clearly mark any direct quotes taken from your sources with quotation marks, brackets, or some other kind of distinguishing mark. Then, when you use these materials in your document, make sure you quote, paraphrase, and summarize them using proper citations.

Ideas and Words Taken without Attribution

In college and in the workplace, you will often need to use the ideas, words, phrases, or sentences from a source. When you do this, *you must correctly quote and cite that source*. That is, you must place those words inside quotation marks (or use a block quote) and provide a citation that tells your reader precisely where you got those words. If you use ideas, words, phrases, or sentences without attribution, you could be charged with academic dishonesty or copyright infringement.

Sometimes it is difficult to determine whether someone else "owns" the ideas that you are using in your document. If you aren't sure, cite the source. Citing a source will add support to your work, and it will help you avoid being accused of plagiarism.

The Real Problem with Plagiarism

No doubt, plagiarism is easier than ever with the Internet. It's also easier than ever to catch someone who is plagiarizing. Your professors use Google, Yahoo, and Bing, too, and they have access to plagiarism-checking websites like Turnitin. They also often have access to collections of prior papers that were handed in.

If you plagiarize, there is a good chance you will get caught, and the price will be steep. But the real problem with plagiarism is that you are cheating yourself. You are probably paying many thousands of dollars for your education. Cheating robs you of the chance to strengthen your communication skills and prepare for advanced courses and your career.

Of course, there is pressure to do well in your classes, and you don't always have enough time to do everything as well as you could. In the end, though, doing your own work will help you improve and strengthen your mind and abilities. Don't miss that opportunity.

Using sources properly is critical to making a reasonable and credible argument. Here are the basics.

1 There are four primary ways to use sources to support an argument: crediting, quoting, paraphrasing, and summarizing.

2 Crediting is the use of parenthetical citations to signal places where information was taken from an exclusive source.

3 Quoting is the use of keywords, phrases, sentences, and longer passages to explain or support your argument or someone else's argument.

4 Paraphrasing is the use of your own words to restate or interpret the ideas of someone else, usually to make those ideas easier to understand.

5 Summarizing is the use of your own words to explain the ideas of someone else while also rearranging those ideas to highlight the ones most important to your argument.

6 Common knowledge includes any information that is generally known to most people or can be found in numerous independent sources.

7 Framing quotes, paraphrases, and summaries involves using signal phrases, citations, and connections to develop a context for a source's words or ideas.

8 An annotated bibliography is a useful tool for keep track of your sources and gaining a deeper understanding of the issues related to your topic.

9 Patchwriting is a form of plagiarism in which a writer loosely rewrites the ideas and words of others and presents them as his or her own.

10 Plagiarism, whether intentional or unintentional, robs writers of the opportunity to strengthen their own writing skills and express their own ideas.

1. Find an argument on the Internet that you want to discuss with your group. Go through the argument and highlight any words, phrases, or sentences that you might quote in an argument of your own. Then, in a different color, highlight information that you might paraphrase, summarize, or just cite. With your group, discuss the differences between the information that you would quote directly and the information that you would paraphrase or summarize. With your group, come up with a list of five reasons you might quote something instead of summarizing or paraphrasing it.

2. On the Internet, find a document that quotes sources. Look at how the author of the document frames quotations and other material taken from sources. Did the author do a good job of framing the material from sources? Are there any awkward places where the framing does not work? Write an e-mail to your instructor in which you critique the document's framing of source material. Explain what the author did well and what could be improved.

3. Find an argument that is 1,000 words or more on a topic that interests you. Write a summary that boils the argument down to 500 words. Then write a summary that boils the argument down to 200 words. Then summarize the argument in 50 words. Finally, summarize the argument in 10 words or less. With your group, talk about what kinds of information was left out of each successive summary as you were forced to use fewer and fewer words.

1. Sometimes it seems like our concerns about plagiarism are overblown, especially in the age of remixing, reposting, sampling, and cutting and pasting. Write an argument in which you explore both sides of the plagiarism issue. Start with the definition of plagiarism from the Council of Writing Program Administrators that is printed in this chapter. Then explore the pros and cons of holding to this kind of definition. At the end of your argument, discuss whether you believe the concept of plagiarism needs to change as communication technologies evolve.

2. As more texts are read on screen, citing sources can be handled effectively through links. In other words, a citation could simply be a direct link to the source itself, not a reference to the bibliography in the Works Cited list. Write an argument in which you come up with an electronic alternative to MLA and APA bibliographic styles for citing sources. What are the advantages of using links, and what are some of the potential disadvantages?

3. On the Internet, find an argument you disagree with that uses sources. In a rebuttal to the argument, directly challenge its use of sources. You might point out that its sources are weak or unsubstantiated, which allows the argument to make some unsubstantiated claims. Or you could point out that the author does not use sources from the other side of the issue, which is why the argument is biased or one sided. In your rebuttal, your goal is not to argue against the argument itself. Instead, challenge the argument by undermining its sources.

Using MLA Style

IN THIS CHAPTER YOU WILL LEARN HOW TO—

18.1 Use MLA parenthetical citations in your texts

18.2 Prepare a Works Cited list

18.3 Format sources in the Works Cited list in MLA style

M odern Language Association (MLA) documentation style helps you to keep track of your sources while showing your readers where you found the supporting information in your document. MLA style is most commonly used in the humanities (i.e., English, history, political science, philosophy, languages, art history). This style is also used in other scholarly fields because of its flexibility and familiarity.

In the previous chapter, you learned how to credit, quote, paraphrase, and summarize your sources. In this chapter, you will learn how to use MLA style to reference your sources and create a list of Works Cited at the end of your document. The models of MLA citations shown here demonstrate the ones most commonly used in college and in the workplace. If you cannot find a model that fits the source you are trying to cite, you should turn to the *MLA Handbook for Writers of Research Papers*, 7th ed. (2009). The Purdue Online Writing Lab (OWL) is also a reliable source if you don't have access to the *MLA Handbook*.

On the Internet, an increasing number of online citation generators are available, or your word-processing software may include one. We recommend using these online tools because they can help you quickly generate MLA-style documentation. However, you should always make sure the generator is following the most up-to-date MLA documentation style. Also, double-check all citations to make sure they were created correctly.

Parenthetical Citations

When citing a source with MLA style, you first need to include a *parenthetical reference.* A parenthetical reference appears in the text of your document, usually at the end of the sentence in which the information that you took from another source appears. For example:

> Archeologists have shown that wild dogs diverged from wolves about ten thousand years ago (Jones 27).

> For example, in *The Robber Bride,* Atwood depicts the response of second-wave feminism to postfeminism through the complex interactions of three friends and an aggressive vampire, Zenia, who has recently returned from the dead (Tolan 46).

Note: For a key to the color highlighting used here and throughout this chapter, see the bottom of the right-hand pages in this chapter.

As shown in these examples a parenthetical reference includes two important pieces of information: the source's name (usually an author's name) followed by a single space with no comma and the page number from the source in which the information appeared. The first parenthetical reference above signals that the information was taken from page 27 in a work from someone named Jones. The second parenthetical reference signals that its information can be found on page 46 in a source written by someone named Tolan.

An in-text citation tells readers they can then turn to the Works Cited list at the end of the document to see the full citation, which will look like these

> Jones, Steve. *Darwin's Ghost.* New York: Ballantine, 2000. Print.

> Tolan, Fiona. "Sucking the Blood Out of Second Wave Feminism: Postfeminist Vampirism in Margaret Atwood's *The Robber Bride.*" *Gothic Studies* 9.2 (2007): 45-57. Print.

The parenthetical reference and the full citation work together. The reference points readers to the Works Cited list, which provides the information needed for locating the source.

When the Author's Name Appears in the Sentence

If you name the author in the sentence, you need to provide only the page number in parentheses. For example:

> According to Steve Jones, a genetic scientist, archeologists have shown that wild dogs diverged from wolves about ten thousand years ago (27).

> In her recent article, Tolan argues that Atwood's *The Robber Bride* is really an allegory of postfeminism, in which three second-wave feminists are confronted with the anxieties brought about by the postfeminist backlash (46).

Typically, a parenthetical reference appears at the end of the sentence, but it can also appear immediately after the name of the source.

If the first part of your sentence draws information from a source but the remainder of the sentence represents your own thoughts, you should put the reference immediately after the source's material is used. For example:

> Glassner argues that naive Americans are victimized by a news media
> that is engaged in "fear-mongering" and other scare tactics (205), but I
> believe the American people are able to distinguish between real news and
> sensationalism.

Citing More Than One Source in the Same Sentence

If you want to cite multiple sources that are basically saying the same thing, you can use one parenthetical reference, separating the sources with semicolons:

> George Washington was the only logical choice for president of the United
> States because he had the respect of the competing political factions that
> emerged after the signing of the Treaty of Paris in 1783 (Irving 649;
> Ellis 375).

If you are citing more than one source in the same sentence but the sources are making different points, you should put the parenthetical reference as close as possible to the information taken from each source. For example:

> Some historians view Cicero as a principled defender of the dying Roman
> Republic (Grant 29), while others see him as an idealistic statesman who
> stood helplessly aside as the Republic crumbled (Everett 321).

Citing a Source Multiple Times

In some situations, you will need to cite a source multiple times. If your document continues using a single source, you only need to include the page number in following references as long as no other source comes between them.

> New owners often misread the natural signals from their puppy (Monks
> 139). One common problem is submissive urination in which a puppy
> shows submission by peeing. Owners often believe the puppy is acting
> defiantly, but it is really trying to signal submission. So punishing the dog
> is exactly the wrong thing to do because it only encourages the puppy
> to be even more submissive, resulting in even more puddles on the
> floor (140).

In the example shown, the full parenthetical reference is included early in the paragraph. The second reference, which is only a page number, is clearly referring to the source in the previous reference.

However, if another source is cited between two parenthetical references to the same source, the author's name from the first source would need to be repeated in a subsequent reference. For example:

New owners often misread the natural signals from their puppy (Monks 139). One common problem is submissive urination in which a puppy shows submission by peeing. Owners often believe the puppy is acting defiantly, but it is really trying to signal submission (Kerns 12). So punishing the dog is exactly the wrong thing to do because it only encourages the puppy to be even more submissive, resulting in even more puddles on the floor (Monks 140).

In the example above, the author includes "Monks" in the last sentence's reference because the reference "(Kerns 12)" appears between the two references to the source written by Monks.

Other Parenthetical References

A wide variety of parenthetical references is possible. Figure 18.1 shows models of some common parenthetical references. Choose the one that best fits your source. If none of these models fits the source you are trying to cite, you can use combinations of these models. If you still cannot figure it out, turn to the *MLA Handbook* for help or you can consult the Purdue OWL.

 18.2 Prepare a Works Cited list

Preparing the List of Works Cited

Your list of Works Cited appears at the end of your document. In this list, you should include full citations for all the sources you cite. A typical entry includes the name of the author, the name of the text, the place it was published, the medium in which it was published, and the date it was published. Here are three entries from three types of sources:

Chew, Robin. "Charles Darwin, Naturalist, 1809-1882." *Lucidcafe* 1 Feb. 2008. Web. 8 Feb. 2009.

Poresky, Louise. "Cather and Woolf in Dialogue: The Professor's House to the Light House." *Papers on Language and Literature* 44.1 (2008): 67-86. Print.

Shreve, Porter. *When the White House Was Ours*. Boston: Houghton, 2008. Print.

Type of Source	Example Parenthetical Reference
Single author	(Gerns 12)
Single author, multiple pages	(Barnes 5-9) or (Barnes 34, 121) *The hyphen signals a range of pages. The comma suggests similar information can be found on two different pages.*
Two authors	(Hammonds and Gupta 203)
Three authors	(Gym, Hanson, and Williams 845)
More than three authors	*First reference:* (Wu, Gyno, Young, and Reims 924) *Subsequent references:* (Wu et al. 924)
Multiple sources in same reference	(Yu 34; Thames and Cain 98; Young, Morales, and Cato 23) *The semicolon divides the sources.*
Two or more works by the same author	(Tufte, *Visual* 25) and (Tufte, "Powerpoint" 9) *The first prominent word in the source's title is used. Italics signals a book, while quotation marks signal an article.*
Different authors with the same last name	(M. Smith 54) and (A. Smith 34) *The first letter abbreviates each author's first name.*
Corporate author	(NASA 12) or (Amer. Beef Assn. 232) *Abbreviate as much of the corporate name as possible. Periods are needed with abbreviations that are not known acronyms.*
No author for book	(*Handling* 45) *Use the first prominent word in the title and put it in italics.*
No author for journal article or newspaper article	("Genomics" 23) *Use the first prominent word in the title and put it in quotation marks.*
No author for newspaper article	("Recession" A4) *The letter "A" is the section of the newspaper and the number is the page.*
Quoted in another source	(qtd. in Franks 94) *"qtd." stands for "quoted."*
Web page or other document with numbered paragraphs	(Reynolds, par. 3) *"par." stands for paragraph, as counted down from the top of the page. The comma separates the name from the paragraph number.*
Web page or other document with no author and no paragraph numbers	("Friendly") *Put the first prominent word in the title in quotes. If paragraph numbers are not included, then cite the whole source without page or paragraph numbers.*

According to the *MLA Style Guide* 7.4.2, "When a source has no page numbers or any other kind of reference numbers, no number can be given in the parenthetical reference.... Do not count unnumbered paragraphs."

Not all possible parenthetical references are shown here. If you have a source that doesn't fit these examples, you can usually figure out how to cite it by combining the above reference models. If you still cannot figure out how to cite your source, turn to the *MLA Handbook* for help.

FIGURE 18.1 Types of MLA Parenthetical References

Only sources you reference in your document should appear in your Works Cited. The works-cited list is not a bibliography of all the sources you consulted but did not cite.

List the entries in alphabetical order by the authors' last names. When the author's name is not known, alphabetize by the first prominent word in its title. Ignore *The, A,* or *An* if it is the first word in the title.

Including More Than One Source from an Author

If your works-cited list includes two or more sources from the same author, only the first entry should include the author's name. Afterward, entries should use three hyphens instead of the name. Multiple entries from one author should be alphabetized by the first prominent words in the titles.

Murphy, James. *Rhetoric in the Middle Ages: A History of Rhetorical Theory from Saint Augustine to the Renaissance.* Berkeley: U of California P. 1974. Print.

---. *A Short History of Writing Instruction: From Ancient Greece to Modern America.* 2nd ed. Mahwah: Erlbaum, 2001. Print.

---, ed. *Three Medieval Rhetorical Arts.* Berkeley: U of California P. 1971. Print.

Murphy, James, Richard Katula, Forbes Hill, and Donovan Ochs. *A Synoptic History of Classical Rhetoric.* 3rd ed. Mahwah: Erlbaum, 2003. Print.

As shown, if a single author is also listed as a coauthor for another entry, you should include the full name again without the three hyphens.

Formatting a List of Works Cited

Start the works-cited list on a new page with the centered heading "Works Cited" at the top (Figure 18.2). Entries are double-spaced, in hanging indent format, which means the first line of each entry is not indented, but the rest are indented a half inch.

In workplace texts, however, your works-cited list should match the design of your document. The "Works Cited" heading should be consistent with other headings. If you are single-spacing the rest of your document, the works-cited list should be single-spaced, too, perhaps with spaces between entries.

Torres 12

Works Cited

Barber, Paul. *Vampires, Burial, and Death*. New Haven: Yale UP,
1989. Print.

Bluestein, Gene. *Poplore: Folk and Pop in American Culture*.
Amherst: U of Massachusetts P, 1994. Print.

Keyworth, Donald. "Was the Vampire of the Eighteenth Century a
Unique Type of Undead Corpse?" *Folklore* 117.3 (2006): 1-16.
Print.

Todorova, Maria. *Imagining the Balkans*. Oxford: Oxford UP, 1996.
Print.

FIGURE 18.2
Formatting a
List of Works
Cited
MLA style requires
that the heading
"Works Cited"
be centered on
the page. The
margins should
be one inch on all
sides. The entries
should be double
spaced.

Citing Sources in the List of Works Cited

18.3 Format sources in the Works Cited list in MLA style

The following examples of MLA citations are based on the guidelines in the *MLA Handbook for Writers of Research Papers* (7th ed., 2009). This list is not comprehensive. However, we have included models of the most common kinds of entries in a works-cited list. You can use these examples as models for your own citations. If you do not find a model for a source, you should turn to the *MLA Handbook*.

MLA List of Works Cited

Books and Other Nonperiodical Publications

1. Book, One Author
2. Book, Two Authors
3. Book, Three Authors
4. Book, Four or More Authors
5. Book, Corporate or Organization Author
6. Book, Edited Collection
7. Book, Translated

8. Book, Author Unknown
9. Book, Second Edition or Beyond
10. Book, in Electronic Form
11. Document, Government Publication
12. Document, Pamphlet
13. Foreword, Introduction, Preface, or Afterword
14. Sacred Text
15. Dissertation, Unpublished

Author Title Publication Online Source

Citing Books and Other Nonperiodical Publications

Books and other nonperiodical publications are perhaps the easiest to list in the works-cited list. A book citation will have most of the following features:

1. Name of the author, corporation, or editor with last name first (add "ed." or "eds." if the work is listed by the name of the editor)

2. Title of the work

3. City in which the work was published

4. Publisher

5. Year of publication

6. Medium of publication

① ② ③ ④ ⑤ ⑥

Author. Title. City of publication: Publisher, year of publication. Medium of publication.

1. Book, One Author

Ambrose, Stephen. *Band of Brothers*. 3rd ed. New York: Simon, 2001. Print.

2. Book, Two Authors

Brett, Michael, and Elizabeth Fentress. *The Berbers: The Peoples of Africa*.
    Malden: Wiley-Blackwell, 1996. Print.

3. Book, Three Authors

Fellman, Michael, Daniel E. Sutherland, and Lesley J. Gordon. *This Terrible
    War: The Civil War and Its Aftermath*. New York: Longman, 2007. Print.

4. Book, Four or More Authors

Huss, Bernard, et al. *The Unknown Socrates*. New York: Bolchazy-Carducci,
    2002. Print.

5. Book, Corporate or Organization Author

American Psychiatric Association. *Diagnostic and Statistical Manual of
    Mental Disorders*. 4th ed. Washington: APA, 1994. Print.

6. Book, Edited Collection

Mueller-Vollmer, Kurt, ed. *The Hermeneutics Reader*. New York: Continuum,
    1990. Print.

7. Book, Translated

Dostoevsky, Fyodor. *Notes from Underground*. Trans. Michael Katz. 2nd ed.
    New York: Norton, 2001. Print.

8. Book, Author Unknown

Physical Science. New York: McGraw, 1998. Print.

9. Book, Second Edition or Beyond

Kottak, Conrad. *Anthropology: The Exploration of Human Diversity*. 12th
    ed. New York: McGraw, 2008. Print.

10. Book, in Electronic Form

Darwin, Charles. *On the Various Contrivances by Which British and Foreign Orchids Are Fertilised by Insects.* London: Murray, 1862. PDF file.

11. Document, Government Publication

Arguin, Paul M., Phyllis E. Kozarsky, and Ava W. Navin, eds. *Health Information for International Travel 2007–2008: The Yellow Book.* St. Louis: Centers for Disease Control, 2007. Print.

12. Document, Pamphlet

Historians Against the War. *Torture, American Style.* Somerville: Historians Against the War, 2006. Print.

13. Foreword, Introduction, Preface, or Afterword

Parker, Hershel. Foreword. *Moby-Dick: Or the Whale.* By Herman Melville. Evanston: Northwestern UP, 2001. xiii-xvi. Print.

14. Sacred Text

The New Oxford Annotated Bible. 3rd ed. New York: Oxford UP, 2001. Print.

15. Dissertation, Unpublished

Charlap, Marie-Helene. "Once with Women, Now with Women: A Qualitative Study of Identity." Diss. New York U, 2008. Print.

Citing Journals, Magazines, and Other Periodicals

Citations for periodicals, such as journals, magazines, and other regularly published documents, need to include additional information. The title of the article should appear in quotation marks. The volume number and issue number appear after the title of the periodical. The page numbers follow the year the work was published.

A citation for a journal, magazine, or other periodical publication includes the following features:

1. Name of the author, corporation, or editor with last name first

2. Title of the work in quotation marks

3. Name of the periodical in italics

4. Volume number and issue number

5. Date of publication (year for scholarly journal; day, month, year for other periodicals)

6. Range of page numbers for whole article

7. The medium in which the work was published ("Print" for a journal, periodical, or newspaper)

    ①   ②   ③   ④   ⑤   ⑥

Author. "Article Title." *Journal Title* Date or Volume.Issue (Year): page numbers.
    ⑦

Medium of publication.

16. Article, Journal with Volume and Issue Numbers

Jovanovic, Franck. "The Construction of the Canonical History of Financial
    Economics." *History of Political Economy* 40.2 (2008): 213-42. Print.

17. Article, Journal with Issue Number Only

Lee, Christopher. "Enacting the Asian Canadian." *Canadian Literature* 199
    (2008): 28-44. Print.

18. Article, Edited Book

Goodheart, George. "Innate Intelligence Is the Healer." *Healers on Healing.*
    Ed. Richard Carlson and Benjamin Shield. New York: Putnam, 1989.
    53-57. Print.

19. Article, Magazine

Zakaria, Fareed. "Obama's Vietnam: How to Salvage Afghanistan." *Newsweek*
    9 Feb. 2009: 36-37. Print.

20. Article, Newspaper

Herszenhorn, David. "Bipartisan Push to Trim Size of Stimulus Plan."
    New York Times 5 Feb. 2009, late ed.: A1. Print.

21. Article, Author Unknown

"The Big Chill Leaves Bruises." *Albuquerque Tribune* 17 Jan. 2004: A4. Print.

Author Title Publication Online Source

22. Article, CD-ROM

Hanford, Peter. "Locating the Right Job for You." *The Electronic Job Finder*.
San Francisco: Career Masters, 2001. CD-ROM.

23. Editorial

"A Vital Boost for Education." Editorial. *New York Times* 4 Feb. 2009,
natl. ed.: A30. Print.

24. Letter to the Editor

Bertin, Joan. Letter. *New York Times* 6 Feb. 2009, late ed.: A22. Print.

25. Review

Leonhardt, David. "Chance and Circumstance." Rev. of *Outliers*, by Malcolm
Gladwell. *New York Times Book Review* 30 Nov. 2008: 9. Print.

Citing Web Publications

In the most recent update of the *MLA Handbook* (2009), Web addresses (URLs) have
been removed from citations. When possible, you should include two dates: the date
the material appeared on the Internet, and the date you accessed the material. If you
cannot find the first date, then put *n.d.* for "no date." If you cannot find the publisher
of the information, put *n.p.* for "no publisher."

26. Website, Author Known

Nagel, Michael. "Biography." *The Official Mark Twain Website*. CMG
Solutions, n.d. Web. 2 Feb. 2009.

27. Website, Corporate Author

United States Fish and Wildlife Service. *Arctic National Wildlife Refuge*.
Dept. of the Interior, 12 Sept. 2008. Web. 12 Mar. 2009.

28. Website, Author Unknown

"Pentagon Sets Sights on Public Opinion." *MSNBC.com*. Microsoft, 5 Feb.
2009. Web. 6 Feb. 2009.

29. Article from an Online Periodical

Leier, Andrew. "How Martian Winds Make Rocks Walk." *ScienceDaily*.
ScienceDaily, 12 Jan. 2009. Web. 4 Feb. 2009.

A citation for a Web publication will have most or all of the following features:

①   Name of the author, corporation, editor, webmaster with last name first

②   Title of the work (in quotation marks if an article; italicized if a stand-alone work)

③   Name of the website in italics if different than the title of the website

④   Publisher of the website. (If not available, use *n.p.* for "no publisher.")

⑤   Date of publication, including day, month, year. (If not available, use *n.d.* for "no date.")

⑥   The medium in which the work was published ("Web" for websites)

⑦   Date on which you accessed the website

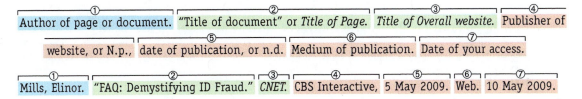

Author of page or document.   "Title of document" or *Title of Page*.   *Title of Overall website*.   Publisher of website, or N.p.,   date of publication, or n.d.   Medium of publication.   Date of your access.

Mills, Elinor.   "FAQ: Demystifying ID Fraud."   *CNET*.   CBS Interactive,   5 May 2009.   Web.   10 May 2009.

③ Name of website

② Title of work

① Author

⑤ Date of publication

⑥ Medium of publication

⑦ Date of access

④ Publisher of website

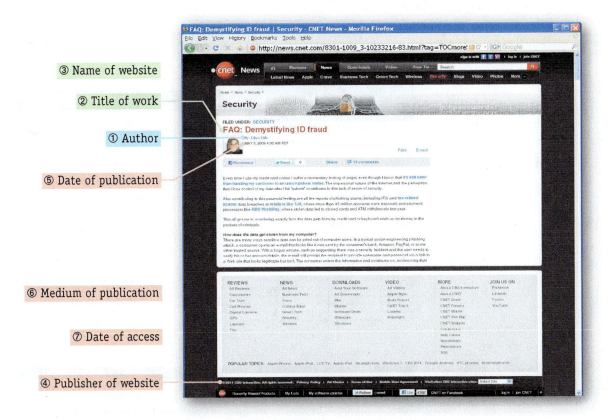

FIGURE 18.3 CITATION MAP: Citing All or Part of a Website

Author   Title   Publication   Online Source

A citation for an article from a scholarly journal on the Web includes the following features:

① Name of the author, last name first   ⑤ Date of publication (year for scholarly journal)

② Title of the work in quotation marks   ⑥ Range of page numbers for whole article

③ Name of the journal in italics   ⑦ The medium in which the work was published

④ Volume number and issue number   ⑧ Your date of access

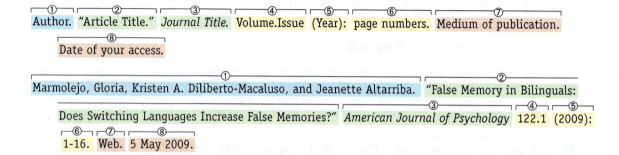

Author. "Article Title." *Journal Title.* Volume.Issue (Year): page numbers. Medium of publication. Date of your access.

Marmolejo, Gloria, Kristen A. Diliberto-Macaluso, and Jeanette Altarriba. "False Memory in Bilinguals: Does Switching Languages Increase False Memories?" *American Journal of Psychology* 122.1 (2009): 1-16. Web. 5 May 2009.

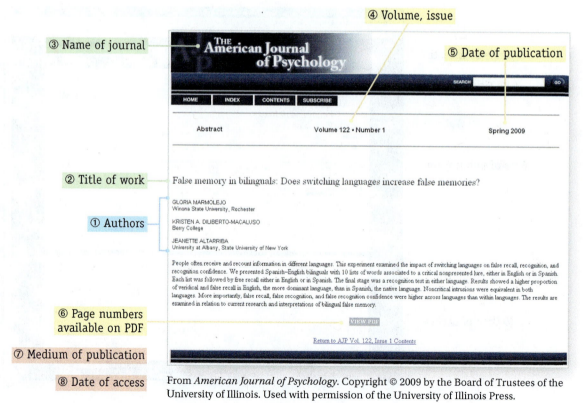

③ Name of journal

④ Volume, issue

⑤ Date of publication

Abstract   Volume 122 • Number 1   Spring 2009

② Title of work — False memory in bilinguals: Does switching languages increase false memories?

GLORIA MARMOLEJO
Winona State University, Rochester

① Authors —
KRISTEN A. DILIBERTO-MACALUSO
Berry College

JEANETTE ALTARRIBA
University at Albany, State University of New York

People often receive and recount information in different languages. This experiment examined the impact of switching languages on false recall, recognition, and recognition confidence. We presented Spanish–English bilinguals with 10 lists of words associated to a critical nonpresented lure, either in English or in Spanish. Each list was followed by free recall either in English or in Spanish. The final stage was a recognition test in either language. Results showed a higher proportion of veridical and false recall in English, the more dominant language, than in Spanish, the native language. Noncritical intrusions were equivalent in both languages. More importantly, false recall, false recognition, and false recognition confidence were higher across languages than within languages. The results are examined in relation to current research and interpretations of bilingual false memory.

⑥ Page numbers available on PDF

VIEW PDF

Return to AJP Vol. 122, Issue 1 Contents

⑦ Medium of publication

⑧ Date of access

From *American Journal of Psychology.* Copyright © 2009 by the Board of Trustees of the University of Illinois. Used with permission of the University of Illinois Press.

FIGURE 18.4 CITATION MAP: Citing a Scholarly Journal on the Web

A citation for an article from a scholarly journal accessed through a database includes the following features:

① Name of the author, last name first
② Title of the work in quotation marks
③ Name of the journal in italics
④ Volume number and issue number
⑤ Date of publication (year for scholarly journal)

⑥ Range of page numbers for whole article
⑦ Name of database
⑧ Medium of publication
⑨ Your date of access

①   ②   ③   ④   ⑤   ⑥   ⑦   ⑧
Author. "Article Title." *Journal Title.* Volume.Issue (Year): page numbers. *Database.* Medium of
                                          ⑧
publication. Date of your access.

①   ②
McGee, Elizabeth, and Mark Shevlin. "Effect of Humor on Interpersonal Attraction and Mate Selection."
    ③   ④   ⑤   ⑥   ⑦   ⑧   ⑨
Journal of Psychology 143.1 (2009): 67-77. *Academic Search Premier.* Web. 4 Apr. 2009.

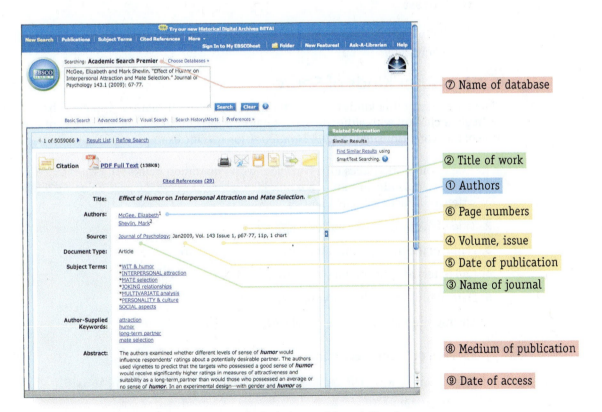

FIGURE 18.5 CITATION MAP: Citing a Scholarly Journal from a Database

30. Article from an Online Scholarly Journal without Page Numbers

Ochiagha, Terri. "The Literary Fantastic in African and English Literature."
    CLCWeb 10.4 (2008): n. pag. Web. 5 Feb. 2009.

31. Periodical Article Accessed through a Database (Web)

Sklansky, David. "Police and Democracy." *Michigan Law Review* 103.7
    (2005): 1699-1830. *JSTOR*. Web. 5 Feb. 2009.

32. Blog Posting

Isaacson, Walter. "A Bold Idea for Saving Journalism." *The Huffington Post*.
    HuffingtonPost.com, 5 Feb. 2009. Web. 5 Feb. 2009.

33. Wiki Entry

"Galileo Galilei." *Wikipedia*. Wikimedia, n.d. Web. 5 Feb. 2009.

34. Podcast

"Interview with Neil Gaiman." *Just One More Book*. N.p., 27 Jan. 2009. Web.
    3 Feb. 2009.

Citing Other Kinds of Sources

There are many other kinds of sources. Especially for performances, you may choose
to begin a citation with either an artist's name, a director or producer's name, or the
title of the work. Consult the *MLA Handbook* for specific examples.

1. Title of the work (italics for a complete work; quotation marks for a work that is a
   segment, episode, or part of a whole) OR name of a specific performer, director,
   writer, etc. (last name, first name)

2. Title of the program, in italics, if applicable

3. Name of the network that aired or produced the work

4. Call letters and city of the station that aired the work, if available

5. Date of broadcast (day, month, year)

6. The medium of the work (e.g., television, radio, DVD, CD, film)

35. Film or Video Recording

Fiddler on the Roof. Dir. Norman Jewison. Prod. Norman Jewison. Mirisch,
    1971. Film.

Harris, Rosalind, perf. *Fiddler on the Roof.* Dir. Norman Jewison. Mirisch, 1971. Film.

36. Television or Radio Program

"Destination: The South Pole." Narr. Richard Harris. *All Things Considered.* Natl. Public Radio. 6 Jan. 2003. Web. 4 Feb. 2004.

37. Song or Audio Recording

Myer, Larry. "Sometimes Alone." *Flatlands.* People's Productions, 1993. CD.

38. CD-ROM

Lilley, Linda, Scott Harrington, and Julie Snyder. *Pharmacology and the Nursing Process Companion CD.* 5th ed. St. Louis: Mosby, 2007. CD-ROM.

39. Personal Correspondence, E-Mail, or Interview

Schimel, Eric. Personal interview. 12 Dec. 2008.

40. Work of Art

Vermeer, Johannes. *Girl with a Pearl Earring.* N.d. Oil on canvas. Mauritshuis, The Hague.

41. Print Advertisement

Sprint. Advertisement. *Newsweek* 9 Feb. 2009. P. 25–26, Print.

42. Commercial

Toyota. Advertisement. MSNBC. 5 Feb. 2009. Television.

43. Speech, Lecture, or Reading

Obama, Barack. "Inauguration Address." Capitol Building, Washington DC. 21 Jan. 2009. Address.

44. Map

"Japan." Map. *Rand McNally World Atlas.* New York: Rand, 2004. 31. Print.

45. Cartoon

Adams, Scott. "Dilbert." Comic strip. *Journal and Courier (Lafayette)* 8 Apr. 2009: C8. Print.

Author   Title   Publication   Online Source

A Student's MLA-Style Research Paper

The document shown here uses MLA citation style. You can use this document to observe how an author uses MLA citation style under real conditions, including parenthetical references and a list of works cited.

Joey Van Note
Instructor Anna Derlaga
ENGL 1106
31 May 2013

Enhancing Engineers' Communication Abilities at Virginia Tech Engineering requires excellence in the fields of math and science, along with exceptional problem-solving skills. As a result, students receiving a higher education in the field of engineering at a school such as Virginia Tech are forced to spend the majority of their time intensively studying formulas, equations, and chemical reactions. This leaves minimal extra time for engineers to work on their communication skills. Because engineers continue to lack good communication skills, the Virginia Tech administration should modify the engineering curriculum to include more social-oriented classes that are focused on teaching communication skills. This change will allow engineers to better develop their abilities to convey their thoughts and ideas with one another.

COMMUNICATION AS PROBLEM-SOLVING FOR ENGINEERS

From my experience as an engineering student, for the typical engineer, anything that doesn't involve solving a problem or improving inefficiencies within a system carries little importance. Students studying engineering are doing it because of the rush they feel after successfully solving a problem. Even if it is a small task, such as making a paper airplane that will fly the furthest and for the longest time, engineers will jump at the chance to tackle this challenge.

The issue with this fascination is that engineers may have the inability to communicate effectively with others when trying to solve a problem. Communicating is required in order to collaborate with teammates and co-workers and optimize efficiency in the work place.

Van Note 2

Pia Lappalainen, a communication researcher, backed up this claim by saying, "Ultimately this [organizational communication] leads to good performance, through a connection between the human aspects of work and organizational productivity" (125). Engineers don't need to be poetic, but they do need to be efficient, effective, and honest when communicating with others.

Besides this general need to communicate one's findings, communication matters for engineers because many employers are seeking this ability in their new hires (see fig. 1).

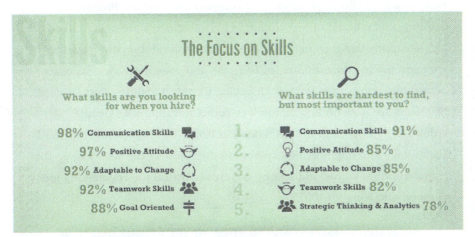

Fig. 1 Top skills employers were seeking in a 2012 survey by Millennial Branding. *Source:* "Millennial Branding Student Employment Gap Study"; *Millennia/Branding*; n.p., 14 May 2012; Web; 30 May 2013.

If you provide a citation for the figure in the caption and do not refer to the figure elsewhere, you don't need to include it on your Works Cited page.

Engineers are required to have social and business skills. Simply writing lab reports, remembering equations, and gathering data is not enough; today's engineers need to be able to interpret as well as present data to other audiences with less known information on the topic in a way in which they understand. An article from the University of South Carolina mentioned how engineers need to do more than just be good at math and science in order to be successful, stating that "students need to move beyond the first stage so that they can begin to assess, interpret, and shape messages" (Bonk et al. 152). Being good at math and science is only the first stage of being an engineer; now, being able to interpret the data collected and being able to present that data to others is what the real challenge.

In order to differentiate oneself from the mass of other engineers trying to become successful in the current job market, aspiring engineers need to show that they have the ability to communicate and collaborate effectively with others and work in teams. According to Lappalainen, "engineers no longer manage their daily tasks with plain substance expertise; instead they must be adept at communication, collaboration, networking, feedback provision and reception, teamwork, lifelong learning, and cultural understanding" (123). Engineers are being forced into situations that they have not been forced into in the past. Now they are expected to communicate, collaborate, and even network with other people and companies along with having technical abilities. Furthermore, engineers are now finding themselves communicating with people around the globe. Both the Accreditation Board for Engineering and Technology and engineering experts in other parts of the world agree that communication within and among cultures is critical for engineering today (Tenopir and King 99-100).

ADDING MORE COMMUNICATION TO THE ENGINEERING
CURRICULUM AT VIRGINIA TECH

Because a change in the workplace is forcing new engineers to have a wider range of skills, there should also be a change in the engineering curriculum that helps prepare them for this aspect of their careers. It should be the job of the Virginia Tech administration to understand these engineering stereotypes as well as the changing workplace and to formulate a new curriculum that integrates communication skills along with the already technically filled education set in place. The College of Engineering and the English Department specifically should collaborate to create a new curriculum that teaches better writing skills to engineers, specifically technical writing, within the first two years of their

Van Note 4

education at Virginia Tech. This would allow students to better develop their technical communication skills early so they can utilize these skills moving forward, as well as leave room in students' schedules to take specific in-major engineering classes during their junior and senior years.

By involving both the College of Engineering and a Technical Writing Program within the English Department, new students can work on their writing skills while being introduced to the engineering profession. A modified version of this plan has already been implemented by the University of Delaware, where "First-year engineering classes, for example, offer opportunities to introduce these key elements of technical communication" as they teach students about careers in engineering (Bonk et al. 152). These types of programs can achieve two purposes at the same time by allowing students to learn about the engineering profession from high-level engineering professors while they improve their technical writing skills by implementing methods used within the English Department.

Within the current engineering curriculum at Virginia Tech, the only classes that engineers are required to take that would help their communication skills directly are two first-year writing courses (which students can test out of in high school). This means that out of the 136 required credits to graduate as an engineer, only six of them have a main focus on communication skills. This forces students to put forth the majority of their effort towards math and science courses, and less towards their communication skills.

In order to compensate for this lack of writing education, the new curriculum would require students to take at least 12 credits of English before graduation. This ensures that even if students received AP credit in high school, they cannot test out of the entire English requirement as an engineer. Beyond first-year writing, students would still need to take another English course that is more directly focused on technical writing because the majority of the writing a future engineer will be required to do is technical in nature. This would allow students to better develop their writing abilities, and in turn be able to use them in other areas of their education, such as lab reports or project write-ups. Though not technically another English course, a modified literacy course like this has already been tested at the University of New South Wales. The results from the students came back saying that "more work was required in the literacy support course than in other, comparably weighted courses, however the students reacted positively to the learning activities and agreed that it was generally useful" (Skinner and Mort 553). Even though learning more about literacy and communication skills adds a little to the already strenuous schedule for an engineer, it will be greatly beneficial when they are finally able to apply these communication skills in the workplace.

Along with this extra English requirement, engineering students should be required to take a public speaking class. The only practice with verbal communication that engineers currently have throughout the Virginia Tech curriculum is in their work on group projects. Unlike working in groups with other engineers, public speaking would teach students how to communicate the same ideas to non-engineers, who have less background information on the topic. As one science writer has pointed out: "Not only must they [engineers] present research results to others with technical training, they may have to make presentations to, and write for, non-engineers. Unfortunately, few engineering colleges prepare students to communicate well" (Titus 5). This class will also teach presentation skills so future engineers will know how to present technical information to a variety of people and groups. Such a class would allow the opportunity for engineers to learn how to present themselves to a group, as well as how to clearly describe their thoughts when in front of others.

CREATING A CAPSTONE PROJECT EXPERIENCE

Building off this strong start of enhancing the textual and verbal communication components within the curriculum, the College of Engineering should require a final capstone project for all engineering students. This capstone project can consist of a collaboration of engineers constructing a device that will make people's lives easier with people

Van Note 6

within the marketing department who will promote the product. This would give engineers experience communicating with business-oriented people on a real-life basis, while putting their creative and technical minds to the test.

This capstone project would require a slight modification within the College of Business curriculum as well, so it might be difficult to implement. If Virginia Tech administration realizes that this change isn't reasonably possible, then this capstone project can be modified to still require a high level of communication skills. To do this, teams would be formed consisting of different types of engineers on each team, such as one Industrial and Systems Engineer, one Materials Engineer, one Mechanical Engineer, etc. These teams would need to produce a device that makes people's lives easier, while forcing them to collaborate with each other on specifically how to make the device, how much it will cost, and how to manufacture it.

Requiring graduating engineers to produce and present a project such as this would build upon and implement everything they have learned about communication, collaboration, and the engineering design process. It will also prepare and present them with a real-world challenge within their profession and better prepare them for jobs in the workplace. This will also reinforce the knowledge and skills that these students learned throughout their English and public speaking classes that provided the foundation for their communication skills.

CONCLUSION: PREPARING ENGINEERS FOR THEIR FUTURES

By Virginia Tech's making these specific three changes within the curriculum, students will find themselves having much better communication skills, while improving their analytical and problem-solving skills. Modifications like this have already been made at other universities, and researchers of the programs have found that "most graduates felt that they had gained analytical and problem-solving skills, subject-specific knowledge, research and improved decision-making abilities through their degree" (Seetha 2). This new curriculum has already been tested, and now it should be implemented by Virginia Tech in order to enable better communication education across graduating engineers.

Too many engineers are lacking in interpersonal skills. The world revolves around interpersonal relationships, so not being able to have those skills would take away from one's ability to be at peak productivity. As a communication specialist notes, "If you are a great engineer and you or your team have an exciting way to solve a problem or execute on a potential project but you cannot communicate the key points of your solution, you are not likely to be chosen for the contract" (Doward). The best engineers are going to be working at this peak productivity, and requiring students to take classes focused on communicating effectively is going to enable that.

Good communication will also maximize efficiency by allowing teams to be comfortable working with each other. When teams are comfortable working with each other, they feel more comfortable stating their opinions and developing collaborative solutions. The more opinions and ideas created within a group, the greater the chance of a high-quality product. Forcing engineers to take more social-oriented classes will increase this comfort level, allowing them to be the best engineers they can be.

Engineers today are required to take an overdose of math and science courses, and as a result they have minimal extra time to work on their communication skills. In order to prevent engineers from becoming poor communicators, Virginia Tech's engineering administration should modify the curriculum by adding more English courses, requiring a public speaking course, and implementing a final capstone project to force engineers to practice and improve their communication skills. This would allow engineering students to become well-rounded employees for the future, as well as maximize their ability to solve problems with the greatest efficiency possible.

If you are using a website without page numbers or paragraph numbers, do not include any numbers in the citation.

Van Note 8

Works Cited

Bonk, Robert J., Paul T. Imhoff, and Alexander H. Cheng. "Integrating
Written Communication within Engineering Curricula." *Journal of
Professional Issues in Engineering and Practice* 128.4 (2002):
152-59. *EBSCOhost.* Web. 15 Apr. 2012.

Dorward, Mary Anne. "Why Engineers Need Great Communication
Skills." *My Real Voice.* N.p., 7 Oct. 2008. Web. 20 Apr. 2013.

Lappalainen, Pia. "Communication as Part of the Engineering Skills
Set." *European Journal of Engineering Education* 34.2 (2009):
123-29. Print.

Seetha, Shikha. "Communication Skills for Engineers in Global Arena."
International Journal on Arts, Management and Humanities. 1.1
(2012): 1-5. Print.

Skinner, Iain, and Pam Mort. "Embedding Academic Literacy Support
within the Electrical Engineering Curriculum: A Case Study." *IEEE
Transactions on Education* 52.4 (2009): 547-53. Web. 17
Apr. 2013.

Tenopir, Carol, and Donald W. King. *Communication Patterns of
Engineers.* Hoboken: Wiley, 2004.

Titus, Jon. "Editorial: Engineers Need Writing Skills." *Test &
Measurement World* 22.9 (2002): 5. *ProQuest.* Web. 17 Apr. 2013.

Author Title Publication Online Source

19 Using APA Style

IN THIS CHAPTER YOU WILL LEARN HOW TO—

19.1 Use APA parenthetical citations in your texts

19.2 Create bibliographic entries for a References list

19.3 Prepare a References list in APA style

American Psychological Association (APA) documentation style, like MLA style (Chapter 18), is a method for keeping track of your sources while letting readers know where you found the support for your claims. APA style is commonly used in the social sciences, psychological sciences, physical sciences, and technical fields.

In this chapter, you will learn how to use APA style to reference your sources and create a list of References at the end of your document. The models of APA citations shown here are the ones most commonly used in college and in the workplace. For more information on APA style, consult the *Publication Manual of the American Psychological Association*, 6th ed. (2010). You can also consult reliable online sources like the Purdue Online Writing Lab (OWL).

Parenthetical Citations

When citing a source with APA style, you first need to include a parenthetical citation, which appears in the text of your document, usually at the end of the sentence in which the information that you used from another source appears. For example:

> Children and adults see the world differently, which can make the divorce of their parents especially unsettling (Neuman, 1998, p. 43).

Among Africa's other problems, the one that is most significant may be its
lack of reliable electrical energy (Friedman, 2008, p. 155).

As shown here, a full parenthetical citation includes three important pieces of information: the source's name (usually an author's name), the year the source was published, and the page number from the source in which the information appeared.

If readers want to, they can then turn to the list of References at the end of the document to see the full citation, which will look like this:

Neuman, G. (1998). *Helping your kids cope with divorce the sandcastles way.* New York, NY: Random House.

In other words, the parenthetical citation and the full reference work together. The parenthetical citation points readers to the reference list, where they can find the information needed to locate the source.

Note: For a key to the color highlighting used here and throughout this chapter, see the bottom of this page.

APA style also allows you to refer to a whole work by simply putting the author's name and the year of the source. For example:

Genetics is a new frontier for understanding schizophrenia (Swaminathan, 2008).

Autism and psychosis have been shown to be diametrical disorders of the brain (Crespi & Badcock, 2008).

Parenthetical references without page numbers are common in APA style, but not in MLA style.

In situations in which you are specifically highlighting a study or author, you should move the full parenthetical reference up in the sentence:

According to one study (Adreason & Pierson, 2008), the cerebellum plays a key role in the onset of schizophrenia.

Three books (Abraham & Llewellyn-Jones, 1992; Boskind-White & White, 2000; Burby, 1998) have tried to explain bulimia to nonscientists.

When the Author's Name Appears in the Sentence

If you name the author in the sentence, you need to provide only the year of the source and the page number in parentheses. The year should follow the name of the source and the page number should appear at the end of the sentence. For example:

Neuman (1998) points out that children and adults see the world differently, which can make a divorce especially unsettling (p. 43).

Friedman (2008) argues that Africa's most significant problem may be its lack of reliable electrical energy (p. 155).

If one part of your sentence draws information from a source but the remainder of the sentence states your own thoughts, you should put the reference immediately after the source's material is used. For example:

As Dennet (1995) points out, scientists are uncomfortable with the idea that nature uses a form of reason (p. 213), but I think we must see nature as a life form that is looking out for its best interests.

Citing More Than One Source in the Same Sentence

In APA style, it is common to cite multiple sources making the same point, separated with semicolons:

Several researchers (Crespi & Badcock, 2008; Shaner, Miller, & Mintz, 2004, p. 102; Swaminatha, 2008) have shown the toll that schizophrenia takes on a family.

In the sentence above, the writer is referring to the whole work by Crespi and Badcock and that by Swaminatha, but she is referring only to page 102 in the article by Shaner, Miller, and Mintz.

If you are citing more than one source in the same sentence but they are making different points, you should put the parenthetical reference as close as possible to the information taken from each source. For example:

Depression is perhaps one of the most common effects of bulimia (McCabe, McFarlane, & Olmstead, 2004, p. 19), and this depression "almost always impairs concentration" (Sherman & Thompson, 1996, p. 57).

Citing a Source Multiple Times

In some situations, you will need to cite a source multiple times. If your document continues using a single source, you need to include only the page number in subsequent references as long as no other source comes between them.

The side effects of brain tumor treatment can include fatigue, brain swelling, hair loss, and depression (Black, 2006, p. 170). Hair loss and other outward signs of treatment can be the most disturbing. Depression, however, perhaps needs more attention because it often requires patients to take antidepressants and stimulants (p. 249).

In the previous example on p. 408, the full parenthetical citation is included early in the paragraph. The second reference, which is only a page number, is clearly referring to the source in the first reference.

However, if another source is cited between two parenthetical citations to the same source, the author's name from the first source would need to be repeated in a subsequent reference. For example:

> The side effects of brain tumor treatment can include fatigue, brain swelling, hair loss, and depression (Black, 2006, p. 170). Hair loss and other outward signs of treatment can be the most disturbing. For instance, Becker (2003) discusses her obsession with hiding the incision where the tumor was removed (p. 231). Depression, however, perhaps needs more attention because it often requires patients to take antidepressants and stimulants (Black, 2006, p. 249).

In the example above, the author includes a full parenthetical reference to Black in the final sentence of the paragraph because the reference to Becker (2003) appears between the first and second references to Black.

Other Parenthetical References

Figure 19.1 on page 410 shows models of some common parenthetical citations. Choose the one that best fits your source. If none of these models fits the source you are trying to cite, you can use combinations of these models. If you still cannot figure it out, turn to the APA's *Publication Manual*.

Preparing the List of References

Your list of references appears at the end of your document. In this list, you should include full citations for all the sources you cite. A typical entry includes the name of the author, the date of publication, the title of the text, and the place of publication. Here are three entries from three different types of sources.

> Servan-Schreiber, D. (2008). *Anti-cancer: A new way of life.* New York, NY: Viking.

> Crespi, B., & Badcock, C. (2008). Psychosis and autism as diametrical disorders in the social brain. *Behavior Brain Science, 31*(3), 241–261.

> Chew, R. (2008, February 1). Charles Darwin, naturalist, 1809–1882. Lucidcafe. Retrieved February 8, 2009, from http://www.lucidcafe .com/library/96feb/darwin.html

Author Title Publication Online Source

Type of Source	Example Parenthetical Reference
Single author	(Gerns, 2009, p. 12)
Single author, multiple pages	(Barnes, 2007, pp. 5–9) or (Barnes, 2007, pp. 34, 121) *The dash signals a range of pages. The comma suggests similar information can be found on two different pages. The "pp." signals multiple pages.*
Two authors	(Hammonds & Gupta, 2004, p. 203) *The ampersand (&) is used instead of "and."*
Three authors	(Gym, Hanson, & Williams, 2005, p. 845) *The ampersand (&) is used instead of "and."*
More than three authors	*First reference:* (Wu, Gyno, Young, & Reims, 2003, p. 924) *Subsequent references:* (Wu et al., 2003, p. 924)
Six or more authors	*First and subsequent references:* (Williamson et al., 2004, p. 23)
Multiple sources in same reference	(Thames & Cain, 2008; Young, Morales, & Cato, 2009; Yu, 2004) *The semicolon divides the sources.*
Two or more works by the same author	(Tufte, 2001, p. 23) and (Tufte, 2003) *The author's name is used with the date.*
Two or more works by the same author in the same year	(Tufte, 2001a, p. 23) and (Tufte, 2001b, p. 11) *The "a" and "b" signal two different works and will appear in the list of references also.*
Different authors with the same last name	(M. Smith, 2005, p. 54) and (A. Smith, 2007, p. 34) *The first letters abbreviate each author's first name.*
Corporate author	(National Aeronautics and Space Administration [NASA], 2009, p. 12) or (American Beef Association, 2006, p. 232) *Well-known acronyms, such as NASA, can be put in brackets the first time and then used in any following parenthetical references.* (NASA, 2009, p. 14)
No author for book	(*Handling Bulimia*, 2004, p. 45) *Use the full title of the source in italics.*
No author for journal article or newspaper article	("Genomics as the New Frontier," 2008, p. 23) *Put the full title in quotation marks.*
No author for newspaper article	("Recession," 2009, p. A4) *The letter "A" is the section of the newspaper and the number is the page.*
Cited in another source	(as cited in Franks, 2007, p. 94)
Web page or other document with no pagination	(Reynolds, 2006, para. 3) *"para." stands for "paragraph," as counted down from the top of the page.*
Web page or other document with no author and no pagination	("Friendly," 2008, para. 7) *Put the first prominent word in the title in quotes, with "para." standing for "paragraph," as counted down from the top of the page.*

FIGURE 19.1
Types of APA Parenthetical References
Not all possible parenthetical references are shown here. If you have a source that doesn't fit these examples, you can usually figure out how to cite it by combining reference models.

VAMPIRES IN HOLLYWOOD   12
                              References
Arthen, I. (2005, December 9). Real vampires. *FireHeart, 2.*
        Retrieved from http://www.earthspirit.com/fireheart
        /fhvampire.html
Barber, P. (1989). *Vampires, burial, and death.* New Haven, CT: Yale
        University Press.
Bluestein, G. (1994). *Poplore: Folk and pop in American culture.*
        Amherst, MA: University of Massachusetts Press.
Keyworth, D. (2006). Was the vampire of the eighteenth century a
        unique type of undead corpse? *Folklore, 117*(3), 1–16.

FIGURE 19.2
Formatting a List of References
The APA *Publication Manual* specifies that the heading "References" be centered on the page. The margins should be one inch on all sides. The entries should be double spaced.

Only sources you reference in your document should appear in your References. The reference list is not a bibliography of all the sources you found on your topic.

In a reference list, the entries are listed in alphabetical order, by the authors' last names. When an author's name is not known, the work is alphabetized by the first prominent word in its title. When alphabetizing, ignore *The, A,* or *An* if it is the first word in the title.

If you are listing two works by the same author in the same year, they should be alphabetized by the first prominent words in their titles and then distinguished by "a," "b," "c," and so on (e.g., 2007a, 2007b, 2007c).

Formatting a List of References in APA Style

Start the reference list on a new page with the centered heading "References" at the top (Figure 19.2). Entries are then listed double spaced, in hanging indent format, which means the first line of each entry is not indented, but the rest are indented a half inch.

In workplace texts, however, your reference list should match the design of your document. The "References" heading should be consistent with other headings. If you are single spacing the rest of your document, the reference list should be single-spaced, too, perhaps with spaces between entries.

Citing Sources in the List of References

The following list is not comprehensive. However, we have included models of the most common kinds of entries in a reference list. You can use these examples as models for your own citations. If you do not find a model for a source, you should turn to the APA's *Publication Manual,* 6th ed. (2010).

Author   Title   Publication   Online Source

APA List of References

Books and Other Nonperiodical Publications

1. Book, One Author
2. Book, Two Authors
3. Book, Three or More Authors
4. Book, Corporate or Organization Author
5. Book, Edited Collection
6. Book, Translated
7. Book, Author Unknown
8. Book, Second Edition or Beyond
9. Book, Dissertation or Thesis
10. Book, in Electronic Form
11. Document, Government Publication
12. Document, Pamphlet

Journals, Magazines, and Other Periodical Publications

13. Article, Journal with Continuous Pagination
14. Article, Journal without Continuous Pagination
15. Article, Edited Book
16. Article, Magazine
17. Article, Newspaper
18. Article, Author Unknown
19. Article, CD-ROM
20. Review

Web Publications

21. Website, Corporate Author
22. Website, Author Unknown
23. Article from an Online Periodical
24. Scholarly Journal Article with a Digital Object Identifier (DOI)
25. Scholarly Journal Article
26. Podcast

Other Kinds of Sources

27. Film or Video Recording
28. Television or Radio Program
29. Song or Recording
30. CD-ROM
31. Personal Correspondence, E-Mail, or Interview

Citing Books and Other Nonperiodical Publications

A book citation will have most of the following features:

1. Name of the author, corporation, or editor with last name first (include "(Ed.)" or "(Eds.)" if the work is listed by editor)

2. Year the work was published, in parentheses (if unknown, use "n.d." for "no date")

3. Title of the work, in italics (capitalize only first word, proper nouns, and any word that follows a colon)

4. City and state or country in which the work was published (use standard U.S. Postal Service abbreviations for states; spell out the full names of countries outside the United States)

5. Publisher

   ①   ②   ③   ④

Author. (Year of publication). *Title of work.* City and state (or country) of
                                    ⑤

publication: Publisher.

1. Book, One Author

Jones, S. (2001). *Darwin's ghost: The origin of species updated.* New York, NY: Ballantine Books.

2. Book, Two Authors

Pauling, L., & Wilson, E. B. (1935). *Introduction to quantum mechanics.* New York, NY: Dover.

3. Book, Three or More Authors

Newnan, D. G., Eschenbach, T. G., & Lavelle, J. P. (2008). *Engineering economic analysis* (10th ed.). Oxford, England: Oxford University Press.

4. Book, Corporate or Organization Author

American Psychiatric Association. (1994). *Diagnostic and statistical manual of mental disorders* (4th ed.). Washington, DC: Author.

5. Book, Edited Collection

Mueller-Vollmer, K. (Ed.). (1990). *The hermeneutics reader.* New York, NY: Continuum.

6. Book, Translated

Habermas, J. (1979). *Communication and the evolution of society* (T. McCarthy, Trans.). Boston, MA: Beacon Press.

7. Book, Author Unknown

Handbook for the WorkPad c3 PC Companion. (2000). Thornwood, NY: IBM.

8. Book, Second Edition or Beyond

Williams, R., & Tollet, J. (2008). *The non-designer's web book* (3rd ed.). Berkeley, CA: Peachpit.

9. Book, Dissertation or Thesis

Simms, L. (2002). *The Hampton effect in fringe desert environments: An ecosystem under stress* (Unpublished doctoral dissertation). University of New Mexico.

10. Book, in Electronic Form

Darwin, C. (1862). *On the various contrivances by which British and foreign orchids are fertilised by insects.* London, England: John Murray. Retrieved from http://pages.britishlibrary.net/charles.darwin3/orchids /orchids_fm.htm

11. Document, Government Publication

Greene, L. W. (1985). *Exile in paradise: The isolation of Hawaii's leprosy victims and development of Kalaupapa settlement, 1865 to present.* Washington, DC: U.S. Department of the Interior, National Park Service.

12. Document, Pamphlet

The Colorado Health Network. (2002). *Exploring high altitude areas.* Denver, CO: Author.

Citing Journals, Magazines, and Other Periodical Publications

A citation for a journal, magazine, or other periodical publication includes the following features:

1. Name of the author, corporation, or editor; last name first, followed by initial of first name and any middle initials

2. Date of publication (year for scholarly journal; year, month, day for other periodicals)

3. Title of the work, not enclosed in quotation marks (capitalize only first word, proper nouns, and any word that follows a colon)

4. Title of the periodical in italics (capitalize all significant words)

5. Volume number (italicized) and issue number (not italicized, but enclosed in parentheses). If each issue begins with page 1, include the issue number.

6. Range of page numbers for whole article

①   ②   ③   ④   ⑤

Author. (Date of publication). Title of article. *Title of Journal, volume number*

⑥   ⑦

(issue number), page numbers.

13. Article, Journal with Continuous Pagination

Boren, M. T., & Ramey, J. (1996). Thinking aloud: Reconciling theory and practice. *IEEE Transactions on Professional Communication, 39,* 49–57.

14. Article, Journal without Continuous Pagination

Kadlecek, M. (1991). Global climate change could threaten U.S. wildlife. *Conservationist, 46*(1), 54–55.

15. Article, Edited Book

Katz, S. B., & Miller, C. R. (1996). The low-level radioactive waste siting controversy in North Carolina: Toward a rhetorical model of risk communication. In C. Herndl & S. C. Brown (Eds.), *Green culture: Environmental rhetoric in contemporary America* (pp. 111–140). Madison, WI: University of Wisconsin Press.

16. Article, Magazine

Appenzeller, T. (2008, February). The case of the missing carbon. *National Geographic,* 88–118.

17. Article, Newspaper

Hall, C. (2002, November 18). Shortage of human capital envisioned, Monster's Taylor sees worker need. *Chicago Tribune,* p. E7.

18. Article, Author Unknown

The big chill leaves bruises. (2004, January 17). *Albuquerque Tribune,* p. A4.

Author Title Publication Online Source

A citation for a Web publication will have most or all of the following features:

① Name of the author, corporation, organization, editor, or webmaster. For authors and editors, last name first followed by initials.

② Date of publication, in parentheses (year, month, date). If no date is given, write (n.d.) to indicate "no date."

③ Title of the individual page, document, or article.

④ Title of the website, in italics.

⑤ Retrieval information: the site's URL; the date retrieved (include only if the source could change, e.g., a corporate website or wiki); do not add a period at the end of the URL.

①　　　　　　②　　　　　　③　　　　　④
Author of website. (Date published). Title of document or *Title of page*. *Title of Overall website*.
⑤
Retrieved (month date, year) from URL

①　　　　　　　　　　　　　　　②　　　　③
Pueblo Grande Museum and Archaeological Park. (n.d.). *Doorways to the past: Hohokam Houses.*
④　　　　⑤
City of Phoenix. Retrieved April 9, 2009, from http://phoenix.gov/PUEBLO/exhouses.html

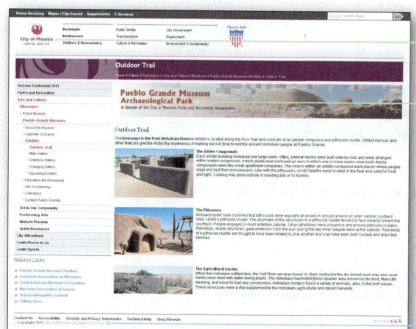

② Date of publication
④ Title of website

⑤ Date retrieved and URL
③ Title of page

① Author (organization)

FIGURE 19.3 CITATION MAP: Citing Part or All of a Website

An article with a DOI retrieved from a database does not require either the database name or retrieval date. A citation for such an article needs to include the following features:

① Name of the author (last name, initials)

② Publication date

③ Title of article

④ Title of the journal in italics

⑤ Volume number in italics, and issue number (in parentheses, not italicized)

⑥ Page numbers

⑦ Digital Object Identifier. (It is easiest to cut and paste the DOI directly from the original document into your text.)

        ①   ②   ③   ④   ⑤

Author of article. (Publication date). Title of article. *Title of Journal, volume number*(issue number),

     ⑥   ⑦

page numbers. DOI

      ①   ②   ③

Pyles, L., & Cross, T. (2008). Community revitalization in post-Katrina New Orleans: A critical analysis of

                                 ④   ⑤

social capital in an African American neighborhood. *Journal of Community Practice, 16*(4),

     ⑥   ⑦

383–401. doi:10.1080/10705420802475050

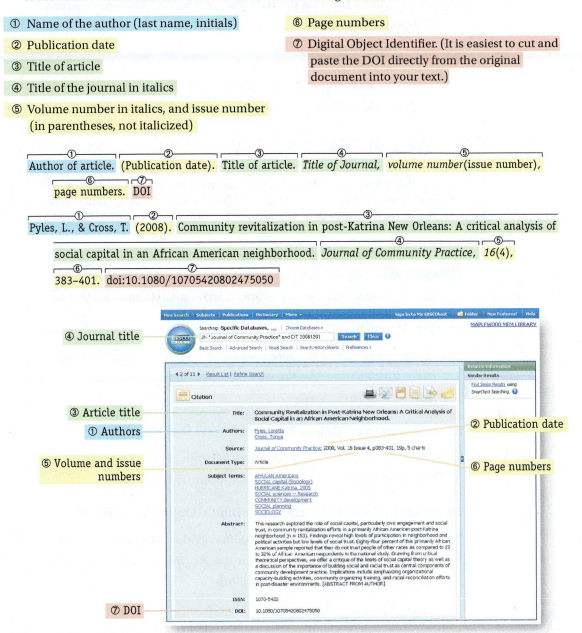

④ Journal title

③ Article title

① Authors

⑤ Volume and issue numbers

② Publication date

⑥ Page numbers

⑦ DOI

FIGURE 19.4 CITATION MAP: Citing a Journal Article with a DOI

Author Title Publication Online Source

19. Article, CD-ROM

Hanford, P. (2001). Locating the right job for you. *The electronic job finder* [CD-ROM]. San Francisco, CA: Career Masters.

20. Review

Leonhardt, D. (2008, November 30). Chance and circumstance [Review of the book *Outliers*, by M. Gladwell]. *New York Times, Book Review.*

Citing Web Publications

Citations for Web documents do not need to include your date of access if you can provide a publication date. However, you do need to provide either the URL from which a source was retrieved or a Digital Object Identifier (DOI). When you need to break a URL or DOI, always do it *before* a slash, period, or other punctuation mark.

21. Website, Corporate Author

U.S. Fish and Wildlife Service. (2008). *Estuary restoration act of 2000.* Retrieved from http://www.fws.gov/coastal/estuaryRestorationAct.html

22. Website, Author Unknown

Clara Barton: Founder of the American Red Cross. (n.d.). *American Red Cross Museum.* Retrieved from http://www.redcross.org/museum /history/claraBarton.asp

23. Article from an Online Periodical

Vaitheeswaran, V. (2009, April 16). Medicine goes digital. *The Economist.* Retrieved from http://www.economist.com/specialreports

24. Scholarly Journal Article with a Digital Object Identifier (DOI)

Blake, H., & Ooten, M. (2008). Bridging the divide: Connecting feminist histories and activism in the classroom. *Radical History Review, (102)*, 63–72. doi:10.1215/01636545-2008-013

25. Scholarly Journal Article

The APA no longer requires you to include the name of a database from which you retrieve a journal article. Use the DOI, if available, for such an article.

Ankers, D., & Jones, S. H. (2009). Objective assessment of circadian activity
and sleep patterns in individuals at behavioural risk of hypomania.
Journal of Clinical Psychology, 65, 1071–1086. doi:10.1002/jclp.20608

26. Podcast

Root, B. (2009, January 27). *Just one more book* [Podcast]. Retrieved from
http://www.justonemorebook.com/2009/01/27/interview-with-neil
-gaiman

Citing Other Kinds of Sources

A variety of other sources is available, each with its own citation style. The citations
for these sources tend to include most of the following information:

1. Name of the producers, writers, or directors with their roles identified in parentheses (Producer, Writer, Director)
2. Year of release or broadcast, in parentheses
3. Title of the work (italics for a complete work; no italics for a work that is a segment, episode, or part of a whole)
4. Name of episode (first letter of first word capitalized)
5. Title of the program (italicized)
6. Type of program (in brackets), e.g., [Film], [Television series], [Song]
7. City and state or country where work was produced
8. Distributor of the work (e.g., HBO, Miramax, New Line)
9. Retrieval information, for works accessed online

27. Film or Video Recording

Osborne, B., Walsh, F., and Sanders, T. (Producers), & Jackson, P. (Director).
(2002). *The lord of the rings: The fellowship of the ring* [Motion picture].
Hollywood, CA: New Line.

28. Television or Radio Program

Paley, V. (Writer). (2009). Human nature, the view from kindergarten [Radio
series episode]. In I. Glass (Producer), *This American Life.* Chicago, IL:
WBEZ/Chicago Public Radio.

29. Song or Recording

Myer, L. (1993). Sometimes alone. On *Flatlands* [CD]. Ames, IA: People's
    Productions.

30. CD-ROM

Geritch, T. (2000). *Masters of renaissance art* [CD-ROM]. Chicago, IL:
    Revival Productions.

31. Personal Correspondence, E-Mail, or Interview

Personal correspondence is not listed in the reference list. Instead, the information from the correspondence should be given in the parenthetical citation:

This result was confirmed by J. Baca (personal communication, March 4, 2004).

A Student's APA-Style Research Paper

The document shown here uses APA style for parenthetical citations and the References list. The student writer followed the professor's requirements for formatting his paper; formatting guidelines in the APA *Publication Manual* are intended for submissions to professional journals.

A header with an
abbreviated title
and page number is
included on all pages.

RUNNING HEAD: HEALTHY FAST FOOD   1

Healthy Fast Food: A Fast Food Revolution

Caitlin K. Foley

La Salle University

Throughout the last two decades, America has transformed into a very fast-paced society where people are constantly on the go. With this transformation came the well-known and very popular option of dining at fast food restaurants. Although these restaurants provide the convenience of quick and cheap food, there are many negative consequences that result from eating fast food, such as a lack of good nutrition. Fast food restaurants came up with "healthy" options that were still able to be served quickly and cheaply, but these options were not truly better for the consumer. New restaurants serving truly healthy food started appearing all over the country, but not many were able to incorporate reasonably priced, fast, and healthy food. More recently, this new concept of healthy fast food has begun to successfully reach the same goals as typical fast food restaurants. By changing various factors such as cost, quality, and convenience of fast food, false health claims, and advertisements towards children, healthy fast food restaurants have the potential to become as prevalent in consumers' lives as regular fast food chains.

Distinctions between Typical Fast Food and Healthy Fast Food

For the purposes of my research, typical fast food is defined as food that is cooked in unhealthy oils to produce greasy and fattening foods. More often than not, food served from typical fast food restaurants like McDonald's and Burger King is very high in calories and prepared in a way that allows for quick service. On the other hand, healthy fast food restaurants can be described as serving nutritionally beneficial food that has not been cooked in fats or oils. Ingredients added to the food are often low-calorie and are real ingredients rather than artificial ingredients filled with preservatives and chemicals. Healthy fast food, although currently rare, may have the same convenience factor as typical fast food restaurants such as quick service and a drive thru option; however, this industry is known as being a little more costly. While typical fast food restaurants are

Main headings are centered and boldfaced, using both uppercase and lowercase letters.

The author defines major terms that will be used throughout the essay.

Fig. 1   Simple secrets to portion control and healthy eating. Most Americans struggle with choosing between healthy, "bland" food and "tastier," albeit unhealthy fast food.

beginning to attempt to transform into something with a healthier image, a clear distinction between the two industries does still exist.

Typical fast food restaurants have always had the advantage of providing cheap food for their customers—a contributing factor to the success of the business. America's current economic crisis has created a society of people who now may be living paycheck to paycheck and having to make many difficult financial decisions. Various aspects of peoples' lives have been affected and altered, including budgets available for food each day. This crisis, along with the surrounding fast-paced society, has made Americans more conscious of what they are spending each day on food. Fast food restaurants have been able to fulfill that financial need by providing fast and cheap food for customers. However, with the always-present pressure surrounding people to be healthy and to make healthy eating choices, many Americans face the dilemma of cheap, unhealthy food and supposedly more expensive, healthy food.

Cost and Quality of Fast Food

The question then comes up of whether restaurants are able to make truly healthy food options inexpensive and of good quality. A healthy fast food restaurant owner, Bryn Davis of BRYN and DANE'S, believes Americans are no longer making cost-sensitive purchases despite the current economic situation. People have become so linked to brands and make purchases that are essentially investments for their future, or in this case, an investment towards health (B. Davis, personal communication, April 1, 2013). Davis believes in the importance of ensuring that good quality food is being served and an extra cost will not outweigh the benefits of eating healthy. Much like Davis, Mark Bittman, Writing in *The New York Times*, talked about his personal experience with healthy fast food and expressed his willingness to spend a few extra dollars for healthier food. Bittman's (2013) vision of a healthy food restaurant is "a place where something like a black-bean burger piled with vegetables and baked sweet potato fries—and, hell, maybe even a vegan shake—is less than 10 bucks and 800 calories (and way fewer without the shake)" (para. 5). As long as good quality food is being presented to the consumers, many may be willing to pay a few extra dollars for that meal. Given this set of standards, healthy fast food restaurants have the potential to become prevalent in people's lives despite added costs that may come along with eating at these restaurants.

Convenience and Quality of Fast Food

The quality of convenience for fast food restaurants is another major component that draws many people to choose unhealthy fast food rather than healthy food. Researchers and business owners have questioned

While cited parenthetically, personal communication is not included in the reference list.

When the author's name appears in the sentence, only the year is parenthetically cited, and the page number is cited at the end of the sentence. When no page number is available, use the paragraph in which the quote can be found.

why there are so few healthy fast food restaurants currently in America. One theory as explained by Joyce Slaton (2011) suggests that healthy restaurants are unable to keep up with the well-known speed that is provided for customers when ordering through a fast food drive thru. Healthy fast food restaurants have adapted to cooking as quickly as they can with the belief that food can be served within anywhere from three and a half to four minutes (Slaton, 2011, para. 12). Similarly, Davis has adapted his business to work under these same goals. The main location of BRYN and DANE'S in Horsham, Pennsylvania, has a drive thru, providing customers with the fast food experience and serving truly healthy food. Having personally worked in the drive thru at BRYN and DANE'S, I know that healthy fast food is definitely possible and successful because of the way Davis has revolutionized Horsham, Pennsylvania.

> When it would be unclear what source is cited, the author's name is included in the parenthetical citation.

False Health Claims of Fast Food

Although cost is a large factor in the fast food industry today, health claims made by the industry also appear to be of great importance for the decision of someone choosing between unhealthy fast food and healthy fast food. Recently, trends have shown that consumers tend to gravitate towards restaurants that claim to be serving lower calories and healthier foods. Studies have shown that "in the past 5 years, fast-food restaurants positioned as healthy (e.g., Subway) have grown at a much faster rate than those not making these claims (e.g., McDonald's)" (Chandton & Wansink, 2007, p. 301). Pierre Chandton and Brian Wansink (2007) argue that restaurants claiming to be healthy lead consumers to "underestimate the number of calories contained in their main dishes and order higher-calorie side dishes, drinks, or desserts" (p. 302). Together, these two aspects potentially lead to overeating at restaurants claiming to be healthy, which turns this idea of healthy fast food into something that may be harming the consumer.

> The findings of credible sources help the author make her point with greater authority.

Not only do health claims made by these restaurants often lead to overeating, they also attempt to convince customers that the food they are eating is both healthy and delicious. Stacey Finkelstein and Ayelet Fishbach (2010) believe that although "it is generally the case that people eat because they need to fulfill their appetite, another major goal many people hold when selecting food is to maintain good health" (p. 357). Rather than choosing food that would satisfy their appetite, people are forcing themselves to choose foods that follow the guidelines towards maintaining good health. In this situation, people experience a desire to eat healthy competing with a desire to fulfill their appetite. Furthermore, when consumers appear to be "giving the thumbs down to supposedly healthier choices [they] have clearly demonstrated they are unwilling to sacrifice taste—not even if the trade off results in improved health" ("McDonald's and Healthy Eating," 2005, p. 10). By making food both delicious and healthy, healthy fast food restaurants have the ability to overcome this concern that the consumers deal with every day and become more prevalent in each of their lives.

The Relationship between Fast Food and Children

Advertisements

The factors of fast food previously described typically affect the relation between teenagers and adults and the fast food industry; however, children are also directly affected by advertisements made by the industry. Throughout the last decade, America has come to realize the connection between the childhood obesity epidemic and fast food restaurants. Berg (2004) argues that the most influential culprit for the obesity epidemic stems from a combination of school and family eating habits. Because of these outside influences, the fast food industry has become conscious of the benefits from focusing advertising towards families with children. According to Kurtis Hiatt (2010), a writer for *U.S. News Health*, fast food

Use of multiple heading levels proves access points and makes the text easier to read.

Secondary headings are flush left and boldfaced, using both uppercase and lowercase letters.

advertisements towards children have intensified despite growing concerns of childhood obesity (para. 1). *Los Angeles Times* reported that in 2009, "preschoolers saw 21 percent more ads for McDonald's, 9 percent more ads for Burger King, and 56 percent more ads for Subway compared to 2007" (Hiatt, 2010, para. 1). Hiatt also points out that "exposure to these ads was even greater among kids ages 6 to 11… with black children seeing 50 percent more of these ads than whites" (para. 1).

Nutritional Standards

One of the biggest differences between restaurants like McDonald's and those like BRYN and DANE'S are the options offered to children that meet or do not meet nutritional standards. When menus at typical fast food restaurants were examined by Yale University's Rudd Center for Food Policy and Obesity, "just 12 of 3,039 meal combinations met the nutritional standards for preschoolers, and just 15 met the standards for older children" (Hiatt, 2010, para. 1). Although these restaurants do provide healthier meals and side dishes, those alternatives are very rarely offered as an alternative for children. Meals included French fries 86% of the time, and 55% of the time these meals included soda (Hiatt, 2010, para 1). Unlike typical fast food restaurants, BRYN and DANE'S do not offer items, that do not meet nutritional standards. Davis spends the time to research and make sure that all of the food offered at his restaurant is organic and locally produced. One of the biggest concerns for Davis is not only making sure he is able to provide his customers with a quality product, but also confirming that the customers know exactly what they are eating (B. Davis, personal communication, April 1, 2013). Therefore, if parents are convinced of the benefits of eating at a healthy fast food restaurant rather than McDonald's, they are more likely to make healthier choices when it comes to choosing what their children consume.

It is effective to include both paraphrases and direct quotations to demonstrate a solid understanding of sources.

HEALTHY FAST FOOD   8

Conclusion

Healthy fast food is a concept that continues to grow, and many, including myself, question whether healthy fast food outlets have the ability to incorporate themselves into the lives of people all over America. Although cost is one of the bigger concerns against this new concept, America has become a society that is very brand oriented, despite added costs. Unhealthy fast food restaurants also create health claims that convince customers that they are eating healthier food; however, truly healthy fast food restaurants ensure that customers are eating real ingredients. In addition, generating a target audience of more than just children allows healthy fast food restaurants to make a statement for themselves not only through television and magazines, but also via social media integration. By creating healthy fast food that proves to meet nutritional standards with the convenience factor of a drive thru, these restaurants are likely to become prevalent in people's lives. Like many other healthy food business owners, Davis has turned this concept into a way of thinking instead of just a restaurant. Davis states, "People want to feel part of something, a movement, and what better way to help with a campaign to help people eat healthy" (personal communication, April 1, 2013). Only time will determine whether healthy fast food will become a concept just as prevalent in people's lives as the current fast food industry.

Final analyses and conclusions are stated succinctly and prominently.

References begin
on a new page.
All cited works
are included
and listed in
alphabetical order
by author.

References

Berg, F. M. (2004). *Underage & overweight: America's childhood obesity crisis—what every family needs to know.* New York: Hatherleigh Press.

Bittman, M. (2013, April 3). Yes, healthful fast food is possible. But edible? Retrieved from http://www.nytimes.com/2013/04/07 /magazine/yes-healthful-fast-food-is-possible-but-edible .html?pagewanted=all&_r=0

Chandton, P., & Wansink, B. (2007). The biasing health halos of fast-food restaurant health claims: Lower calorie estimates and higher side-dish consumption intentions. *Journal of Consumer Research, 34*(3), 301–314. Retrieved from http://www.ejcr.org/

Finkelstein, S. R., & Fishbach, A. (2010). When healthy food makes you hungry. *Journal of Consumer Research, 37*(3), 357–367. doi:10.1086/652248

Hiatt, K. (2010). Health buzz: Fast food restaurants increase ads aimed at kids. Retrieved from http://health.usnews.com /health-news/diet-fitness/diet/articles/2010/11/08/health-buzz -fast-food-restaurants-increase-ads-aimed-at-kids

McDonald's and healthy eating. (2005). *Strategic Direction, 21*(4), 9–12. doi:10.1108/02580540510589639

Slaton, J. (2011). Where are the healthy drive-thrus? Retrieved from http://www.chow.com/food-news/71229/where-are-the-healthy -drive-thrus/

When the DOI of
an article is not
provided, use the URL
of the journal home
page.

The DOI is provided
whenever available,
even for print articles.

Style, Design and Medium

Why Adaptive Planning?

- Significant climate change impacts are projected, and impacts over the next few decades are virtually certain.

- Washington's residents, businesses, and local and state governments are on the "front line" for dealing with climate change.

- Decisions with long-term impacts are being made every day. Today's choices will shape tomorrow's vulnerabilities.

- Significant time is requi_____ ___te and develop adaptive capacity, and ___ _____ _anges.

- Proactive planning is/___ ____ ___ _stly than reactive plannin_ ___ _oday.

STYLE *allows you to argue with clarity and power. Design helps you present your argument in an accessible and attractive way.*

20 Arguing with Style

IN THIS CHAPTER, YOU WILL LEARN—

20.1 How to use good style to improve the clarity and power of your arguments

20.2 How to train yourself to write plainly while arguing

20.3 Techniques for using tropes and schemes to create an "elevated" style

20.1 How to use good style to improve the clarity and power of your arguments

Good style allows you to argue with clarity and power. Your style is the tone and voice your audience will hear as they read your text or listen to your presentation. Your style enhances the clarity of your argument, helping your good ideas shine through. Style is also the mental imagery and emotions your audience will experience as they consider your points and weigh the merits of your argument.

Style alone won't compel people to agree with you. In generative arguments, you still need to frame issues properly, build a sense of identity, tell interesting stories, and negotiate differences with your audience. In persuasive arguments, you still need use solid reasoning, good evidence, appeals to authority, and emotional appeals. But good style will help your audience better understand your argument and be more inclined to consider your point of view.

Some people mistakenly believe that style is something a person is born with. That's not true. Writing and speaking with good style are abilities that you can develop. In this chapter, you will learn how to argue in both the *plain style* and the *elevated style*. Choose the plain style when you want to present your ideas in a clear and straightforward way. The elevated style helps you capture and hold your audience's attention with color, imagery, sounds, and contrasts.

Using the Plain Style

20.2 How to train yourself to write plainly while arguing

Arguing plainly is harder than it looks, especially when you are discussing contentious issues with others. You have probably been advised to write concretely or speak clearly as though it was simply a matter of choosing to do so. Actually, writing and speaking clearly takes practice and awareness.

For the most part, plain style happens at the sentence level. If your sentences are straightforward and clear, chances are good your audience will understand what you are saying and what you are trying to accomplish. If your sentences are muddled or convoluted, your audience is likely to conclude that your thinking is muddled, too.

Here's how to write plainly. When you are drafting, just write down your ideas without worrying about how clearly you express them. Then, revise and edit at the sentence level to improve the clarity of your argument. When you come across a sentence that should be simpler, follow these six steps.

FIGURE 20.1 Practice Speaking Plainly with Your Friends and Family
Speaking plainly takes practice. You can work on speaking plainly when you discuss issues with your friends.

1. Find the action in the sentence and state it as a verb.

2. Put the "doer" of that action in the subject of the sentence.

3. Move the subject of the sentence (the doer) to an early place in the sentence.

4. Minimize the use of prepositional phrases.

5. Replace complex words with simpler, common words.

6. Make your sentences *breathing length*.

You can use these guidelines as a step-by-step method for revising your sentences to make them plain.[1] Let's look at each of these guidelines in more depth.

---

[1] These steps are a modified version of Richard Lanham's "paramedic method" that can be found in his book *Revising Prose* (20.06).

Step 1: Find the action in the sentence and state it as a verb.

Weak style often happens because the sentence's action is not expressed as a verb. As a result, readers struggle to understand what is happening and who is doing it.

> **Weak:** To make a determination about the vulnerability of archeological sites to thievery, it is important that an investigation be commissioned by the U.S. Interior Department.

> **Revised:** The U.S. Interior Department should **investigate** why archeological sites are vulnerable to thieves.

The meaning of the weak sentence is unclear because several words are competing to be the action of the sentence ("make," "determination," "investigation," "commissioned"). However, the actual verb in this weak sentence, "is," does not express an action. In the revised sentence, the action of the sentence, "investigate," is easy to find. Putting the action in the verb makes the sentence much easier to read.

Step 2: Put the "doer" of the action in the subject of the sentence.

When you have identified the action of the sentence, you can determine who or what is doing the action (the "doer"). Then make that doer the subject of the sentence.

> **Weak:** It is widely known that the political landscape experienced a significant alteration with the Supreme Court's *Citizens United* ruling, which removed almost all restrictions on independent campaign spending by corporations, unions, and individuals.

> **Revised:** The **Supreme Court** altered the political landscape significantly with the *Citizens United* ruling, which removed almost all restrictions on independent campaign spending by corporations, unions, and individuals.

In this revised sentence, the Supreme Court is doing the action ("altered").

Step 3: Move the subject of the sentence (the doer) to an early place in the sentence.

Introductory and transitional phrases are important and helpful in sentences. However, an excessively long introductory phrase makes the subject of the sentence difficult to locate.

> **Weak:** At the Seattle-Tacoma International Airport after being pursued for nearly three years by U.S. Immigration and Customs Enforcement, Harold Jenkins was finally arrested.

This sentence is difficult to understand because the readers need to hold all those details from the introductory phrase in mind until they arrive at the subject of the sentence (Harold Jenkins). You can easily revise this sentence to move the subject up front:

Revised: At the Seattle-Tacoma Airport, **Harold Jenkins** was finally arrested after being pursued for nearly three years by U.S. Immigration and Customs Enforcement.

Your subject does not need to appear first in the sentence, but it should be placed early where your readers can easily find it.

Step 4: Minimize the use of prepositional phrases.

Prepositional phrases begin with prepositions, such as "in," "of," "by," "about," "over," "under," "beneath," "during," "across," "after," or "until." These phrases can be useful when needed, but if they are used in excess or chained together, they can make sentences harder to read.

Here is an example sentence with too many prepositional phrases:

Weak: The total amount of debt for students to go to college is increasing at a rate that is alarming.

Let's reduce the number of prepositional phrases by turning them into adjectives and adverbs.

Revised: Total college student debt is increasing at an alarming rate.

By minimizing the prepositional phrases, you can make a sentence shorter and clearer.

Step 5: Replace complex words with simpler, common words.

In *Elements of Style*, Strunk and White famously advised, "Do not be tempted by a twenty-dollar word when there is a ten-center handy, ready and able. Anglo-Saxon is a livelier tongue than Latin, so use Anglo-Saxon words" (111–112). Most people can't tell Anglo-Saxon English words from Latin English words. Still, as Strunk and White advise, you should use simpler and common words when possible.

Complex words make your argument harder to understand. They can also make your argument sound stiff and stuffy. So, as you revise, look for complex words that could be replaced with simpler or more common words. Here are a few examples:

Complex Word	Simple Word	Complex Word	Simple Word
deceased	dead	inquire	ask
altercation	fight	witness	see
vehicle	car or truck	transport	drive or fly
commence	begin	laceration	cut or wound
utilize	use	contusion	bruise
individual	person	endeavor	try
purchase	buy	irritation	ache
reside	live	companion	friend or partner

Step 6: Make your sentences breathing length.

The punctuation mark "period" originally signaled "take a breath" when reading a text out loud. A sentence, therefore, should include only as many words as you can read out loud during a period of a breath. For example here is a passage with sentences that are longer than breathing length:

Too long: Though the legalization of marijuana for medicinal reasons is an issue largely ignored by politicians at the national level due to their fear of the political backlash from special-interest groups who use this bellwether issue as a way to label others as "weak on crime" or just "too liberal," a majority of Americans have begun to tell pollsters that they welcome the legalization of medicinal marijuana, and these poll numbers are climbing quickly, especially as Baby Boomers, who are more familiar with marijuana, become the elderly who are experiencing chronic pain.

Try reading the above sentence out loud. You will probably run out of breath about midway through, causing you to give up on it. Even when you are reading silently, this kind of sentence causes you to mentally gasp for breath. Don't asphyxiate your readers!

A sentence like this one can be carved into two or more sentences that are breathing length. Try reading this revision, paying attention to where each period calls for a breath:

Just right: The legalization of marijuana for medicinal reasons is an issue largely ignored by politicians at the national level. They still fear the political backlash from special-interest groups who use this bellwether issue as a way to label others "weak on crime" or just "too liberal." Recently, though, a majority of Americans have begun to tell pollsters that they welcome the legalization of medicinal marijuana. These poll numbers are climbing quickly as Baby Boomers, who are more familiar with marijuana, become the elderly who are experiencing chronic pain.

Sentences that are too short can be equally problematic for your readers. A series of short sentences signals that they should breathe quickly while they are reading:

Too short: The legalization of marijuana for medicinal reasons is an important issue. This issue is largely ignored by politicians at the national level. They still fear the political backlash from special-interest groups. These groups use this bellwether issue as a way to label others. They call them "weak on crime." They call them "too liberal." Recently, though, a majority of Americans have begun to tell pollsters something new. They welcome the legalization of medicinal marijuana. These poll numbers are climbing quickly. They are rising as Baby Boomers get older. Baby Boomers are more familiar with marijuana. Now they are becoming the elderly who are experiencing chronic pain.

Even if your readers aren't reading the text out loud, these short sentences give them the sense that they are breathing too fast. Don't hyperventilate your readers!

Using Elevated Style

The elevated style allows you to use imagery and the senses to illustrate important points while holding the audience's attention. Writing and speaking in the elevated style does not mean adding in extra adjectives or using fancy words. Instead, the elevated style uses rhetorical techniques called *tropes* and *schemes* to animate and energize your arguments.

Tropes and schemes are *figures of speech*. Tropes are words and phrases that are being used in unusual or unexpected ways. Meanwhile, schemes are used to arrange ideas into interesting patterns that highlight important ideas or use familiar words in intriguing new ways.

Tropes

The word "trope" means "turn" in Ancient Greek. You can use tropes to turn or twist the meanings of words and phrases in interesting and insightful ways. Most tropes are visual, which means they are used to bring images into the minds of the audience. A few are aural, which means they allow the audience to hear what you are describing.

Simile (X is like Y, or X is as Y)

A simile visually compares one thing to something quite different, usually highlighting their similarities.

> My softball team devoured the pizza like a pack of wolves.
>
> Her cat waddled across the room like a walrus.
>
> After lunch, students are as cerebral as well-fed zombies.

Similes are most useful for creating a brief image in the readers' minds. If you want, you can extend a simile for a few sentences:

> My softball team devoured the pizza like a pack of wolves. Frank and Gina were like pups tugging at a slice across the table. Bryan, behaving like a typical omega male, grabbed two pieces and scurried over to a corner. Valerie, the alpha female of the group, glared at Henry before taking a couple slices.

Extended similes are effective for a sentence or two, but you will annoy your audience if you extend a simile too far. They can get tiresome.

Metaphor (X is Y)

Metaphors look like similes, but they have much more power and often work at a deeper psychological level. A metaphor says one thing *is* something else, or it substitutes an unexpected word or phrase into a sentence.

> The depressed mind is a city of ruins. (Comparison: X is Y)
>
> While suffering from depression, she lived among the ruins of her once-happy memories. (Substitution)

There are three main types of metaphors: *novel metaphors, conceptual metaphors,* and *dead metaphors.*

Novel Metaphors

Novel Metaphors—Novel metaphors are new metaphors that you or someone else created to make a specific point.

> The library's Technology Center has been turned into a junkyard for obsolete computers.
>
> She divorced James in the sunset of her life.
>
> They tortured me with their painful lyric poetry.
>
> Sometimes college students just need to be college students.

Each of these new metaphors brings specific images to mind. The first example is a comparison metaphor, linking two dissimilar things ("Technology Center" and "junkyard"). The middle two are substitution metaphors in which an unexpected word ("sunset," "tortured") is substituted for an expected word or phrase ("end," "annoyed"). The last example is a metaphor that makes a trivially true statement ("college students are college students") that invites readers to come up with a deeper meaning than the one on the surface.

Conceptual Metaphors

Conceptual Metaphors—Conceptual metaphors are pre-existing in our culture and our ways of thinking. For example:

> *Thought is light*—He enlightened me. I was in the dark. I couldn't see what she was talking about. It suddenly dawned on them. I saw the light bulb go on when he figured it out. The dog seemed a bit dimwitted.
>
> *Time is money*—She spent a few minutes with me. He was wasting his time. I saved ten minutes by taking a shortcut. Time was precious to them. That mistake cost us five hours.
>
> *Life is travel*—She had a one-track mind. He took a detour instead of going to college. She reached a dead end in her career. When he started talking about marriage, I slammed the brakes on our relationship.

You will find that many of our everyday expressions are rooted in conceptual metaphors. These metaphors guide how we talk about our experiences and the reality around us.

You can use existing conceptual metaphors in your arguments, or you can work against them by calling attention to their inherent contradictions. For example, you can point out that *time* really isn't *money* and that *life* isn't really isn't *travel*. Working against conceptual metaphors is a good way to get people to reconsider things they believe to be true. Most "truths," when considered closely, are really just metaphors that have become part of our everyday lives.

Dead Metaphors

Dead Metaphors—Dead metaphors are expressions that are so common that they no longer seem like metaphors.

> The table was wobbly because one of its legs was too short.
>
> He ran the meeting.

The traffic slowed to a stop at the usual bottleneck.

He lent a hand to the project.

They watched the highlights of the game.

The government has three branches.

I didn't catch her name.

She faced her accusers.

Dead metaphors are so common that we don't even notice that we are using them. A fun thing to do with dead metaphors is "wake them up" by calling attention to them:

He didn't really run the meeting. He wandered through it.

The government may have three equal branches, but the Executive branch has grown far too large and needs some serious pruning.

I didn't catch her name, but I did catch her cold.

When you notice that you are using a dead metaphor in your writing, you might look for a way to wake it up in an ironic or humorous way.

Analogy (X is to Y as A is to B)

An analogy compares two items on parallel levels. For example,

Espresso is to coffee as rocket fuel is to gasoline.

If my ex-girlfriend, Sasha, was like a Cadillac, then my new girlfriend, Katie, is like a Cooper Mini.

The courier rode his bike through the city streets like kayaker paddling through whitewater rapids.

Analogies work much like similes. They offer a quick comparison that creates an image in the minds of the audience. An analogy can be extended beyond one sentence, but extended analogies (like extended similes) soon become tiresome to the audience.

Personification

Personification involves using human characteristics to describe something that is nonhuman:

The face of the stone building glared at us with its many dark windows.

The storm grumbled and groaned as it roamed through the valley.

The soccer ball screamed past my head.

The smaller trees stretched their arms upward, trying to push their leaves up into the sunlight.

When we brought home our new puppy, my five-year-old Labrador acted a like a faithful spouse who had been tossed aside for someone younger.

My dorm couch moaned in agony as my 350-pound father eased himself down for a nap.

Personification can be fun, because it allows you to animate some of the nonhuman features of a scene. But don't overdo it. If you animate too many parts of the scene, your argument will start to resemble a Disney-like cartoon fantasy.

 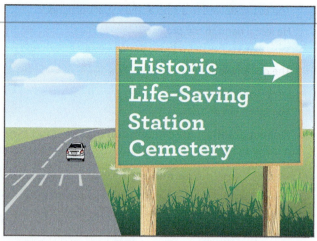

FIGURE 20.2 Accidental Oxymorons Can Be Embarrassing
When used properly, oxymorons can draw attention to inherent contradictions in words and idea. When used accidentally, they can be funny and embarrassing.

Oxymoron

An oxymoron puts two contradictory terms together. As shown in Figure 20.2, oxymorons can be confusing to the audience or even embarrassing to the speaker when used accidentally (e.g., *He was found missing. They were clearly misunderstood. Here's an exact estimate.*). When used intentionally, though, oxymorons can add humor or highlight a subtle point:

> That's when the anarchists started to get organized.
>
> She let out a silent scream.
>
> He gave a definite maybe when I asked him about going to the party.
>
> She's taking one of those so-called working vacations.
>
> Thank God I'm an atheist.
>
> After that quarrel, my roommate and I lived alone together in our dorm room.

You should only use an oxymoron when it is clear that you are doing so intentionally. Otherwise, your audience may think you are not aware of the contradiction in what you are saying.

Onomatopoeia

Onomatopoeia is an aural trope because it helps the audience *hear* what you are explaining or describing. Onomatopoeia involves using words that sound like the things you are describing.

> The tree branch snapped off and then splintered on the ground.
>
> The fire crackled late into the night.

They shuffled the deck of cards.

The speedboat roared by us.

She howled, "I can't take this any more!"

The plates clattered and crashed onto the floor.

The dog wriggled through the tiny opening.

The best time to use onomatopoeia is when you are trying to describe a scene in which sound is an important element. Onomatopoeia will allow your audience to actually hear the scene, not just visualize it.

Schemes

A scheme rearranges the words in a sentence to enhance their meaning or highlight the sentence in a way that grabs the audience's attention. Here are some schemes that you might find helpful.

Antithesis

An antithesis uses two contrasting terms or phrases to describe or explain something:

He wasn't a large man, but he wasn't small man either.

Arriving at college felt like a new beginning, but it also felt like an ending, too.

Would you rather live free as an entrepreneur or die in chains as a corporate employee?

He was good looking, but he wasn't good looking enough for Sally.

High school was the best of times and the worst of times.

Antithesis is a good way to describe something by not directly describing it. By using antithesis to mark the two ends of a range of descriptions, you encourage the audience to use their imagination to fill in the middle with their own description.

Anaphora

An anaphora is a repetition of a word or phrase, usually at the beginning of a series of sentences. Speakers often use anaphora to build up to a climax in their speech (Figure 20.3).

Winston Churchill, June 4, 1940—We shall go on to the end. We shall fight in France. We shall fight on the seas and oceans. We shall fight with growing confidence and growing strength in the air. We shall defend our island, whatever the cost may be. We shall fight on the beaches. We shall fight on the landing grounds. We shall fight in the fields and in the streets. We shall fight in the hills. We shall never surrender.

Martin Luther King, Jr., August 28, 1963—And so even though we face the difficulties of today and tomorrow, I still have a dream. It is a dream deeply rooted in the American dream. I have a dream that one day this nation will rise up and live

FIGURE 20.3 Using Anaphora
Great speakers like Winston Churchill and Martin Luther King, Jr. often use anaphora, the repetition of phrases, to build excitement in a speech.

out the true meaning of its creed: "We hold these truths to be self-evident, that all men are created equal." I have a dream that one day on the red hills of Georgia, the sons of former slaves and the sons of former slave owners will be able to sit down together at the table of brotherhood. I have a dream that one day even the state of Mississippi, a state sweltering with the heat of injustice, sweltering with the heat of oppression, will be transformed into an oasis of freedom and justice. I have a dream that my four little children will one day live in a nation where they will not be judged by the color of their skin but by the content of their character.

Rhetorical Questions

A rhetorical question asks a question that encourages the audience to consider the issue from a new point of view.

How many times have you heard the saying, people kill people, guns don't kill people?

When did Congress become a tribe of brainless zombies?

How much longer do we need to put up with this?

With so many beer ads aimed at college students, is it any wonder college students are so interested in buying the stuff?

How did this idiot ever get elected?

What does it take to become a millionaire?

The key to using a rhetorical question is to ensure that it cannot be answered with a yes or no answer. You also need to be clear that you aren't expecting the audience to actually supply an answer. A rhetorical question fails if the audience answers the question in a way that is opposite to the response you expected.

Alliteration and Assonance

Alliteration and assonance involve using words that have similar sounds. Alliteration is using words that start with the same consonant. In most cases the words are used next to each other in the sentence, but in some cases the words can be separated. Here are a few examples:

The dogs ran roughshod over the plants.

The telescope teetered on the tripod.

The rally cars revved their engines.

The shadow's appearance on the wall sent a shiver up my spine.

Assonance is the use of words that share a vowel sound:

They tried to light the fire.

They grumbled about her blunder.

Last summer was hot and obnoxious.

That's when I figured out that school was cool.

Alliteration and assonance have two effects on the audience. First, when people hear words that sound similar, the sentence feels more logical and meaningful to them. Second, the sounds themselves, whether they are sharp or soft, can be used to set a particular tone or mood. However, don't overdo the use of alliteration and assonance. Too many words that sound the same can make an argument seem silly or trivialize the subject.

Arguing with good style is a skill you can learn. Here's what you need to know.

1 Good style helps you argue with clarity and power.

2 Style is not something you have or don't have. It is a skill that you can develop.

3 Style alone won't persuade people, but it will enhance a well-reasoned argument.

4 To write in the plain style, revise and edit for clarity at the sentence level.

5 Writing plainly often involves figuring out the action of the sentence and moving the doer of that action to the subject of the sentence.

6 To write plainly, you should also minimize prepositional phrases, replace complex words with simpler words, and make your sentences breathing length.

7 The elevated style involves using tropes and schemes to animate and energize your arguments.

8 A trope, which means "turn" in ancient Greek, is used to turn or twist the meanings of words and phrases in interesting and insightful ways.

9 Tropes can be visual or aural.

10 A scheme arranges the words in a sentence in a way that enhances its meaning or highlights the sentence in a way that grabs the audience's attention.

1. With your group, come up with a list of three public figures who speak plainly and three people who don't. Divide your group into two teams. One team should look for clips of the plain speakers on YouTube or another video-sharing site, and one team should look for clips of the nonplain speakers. Using these clips, come up with a list of five characteristics of plain speaking. Then come up with a list of five characteristics of people who don't speak plainly. Share your lists with your group and then e-mail them to your instructor.

LET'S TALK ABOUT THIS

2. With your group, divide up the list of tropes and schemes discussed in this chapter. Then send each person to out to find three examples of each one. (It's cheating to look for examples by finding websites that discuss these tropes. Find your own examples!) Share these examples with the group and explain how they have an effect on the audience.

3. Ask each member of your group to find a "conceptual metaphor" that guides the way we think and talk about some aspect of reality. Your group should come up with several examples of how each conceptual metaphor is used in our culture. Then push the conceptual metaphor to its extremes. Where does the metaphor seem to break down? What kinds of strange conclusions can be drawn if you take the metaphor to its limits? Finally, think of alternative metaphors that would encourage people to see and discuss reality in a way that is different from this conceptual metaphor.

LET'S ARGUE ABOUT THIS

1. Occasionally, you will hear public figures arguing that government and industries need to adopt "plain speech" standards. Usually, these standards involve choosing words from a basic list of terms or only using a specific limit of words in each sentence. In an argument, explore the pros and cons of these kinds of plain-speech movements. What are some of the benefits of restricting vocabulary and the length of sentences? What are some of the problems with these kinds of limitations?

2. Identify a conceptual metaphor that is commonly used, such as "time is money" or "the body is a machine." Write an argument in which you challenge that metaphor and explain why it is problematic in our culture. For example, you could argue that viewing the human body as a machine (the heart is a pump, the brain is a computer, elbows are joints, etc.) can lead people to treat their bodies like they would treat a car or some other machine. In reality, though, the human body is not a machine. The mind is much more than electrical wiring, and we cannot simply replace parts when our bodies break down. Write an argument in which you challenge the assumptions and conclusions of the conceptual metaphor you choose.

3. Write a rhetorical analysis of an argument in which you concentrate exclusively on the author's use of tropes and schemes. Highlight the tropes and schemes and explain how the author uses them effectively (or ineffectively). Don't worry about whether you agree or disagree with the author's argument. In fact, you may find it easier to study the tropes and schemes in an argument that you disagree with because the figures of speech will be more obvious. Explain why you thought the use of elevated style was appropriate or in effective for the author's intended audience.

443

21 Designing Arguments

IN THIS CHAPTER, YOU WILL LEARN—

21.1 About the five basic principles of design

21.2 Strategies for adding photographs and images that support your argument

21.3 Techniques for using graphs and charts to illustrate data

Arguments are becoming increasingly visual and multimodal, especially with the rapid evolution of computers, tablets, and smartphones. Today, effective design is a must. It's not an add-on or a luxury. Your audience will expect your argument to use a practical and attractive page design while including images and color to catch their attention and help them locate the key information they need.

Most people, including you, won't willingly read a document or view a screen that consists of lifeless black-and-white blocks of paragraphs. Your argument's design needs to engage them and capture their attention. You need to present the information in an accessible and attractive way, while using images, illustrations, and graphics to reinforce and clarify what you mean. And, yes, your readers want your argument to look colorful and attractive, not bland and boring.

Arguments are also becoming *multimodal*, which means they give people multiple ways of interacting with the information. Increasingly, arguments will use a variety of "modalities," including words, images, voice, audio, video, and touch to reach their audiences. With multimodal arguments, the "users" of your argument will be able to choose how they want to interact with your text (Figure 21.1).

This trend toward the visual and multimodal will only expand as arguments are viewed more and more on screens rather than on paper.

FIGURE 21.1
Today's
Arguments Are
Increasingly
Visual and
Multimodal
Arguments are
becoming more
multimodal,
allowing users to
interact with the
information in
multiple ways.

21.1 About the five
basic principles of
design

Five Basic Principles of Design

Good design helps your audience see your document's organization by providing *access points* to help them locate the information they need. Here are five basic principles of design that will help you make your documents accessible and attractive:

1. **Balance.** Your text should look balanced from left to right and top to bottom.

2. **Alignment.** Related text and images should be aligned vertically on the page or screen to reveal the text's structure and its hierarchy of information.

3. **Grouping.** Related text and images should be placed near each other on the page or screen so the audience sees them as groups.

4. **Consistency.** Design features should be used consistently and predictably, helping the audience quickly grasp the layout of each page or screen and locate information.

5. **Contrast.** Items on the page or screen that are different should *look* significantly different. Contrast creates a feeling of boldness and confidence.

These five principles are based on the Gestalt theory of design, which is used by many graphic designers, clothing designers, architects, and artists. Once you learn these principles, you will find it easy—and even fun—to design your texts.

Design Principle 1: Balance

To balance a page or screen, imagine it has been placed on a point, like the tip of a pencil. Everything you add to the left side of the page needs to be balanced with something on the right. For example, if you add a picture to the left side, you might need to add a column of written text or perhaps another picture on the right.

Take a look at the page shown in Figure 21.2. The picture of the dog on the right has "weight." This image strongly attracts the readers' eyes, so to offset this photograph, the designers placed a column of text on the left. Meanwhile, the header at the top of the page balances the design from top to bottom, making the design feel stable and steady.

Balance is not a matter of making the page look symmetric (the same on the left and right). The items on the left and right of the page should balance, but they don't need to mirror each other.

Here are some guidelines for balancing a page or screen:

- Pictures weigh more than written text.

- Color items weigh more than black-and-white items.

- Big items weigh more than small ones.

- Strange shapes weigh more than familiar, standard shapes.

- Features on the right side of the page weigh more than features on the left.

- Features on the top of the page weigh more than features on the bottom.

- Moving features, like animations on a Web page, weigh more than static ones.

You can use these guidelines to help you balance any page or screen. Try moving items around on the page or screen to see how they look.

Design Principle 2: Alignment

Your readers will subconsciously search for visual relationships among items on the page or screen. If two items are aligned vertically or horizontally, your readers will assume that those two items are related in some way. If a picture, for example, is vertically aligned with a caption, list, or block of text on the page, readers will naturally assume that they go together.

For example, in Figure 21.3 (page 448), the absence of alignment means the page on the left gives no hint about the levels of information. This makes it difficult for readers to locate the information they are looking for. The page on the right, however, uses vertical alignment to make the levels obvious. The text on the right is easier to read because it visually reveals how the information is structured.

The colorful header and title balance with the bottom of the text.

Livestock and Wolves: A Guide to Nonlethal Tools and Methods to Reduce Conflicts

3. Working with Livestock Guarding Dogs

Livestock producers around the globe have long relied on dogs to protect livestock from carnivores such as wolves, bears and lions. In some instances, the mere presence of dogs seems to help keep wolves away from livestock; in other cases, dogs play a more active role by alerting herders to predators in the area.

The ability of a guarding dog to protect livestock is partly a result of genetics and careful breeding and partly a result of socialization and proper training. Over the centuries, people have selected the best working dogs for breeding purposes to pass along valuable traits to future generations. Dogs that harassed or harmed livestock were typically relieved of duty and not permitted to breed, thereby removing undesirable traits from the gene pool. Socializing and bonding guard dogs with livestock from a young age is a **crucial part of their training (see page 7). The climate and landscape** in which the dogs live, the distances they travel, the diseases they are exposed to and the food supply available to them also influence their behavior.

In North America, the use of livestock guarding dogs has been growing since the mid-1970s, mainly to protect sheep and goats from coyotes and domestic dogs. Great Pyrenees, Anatolian shepherds, Akbash and other breeds that have been used for centuries in Europe, Asia and Africa are now used to protect livestock throughout the United States and Canada.

Breeds that make good livestock guarding dogs are not the ones **that make good livestock herders. The two functions, guarding** and herding, are quite different, and the dogs that do best at each task have been bred for their specific tasks. In other words, border collies and Australian shepherds are born to herd; Great Pyrenees and Anatolian shepherds are born to guard.

How effective are livestock guarding dogs? Researchers at Hampshire College in Amherst, Massachusetts, the U.S. Fish and Wildlife Service's National Wildlife Research Center in Colorado and the United States Sheep Experiment Station in Idaho addressed this question by placing dogs on farms and ranches throughout the United States. Almost immediately, they received reports of fewer livestock losses from predators. Most of the cases studied focused on coyote attacks on sheep and goats, although other predators such as domestic dogs, mountain lions and wolves **were included. The researchers also looked at losses of other** livestock such as turkeys, llamas and ostriches.

The ability of livestock guarding dogs to protect cows from wolves in northern Minnesota and Michigan has also been tested, and some dogs demonstrated that, if managed correctly, they could be effective. Interviews with cattle ranchers in Kenya, Turkey and Italy also suggest that, if properly managed, livestock guarding dogs can play a valuable role in protecting against a wide variety of predators.

The picture of the dog balances with the written text on the left.

The Anatolian shepherd is one of several breeds developed to guard livestock.

Choosing and using guarding dogs

To determine if livestock guarding dogs would be a valuable aid for a specific livestock operation, consider your primary needs and how such a dog could fit into your current operation. Professionals at the U.S. Department of Agriculture, local agriculture extension agents, other livestock producers who work with livestock guarding dogs, and breeders and breed clubs can help you evaluate your situation and advise you on the selection and use of guardian dogs (see the Resource Directory for contact information.)

Selecting your pups from breeding stock that is doing what you want your dog to do is important. Pups learn from their mothers, so make sure she has the characteristics of a good livestock guarding dog. Base your selection on a dog's working potential, rather than the fact that it is registered and meets the breed's physical standards. Pups can learn behavior, but not all registered livestock guarding dogs have the instincts necessary to do well at the work **for which they were bred. The right livestock guarding dog for you** is the one that demonstrates the traits necessary to work well in your particular setting. Desirable livestock guarding dogs stay with their livestock and successfully defend them by alerting people to the presence of threatening predators. Ultimately, the best livestock

6

FIGURE 21.2 A Balanced Design

Balance creates a sense of order in documents. This page is balanced both left to right and top to bottom.

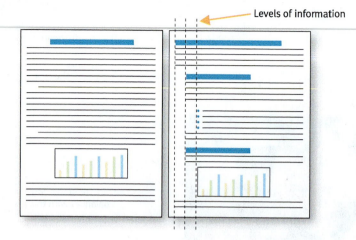

Levels of information

FIGURE 21.3 Using Vertical Alignment
Aligning text vertically allows you to show different levels of
information in the text, making the document easier to read and
scan. The page on the left is harder to read because it has minimal
alignment. The page on the right uses alignment to signal the
levels of information in the text.

To create vertical alignment in your page design:

- Use margins and indentation consistently to highlight the hierarchy of the information.

- Use bulleted lists or numbered lists whenever appropriate to set off related information from the main text.

- Adjust the placement of any photographs or graphics to align vertically with the text around them so readers see them as belonging together.

To check alignment on a page, use a straightedge, like a ruler or the edge of a piece of paper, to determine if items on the page line up. Another technique is the *squint test*. Squint as you are looking at the screen or page. Even though you cannot read the words, the structure of the document's design should be apparent.

Design Principle 3: Grouping

Readers assume that items placed close together belong to the same group. If a photograph appears near a block of text, your readers will naturally assume that the image and text are related. Similarly, if a heading appears near a block of written text, the readers will see the heading as belonging with that text.

Figure 21.4 shows a page design that uses grouping well. The green banner on the top of the page groups several text items together. It is also placed near the photograph, creating another group. The gray-shaded boxes form another group. Finally, the columns of text are naturally seen as a group, too, because they are so close together on the page.

A document's *white spaces* also play a key role in grouping. White spaces are the blank places on the page or screen in which no text or images appear. When areas are left blank, they frame graphics and written words. Look again at Figure 21.4. Notice how the white space on the page draws the readers' attention to the visual elements they frame.

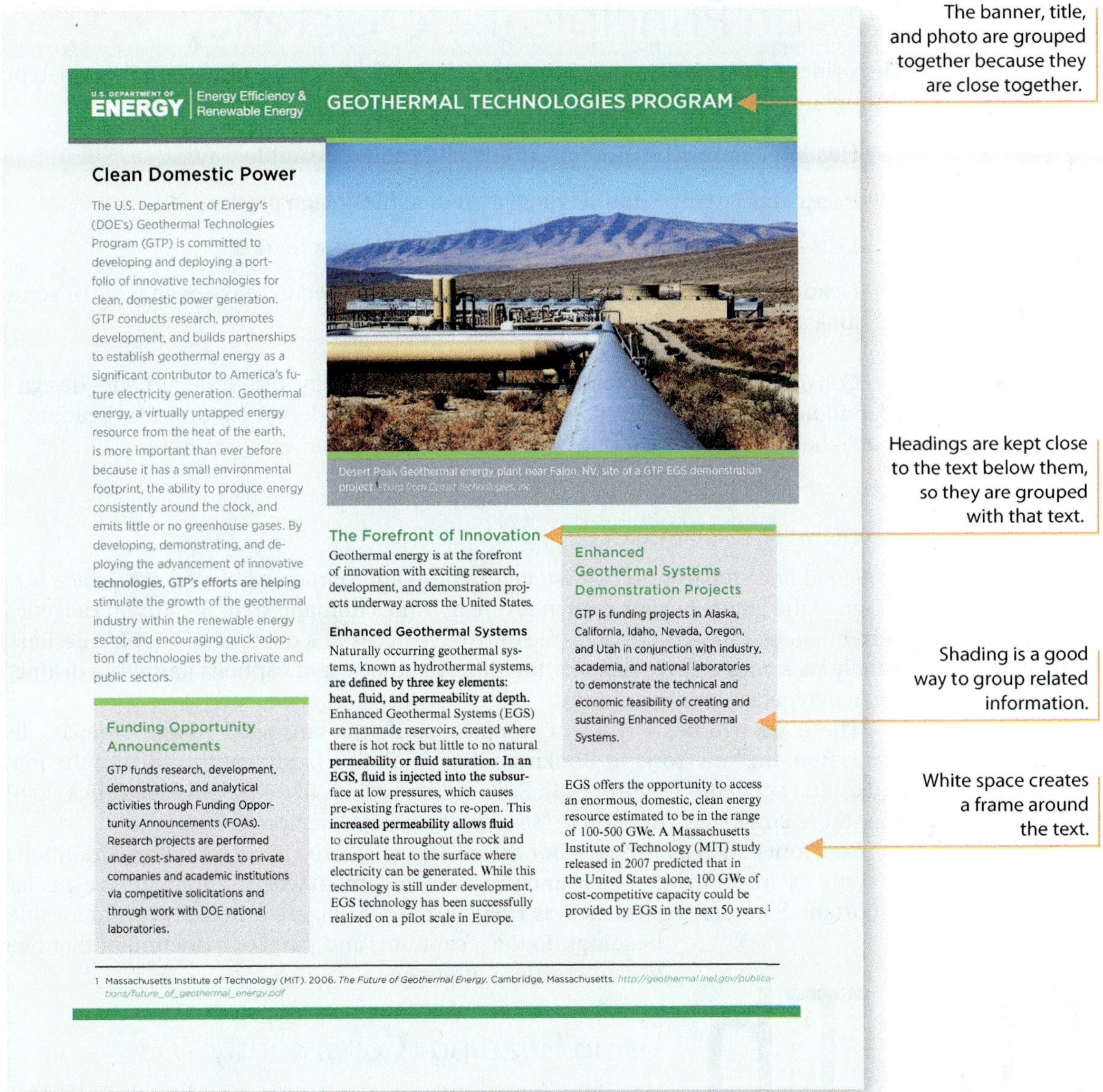

The banner, title, and photo are grouped together because they are close together.

U.S. DEPARTMENT OF ENERGY | Energy Efficiency & Renewable Energy

GEOTHERMAL TECHNOLOGIES PROGRAM

Clean Domestic Power

The U.S. Department of Energy's (DOE's) Geothermal Technologies Program (GTP) is committed to developing and deploying a portfolio of innovative technologies for clean, domestic power generation. GTP conducts research, promotes development, and builds partnerships to establish geothermal energy as a significant contributor to America's future electricity generation. Geothermal energy, a virtually untapped energy resource from the heat of the earth, is more important than ever before because it has a small environmental footprint, the ability to produce energy consistently around the clock, and emits little or no greenhouse gases. By developing, demonstrating, and deploying the advancement of innovative technologies, GTP's efforts are helping stimulate the growth of the geothermal industry within the renewable energy sector, and encouraging quick adoption of technologies by the private and public sectors.

Desert Peak Geothermal energy plant near Falon, NV, site of a GTP EGS demonstration project. *Photo from Ormat Technologies, Inc.*

Headings are kept close to the text below them, so they are grouped with that text.

The Forefront of Innovation

Geothermal energy is at the forefront of innovation with exciting research, development, and demonstration projects underway across the United States.

Enhanced Geothermal Systems

Naturally occurring geothermal systems, known as hydrothermal systems, are defined by three key elements: heat, fluid, and permeability at depth. Enhanced Geothermal Systems (EGS) are manmade reservoirs, created where there is hot rock but little to no natural permeability or fluid saturation. In an EGS, fluid is injected into the subsurface at low pressures, which causes pre-existing fractures to re-open. This **increased permeability allows fluid** to circulate throughout the rock and transport heat to the surface where electricity can be generated. While this technology is still under development, EGS technology has been successfully realized on a pilot scale in Europe.

Funding Opportunity Announcements

GTP funds research, development, demonstrations, and analytical activities through Funding Opportunity Announcements (FOAs). Research projects are performed under cost-shared awards to private companies and academic institutions via competitive solicitations and through work with DOE national laboratories.

Enhanced Geothermal Systems Demonstration Projects

GTP is funding projects in Alaska, California, Idaho, Nevada, Oregon, and Utah in conjunction with industry, academia, and national laboratories to demonstrate the technical and economic feasibility of creating and sustaining Enhanced Geothermal Systems.

EGS offers the opportunity to access an enormous, domestic, clean energy resource estimated to be in the range of 100-500 GWe. A Massachusetts Institute of Technology (MIT) study released in 2007 predicted that in the United States alone, 100 GWe of cost-competitive capacity could be provided by EGS in the next 50 years.[1]

Shading is a good way to group related information.

White space creates a frame around the text.

1 Massachusetts Institute of Technology (MIT). 2006. *The Future of Geothermal Energy.* Cambridge, Massachusetts. http://geothermal.inel.gov/publications/future_of_geothermal_energy.pdf

FIGURE 21.4 Using Grouping in Page Design
To group items on a page, you can put them near each other or use shading and colors to create relationships among them.
Source: U.S. Department of Energy, Geothermal Technologies Program.

Design Principle 4: Consistency

The principle of consistency means that design features should be used consistently throughout the document:

- Headings should be used in a predictable and repeatable way.

- Pages and screens should follow a predictable design pattern.

- Lists should use consistent bullets or numbering schemes.

- Headers, footers, and page numbers should be used to make each page or screen look similar (not identical) to the others.

Consistency creates a sense of order and predictability in your document's design so your audience knows what to expect. Consistent page-design features like headings or images help your audience readily understand your document's structure.

Choosing Consistent Typefaces

As a good first step toward consistency, choose appropriate typefaces. A typeface is the design of the letters in your written text (e.g., Times Roman, Arial, Bookman, Helvetica). Most often, you should use only one or two typefaces in a document. Graphic designers usually stick with one typeface for the titles, headings, and captions and use a distinctly different typeface for the main text.

There are two basic types of typeface: serif and sans serif. A serif typeface, like Times Roman, New York, or Bookman, has small tips (serifs) at the ends of the main strokes in each letter (Figure 21.5). Sans serif typefaces like Arial and Helvetica do not have these small tips. (In French, "sans serif" means "without serifs.")

Serif fonts, such as Times or Bookman, are considered more formal and traditional. They are useful for the main text and parts of a document where readability is especially important. Sans serif fonts, such as Helvetica and Arial, are especially useful for titles, headings, footers, captions, and parts of a document that need to catch readers' attention.

Serifs   Sans Serifs

FIGURE 21.5 Serif vs. Sans Serif Typefaces
Serif fonts, like Times Roman on the left, have serifs, while sans serif fonts, like Arial on the right, do not have them.

Using Headings Consistently

Headings are useful visual elements in any kind of document, but you need to use them consistently (Figure 21.6). Make some decisions up front about the levels of headings you will use.

Title

The title of the document should be sized significantly larger than other headings in the text. You might consider using color to set off the title, or you could center it.

First-Level Headings ("A Heads")

First-level headings divide your text into major sections. First-level headings are often bold and should be noticeably larger than the main text and lower-level headings.

Second-Level Headings ("B Heads")

Second-level headings divide large sections into smaller subsections. These headings tend to use italics and can be the same size as the body text.

Third-Level Headings ("C Heads")

Third-level headings should be the smallest level of headings. They are often italicized or boldfaced and placed on the same line as the body text.

Headings help your audience navigate your document. First, they offer access points into the argument, giving the audience obvious places to locate the information they need. Second, they highlight the structure of the argument, breaking down larger chunks of information into smaller blocks. Third, they give the audience places to take breaks from reading sentence after sentence, paragraph after paragraph.

Headings are also beneficial to you as the writer because they help you transition between sections of the document.

**Document Title:
The Best College Paper
Ever Written**

First-Level Headings

These "A heads" divide a document into its major sections. They are usually significantly larger and bolder and use a different font than the body text.

Second-Level Headings

These "B heads" divide sections into smaller subsections. While these use the same font as the first-level headings, they should differ significantly in size or style (such as italics).

Third-Level Headings. These "C heads" might be the same font and size as the body text (and appear on the same line), but use bold or italics to distinguish them.

FIGURE 21.6 Levels of Headings
Headings should be clearly distinguishable from the body text and from other heading levels. That way, your readers can clearly see the hierarchy of your text.

Design Principle 5: Contrast

The fifth and final design principle is *contrast*. Items that are different should look noticeably different. Your headings, for example, should look significantly different from the main text and from other heading levels.

You can create contrast by changing the size of the font or adding color, shading, and highlighting features like boldface, italics, or underlining. The sample report shown in Figure 21.7 (page 452) uses several of these contrast strategies.:

- With its white lettering and bold color, the green banner across the top, "U.S. Fish & Wildlife Service," clearly contrasts with the rest of the items on the page.

- The title, "Proposed Expansion of Conservation Easement Program," with its large and in a sans serif font, pops off the page and contrasts with the body text and the italics below it.

- Below the title, the italicized text contrasts sharply with the body text, helping it stand out on the page.

The green banner stands out against the lighter background.

This large, bold font makes the title "pop" from the page.

U.S. Fish & Wildlife Service

Proposed Expansion of Conservation Easement Program

Blackfoot Valley Wildlife Management Area

The U.S. Fish and Wildlife Service is proposing to protect one of the last undeveloped, low-elevation, river valley ecosystems in western Montana by expanding the existing boundary of the federally designated Blackfoot Valley Wildlife Management Area from 165,000 acres to 824,024 acres.

The federal Blackfoot Valley Wildlife Management Area ("Blackfoot Valley area") is managed through a conservation easement program where easements are purchased from willing sellers within the wildlife management area. Started in 1994, the purpose of the program is to protect a vital habitat corridor between federally protected lands, state wildlife management areas, waterfowl production areas, voluntary perpetual easements, and private lands that are part of Partners for Fish and Wildlife projects.

Expansion of the Blackfoot Valley area boundary and associated easement program would protect unique plant communities and help prevent the listing of several candidate species. The program would continue to complement other components of a broad partnership known as the "Blackfoot Challenge."

The Blackfoot Challenge is a landowner-based group that coordinates management of the Blackfoot River, its tributaries, and adjacent lands. Organized locally, the group is known nationally as a model for preserving the rural character and natural beauty of a watershed. Expansion of the easement program boundary for the Blackfoot Valley area supports the vision of the Blackfoot Challenge.

How would the conservation easement program work?

The proposed expansion encompasses an 824,024-acre ecosystem that includes portions of Missoula, Powell, and Lewis and Clark counties. The boundary expansion would provide opportunities for easement acquisition from willing sellers.

Conservation easements are voluntary legal agreements between landowners and government agencies or qualified conservation organizations. These easements limit the type and amount of development that may take place on a property in the future. Service easements are perpetual and typically prohibit subdivision and commercial development activities but allow for continued agricultural uses such as livestock grazing and haying. Conservation easements not only protect important wildlife habitat but also help maintain the working ranches and agricultural lifestyle of the area.

Under conservation easements, the land ownership and property rights including control of public access would remain with the participating landowner. In addition, participating properties remain on local tax rolls. Easement values are determined by appraisal and typically are about one-third of the property's full-market value.

The color in this image contrasts sharply with the black text.

FIGURE 21.7 Using Contrast
Contrast makes a page look more readable and attractive. This page uses several kinds of contrast to capture the readers' attention.

- The green heading, "How would the conservation easement program work," is clearly distinguishable from the body text because it is larger and uses color.

- The photo at the bottom of the page contrasts sharply with the black wording on most of the page.

You can experiment with contrast to make items stand out.

Using Photographs and Images

21.2 Strategies for adding photographs and images that support your argument

With today's computers, it's easy to add photographs and other images to your argument. You can use a digital camera or a mobile phone to take your own pictures. Then download these pictures and insert them into your document.

Downloading Photographs and Images from the Internet

You can also download photos and other images from the Internet. When you find an image that supports your argument, you can copy it or use your cursor to drag the image to your desktop. Then you can insert this file into your document.

Some good sources for photographs include Flickr.com, Photobucket.com, Google Images, and Zooomr.com. The Library of Congress (http://www.loc.gov) offers many historical pictures that you can use free of charge.

When using photographs and images from the Internet, remember that the majority of them are protected by copyright law. According to copyright law, you can use photographs and images for academic purposes. This is called "fair use." (Information about fair use and copyright law is available at the U.S. Copyright Office at copyright .gov). However, if you want to publish your argument or put it on the Internet, you will need to obtain permission to use the photograph or image from the person or organization that owns it. You can ask permission simply by sending an e-mail to the website's manager. Explain how you want to use the image, where it will appear, and how you will identify its source.

In most cases, the website owner will give you permission or explain how you can get permission. If the owner denies you permission or does not respond to your inquiry, you won't be able to use the photograph or image in any nonacademic way.

Labeling a Photograph or Image

Label each photograph or image by giving it a figure number and a title (Figure 21.8, page 454). The figure number should be mentioned in the written text so your readers know when to look for the photograph.

Captions are not mandatory, but they can reinforce an important point by explaining how the image relates to main text and what readers should notice about the image.

FIGURE 21.8
Labeling a
Photograph
Proper labeling
will help readers
understand how the
graphic supports the
written text.

Figure number
and title

▶ Fig. 2: A Gray Wolf

The Gray Wolf is one of the comeback success stories of the Endangered Species Act. In August 2012, it was "delisted" as an endangered species in Wyoming.

Caption and source
information

▶ *Source:* Hollingsworth, John and Karen Hollingsworth, U.S. Fish & Wildlife Serv., Jan. 2007; Web; Oct. 2012.

21.3 Techniques for
using graphs and charts
to illustrate data

Using Graphs and Charts

Graphs and charts are helpful for presenting data. They are especially common in genres like reports and proposals but are becoming increasingly common in all argument genres.

Creating a Graph or Chart

If you need to make your own graph or chart, your best option might be to use the spreadsheet program, such as Excel, Numbers, or Quattro Pro, that came bundled with your word-processing software (Figure 21.9). Less complex graphs can be made with presentation software, such as PowerPoint or Keynote.

These spreadsheet and presentation software packages can help you make graphs and charts quickly and easily. Then you can insert the graphic into your document. (Your word processor will probably have a Chart feature that connects you to the spreadsheet program.) Once you have created the graph, you should add a title and label the horizontal x-axis and vertical y-axis (Figure 21.9). These axes need to be clearly marked so readers know exactly what each axis signifies.

After you have inserted your graph or chart into your document, label it properly and cite the source of the data. To label the graphic, give it a number or letter and a title. For example, the graph in Figure 21.9 is called "Smokers in DuPage County." Finally, name your source below the graphic using a common citation style (e.g., MLA, APA).

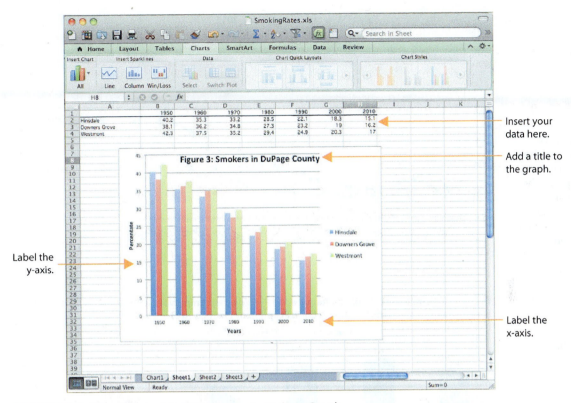

Insert your data here.

Add a title to the graph.

Label the y-axis.

Label the x-axis.

FIGURE 21.9 Using Spreadsheet Software to Make a Graph
A spreadsheet is a helpful tool for creating a graph. Enter your data and then click the graphing button to create a graph. Then you can insert the graph into your document.

In the written part of your document, refer to the graphic by its number so readers know when to consider it. When you want the readers to refer to the graphic, write something like, "As shown in Figure A, the local smoking rate…" Or, you can simply put "(Figure A)" at the end of the sentence where you refer to the graphic.

Choosing the Appropriate Graph or Chart

Various graphs and charts allow you to tell your story in different ways.

Line Graph

A line graph is a good way to show measurements or trends over time. In a line graph, the vertical axis (*y*-axis) displays a measured quantity, such as temperature, sales, growth, and so on. The horizontal axis (*x*-axis) is usually divided into time increments such as years, months, days, or hours. See Figure 21.10 (page 456).

Bar Chart

Bar charts are used to show quantities, helping readers to make visual comparisons among different amounts. Like line graphs, bar charts can be used to show changes in quantities over time. See Figure 21.11 (page 456).

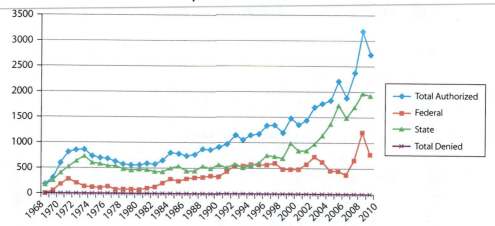

Title III Wiretap Orders 1968–2011

FIGURE 21.10
Line Graph
A line graph is a
good way to show
a trend over time.
In this graph, the
line reveals a trend
that would not be
apparent from the
data alone.

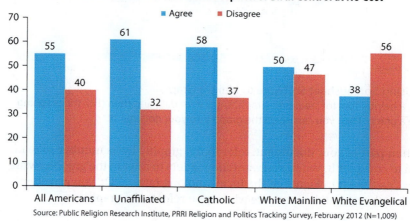

All Employers should be Required to Provide their Employees with Health Care Plans that Cover Contraception or Birth Control at No Cost

■ Agree   ■ Disagree

FIGURE 21.11
Bar Chart
A bar chart
allows you to
show quantities,
especially quantities
changing over time.

Source: Public Religion Research Institute, PRRI Religion and Politics Tracking Survey, February 2012 (N=1,009)

Pie Charts

Pie charts are useful for showing how a whole quantity is divided into parts. These charts are a quick way to add a visual element to your document, but they should be used sparingly. They take up a great amount of space but usually present only a small amount of data. See Figure 21.12.

Tables

A table is one of the most efficient ways to display data or facts. Information placed in horizontal rows and vertical columns allows readers to quickly locate specific numbers or words that address their interests (Figure 21.13).

Where Does My Money Go?

Annual Energy Bill for a typical Single Family Home is approximately $2,200.

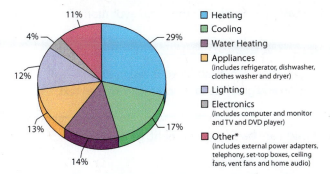

- 29%
- 17%
- 14%
- 13%
- 12%
- 4%
- 11%

- Heating
- Cooling
- Water Heating
- Appliances
  (includes refrigerator, dishwasher, clothes washer and dryer)
- Lighting
- Electronics
  (includes computer and monitor and TV and DVD player)
- Other*
  (includes external power adapters, telephony, set-top boxes, ceiling fans, vent fans and home audio)

FIGURE 21.12 Pie Chart
A pie chart is a good way to show how a whole is divided into parts. When using a pie chart, you should label the slices of the pie and add the numerical information that was used to create the chart.

	Asymmetry - Moles that, if divided in half are not the same on both sides.
	Border - Moles with edges that are jagged like a coastline.
	Colour - Moles gaining or losing colour, or multicoloured.
	Diameter - Moles more than 1/2 cm in diameter (*especially if uneven colour*).
	Evolution - Moles that have changed size, shape, colour or risen.

FIGURE 21.13 Table
A table offers a great way to present information efficiently. This table combines words and images to illustrate indicators of early-onset melanoma.

Diagrams

Diagrams are drawings that show features or relationships that might not be immediately apparent to the audience. The diagram in Figure 21.14, for example, shows the different parts of DNA. In reality, DNA does not look exactly like this colorful diagram, but the double-helix image helps the audience visualize how DNA is constructed.

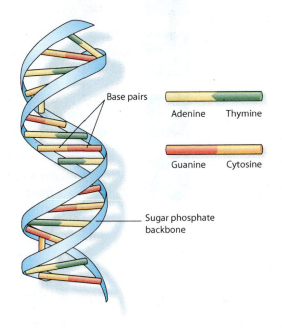

Base pairs

Adenine   Thymine

Guanine   Cytosine

Sugar phosphate backbone

FIGURE 21.14 A Diagram
A diagram is only partially realistic. It shows only the most important features and focuses on relationships instead of showing exactly what the subject looks like.

Don't design boring documents! Here's what you need to know about designing arguments:

1 Arguments have become increasingly visual with the rapid evolution of computers.

2 Before drafting any argument, you should think about your *design strategy*— how you will use document design and graphics to support your written text.

3 The five basic principles of design are balance, alignment, grouping, consistency, and contrast.

4 Balance involves placing visual elements on a page so that it feels balanced from side to side and top to bottom.

5 Alignment means lining up related items on a page so they are viewed as related to each other.

6 Grouping involves putting related items near each other so the audience will see them as a unit.

7 Consistency is the use of design features in a predictable and constant way.

8 Contrast means making different items on the page look significantly different.

9 To add photographs and images, you can make your own with a digital camera or mobile phone or download them from the Internet.

10 Graphs and charts can be especially helpful for presenting data in ways that illustrate trends or relationships.

1. Ask each member in your group to bring a favorite magazine to class. Discuss the magazine's full-page advertisements and how they use design features. Pay special attention to the use of balance, alignment, grouping, consistency, and contrast.

2. On campus or in the community, find a flyer or brochure that you think is unattractive or that fails to use good design. You can look on the corkboards that are probably on the walls in just about any building. With your group, discuss how you could do a makeover on this unattractive or badly designed document to make it more accessible and attractive.

3. Ask the members of your group to find and bring to class two graphs or charts from the Internet. Each member should find one graph that illustrates data in a fair and honest way and one that presents data in a distorted or manipulated way. With your group, make a list of five guidelines for identifying misleading graphs.

1. Write a brief rhetorical analysis of the visual elements of a poster you found on campus or at your workplace. In your analysis, use the five principles of design (balance, alignment, grouping, consistency, and contrast) to explain why you felt the poster's design was effective or ineffective.

2. Imagine a college writing course twenty years from now. As our society continues to evolve toward a visual and digital culture, how do you think the teaching of design will need to change? What kinds of training do you think will be needed for this new visual culture? To make room for this new training in a busy college semester, what aspects should be given less attention and time?

3. Make a visual argument on a topic of your choice. Collect a series of about twenty images or graphics that illustrate your views on this topic. Then add a one-sentence caption for each image or graphic that verbalizes your argument. You might find presentation software like PowerPoint, Keynote, or Prezi helpful for organizing the content and adding captions to your images.

22 Presenting Your Argument

IN THIS CHAPTER, YOU WILL LEARN—

22.1 How to plan out your presentation

22.2 Strategies for organizing the content of your presentation

22.3 Techniques for designing effective visual aids

22.4 How to deliver your presentation in a positive way

22.5 The importance of practicing and rehearsing your argument

The ability to present arguments clearly and persuasively has always been an important part of college and the workplace. The rise of new media, though, has only increased the importance of presenting your ideas effectively and persuasively. Today, video and audio applications like Skype, Facetime, Google Talk, GoToMeeting, and ooVoo give people the ability to collaborate in virtual teams and make video presentations long distance (Figure 22.1). Likewise, video-sharing websites, such as YouTube, Hulu, and Dailymotion, allow you archive and distribute presentations worldwide.

Meanwhile, the ability to speak in front of physical audiences is still important. Your professors will ask you to explain your research, exhibit your projects, and debate publicly with others. In your career, you will be asked to pitch new ideas, demonstrate products and services, and present your reports, proposals, and other arguments. Public speaking is an essential skill to master in just about any career.

FIGURE 22.1
New Media
Are Making
Presentations
More Common
The ability to
videoconference
through the
Internet means
presentations
are becoming
an everyday
experience.

You will need to make a few different types of presentations:

Lecture—a presentation that is typically made to a larger group of people, often followed by a question-and-answer session.

Demonstration—an exhibition in which products, services, or projects are explained to an audience.

Team meeting—a project-centered discussion in which team members briefly present new ideas, pitch projects, share information or opinions, and receive updates on individual progress.

Poster session—a showcase in which the speaker uses a large poster or three-panel display board to exhibit research, describe new ideas, or provide information.

In this chapter, you will learn some helpful strategies for turning your arguments into engaging, persuasive presentations.

Planning Your Presentation

22.1 How to plan out your presentation

As you begin planning your presentation, keep in mind that your audience doesn't want you to just read a document aloud. Instead, they want you to *perform* the material for them and *interact* with them.

Answer the Five W and How Questions

The Five-W and How questions are an easy and memorable way to begin the planning process. Ask yourself these kinds of questions:

- *What* do I want to accomplish with my presentation?

- *Who* will be in my audience and what do they need?

- *Why* am I presenting this information to this audience?

- *Where* will I be giving my presentation?

- *When* will I be asked to speak?

- *How* should I give the presentation?

You should answer these questions separately and in depth. Specifically, you want to figure out what your audience needs to know to make a decision or take action. In most cases, your original written argument will contain more information than the audience wants or needs. So you need to figure out how you can highlight the information your audience wants while trimming out any extraneous details that your audience doesn't need.

Choose the Appropriate Presentation Technology

The next stage in the planning process is to figure out which presentation technology would work best for your argument. As shown in Figure 22.2, a variety of presentation technologies are available, but each one has its advantages and disadvantages. You want to choose the technology that best fits your topic, purpose, audience, and the place in which you will give your presentation.

22.2 Strategies for organizing the content of your presentation

Organizing Your Presentation's Content

Your presentation should have a distinct beginning, middle, and end. These three parts might seem obvious, yet public speakers often forget one or more of them. They dive into the details without first identifying the topic or stating their purpose. Or, they end their presentation abruptly without a conclusion that restates their main point.

To help you remember to include all three parts, you can, memorize the well-worn speechmaking advice:

Tell them what you're going to tell them. Tell them. Tell them what you told them.

	Advantages	Disadvantages	Genres
 **Digital Projector**	• Can be dynamic and colorful • Allows for animation and sound • Creates a more formal atmosphere	• Requires a darkened room, which might inconvenience your audience • Diverts attention from the speaker to the screen • Computers are not completely reliable	Narratives Profiles Reviews Evaluations Proposals Rhetorical Analyses Commentaries Research Papers, and Reports
 **Overhead Projector**	• Projectors are available in most workplaces and classrooms • Easy to print transparencies from most home printers	• May seem static and lifeless • Need to manually change transparencies during your presentation	Evaluations Proposals Rhetorical Analyses Commentaries Research Papers and Reports
 **Whiteboard, Chalkboard, Notepad**	• Allows speaker to create visuals on the spot • Audience pays more attention because speaker is moving	• Cannot be used with a large audience • Writing on board requires extra time • Ideas need to be transferred clearly to the board	Evaluations Commentaries Position Papers Proposals Research Papers and Reports
 **Poster Presentation**	• Allows audience to see whole presentation • Presents highly technical information clearly • Allows audience to ask specific questions	• Cannot be presented to more than a few people at a time • Can be hard to transport	Narratives Descriptions Reviews Evaluations Proposals Rhetorical Analyses Commentaries Research Papers, and Reports
 **Handouts**	• Helps reinforce major points • Can offer more detail, data, and statistics • Audience has something to take home	• Handing them out can be distracting in large presentations • Audience members may read the handouts instead of pay attention to the talk	Reviews Evaluations Proposals Rhetorical Analyses Commentaries Research Papers, and Reports

FIGURE 22.2 Pros and Cons of Presentation Technologies

Each presentation technology has its strengths and weaknesses, depending on your audience and the place where you will give your presentation.

The Beginning: Tell Them What You're Going to Tell Them

A good introduction is an essential part of any presentation. At the beginning of your speech, you have a small window—perhaps a minute or two—to capture the audience's attention while stating your topic, purpose, and main point.

In your introduction, you should make some or all of the following moves:

Use a grabber to start your argument—Start out with an anecdote, rhetorical question, startling statistic, or a compelling statement. You can also ask for a show of hands, "Let's see a show of hands. Who thinks...?" *Note*: Starting with joke is risky because attempts to be funny often fall flat or offend people.

Identify your topic—Tell your audience what your presentation is about by identifying and defining your topic.

State the purpose of your presentation—In one sentence, explain what you are trying to achieve in your talk.

State your main point (thesis)—State the claim that you want to prove or support. You can also use a thesis question if you want to reveal your main point in the conclusion.

Stress the importance of your topic to the audience—Explain why this issue is important to the audience and why they should pay attention.

Offer background information on the subject—Provide just enough historical information to familiarize the audience with your topic.

Forecast the structure of your talk—Identify the major sections of your talk so the audience understands its structure from the start.

You don't need to make all seven moves, and they can be made in almost any order. Minimally, you should identify your topic and purpose. The other moves are helpful for building a framework that prepares your audience for your argument. Typically, an effective introduction for a presentation lasts two to three minutes.

The Middle: Tell Them What You Want to Tell Them

In the body you will present your major points and support them with facts, reasoning, examples, data, quotations, and other forms of proof. In most situations, the body of your presentation should follow the same pattern as the body of your written argument.

Divide your argument into two to five major issues that you want to discuss with the audience. If you have more than five major issues, you might try to consolidate some of the smaller points or remove them from your talk. You're better off giving adequate time to the most important two to five issues than trying to cover everything.

Now it's time to make some tough decisions. Look through your written argument and ask yourself, "What information and facts do my readers *need to know* in order to make a decision or take action about this issue?" Then cross out any material that they do not need to know.

The End: Tell Them What You Told Them

Inexperienced presenters regularly make this mistake: They finish the body of their talk and then shrug their shoulders and say something like, "That's all I have to say. Any questions?" An abrupt ending to a presentation feels awkward and misses the opportunity to drive home the argument's main point.

Here's a better way. Once you signal that you are about to conclude, you will have the audience's heightened attention for a couple minutes. Take advantage of their attentiveness by restating your main point and emphasizing its importance. A typical conclusion will include some or all of these moves:

Signal clearly that you are concluding—Make an obvious transition that signals the end of your talk, such as "In conclusion," "Let me wrap up now," or "Finally." This transition will perk up your audience because they know you will soon state your main point or reinforce it in a new way.

Restate your main point (thesis)—State your main claim or thesis clearly and with emphasis.

Reemphasize the importance of your topic to the audience—Explain why they should care about your topic and how this issue impacts them or something they care about.

Call the audience to action—If you want your audience to do something, be specific about the actions you want them to take.

Thank the audience—When you are finished, don't forget to say "thank you." This phrase signals that you have completed your argument, and it usually prompts them to applaud. You want that applause because it caps off your presentation and helps you transition to the question-and-answer period.

Remember to keep your conclusion brief. Once you say something like, "In conclusion," you have one or two minutes to finish up. If you ramble beyond a couple of minutes, your audience will become restless and annoyed.

Question and Answer

At the end of your argument, you should be prepared to answer a few questions and clarify your ideas. During the question-and-answer period, you should be ready to answer three types of questions:

A request for clarification or elaboration

These kinds of questions give you opportunities to clarify and reinforce key points. When asked to clarify or elaborate, start out by rephrasing the question. Rephrasing ensures that everyone hears the question, and it allows you to put the issue in your own words, making the question easier to answer.

A hostile question

Occasionally, an audience member will ask a question that challenges the information you provided. Here is a useful three-step strategy for responding:

1. **Rephrase the question.** State the question in terms that will allow you to answer it in ways that reflect your main point.

2. **Validate the question.** Tell the audience that you understand the questioner's concerns or even share them.

3. **Elaborate and move forward.** Explain that the course of action you are supporting is preferable because it addresses the issue more appropriately and is more reasonable than the alternatives.

Keep in mind that a hostile question is not meant to challenge your authority or trip you up. The person asking the question simply has some doubts about your facts or conclusions. Stay positive and don't be defensive.

A heckling question

In rare cases, an audience member may ask a series of heckling questions. In these rare cases, you need to recognize that the questioner is *trying* to sabotage your presentation. This person wants you to become flustered, but don't let a heckler do that to you. Instead, after trying your best to answer one or two questions from a heckler, simply say, "I'm sorry you feel that way. We have other people with questions. Perhaps we can meet after my talk to discuss your concerns." Then look away from that person. Usually, someone else in the audience will ask a question, and you can move on. If nobody steps forward to ask another question, then thank the audience and bring the presentation to an end.

When the question-and-answer period is over, you should thank the audience again. This final "thank you" will usually prompt another round of applause.

Designing Your Visual Aids

22.3 Techniques for designing effective visual aids

Visual aids help you clarify and illustrate your ideas and main points. Perhaps the best way to create visual aids is to make slides with the presentation software (PowerPoint, Keynote, or Presentations) that was packaged with your word-processing software. Slides are some of the best visual aids available, whether you are using a projector to speak in a large lecture hall or using a poster presentation to speak with a few people. (Figure 22.3).

Here are some strategies for formatting your slides:

- Title each slide with an action-oriented heading.

- Put five or fewer major points on each slide. If you have more than five major points, divide that topic into two slides.

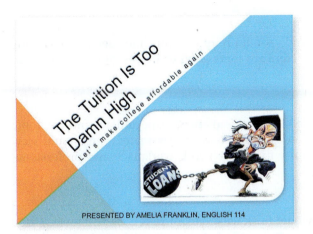

FIGURE 22.3 Creating Slides
Shown here are a title slide and a body slide from a profile paper repurposed as a presentation. The photographs add a strong visual identity to the slides.

- Use left-justified text for most items on your slides. Centered text should only be used for the titles of your slides.

- Use dark text on a white or light background whenever possible. Light text on a dark background can be difficult to read.

- Use bulleted lists of phrases instead of paragraphs or sentences.

- Use photos, icons, and graphics to keep your slides fresh and active. Make sure your graphics look good on the screen. Increasing the size of a Web-based graphic, for example, can make the image look blurry or grainy.

Avoid the temptation to pack too much material onto each slide. Effective slides, like the ones shown in Figure 22.3, need to be simple and easy to interpret. You don't want your audience to waste time puzzling out the meaning of a complicated slide instead of listening to your talk.

If you don't want to use slides, you could draw diagrams on a whiteboard, a large tablet of paper, or a chalkboard. When using these low-tech approaches to creating visuals, you should plan your drawings out before you give your presentation.

Delivering Your Presentation

22.4 How to deliver your presentation in a positive way

How you deliver your argument will have a significant impact on your audience. The usual advice is to "be yourself." Of course, that's good advice if you are already comfortable speaking in front of an audience. Better advice is to "be the person the audience expects." In other words, like an actor, play the role that fits your topic and the situation.

Body Language

Ideally, the movements of your body should reinforce your message and focus the audience's attention (Figure 22.4). Here are some good strategies for enhancing your body language:

Dress appropriately

Your choice of clothing should reflect your audience's expectations and the topic of your talk. Even when you are presenting to your classmates, you should view your presentation as an opportunity to practice your workplace and professional demeanor.

Stand up straight

When speakers are nervous, they tend to slouch, lean, or rock back and forth. These postures look unprofessional and make it difficult to breathe and speak properly. Instead, keep your feet squarely under your shoulders with knees slightly bent. To allow good airflow, keep your shoulders back and down and your head up.

Use open hand and arm gestures

Open hand and arm gestures will convey trust and confidence. Avoid folding your arms, keeping your arms stiff at your sides, or putting both hands in your pockets. These poses will convey a defensive posture and make you seem less trustworthy.

Make eye contact

Everyone in the audience should believe you made eye contact with him or her at least once. If you are uncomfortable making eye contact, you can give the impression of direct eye contact by looking at the audience members' foreheads.

FIGURE 22.4
Your Body Is Part of the Presentation
While in college, you should look for opportunities to speak in public. Public speaking may be uncomfortable, but college is a good place to strengthen this important skill.

Move to reinforce major points or transitions

If possible, step forward toward the audience when you make important points. Move to the left or right when you make transitions from one topic to the next. Your movement across the floor will highlight the transitions in your speech.

Voice and Tone

As you improve your presentation skills, pay attention to your voice and tone.

Speak lower and slower

You will need to speak louder than you normally would, but raising your volume can cause your voice to sound higher pitched than normal. By consciously lowering the pitch of your voice, you will make it sound just about right. Also, nerves may cause you to speak too quickly. Silently remind yourself to speak slowly.

Use pauses to reinforce your major points

Each time you make a major point, pause for a moment to let the audience commit it to memory.

Use pauses to eliminate verbal tics

Verbal tics like "um," "ah," "like," "you know," "OK?" and "See what I mean?" only distract your audience. If you have a verbal tic, train yourself to pause just before you feel a verbal tic coming on. Before long, you will find they've disappeared from your speech.

Minimize how often you look down at your notes

When you look down at your notes, your neck bends, restricting your airflow and lowering your volume. Plus, notes can become a distracting "safe place" that keeps you from engaging visually with your audience. You should look at them only when needed.

Practicing and Rehearsing

You should leave plenty of time to practice and rehearse your presentation out loud. Speakers are often advised to "practice, practice, practice" so their presentations are fluid and natural. Even better advice, though, is to "rehearse, rehearse, rehearse." Rehearsal will help you figure out how you are going to present your argument in a more realistic setting.

22.5 The importance of practicing and rehearsing your argument

Practice, Practice, Practice

Practice involves speaking out loud to yourself, usually at your desk or in front of a mirror. Practicing out loud helps you memorize your presentation's major points and enhance your feel for its organization and flow. While practicing, you should:

- Correct any problems with content, organization, and style.

- Edit and proofread your visuals and handouts.

- Decide which movements and gestures you will use during your actual delivery and practice them.

- Pay attention to your body language and voice.

If you notice any problems as you are practicing your presentation, you can stop and fix them right away.

Rehearse, Rehearse, Rehearse

The secret to polishing your presentation is to rehearse it several times. Unlike practice, rehearsal means giving the presentation from beginning to end *without stopping*.

As much as possible, you want to replicate the experience of giving your real talk. So don't stop to correct any mistakes or start over. Instead, make revisions or corrections after each rehearsal session.

Your friends can provide you with a live audience so you can gauge their reactions to your ideas. They can also give you constructive feedback. If available, you should record your presentation with a video camera or an audio recorder. If you have a mobile phone that can record video or audio, you can make a quick recording of yourself.

Practicing will help you identify any major problems with your talk, but rehearsal will help you turn the whole package into an effective presentation.

Let's turn your written argument into a presentation. Here's what you need to know.

1 Presentations are becoming more common in advanced college courses and will be critical to your successful career.

2 Technologies like Skype and Facetime make it easier than ever to communicate with others through the Internet, which also means people are giving more presentations than ever.

3 While planning out your presentation, first ask the Five-W and How questions: What is my purpose? Who is my audience? Why am I presenting? Where and when will I be presenting? How should I give the presentation?

4 Your audience wants more than just information; they want you to *perform* the material and *interact* with them.

5 To organize your presentation, remember to "Tell them what you are going to tell them, tell them, and tell them what you told them."

6 Your introduction should make some or all of these moves: use a grabber, identify your topic, state your purpose, state your main point, stress the importance of the topic, offer background information on your topic, and forecast the structure of your talk.

7 Your conclusion should make all of some of these moves: signal that you are concluding, restate your main point, stress the importance of your topic to the audience, call the audience to action, and thank the audience.

8 Audience members ask three types of questions: a request for clarification or elaboration, a hostile question, and a heckling question.

9 Your visual aids should be simple, and they should reinforce your argument by highlighting your major points, adding images, and including graphs.

10 You should "practice, practice, practice" as well as "rehearse, rehearse, rehearse."

1. In a small group, share your opinions about what works well in a presentation. Discuss the effective and ineffective presenters you have seen in the past (coaches, teachers, public speakers). What traits made these speakers effective or ineffective?

2. Find a video clip online of a particularly problematic speech. (You can search YouTube for "Worst Speech" or "Boring Speech" to find examples). Imagine that you and your group are coaching this person on his or her speaking skills. Being as helpful as possible, what advice would you give this person to improve his or her future presentations?

3. With your group, choose three strategies from this chapter that you would like to use to improve your presentation skills. Then take turns presenting these three strategies to your group.

1. Outline a two-minute speech on a subject that you know well. Then without much further thought, give a presentation to a small group of people from your class. Practice making the seven introductory moves mentioned in this chapter and the five concluding moves.

2. Set up a group discussion over a video chat system like Skype, Google Talk, or Facetime. Choose a campus-related topic that you can debate with your group. For example, you might debate whether the campus has enough food options or whether more classes should be put online. As you are debating, think about the differences between face-to-face debates and video chat debates. What are some advantages and disadvantages of discussing issues through video chats?

3. Do some research on the need to give presentations in careers that are related to your major. Use the Internet to collect information and interview someone personally or via e-mail about the importance of presentations to this career. Then create a two-minute presentation in which you explain how giving public presentations will be a part of your possible career.

Arguing in Virtual Spaces

23

IN THIS CHAPTER, YOU WILL LEARN—

23.1 Strategies for starting and posting arguments on social networking sites

23.2 How to start your own blog for posting longer arguments

23.3 How to write an article for a wiki

23.4 Strategies for posting videos and podcasts on video and audio sharing websites

23.5 The importance of thinking of arguments as multimodal

If you're looking for an argument, you only need to turn to Facebook, Twitter, Tumblr, YouTube, blogs, or just about any place on the Internet. The Internet is designed for people who want to discuss and argue about both important and not-so-important issues. Social networking sites are now the primary places where people share ideas and advocate for the issues they care about.

Learning how to generate ideas and persuade people in virtual spaces will become more and more important as arguments go increasingly online. Not long ago, college students were mostly restricted to two media: oral arguments in classrooms and written arguments on sheets of paper. Today in college, people are using new media to argue about serious issues and have fun discussing what is going on. Similarly, in the workplace, social media sites are being used to develop plans, discuss trends, promote new ideas, and work out differences (Figure 23.1).

Arguments in virtual spaces are often more dynamic than paper-based arguments because people can respond to others' comments quickly. These virtual arguments can then be modified or revised in ways that respond to emerging information and audience reactions. You need to know how to maneuver and communicate in these new argumentative spaces, which each year become more dynamic and important.

FIGURE 23.1 Virtual Arguments Are Dynamic
Increasingly, arguments are happening in virtual spaces. These arguments are far more fluid and dynamic than paper-based arguments.

23.1 Strategies for starting and posting arguments on social networking sites

Creating a Social Networking Site

Let's start with the easiest way to go public with your arguments—creating a site on a social networking website like Facebook, Tumblr, Pinterest, Bebo, LinkedIn, or Spoke.

You probably use these sites for staying in touch with friends already, but nonprofit organizations, political movements, and companies also use them to stay connected with supporters, customers, and clients. For example, your college or university probably has a Facebook, Tumblr, or Pinterest site that helps students keep in touch with what is happening on campus. LinkedIn and Spoke are career-related sites that can help you connect with colleagues, business associates, and potential employers.

Choose the Best Site for You

Each social networking site offers something different. As you choose the sites that are best for you, think about your long-term goals. Right now, you mostly want to keep in touch with your friends. But as you move through college and into the work-place, your social networking sites will become part of your network for connecting with other professionals in your field and sharing your ideas.

Develop a "Posting Strategy"

You should think about your *posting strategy*, which means staying focused on a few topics you want to comment upon regularly. For example, let's say you are primarily interested in posting about three major topics: video games, fashion, and local live music. Your posting strategy means you will concentrate most of your comments in these areas of interest.

You should start thinking of your social networking site as more than a way to keep in touch with friends. Your site will likely evolve into a tool for staying in touch with people in your career field, other professionals and clients, and people in your community. It will be less about what you did last weekend and more about your passions, your long-term interests, your career, and how you're making a difference in the world.

Starting Your Own Blog

A blog is a website in which a writer keeps a public journal of his or her experiences, thoughts, and opinions. Blogs are usually made up of words and sentences, but an increasing number of photo blogs, video blogs, and audio blogs are coming online.

Blogs are good places for presenting longer arguments. Unlike Facebook or Tumblr, where long posts are often ignored, a blog gives you a chance to write hundreds of words about the issues you care about. Your blog is a good place to make extended arguments because blog audiences tend to be more patient.

23.2 How to start your own blog for posting longer arguments

Choose a Host Site for Your Blog

Don't pay for a blogging site. Some popular free host sites include Blogger, Word-Press, Blogsome, and Moveable Type. Each one has strengths and weaknesses, so you might look at them all to determine which one fits your needs and will allow you to reach the people you want.

Another kind of blog is a "microblog," which allows only a small number of words per post. Twitter was the groundbreaking microblogging site, but other microblogging sites are now available, such as Blauk, Plurk, or Instagram.

Begin Your Blog

Once you choose a host for your blog, the site will ask you for some basic information, such as your name, your blog's name, and an e-mail address. You will then be shown a menu of templates that are available (Figure 23.2). Pick one that fits your personality and the kinds of topics you want to discuss and argue about.

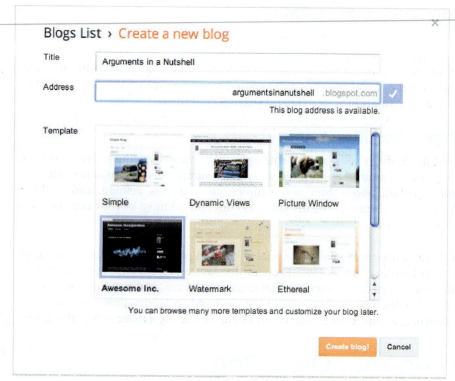

FIGURE 23.2
Choosing a Blog
Template
The template you
choose for your
blog should fit your
personality and the
kinds of topics you
want to discuss on
your blog.

Compose, Edit, and Publish Your Ideas

On your blogging site, you will see tabs or buttons on the screen that allow you to
"compose," "edit," and "publish" your comments. Type some of your thoughts into
the Compose screen and hit the Post or Publish button. Your words should appear on
your blog. Keep adding more comments regularly.

Personalize Your Blog

Blogging sites allow you to add photographs, profiles, polls, newsreels, icons, and
other gadgets. Don't go overboard. You don't want the extra gadgets on your site to
distract your audience from your main ideas and arguments.

Let Others Join the Conversation

The initial settings for your blogging site strictly limit access. You and you alone will
be able to post comments. As you grow more comfortable with your blog, though, you
might want to loosen up your settings to allow others to contribute comments.

At first, you should allow only "registered users" to add comments. Mistakenly,
some bloggers set their blog to allow "anyone" to comment. That's risky, because
strangers, spammers, and "trolls" may contribute posts that annoy or embarrass you.
A troll is someone who posts inflammatory, hostile, or upsetting statements and photos. If you allow *everyone* to comment, you will need to regularly monitor your blog
for inappropriate posts.

Develop Your Blogging Strategy

Choose a few topics that you really care about and make them the center of your blogging strategy. Concentrate on making substantive arguments about those topics.

As you add posts, keep in mind that your blog is a public site. In other words, anyone can read what you have put on your page. So keep the blog interesting, and be careful about making any arguments that would put you in a bad light. Always remember that people you care about, such as family, friends, and current or future employers, may discover your blog. So you want to only say things that you would say directly to these people, including your current or future boss. Plus, always remember that you can be sued for writing slanderous or libelous things about other people. So keep your blog appropriate and truthful.

Writing Articles for Wikis

23.3 How to write an article for a wiki

Wikis are collaboratively written Internet sites that allow users to add and edit content. Wikipedia is, of course, one of the more popular wikis. It is an online encyclopedia that allows users to add, edit, and manage information on just about any topic. Other popular wikis include eHow, WikiHow, CookbookWiki, ProductWiki, Uncyclopedia, and Wikicars. For example, Figure 23.3 shows an entry from Wikitravel that was written by a user of the site. Your professors may ask you to add material to one of these popular wikis or contribute to a wiki created for your class.

Wiki articles might not seem like arguments on the surface, but there are plenty of arguments going on behind them. Wikipedia is a constant battleground for people who want to "tell the truth" from their perspective.

Like any user, you have the ability to add articles to these wikis and edit the existing content. Here's how to add an article to the wiki of your choice.

FIGURE 23.3

Writing for a Wiki A wiki is a collection of articles written and edited by users. Here is an article about travelling to Barcelona, Spain, from Wikitravel.

Write the Wiki Article

You should begin planning your wiki article by thinking about your topic, angle, purpose, audience, and the contexts in which it will be needed or used. Research your topic thoroughly, draft the article, and edit it carefully. Include any appropriate graphics. You should also have your sources available so you can cite and list them in "References," "External Links," and "Further Reading" sections of the article.

Above all, you want to make sure your article is interesting and factually accurate. If your article is about something trivial or mundane, the wiki administrator may simply delete it. If your article is factually wrong or contentious, other wiki users will rewrite your work.

Add Your Article to the Wiki

Most wikis will expect you to have an account if you want to add an article. Once you log in, look for a button that says something like "Create an article," "Add a listing," or "Create a page." Some wikis provide a box in which you can cut and paste your article from your word processor.

Edit and proofread your article. Then click the "Save" or "Publish" button. At this point, your article will be added to the wiki.

Other users can revise and edit your article, so you should return to your article periodically to make sure someone hasn't altered it to say something inaccurate. You might even be pleasantly surprised to find that someone has expanded your article, providing information you didn't know about.

23.4 Strategies for posting videos and podcasts on video and audio sharing websites

Putting Videos and Podcasts on the Internet

You can upload videos to websites like YouTube, MySpace Videos, MSN Video, Yahoo! Video, Veoh, Joost, iFilm, Hulu, Metacafe, and blip.tv. Some popular podcasting sites include Podcast Alley, iTunes, Digg, and Podcast Pickle. Many individuals and corporations are now using these websites to upload documentaries, speeches, and other kinds of arguments. Movies and podcasts are powerful tools for reaching the broader public with your views. Here is how to put your video or podcast on one of these sites.

Create Your Video or Record Your Podcast

Making a video or podcast takes some preparation if you want to produce something worth watching or hearing. As with any kind of writing, you should first consider your topic, angle, purpose, audience, and the contexts in which your video or podcast will be experienced. Then invent the content and draft a script.

Edit Your Work

After you have shot your video or recorded your podcast, edit your work with video or sound editing software. Some good video editing software packages include Corel VideoStudio, MS Movie Maker, Adobe Premiere, Final Cut, and iMovie. For editing podcasts, the most common software packages are Adobe Audition, Audacity, Garage Band, and Cubase. One or more of these editing tools may have already been pre-loaded onto your computer, so look for them among your applications before you buy something new.

Add Music or Other Sounds

After you've recorded your podcast or vidcast, you can use your editing software to add music, the spoken words of others, and other background sounds. Background music and other sounds can help create the mood you want to get across. Also, you can include the spoken words of someone you've interviewed (similar to the way you would quote others in a written argument). Live quotes give your audience a better sense of who you are quoting and using as a source.

Upload Your Video or Podcast

If your video or podcast is ready to be uploaded, then go to the "upload" link in your account. The site will ask you for a title and description, as well as some keywords called "tags." Try to include as many keywords as you can. That way, people who are searching the Internet will be more likely to come across your video or podcast.

Again, always remember that these sites are public. So don't show, do, or say anything that is illegal, unethical, or embarrassing. Be very careful not to give away personal information. Even if you put limits on who can access your videos and podcasts, someone else, including your friends, might share them with others.

Multimodal Arguments

23.5 The importance of thinking of arguments as multimodal

Increasingly, arguments are becoming "multimodal," which means they are happening in a variety of media. A multimodal argument might start with a YouTube video, which is picked up by the television media. Before you know it, people are talking about it on blogs and tweeting about it on Twitter. Your friends are discussing it on Facebook, Tumblr, LinkedIn, or Google+. This "viral" reaction to an argument is one kind of multimodal argument.

Another kind of multimodal argument happens when you, as an author, use more than one medium to express your ideas. For example, your original argument might have been written as a paper for a college course. Then you turn it into a presentation with Prezi or PowerPoint, or you make a podcast or video documentary from it. You might use a combination of these media to help you argue for a specific point or engage in a multimodal conversation.

Are these "multimodal" discussions and texts really arguments? Of course they are. Arguments have never been restricted to the spoken or written word. Within your lifetime, arguments will continue to evolve to take advantage of new technologies. What's important is whether you can get your message out there in ways that allow you to engage in conversations and persuade others.

It's time to get your ideas out there. Here's how to reach the public with your arguments.

1 The Internet seems to be designed for people who want to discuss and argue about important issues (and not-so-important issues, too).

2 Creating a social networking site involves choosing the best site for you, being selective about friends, and developing a posting strategy.

3 Social networking sites are good for having conversations about an issue, and a blog is a good way to make longer arguments.

4 When creating a blog, you should personalize it and choose a few topics about which you want to blog on a regular basis.

5 Articles written for wikis may not seem like arguments, but they indirectly offer a point of view on each topic or offer recommendations and points of view.

6 The arguments about the contents of wiki articles often happen behind the scenes, where people with different views compete to tell the truth from their point of view.

7 Putting videos and podcasts on the Internet is becoming one of the most popular ways to make arguments available to the broader public.

8 Remember that anything on the Internet is accessible to people you didn't expect, so make sure you do not post information or arguments that put you in a bad light or allow people to harm you.

9 Increasingly, arguments are becoming "multimodal," which means they are using a variety of media.

10 The ability to use a variety of media tools is important because of the rise of multimodal forms of argument.

1. With your group, talk about the different ways you use the new media tools discussed in this chapter. What changes have you noticed in the last year, five years, and ten years? Discuss how these media tools have changed the way people communicate in your lifetime.

2. How are social networking sites like Facebook, Tumblr, Twitter, and Pinterest changing the ways people argue? What are some of the advantages of being able to argue through social networking sites? What are some of the disadvantages? Discuss these advantages and disadvantages with your group.

3. You probably know some people who say inappropriate things on their social networking sites or a blog. With a group, make a list of five kinds of issues that you find inappropriate on social networking sites or blogs. How do others respond to these kinds of arguments? Can you think of a good way for people to curb others who make inappropriate, offensive, or inflammatory arguments?

1. With a group of people from your class, choose a topic and shoot videos or record podcasts that express your different opinions on this issue. You can probably use your mobile phone to make these movies or audio files. Otherwise, you can use a video camera or an audio recorder. Each person should briefly express his or her opinion. Then use video or podcasting software to put these statements into one file. If you're feeling ambitious, add music and other sounds. Upload the video or podcast to a video-sharing website and send a link to your instructor.

2. With a group in your class, think of a topic that people often argue about. Then, using three different wikis, read the articles written about that topic. What facts do these wiki articles have in common? What facts are different or missing from one or more of the articles? How do the articles approach the topic from different angles, and what do they choose to highlight? Finally, try to imagine the arguments that seem to be going on "behind the scenes" about this topic. Write a comparison argument in which you highlight the similarities and differences in these wiki articles and explain why those differences exist.

3. Find an argumentative article that you disagree with that was posted recently on the Internet. Go to the comments section below the article and read the most recent ten responses from audience. Then write a brief (200-word) rebuttal to the author's argument in which you point out its flaws and offer a different view. Send your rebuttal and a link to the article to your instructor.

Photo Credits

Text Credits

Chapter 1

Screen Capture, "21 Is It Time to Lower the Drinking Age?" Used by permission from Reason.com and Reason TV.

Chapter 2

From "Eating Disorder Stories: Kathy Carey" by Teresa Joerger, www.caringonline.com. Used by permission of The Center, Inc.

Graphic from "Understand What the Bible Really Says About The Future..." by Andrew Corbett, www.andrewcorbett.net. Courtesy of Andrew Corbett.

Chapter 3

2010 Iowa Gross Greenhouse Gas Emissions.

Chapter 4

"Effective Diplomacy: Examining the Rhetorical Elements of Obama's 2009 Cairo Speech" by Jeremy Dellarosa.

Chapter 5

From "J.K. Rowling's Harry Potter Novels to Real Life: The Sport of Quidditch Takes Flight" by Jace Lacob, *Newsweek*, March 14, 2012, © 2012 The Newsweek/Daily Beast Company LLC. All rights reserved. Used by permission and protected by the Copyright Laws of the United States. The printing, copying, redistribution, or retransmission of this Content without express written permission is prohibited.

Chapter 6

"Why 'The Hunger Games' Isn't 'Twilight' (And Why That's a Good Thing)" by Kate Erbland, Film School Rejects (www.filmschoolrejects.com). Used by permission.

"Conservatives are from Mars, Liberals are from Venus" by Riley Schenck, *The Daily Nexus*, April 23, 2012. Used by permission of The Daily Nexus, University of California Santa Barbara.

Chapter 7

Figure from "Millennials' Judgments About Recent Trends Not So Different." Pew Research Center, Washington, D.C. (2010) http://www.pewresearch.org/2010/01/07/millennials-judgments-about-recent-trends-not-so-different/, accessed June 1, 2013. Reproduced with permission of Pew Research.

Fig 1, Tatoo Design from "Differences in Personality Characteristics Between body-modified and Non-Modified individuals" by Silke Wohlrab et a., from *European Journal of Personality*, Vol. 21, Issue 7 Edition, © 2007, pp. 938. Used by permisson of John Wiley & Sons.

"Why Working-Class People Vote Conservative" by Jonathan Haidt, *The Guardian*, June 5, 2012. Copyright Guardian News & Media Ltd., 2012. Used by permission.

"Religiously Yours" by Hemang Sharma, *Minnesota Daily*, October 18, 2012. Used by permsision of Minnesota Daily, University of Minneapolis.

Chapter 8

"Mongolia: Children and the 'Dzud'" UNICEF, www.unicef.org/photoessays/53579.html. Used by permission.

Chapter 9

"Workers" from *Hunger of Memory: The Education of Richard Rodriguez* by Richard Rodriguez. Copyright 1982 by Richard Rodriguez. Reprinted by permissions of David R. Godine, Publisher, Inc.

Screen Capture from MSU Press - Fourth Genre, http://msupress.org. Used by permission of Michigan State University Press.

Courtesy NASA/JPL-Caltech, http://www.nasa.gov/offices/ducation/programs/descriptions/INSPIRE_Project.html#.mmgjVOCdNo.

Courtesy NASA/JPL-Caltech, http://www.nasa.gov/offices/education/programs/descriptions/INSPIRE_Project.html#.UmmgjVOCdNo.

Chapter 10

Screen Capture from University of Mississippi, http://news.olemiss.edu.

"Dining Review: Masullo Up with the Best Pizza " by Blair Reitman, *The Sacramento Bee*, July 8, 2012. © 2012 The Sacramento Bee. All rights reserved. Used by permission and protected by the Copyright Laws of the United States. The printing, copying, redistribution, or retransmission of this Content without express written permission is prohibited.

Chapter 11

Screen capture from www.cars.com. Courtesycars.com.

"iPhone 5 Review" by Tim Stevens from www.engadget.com. September 18, 2012. © 2012 AOL Inc. All rights reserved. Used by permission and protected by the Copyright Laws of the United States. The printing, copying, redistribution, or retransmission of this Content without express written permission is prohibited.

"How We Ended Up in Louisville: An Evaluation of Spring Break Options" by Danielle Cordaro. Used by permission of the author.

Chapter 12

"Is It Really the End of Men?" by Erika and Nicholas Christakis as appeared in *TIME Magazine*, September 11, 2012. Reprinted by permission of the authors.

"Affirmative Action Creates False Stigmas" by Mpaza Kapembwa as appeared on *USA Today College*, www.usatodayeducate.com, May 30, 2012. Used by permission of the author.

Chapter 13

Screen Capture from www.lib.msu.edu. Used with the permission of The Michigan State University Libraries.

Figure from "Unauthorized Immigrant Population: National and State Trends, 2010" by Jeffrey S. Passel and D'Vera Cohn, Pew Research Center, Washington, D.C. (2010) http://www.pewhispanic.org/2011/02/01/unauthorized-immigrant-population-brnational-and-state-trends-2010/, accessed June 1, 2013. Reproduced with permission from Pew Research.

"The Atheist Crusade" by Sara Yoheved Rigler and Rabbi Moshe Zeldman, *Aish*, n.d. Used by permission of Aish.com.

"Against Capital Punishment " by Angela J. Moore. Used by permission of the author.

Chapter 14

"The End of Poverty" by James D Sachs as appeared in *TIME Magazine*, TIME, March 6, 2005. Copyright TIME INC. Reproduced by permission. TIME is a registered trademark of TIME Inc. All rights reserved.

Chapter 15

"Does TV Help Make Americans Passive and Accepting of Authority?" by Bruce E. Levine, *AlterNet*, October 26, 2012. Used with permission of AlterNet, www.alternet.org.

"Concussions in Ice Hockey" Is It Time to Worry?" by Khizer Amin, *The Meducator*. Vol. 1: Issue 20. Used by permission of *The Meducator, McMaster Undergraduate Health Sciences Journal*. Reproduction or retransmission of the materials, in whole or in any part, requires prior written consent of the copyright holder, *The Meducator*.

Chapter 16

Screen Capture from http://www.lib.iastate.edu. Courtesy Iowa State University Library.

Screen Capture, www.dogpile.com. Courtesy Blucora, Inc.

Chapter 17

Reprinted with permission from *Science as a Contact Sport : Inside the Battle to Save Earth's Climate*. By Stephen Schneider. Copyright © 2009 Stephen H.Schneider.

From Council of Writing Program Administrators, www.wpacouncil.org. Licensed under a Creative commons Attribution - No Derivative Works 3.0 United States License, http://creativecommons.org/licenses/by-nd/3.0/us/

Chapter 18

Screen Capture from CNET.com. Used by permission of the YGS Group.

Screen Capture from www.press.uillinois.edu/journals/ajp.html, *American Journal of Psychology*. Copyright 2009 by the Board of Trustees of the University of Illinois. Used with permission of the University of Illinois Press.

Screen Capture from EBSCO. © EBSCO Publishing, Inc. All rights reserved. Used by permission.

"Enhancing Engineers' Communication Abilities at Virginia Tech" By Joseph Van Note. Used by permission of the author.

"The Focus on Skills" by Daniel Schawbel, from *Millennial Branding Student Employment Gap Study*. May 14, 2012. Used by permisson of Millennial Branding, LLC.

Screen Capture from www.phoenix.gov/recreation/arts/museums/pueblo/index.html. Courtesy Phoenix Parks and Recreation Department.

Chapter 19

Screen Capture from EBSCO. © EBSCO Publishing, Inc. All rights reserved. Used by permission.

"Healthy Fast Food: A Fast Food Revolution?" by Caitlin Foley. Used by permission of the author.

Chapter 20

From "I Have a Dream" by Martlin Luther King, Jr. Reprinted by arrangement with The Heirs to the Estate of Martin Luther King Jr., c/o Writers House as agent for the proprietor New York, NY. Copyright © 1963 Dr. Martin Luther King, Jr; copyright renewed 1991 Coretta Scott King.

Chapter 21

"Working with Livestock Guarding Dog" from *Livestock and Wolves* by Suzanne Asha Stone, et al. Copyright © 2008 Defenders of Wildlife. Courtesy of Defenders of Wildlife.

Public Domain. "Clean Domestic Power" by the Geothermal Technologies Program, U.S. Department of Energy.

Public Domain. "Proposed Expansion of Conservation Easement Program" by the U.S. Fish and Wildlife Services.

Graph from www.epic.org. Courtesy Electronic Privacy Information Center.

Graph from "Survey, Majority of Catholics Think Employers Should be Required to Provide Health Care Plans that Cover Birth Control at No Cost" from www.publicreligion.org. Reproduced by permission of Public Religion Research Institute.

From "Reduce Your Risk" from *The Dark Side of Tanning*, www.arksideoftanning.com. Courtesy of The Cancer Institute NSW.

Public Domain. Graphic, "Base Pair - Sugar Phosphate Backbone" by the National Library of Medicine.

Index